THE ATOMIC BOMB
IN JAPANESE CINEMA

ALSO EDITED BY MATTHEW EDWARDS

*Film Out of Bounds: Essays and Interviews
on Non-Mainstream Cinema Worldwide*
(McFarland, 2007)

THE ATOMIC BOMB IN JAPANESE CINEMA

Critical Essays

Edited by
Matthew Edwards

McFarland & Company, Inc., Publishers
Jefferson, North Carolina

LIBRARY OF CONGRESS CATALOGUING-IN-PUBLICATION DATA

The atomic bomb in Japanese cinema : critical essays /
edited by Matthew Edwards.
p.   cm.
Includes bibliographical references and index.

ISBN 978-0-7864-7912-2 (softcover : acid free paper) ∞
ISBN 978-1-4766-2020-6 (ebook)

1. Nuclear warfare in motion pictures.   2. Atomic bomb victims in
motion pictures.   3. Motion pictures—Japan—History and criticism.
4. Motion picture producers and directors—Interviews.
I. Edwards, Matthew.

PN1995.9.W3A86 2015   791.43'658—dc23   2015015609

BRITISH LIBRARY CATALOGUING DATA ARE AVAILABLE

Printed in the United States of America

*McFarland & Company, Inc., Publishers
Box 611, Jefferson, North Carolina 28640
www.mcfarlandpub.com*

For my wife, Johanna

This book is also dedicated to all those
who were killed, or whose lives were affected,
by the atomic bombings of Hiroshima and Nagasaki

Acknowledgments

This book would not have been possible without the support and help of my family and friends who have assisted me at various stages throughout the book's conception. I would like to thank all the contributors for their essays and their patience and support in getting this book realized and published. Without their hard work and their desire to tackle such a sensitive and vital subject as the atomic bombings, this book would never have had come to fruition. I would like to thank Johannes Schönherr for all his support during the writing of the book and agreeing to contact Gō Shibata to interview him for the volume. I would also like to express my thanks and gratitude to Gō Shibata, Steve Nguyen, Steven Okazaki, David Rothauser, Roger Spottiswoode and Dominic and Ian Higgins for giving up so much of their limited time to be interviewed for this project.

I would like to offer my thanks to my parents and brothers Paul, Mark and Daniel for their encouragement and support during the writing of this book. Thanks also to my sister-in-law Mandy, Kate Long and my nieces Lily, Poppy, Naomi and Eliza. A special thank you to Patrick Prescott for listening to me ramble on about this project and for his continued support as my "unofficial book agent" in promoting (or bullying people into buying) *Film Out of Bounds* (McFarland, 2007) and for visiting me in Japan, with Alex Whiting. It was during this trip that I visited Hiroshima for the first time and helped sow the seeds for this collection. Thank you also to Jasper Sharp for his excellent writings on Japan which helped me enormously with this project; Darren and Beth Harris; Doug and Rosemary; Jenny Hutcheson; Kate Ellis and my friends in Tahara, Aichi, Jimbo-sensei; the JET Programme and Stuart and Emma Pearce.

Finally, lots of love to my wife Johanna as this book could not have been completed without her. Her patience, advice, support, and encouragement have been invaluable from the initial concept of this book to its conclusion. Without her this book would not have been possible. I am grateful to be lucky enough to have her at my side every step of way and for her kindness in allowing me to watch film after film about the atomic bombs. Johanna, this book would not have been possible without your support or guidance. It is to her that this book is dedicated.

Table of Contents

Acknowledgments   vi

Preface • MATTHEW EDWARDS   1

Introduction • MATTHEW EDWARDS   5

Prologue: Hiroshima/Nagasaki • MATTHEW EDWARDS   11

PART I: GOJIRA AND THE BOMB

The Rhetorical Significance of *Gojira*: Equipment for Living
    Through Trauma • SHANNON STEVENS   17

Japan Removed: *Godzilla* Adaptations and Erasure of the Politics
    of Nuclear Experience • JASON C. JONES   34

Atomic Reaction: *Godzilla* as Metaphor for Generational Attitudes
    toward the United States and the Bomb • JOHN VOHLIDKA   56

PART II: JAPANESE ATOMIC CINEMA, 1945–2014

Suppression and Censorship: Japanese Cinema During the
    Occupation • MATTHEW EDWARDS   69

Pica-don: Japanese and American Reception and Promotion
    of Hideo Sekigawa's *Hiroshima* • MICK BRODERICK *and*
    JUNKO HATORI   77

The Shadow of the Bomb in Hiroshi Teshigahara's *The Face
    of Another* • TONY PRITCHARD   88

Nuclear Skin: Hiroshima and the Critique of Embodiment in
    Affairs Within Walls • JULIA ALEKSEYEVA   99

The Atomic Bomb Experience and the Japanese Family in
    Keiji Nakazawa's Anime *Hadashi no Gen* (*Barefoot Gen*)
    • KENJI KANEKO   111

Yuichi and Jizō in *Black Rain*: Imamura's Phenomenological
    Attempt to Render a Hiroshima Wormhole Experience Among
    His Audience • KEIKO TAKIOTO MILLER   124

Trauma and Witness in Hideo Nakata's *Ring* • Tienfong Ho   140

The Fragile Roots of Memory • Robert McParland   150

Inconceivable Anxiety: Representation, Disease and
Discrimination in Atomic-Bomb Films • Yuki Miyamoto   157

Kazuo Kuroki and Hisashi Inoue's *Chichi to kuraseba*: Remember,
Protest and Return to Ordinary Life • Yoshiko Fukushima   171

Breaking the Silence of the Atomic Bomb Survivors in the Japanese
Graphic Novel *Town of Evening Calm, Country of Cherry
Blossoms* and the Film Adaptation • Senjo Nakai   184

The Sound of the Bomb: Gō Shibata's *NN-891102*
• Johannes Schönherr   200

PART III: WESTERN PERSPECTIVES

Hiroshima Films: Cultural Contexts Before, During and After
the Cold War • Greg Nielsen *and* Margaret M. Ferrara   211

Hiroshima: An Interview with Director Roger Spottiswoode
• Matthew Edwards   228

White Light/Black Rain: The "Atomic Films" of Steven Okazaki
• Matthew Edwards   240

A[nime] Bomb: An Interview with *Hibakusha* Director Steve
Nguyen • Matthew Edwards   246

Hibakusha: Our Life to Live: An Interview with Director David
Rothauser • Matthew Edwards   254

All That Remains: An Interview with Ian and Dominic Higgins
• Matthew Edwards   267

Appendix: Japanese Titles of Films Referenced in Text   281

About the Contributors   283

Index   285

"There's something white falling…!"

Flash

Forty-three seconds later, 1,800 feet above Hiroshima, the atomic bomb named Little Boy exploded with a white-hot light. It was like a million flashbulbs going off at once…

—*Kenji Nakazawa,*
Barefoot Gen (Hadashi no Gen)

"The first Atomic Bomb was an unnecessary experiment…. It was a mistake to ever drop it…. It killed a lot of Japs, but the Japs had put out a lot of peace feelers through Russia long before."

—*Admiral William "Bull" Halsey,*
Commander of the South Pacific Fleet

EDWARD R. MURROW: "Any regrets?"

HARRY S TRUMAN: "Not the slightest—not the slightest in the world."

—*Harry S Truman on his decision to drop the atomic bomb*
during an interview with Edward R. Murrow

Preface

MATTHEW EDWARDS

The genesis of this book happened in 2008, when I was teaching English in the Japanese government-sponsored JET Programme. Living in the small town of Tahara-shi, located on the Atsumi Hantō (Atsumi Peninsula) in Aichi-Ken, I was invited to dinner with a small group of Japanese English teachers where we enjoyed copious amounts of fried tako, sushi and sake. As the night wore on, and the sake took hold of my work colleagues, the conversation shifted to the atomic bombs and their use against Japan during World War II. Usually inhibited by the strict conventions dictated in social situations and in public (*tatemae*), my colleagues were forthright with their true feelings in regard to this contentious and sensitive issue. They vehemently argued that the atomic attacks on Hiroshima and Nagasaki were acts of genocide and that the U.S. had deliberately tried to wipe out the Japanese. I was taken aback by this response, and strongly disagreed with their stance. It also struck me as very hypocritical, especially when one considers Japanese genocide in China and throughout Asia. I also argued that America and its allies plowed huge amounts of money into rebuilding Japan and steering it towards a path of democracy and away from its militaristic designs. Yet that was their opinion and they felt much aggrieved, at once highlighting an underlining tension that co-exists today despite the two countries on the surface having strong international and cultural relations.

Their response continued to intrigue me. What were the Japanese people's true feelings toward the bombings and how have they come to terms with the bombings of Hiroshima and Nagasaki? Along with this my passion for Japanese cinema spawned an interest in how this has been expressed in their national cinema. I became fascinated with how the Japanese have sought to understand, comment on and explore the use of atomic warfare and the plight of the *Hibakusha* through cinema and other media associated with its national output. Is there a raging fury, a sense of outrage, or a sad reflection that such an atrocity should never be seen again? Has the issue been treated with sensitivity or has it been used as an exploitative device in more subversive genres?

With these questions in mind, this collection explores a wide variety of films associated with the *Genbakudan* spectrum of Japanese films, through new scholarship from a number of writers connected to Japanese studies or atomic warfare. Equally important, the book includes a number of exclusive interviews with both Japanese and Western filmmakers who have tackled this sensitive question.

The collection starts with three essays tackling the spectrum of *Gojira* films, exploring the trauma of the bombings (Shannon Stevens), the erasure of the atomic question from subsequent adaptations and remakes of *Gojira* both in Japan and in the West (Jason C.

Jones) and the general attitude to the bombings in America, through close examination of the *Godzilla* cycle of films (John Vohlidka). The collection delves into the suppression and censorship of Japanese films on the atomic issue during the occupation (Matthew Edwards) and includes an excellent study of Hideo Sekigawa's *Hiroshima* and its promotion and reception in both Japan and the U.S. (Mick Broderick and Junko Hatori) and close-contextual studies of the films *The Face of Another* (Tony Pritchard), the cult Japanese pink film *Affairs Within Walls* (Julia Alekseyeva), *Barefoot Gen* (Kenji Kaneko), *Black Rain* (Keiko Takioto Miller) and *Ring* (Tienfong Ho), all of which deal with their relationship to the trauma caused by the atomic bombings. Robert McParland's study sheds light on how the profound memory of the bombings is remembered in Japanese cinema. With particular emphasis on the films *Children of Hiroshima*, *Women in the Mirror* and *The Face of Jizō*, the essay explores the human factor in the wake of the bombings. Japanese scholars Yuki Miyamoto, Yoshiko Fukushima and Senjo Nakai focus their attention on Japanese atomic cinema through the suffering of the *Hibakusha* and the discrimination, disease, protest and silence they have had to endure. Johannes Schönherr provides an exclusive interview with cult film director Gō Shibata on his experimental atomic bomb film *NN-891102*, exploring the filmmaking process and why he felt prompted to make a film about the Nagasaki atomic bombing. Greg Nielsen and Margaret M. Ferrara provide an insightful history of the atomic bomb in American cinema before, during and after the Cold War. The book finishes with a number of exclusive interviews conducted by Matthew Edwards with Western filmmakers who have tackled the subject in their own work. They include interviews with Roger Spottiswoode on his brilliant docudrama *Hiroshima*, award-winning documentary filmmaker Steven Okazaki, David Rothauser on his documentary *Hibakusha: Our Life to Live*, animator Steven Nguyen and finally British filmmakers Ian and Dominic Higgins on their new film *All That Remains*, an adaptation of the tragic story of Dr. Takashi Nagai.

This book is aimed at researchers, students, teachers and readers interested in Japanese cinema or cinema related to the atomic bombings. It provides an introductory point of entry into this sub-genre of Japanese cinema. While the collection is not an exhaustive study on the topic, it is intended to provide further comment and discussion on the atomic bombings and how they have been represented and portrayed in Japan's national cinema. It will hopefully lead to further research on the topic and encourage more scholars and writers to study the background of Japan's relationship with the bombings of Nagasaki and Hiroshima through its cinema.

As this book is released near the 70th anniversary of the bombings, my time in Japan and the responses of Japanese people that I have met clearly indicate that this is still an emotive issue in Japan and one that produces wide and varying opinions. It is these opinions that I and my fellow contributors have looked to explore.

It would be wrong to neglect the plight and suffering of all those who were killed or injured during the bombings of Hiroshima and Nagasaki. To this day, people suffer the consequences of the atomic bomb through disease and the mental and physical scars brought about by the bomb's use. That is truly horrifying. We debase ourselves if we think that the dropping of the bombs on innocent women, children and the elderly was a fitting response to the attack on Pearl Harbor and Japanese atrocities, and so this book is dedicated to all those who died in the blast and those *Hibakusha* who continue to suffer. The personal and cinematic essays in this book one hopes will guide the reader to realize that whatever his or her personal angle on the atomic bombings may be, that such a weapon should never again be used on mankind.

A Note on Terms and Transcription

Because the Japanese language and writing system is alien to most Western readers, this book follows the revised Hepburn system to transcribe Japanese words, places and people into the Roman alphabet. The Hepburn system uses macrons on vowels to denote a long vowel sound (as in *Ōta*, as opposed to *Ohta*, or *obāsan* [grandmother] instead of *obaasan*). The modified Hepburn system's spelling follows English phonology, however, for clarity for the reader, this convention has been eschewed for the international spellings of such familiar places as Tokyo instead of *Tōkyō*, Osaka instead of *Ōsaka* and Kyoto instead of *Kyōto* (and for all other place names in Japan). Likewise, to avoid confusion of Western readers who are familiar with Japanese cinema, I have used nonmacronized international spellings to denote Japanese companies such as Toho (*Tōhō*) and Toei (*Tōei*). Equally, I have used the common English forms when referring to *Noh*, as opposed to macronized form Nō.

Japanese terms such as anime and manga which are familiar in English are not italicized, but Japanese terms less widely known, such as *Hibakusha* are. All Japanese terms include an English definition and in some essays the original Japanese characters are provided for those familiar with the language and its use.

As the collection is aimed primarily at non–Japanese readers, the book has adopted the Western standard of given name followed by family name, as opposed to the standard Japanese practice of family name first and given name second (for example, in the West, the director of *Gojira* (1954) is referred to as Ishirō Honda, while in Japan it is Honda Ishirō). Again, this editorial decision was made to avoid confusion for readers who are already familiar with names such as Hideo Nakata instead of Nakata Hideo and Akira Kurosawa instead of Kurosawa Akira.

All film titles are referred to in their English titles and are preceded by the transliterated title. In some cases the original title in Japanese is included. Alternative titles have been provided for those films known by multiple names, as is the case when foreign distribution labels retitle the films in English. The exception to this rule is referring to film *Godzilla* by its original Japanese title *Gojira*. This decision has been made to avoid confusion with Ishirō Honda's original film and subsequent re-imaginings of the franchise, most notably Roland Emmerich's American remake and the Frank Darabont/Warner Bros.–produced *Godzilla*, directed by Gareth Edwards of *Monsters* fame (2014). The term Godzilla has become synonymous with everything that is of enormous size and considerable strength, and is so embedded in popular culture through a slew of remakes, sequels, comics, parodies and advertisements that for the purposes of this book the original film will be referred to simply as *Gojira*, especially when discussed in the wider Godzilla spectrum of films. The book follows standard American English except when using official titles or organizations such as Japanese National Theatre.

Introduction

Matthew Edwards

As this collection marks the 70th anniversary of the atomic bombings of Hiroshima and Nagasaki, it highlights the continued profound effect that this traumatic event has had on the Japanese people, artists, filmmakers and national cinema. The bombings left an indelible mark on the Japanese psyche, not to mention the physical scars of *Hibakusha* (literally translated, bomb-affected people). The issue of the bombings is still a contentious one wrought with emotion and sensitivity. Yet it is an issue worthy of further discourse and exploration. With each passing year, more and more *Hibakusha* and survivors of the Hiroshima and Nagasaki bombings pass away, taking with them their stories.

Keeping the tragic events of August 6 and 9, 1945, alive for future generations to understand is imperative in academia, education and the arts. With this in mind it is important to ask if this emotive topic can be tackled adequately in a cinematic dramatization. Just how have the Japanese dealt with this monumental national trauma in their national cinema? Have they addressed the many issues that have been raised as a result of the nuclear attacks?

The collection of essays and interviews herein tackle this complex subject and engage with specific Japanese cinematic works as a means of attempting to dissect these questions. The essays will study to what extent the Japanese have addressed the horrors of those fateful days and the tragic stories that emerged from the bombings. We ask if the bombings have become politicized and whether they address the sensitive subject of discrimination against *Hibakusha*. How have the resulting anxieties and fears been addressed and played out in Japanese cinema? How can these films point toward Japanese society's reaction, interpretation and understanding of the events that transpired in Hiroshima and Nagasaki?

An academic study is therefore important, especially in an era when some countries, particularly Iran and North Korea, continue to develop nuclear weapons.

Through close analysis of popular culture mediums such as films, comic books and literature we can see how the prevailing message and response to Hiroshima and Nagasaki have evolved over the last seventy years. It is important to remember that these films are wrought with the political, social, military and psychological issues of their time. For example, latent fears with regard to nuclear weapons were shown in '50s and '60s Japanese cinema where the threat of nuclear obliteration and fear of radiation sickness were widely prevalent in *Genbakudan* (atomic bomb) cinema. Kurosawa's superb *I Live in Fear* (*Ikimono no kiroku*, 1955) is one of the most well known films centering on the *Hibakusha* experience. Like many of his contemporaries, Kurosawa was a cinematic visionary whose work was touched by the personal tragedies of ordinary people. Personally incensed that during the occupation the atomic question was suppressed in its own national cinema, Kurosawa sought to address his concerns post-occupation by highlighting the consequences of the bombings. *Rhapsody in August* (*Hachigatsu no kyōshikyoku*), starring Richard Gere, was an international hit about an elderly lady whose husband was killed in the atomic attacks.

What is for certain is that Hiroshima and Nagasaki have come to represent the dangers of nuclear warfare and serve as microcosms of a post-apocalyptic and nuclear holocaust landscape that we are teetering on the edge of. Images of a nuclear holocaust and post-apocalyptic world have been articulated and explored extensively in Japanese anime and science fiction cinema, like Ishirō Honda's *Gojira* and *The Mysterians* (*Chikyū bōeigun*, 1957). The legacy of the bombings casts a long shadow over the cinematic work of Honda, who was deeply influenced by the atomic bombings and the fear of nuclear Armageddon and radiation sickness. The images that he saw in Hiroshima were burned into the soul of the gentle and soft-spoken Honda. Honda's career took a different trajectory resulting in a large percentage of his work being influenced by the bombings of Nagasaki, Hiroshima and the Lucky Dragon No. 5 incident in 1954. *H-Man* (*Bijo to ekitaningen*, 1958) in particular was inspired by the tragic exposure of the crew of the tuna fishing boat *Fukuryu-maru No. 5* to the radiation fallout as a result of American nuclear testing in the Pacific. In Honda's film, which opens with footage of a hydrogen bomb being detonated, the effects of the radiation contaminates a small fishing vessel which turns the humans into frothing green subhuman slime creatures that return to mainland Japan and dwell in Tokyo's sewer system wreaking havoc to the populace and the initially skeptical police force. It has some creepy special effects and its central theme is the fear of radiation and radiation's impact on living organisms. This fear can be translated as a primary concern many Japanese harbored about the effects of radiation poisoning and is consistent with many Japanese genre films that explored this idea. One critique of these genre films, like Honda's, is that those unfortunate to be afflicted with radiation poisoning or sickness are generally transformed into grotesque monsters or creatures or killers. *Hibakusha* have long been discriminated against in Japanese society and looked down on as outcasts or seen as carriers of hereditary diseases. Such depictions of *Hibakusha*, especially in genre fare such as *H-Man,* and Honda's film *Matango* (1963), certainly would not have done the public perception of *Hibakusha* any good, despite the best intentions of Honda in raising awareness of the horror of nuclear warfare. It merely helped reinforce the notion of the *Hibakusha* as a threat, thus society would shun them from all aspects of life, from employment to marriage. *Hibakusha* came to represent the monstrous in a number of Japanese films over the years. Out of the 25 genre films that Honda was to direct, 18 dealt overtly or indirectly with the nuclear question and the dangers of nuclear warfare. Aside from *Gojira* and the subsequent Godzilla sequels, other Honda films that fall into the *Genbakudan* category include *Rodan* (1956), *Mothra* (1961) and the *Human Vapor* (*Gasu ningen dai ichigō*, 1960), to name but a few.

Japanese anime and manga are littered with post-holocaust imagery, nuclear destruction and post-apocalyptic worlds from *Akira, Neon Genesis Evangelion* to the late Satoshi Kon's seminal *Paranoia Agent* (*Mōsō dairinin*, 2004) in which remnants of the bomb hang over Japanese society. Yet these apocalyptic films come with the overriding message of the need for peace and nuclear disarmament, an idea that prevails strongly not only in Japanese cinema but Japanese society as the whole.

Noteworthy additions in the field of anime and the depiction of the atomic bombings include the classic adaptation of Keiji Nakazawa's seminal manga *Barefoot Gen* (*Hadashi no Gen*). Directed by Mori Masaki in 1983 for Madhouse, the cinematic version brought

Nakazawa's moving semi-autobiographical story of his childhood in Hiroshima to a wider audience, gaining critical acclaim in Japan and abroad. It omits much of Nakazawa's criticism of Japan's military and aggression during the war and its treatment of non–Japanese subjects, like the Koreans, but it still, for a children's film, does an extraordinarily good job of capturing the horror and devastation inflicted on innocent civilians caught up in the atomic blast. This is best reflected during the sequence in which the bombing is shown passively from the American point of view before the viewpoint changes and the bomb explodes. Masaki does not shy away from presenting the grisly realities to his audience; we see people being vaporized, buildings torn to pieces, charred corpses and eerie precessions of the walking injured with melting skin drooping from their wretched frames.

Barefoot Gen, which was first serialized by *Weekly Shōnen Jump* between 1973 and 1985, made its big screen debut in three live-action films directed by Tengo Yamada: *Barefoot Gen* (*Hadashi no Gen*, 1976); *Barefoot Gen: Explosion of Tears* (*Hadashi no Gen: Namida no bakuhatsu*, 1977), and *Barefoot Gen: Battle of Hiroshima* (*Hadashi no Gen Part 3: Hiroshima no tatakai*, 1980). After the success of Masaki's adaption, a sequel was commissioned and filmed in 1986 and directed by Toshio Hirata: *Barefoot Gen 2* (*Hadashi no Gen 2*, 1986). The sequel is set three years after the original and focuses its attention on Gen's survival in post-war Hiroshima and the devastated ruins of his city.

The atomic bombings have also been featured in the work of Seiji Arihara, particularly *On a Paper Crane: Tomoko's Adventure* (*Tsuru ni notte*, 1993) and *Nagasaki Angelus Bell 1945* (*Nagasaki 1945: Angelus no kane*, 2005). The former is a charming and moving anime about a young girl named Tomoko who visits the Hiroshima Peace Memorial and comes to understand the harrowing truth of what happened at Hiroshima and the deadly effects of radiation poisoning through a ghostly encounter with a girl named Sadako. Loosely inspired by the tragic true-life experiences of Sadako Sasaki, who was two years old when she was caught up in the atomic blast in Hiroshima and later died of radiation poisoning, the film is an exceptional educational film for children as it highlights the dangers of nuclear warfare and the necessity of peace. An interesting aspect of the film is that the younger generation is portrayed as ignorant and having little understanding of the bombings of Hiroshima and Nagasaki. Arihara was clearly upset by this lack of understanding. Equally appalled was Miho Cibot-Shimma, who was horrified at seeing children in France playing atomic war games. She was instrumental in helping raise money for the film and in Arihara realizing his vision.

The latter film by Arihara drew inspiration from the real-life experiences of Dr. Akizuki who was caught up in the bombing of Nagasaki as he wrestled to save his patients. What really hits home in this film is how Dr. Akizuki and his staff, despite being so overwhelmed with critically injured and dying patients, do everything in their power to save them with such dignity and spirit. Arihara's film again shows the power of animation as a tool for spreading the message of peace to younger generations of moviegoers. The film was screened October 25, 2007, to the UN by the Permanent Mission of Japan, NGO Committee for Disarmament, Mushi Productions and UNODA and through financial support from the Japan Foundation.

Less widely known are the animated films of author Tatsuharu Kodama. Inspired by his own interviews with A-bomb survivors, his trilogy of films on the Hiroshima bombings include *Shin's Tricycle* (*Shin-Chan no san rin sha*, 1995), *The Lunch Box* (1990) and *A Boy's Marbles* (1994). *Shin's Tricycle* is inspired by the true story of Shinichi Tetsutani who was killed in the atomic blast while riding his beloved tricycle. His distraught father, unable to bury his three-year-old son alone, buried Shin with his prized possession. Forty years later, his father dug up his grave and moved his body to the family cemetery. The tricycle was donated to the Hiroshima Peace Memorial Museum. The animation is based on Kodama's graphic and controversial children's book of the same name. Kodama's refusal to dilute the horror of the bombings for his target audience of young children caused some critics to criticize the film. Kodama's refusal to compromise on this matter saw subsequent film backers shy away from the film (the first two animated films had received sponsorship). Kodama was forced to fund *Shin's Tricycle* himself. Though flying under the radar of *Genbakudan* cinema, Kodama's trilogy is both profoundly moving and unflinching in its depiction of the human cost of nuclear warfare. All three films deserve a wider audience in the West (his print books have received English translations).

Countless Japanese films have dealt with or made reference to the bombings, many of which are explored in this collection such as *Black Rain* (*Kuroi ame*, 1989), and *The Face of Jizō* (*Chichi to kuraseba*, 2004) to more experimental and lesser known films such as Gō Shibata's *NN-891102*. J-Horror has conjured up any number of "Hiroshima Horrors" that can be interpreted as having some legacy of the atomic bombing wrapped up in their narrative, as shown in horror films such as *The Ring* (*Ringu*, 1998). Other references to the bomb can be found in Shinji Aoyama's weirdly wonderful *Hibakusha* serial killer flick *An Obsession* (*Tsumetai chi*, 1997), a re-working of Kurosawa's *Stray Dog*, to more moving fare such as *Women in the Mirror* (*Kagami no onnatachi*, 2003) and Kazuo Kuroki's *Tomorrow/Ashita* (*Tomorrow: Ashita*, 1988). In Kenji Fukasaku's *Battle Without Honour and Humanity* (*Jingi naki tatakai*, 1973) warring factions fight for supremacy in post-war Hiroshima. A violent and gritty gangster flick, the film opens with a shot of the atomic bomb exploding over Hiroshima, before depicting a ruined city fueled by hysteria, confusion and violence where rival *yakuza* gangs exploit the situation before descending into all-out war. Such was the success of the series for Toei that the series spawned eight sequels with Fukasaku helming eight of the nine films.

In a country whose national cinema deals with controversial topics such as rape and violence with misogynistic glee, it is unsurprising that the atomic bombings should somewhere along the line fall into the realm of Japanese exploitation and sexploitation. Research into Japanese atomic cinema quickly found references and inspiration in a number of exploitation titles, whether directly or indirectly, that further show the impact the bombings have had on the psyche of filmmakers and scriptwriters working in all areas of the Japanese film industry. The most famous of examples is the late Kōji Wakamatsu's brilliant *Affair Within Walls*. Screened at the Berlin Film Festival, the film's main protagonist is disfigured with a keloid scar from the bombing of Hiroshima. His lover proclaims it to be an emblem of Hiroshima and of Japan.

Julia Alekseyeva examines the film in more depth in her expertly researched essay "Nuclear Skin: Hiroshima and the Critique of Embodiment in *Affairs Within Walls*." She argues that the provocative political issues in the film come to symbolize the keloid-ridden protagonist as an embodiment of the atomic bombings. This idea is supported in Wakamatsu's film when the protagonist's lover caresses his keloid scar and declares him an "emblem of Hiroshima, an emblem of Japan, an anti-war emblem." For Japanese audiences the image of the atomic bombing and *Hibakusha* in a sexual context was surprising and startlingly confrontational, especially when one considers the prejudice shown to *Hibakusha* survivors by the Japanese themselves. Such a film—with a character that is a *communist Hibakusha*—would not have been possible under the auspices of a larger or more commercial

Japanese studio, which would have balked at Wakamatsu's inflammatory and confrontational tone. Such subversive and politically emotive films ended up finding their voices in the *pinku eiga* genre (so long as the director adhered to the standard practice of five to six sex scenes, the filmmakers were generally given free license to explore a wide variety of subjects that were generally prohibited in the mainstream), which accounts for the rise in academic study of this strange and interesting facet of Japanese national cinema. The decision by the Berlin International Film Festival to screen the film in competition is further proof of the validity of some of the films that were produced in the *pinku eiga* genre, and in the case for *Affairs Within Walls*, it proved to be a money-winning hit for Wakamatsu, while garnishing him with international prestige on the film circuit. Back in Japan, the film caused a national uproar, branded a disgrace by a large number of critics who were stunned that a film perceived to be from one of the lowest rungs of Japanese cinema, and one of such questionable content, could be successful.

This anger directed toward Wakamatsu stemmed from Japan's desire to present a more civilized front to the world in the aftermath of its militaristic past, yet *Affairs Within Walls* was certainly showing a side of Japan that it wanted to keep repressed, as well as dispelling connections with Communism and reminders of the war and the bombings of Hiroshima and Nagasaki. The domestic uneasiness with the film can also be attributed to Wakamatsu's female protagonist who is the lover of a *Hibakusha* survivor. Such a notion didn't sit well in Japan, where fear and prejudice ensured that *Hibakusha* were shunned by family and friends and considered "damaged goods" and unworthy to marry for fear of contamination of their offspring. The sequence where the protagonist caresses the keloid scar of her lover with sexual delight was too much for Japanese authorities and some cinemagoers. Japan didn't want to be reminded of the war, its atrocities, and its colonialism. The *Hibakusha* were a painful reminder of its shameful past.

The atomic bombings were again referenced in the cult favorite *School of the Holy Beast* (*Seijū gakuen*, 1974), a strange addition to the *nunsploitation* flicks that features images of the destruction of Nagasaki and a bomb-scarred villain, the wicked Father Kakinuma. He is sent to a convent to restore order after a series of violations are seemingly perpetrated by the nuns. Filmmaker Norifumi Suzuki sets out to shock and upset viewers with scenes of bound nuns urinating on an effigy of Christ, but such images were wasted on the primarily Japanese audience, who are not traditionally Christian. Yet, it is the images of the destruction of Nagasaki and the use of a *Hibakusha* sufferer as the villain that makes the film more than a simply exploitation flick. The film seems to tap into the Japanese fear of the *Hibakusha* as "unpure" or an evil that will contaminate. This idea of *Hibakusha* as a threat is a motif that has been used over and over in Japanese horror cinema or in the work of Honda, as previously detailed.

New films, such as the documentary *Atomic Bomb Home* (*Natsu no inori*, 2012) by Katsumi Sakaguchi, poignantly capture the lives of the patients at Meguminooka Nagasaki Genbaku Home. Particularly moving is the patients re-enacting the tragic events of the Nagasaki bombing to young children who come to visit. The documentary succeeds in showing the daily trauma and survival that the *Hibakusha* patients endure but also their resolution and desire to spread their message of peace and the necessity for such an act to be never repeated again. Of equal importance is Masaaki Tanabe's documentary film *Ground Zero: Documents of Hiroshima*. An orphan to the bomb—both of his parents perished in the blast—Tanabe re-creates pre-war Hiroshima using 3D graphics before it was destroyed by the blast. Using firsthand accounts of survivors, old photographs and his own recollections, the film sets out to look for the lost, not only the human tragedy of the bombing but also the impact it had on the landscape and topography of Hiroshima, its history and cultural landmarks. We forget that the bombings did not only rob survivors of their loved ones, but the beauty of their landscape, their city and their homes. Small wonder the wound of the nation has transcended its national cinema with an affliction that it has been unable to shed.

This book is not designed to be a definitive collection on *Genbakudan* cinema but an academic forum for Pan-Pacific and Western writers to continue scholarly discussion on this area of Japanese cinema and for further academic research and reading on the subject matter. In fact, the book should be read in conjunction with Mick Broderick's seminal *Hibakusha Cinema* (Routledge, 2009) which focuses on elements of Japanese atomic cinema which are not covered in depth in this volume. Further recommended reading on the subject and films relating to Japanese atomic cinema is the entry in Japanese film historian Jasper Sharp's superb *Historical Dictionary of Japanese Cinema* (Scarecrow Press, 2011) which gives an exhaustive list of entries in this genre and the filmmakers behind them. Sharp's book was an invaluable aid during the research of this collection and on Japanese cinema in general as was his excellent book *Behind the Pink Curtain: The Complete History of Japanese Sex Cinema* (Fab Press, 2008). The inclusion of Western perspectives in Part III was necessary to establish a sense of balance to the book and to promote the small band of filmmakers who are actively debating and raising awareness of the atomic threat in the West. Yet, the bigger picture reveals that America and its Western allies have equally been unable to come to terms with the bombings of Hiroshima and Nagasaki and this has been reflective in the lack of films relating to the subject, as detailed by Nielsen and Ferrara in their essay "Hiroshima Films: Cultural Contexts Before, During, and After the Cold War." Unlike Japan, which has used its national cinema as a means of working out the trauma of Hiroshima and Nagasaki, the U.S., in particular Hollywood, has shunned cinematic discourse for it has come to represent a shameful chapter in its history and a trauma it too has had trouble coming to terms with.

Prologue:
Hiroshima/Nagasaki

Matthew Edwards

"Mr. President [Truman], I hope you have your answer ready for that hour when you and I stand before Saint Peter and he says, 'I understand you two are responsible for putting off those atomic bombs. What have you got to say for yourselves?'"[1]

Early on August 6, 1945, the people of Hiroshima rose tentatively from their shelters and homes, after a night interrupted by several air raid warnings, and into the thick, sticky August heat. The previous night, and early morning, air raid sirens had yielded no attack. Tired and weary, the people of Hiroshima set off to aid the war effort. Twelve thousand children went to work at demolition sites around the city, while government clerks filed into their prefectural offices, police and troops assembled around the city center, and doctors and nurses flooded into their hospitals to tend the sick and needy while "volunteer corps and neighbourhood associations went about their duties, morning exercises, prayers, donation collections and defence training."[2]

At 8:15, a B-29 flew high in the blue sky above the city approaching the Aioi Bridge. The B-29, the *Enola Gay*,[3] sped toward the bridge at a ground speed of 285 miles per hour. Some paused to watch the single fighter glint in the sky above them; many proceeded with their work. No alert rang out around the city; no warnings were given. From *Enola Gay*'s underbelly it birthed its light. "Little Boy" fell from the aircraft's undercarriage. The uranium bomb, a long projectile shaped like an "elongated trash can with fins"[4] as described by the crew, fell toward the city below. Scrawled with derogatory messages to the Japanese emperor Hirohito,[5] the bomb nosedived over Hiroshima Shima Hospital where it detonated 1,900 feet above the city. A brilliant noiseless light tore through the city, creating temperatures at "ground zero which reached 5,400 degrees and generated the explosive power of 12,500 tons of TNT."[6] All but 6,000 buildings were destroyed in the blast or by the resulting fire. As the *Enola Gay* turned sharply away from the blast, a mushroom cloud consumed the city and reached 45,000 feet toward the heavens as if to grab those who had unleashed its wrath. Staring out at the smoldering city below, crew member Sergeant George Caron remarked that the city seemed to be consumed in lava and that flames and fires kept springing up in different places before becoming obscured in the billowing smoke.[7]

On the ground, Little Boy's violent destructive force obliterated and charred Hiroshimans within a 500-meter radius of the bomb's epicenter and scorched the uncovered skin of those exposed to the searing heat within two kilometers. The velocity of the shock wave and heat rays subjected those on the ground to either instant or agonizing deaths and to horrendous injuries never before inflicted on humanity. Carbonized corpses littered the streets; mothers clung to their dead or headless babies; some were blinded by a tremendous light akin to that of a thousand suns; ghostly processions of naked and hideously burned people staggered through the smoldering city, their skin drooping from their burned bodies like oiled rags; many were left with severe deformities and keloid scars; thousands were killed through acute radiation poisoning. Scores of survivors lined the streets, desperate to escape the inferno. Lining the walkways they looked like phantoms, the walking dead. Keijiro Matsushima vividly remembers the horrifying injuries and aftermath: "Some were so badly burned from head to toe, their skin peeling from their heads. Their clothes were burned, some were almost naked. I thought to myself, 'Hiroshima is dying.' I could see red muscle under their skin. They held their arms forward, all of them, maybe because of the wounds. They were walking slowly in a long line, hundreds of them, like a procession of ghosts."[8] Hiroshima's rivers boiled. Those seeking sanctuary from the heat crawled to the riverbed, desperate for water. Many drowned. Soon the Aioi River was littered with the dead.

Then the "black rain" fell, a mixture of dust, ash and debris mixed with the atomic radioactive fallout from the initial bomb blast. Survivor Keiko Ogura recalls: "There was black rain falling, black rain mingling with ashes and rubbish and oil, something like that. It smelled bad and there were many spots on my white blouse—sticky, dirty rain."[9] The black rain fell back to earth as dangerously radioactive water that stained clothes, buildings and skin but also contaminated the water and food supply. Ingesting the black rain, either by eating, drinking or simply through breathing, caused radiation poisoning. In the following months and years, those exposed to the fallout experienced slow, agonizing deaths due to acute radiation sickness or their burns. Thousands had been made homeless. Hiroshima had been devastated, destroyed. It had been turned into hell on Earth, its burning city strewn with charred corpses and radioactive waste.

As Truman and America and its allies basked in the glory of the successful implementation of their new super-weapon, confidence was high that the war had been won and that the Japanese would surrender to the terms laid down by the Potsdam Proclamation on July 26, 1945. Japan dithered. Differing factions in the Japanese war cabinet prevented an end to the war, as they argued internally, with one side dragging Japan into a national *seppuku* as they vowed to fight to the death while the other protested that the nation be saved before annihilation by accepting the terms of surrender that had been placed before them, a proposition that many hard-line Japanese perceived be an act of treachery to the revered emperor. Unwilling to surrender, the Japanese sought continued help from the Soviets, believing they would facilitate a peace treaty with the U.S. and Great Britain that would be more favorable to them. On August 8, the Soviets declared war on Japan, pouring more than a million soldiers into Manchuria, a direct violation of the 1941 Soviet-Japanese Neutrality Pact (*Nisso chūritsu jōyaku*).

On the morning of August 9, Nagasaki felt the destructive force of "Fat Man," an implosion plutonium bomb that was initially intended for Kokura (Kyoto and Niigata had been withdrawn from the government's list of targets). Due to poor visibility, a build up of clouds, Kokura was spared Fat Man's atomic wrath and Nagasaki became the primary target. Nagasaki, a city whose topography was riven with hills and valleys that were broken up by stretches of water, was considered a shipbuilding and military port. At 11:02, the B-29 *Bockscar* flew above the city and released the bomb by parachute. The bomb detonated off course and away from its intended target, exploding 500 meters above ground over the district of Urakami (which was home to Japan's largest Christian population, and their spiritual cathedral, the biggest in Asia). Thirty percent of Nagasaki was destroyed during the bombing, including almost all of its industrial districts. While its topography did shield Nagasaki from a similar devastating fate, in that certain parts of the city survived the blast, its people were still subjected to the same horrific deaths and injuries as seen in Hiroshima—phantoms walking through flames, naked torsos covered in red lesions, swollen faces masked in blisters, charred remains. Survivor Katsuji Yoshida recalls the human cost and immediate aftermath of the bombing:

> There was a big bang and I was thrown 40 metres into a rice field. The skin on my arms had peeled off and was hanging down like a torn shirt from my fingertips. We had mud from the paddy all over us, and we pressed leaves on our exposed flesh to make up for missing skin. My right ear was blown off. Two of my ribs were broken and they've never mended, even 60 years later.
> A group of women came down from the fields, screaming, to an area where wooden houses were burning in a huge fire. All those dead and wounded people. Arms and legs cut off. Stomachs split open and intestines hanging out. Heads split open and brains hanging out. Eyes had popped out and I could see the blood vessels still pulsing. I have never seen such a brutal thing. Adults put their heads into the river and never came back up—they died just like that. People in the mountains were hit by black rain and for years they came down with diarrhoea. This is what the atom bomb is: even when you think the worst is over, it comes back to haunt you.[10]

The Urakami Cathedral, situated in the Catholic district of Nagasaki, which had taken more than three decades to build, was flattened in a mere three seconds. Having survived persecution through Catholicism's troubled history in Japan, its monument and grand statement of its faith was ironically destroyed by the winds of the West. As in Hiroshima, its people are still carrying the weight of the bombing to this very day. The physical and mental consequences of radiation still plague its population.

Estimates suggest 60,000 to 80,000 people died instantly in the blast at Hiroshima with the final death toll reaching around 200,000 by 1950. At Nagasaki, estimates suggest 40,000 were killed instantly and the final death toll was around 80,000. America had avenged Pearl Harbor. An eye for an eye mentality had kindled in the U.S. a burning desire to get even with the Japanese, especially after the bloody Pacific war and the appalling atrocities that the Japanese had committed throughout it. The U.S. has always maintained that the bombs were necessary to the end the war and to stop an invasion of Japanese that would have killed millions more people. Revisionist historians, however, have argued that the U.S. had no intention of executing such an operation and that they were fully aware that the Japanese were looking for a way to surrender, through their desperate attempts to get the Soviets to negotiate a more face-saving treaty that would allow them to keep Emperor Hirohito, who the Japanese revered as a god. Max Hastings agrees that "the dropping of the bombs did not represent, as Truman and others later claimed, a direct alternative to a costly U.S. invasion of Japan."[11] The Japanese were already on their knees due to Le May's successful carpet bomb campaign of Japan's major cities and the naval blockade that was starving Japan of vital food, provisions and essential goods and their heavy defeats in Manchuria and throughout Asia. Their last throw of the dice was to insist on Soviet intervention or a national *seppuku* if America invaded Japan where a costly and bloody land battle would leverage Japan with a "formidable bargaining chip."[12] In the end, their delusion and dickering proved their undoing as the U.S. grew impatient with the Japanese defiance and continued pursuit of war and rejection of the Potsdam Declaration. Despite estimates of a human cost between 63,000 and 1 million[13] if America proceeded with a land invasion, in the U.S. the next phase in the campaign against the Japanese was always intended to be the use of atomic weaponry. The invasion debate is a smokescreen; propaganda to justify the bombs' usage.

Ironically, evidence indicates that the dropping of the bombs on Hiroshima and Nagasaki did not force the Japanese to surrender. The decisive blow actually came on August 8, 1945, when the Soviets declared war against them, a direct violation of the Soviet-Japanese Neutrality Pact and the grim reality hit the Japanese government that the game was over. As General Dwight Eisenhower astutely pointed out, "Japan was at that very moment seeking some way to surrender with minimum loss of face. It was not necessary to hit them with that awful thing [the atomic bombs]."[14] Before Japan had time to ingest and react to the news that the Soviets had declared war against them, the U.S. and its allies proceeded with the dropping of the second nuclear weapon on Nagasaki. Historian Paul Ham sums up the folly and barbarism of this act in his horrifying and furious account of the bombings in *Hiroshima Nagasaki*: "Taken together, or alone, the reasons offered in defence of the bomb do not justify the massacre of innocent civilians. We debase ourselves, and the history of civilisation, if we accept that Japanese atrocities warranted an American atrocity in reply."[15]

Max Hastings, in his book on the battle of Japan, *Nemesis*, offers a more understanding view of the complexities of using atomic warfare on civilians (the U.S. had been against the bombing of civilians at the outset of the war but soon abandoned this stance as it got dragged further into the horrors of total war):

> In judging the behaviour of those responsible for ordering the atomic attacks, it seems necessary to acknowledge all this. The bomb was only the foremost of many huge issues with which these mortal men, movingly conscious of their own limitations, strove to grapple. In the course of directing a struggle for national survival, all had been obliged to make decisions which had cost lives, millions of lives, of both Allied servicemen and enemy soldiers and civilians.[16]

To some, the bombings of Nagasaki and Hiroshima were merely an extension of the aerial raids conducted by Le May's campaign in which his B-29s had been successful in reducing Japan's major cities to rubble and displacing millions of civilians. The atomic bombings achieved the same desired effect, yet without the requirement of a bomber force. Hasting also points out that though atomic warfare is horrific, obliteration through "conventional shells and bombs [that] dismember human bodies in the most repulsive fashion"[17] was equally abhorrent.

Evidence from the Japanese suggests that the dropping of the bombs had no immediate impact on Japanese leaders, as news was slow to reach Tokyo on the true nature of the bombs and the destruction they had caused (though news at the time of another burned-out city was unlikely to propel the Japanese leaders from its course of national suicide). When the Soviets entered the war against the Japanese leaders, however, they realized their chances had all but diminished. It was this development, and not that of the atomic bombings, that had been the overriding decisive factor in their surrender, as General Torashiro explained:

> It was only in a gradual manner that the horrible wreckage which had been made of Hiroshima become known…. In comparison, the Soviet entry into the war was a great shock when it actually came. Reports reaching Tokyo described Russian forces as "invading in swarms." It

gave us all the more severe shock and alarm because we had been in constant fear of it with a vivid imagination that "the vast Red Army forces in Europe were now being turned against us."[18]

Likewise, Admiral Toyoda further supports the theory that the Soviets' declaration of war swayed the Japanese cabinet to accept defeat and agree to a halt in the war when he said, "I believe that the Russian participation in the war against Japan rather than the atom bombs did more to hasten the surrender."[19]

For all Japan's atrocities, did an American and Allied atrocity of this magnitude on innocent women and children justify the use of atomic warfare as a means of ending the war? In truth, the bombs' deployment leads us to ask the question whether the bombs' use gave the U.S. an opportunity to showcase its military might to the world and its dominance in the region. A more significant factor was that the dropping of the bombs was a loud statement to their more strategic concern, Stalin and the Soviet Union. Was it a statement of intent to keep an evil they perceived in check? The Soviets' duplicity, self-aggrandizement and a perceived threat to U.S. security had left the Americans sensing the rise of a more formidable foe that needed to be kept in check.

The debate will rage on and opinions will continue to be polarized with regard to this sensitive issue. In the U.S., many still consider Truman's actions were wholly justified in stopping the Japanese war machine and saving the lives of many millions of Americans, despite growing evidence which pointedly indicates that the U.S. was fully aware that Japan was close to capitulation and that they were actively putting out peace-feelers to Moscow to help broker a settlement that was beneficial to the Japanese as opposed to offering submission to Washington. There is an argument as to whether we should hold the actions of those responsible for authorizing the bombings to account purely through hindsight and without the firsthand experience of living through the reality of such a devastating war and an enemy who was prepared to fight bitterly to the last man. Those who lived through the war, experienced firsthand combat with the Japanese and bore witness to Japanese cruelty, barbarism and atrocities believe the bombings were wholly justified in defeating their foe.

Finding a definitive answer to this difficult question is problematic for there are so many facets that led to the bombings. When debating such a sensitive question as to the rights and wrongs of the use of the atomic bombs, the reality paints a more distressing picture: to this day Japanese people are dying as a result of the bombings of Hiroshima and Nagasaki. We debase ourselves if we find such a notion acceptable. The consequences bring to the forefront the human devastation the bombs had on the people of Hiroshima and Nagasaki, and the psychological scars the nation has had to bear. Those exposed to the radioactive aftereffects suffered with a range of illnesses from chronic fatigue to blindness to a plethora of cancers. More explicitly, it reveals to us the true horrors of nuclear warfare. We need to ask ourselves if the toll of the lives lost in the blast and afterward, the bereavement of loved ones, the physical scarring and disfigurement and the psychological trauma on helpless civilians was a justifiable act in revenge for Pearl Harbor, the bloody Pacific War and wartime atrocities of the Japanese.

Ironically, when Japan officially surrendered, the U.S. conceded to the demands of Japan and retained Emperor Hirohito as a sovereign ruler. He was not tried, nor answerable or accountable for war crimes committed by his Imperial forces. Had Truman accepted the original Japanese surrender terms, more than 250,000 lives would have been saved. Telford Taylor, chief prosecutor at the Nuremberg trials, agreed. He believed the dropping of the atomic bomb on Hiroshima was debatable at best while the Nagasaki bombing he viewed as a war crime: "I've never heard a plausible justification [for the bombing on] Nagasaki."[20] Such cruelty and such an atrocity could have been prevented. Radioman Abe Spitzer, who watched the terrifying bombing of Hiroshima from the accompanying plane to the *Enola Gay*, the *Great Artiste*, best sums up the dropping of the bombs when he heard a second city, Nagasaki, had been wiped from the earth. "There was no need for more missions, more bombs, more fear and more dying. Good God, any fool could see that."[21]

Notes

1. P. Kuznick and O. Stone, *The Untold History of the United States* (New York: Simon & Schuster, 2012), p. 180.

2. P. Ham, *Hiroshima Nagasaki* (London: Black Swan, 2011), p. 316.

3. The B-29 was named after pilot Colonel Paul Tibbets' mother, Enola Gay Tibbets.

4. M. Hastings, *Nemesis: The Battle for Japan, 1944–45* (London: Harper Perennial, 2008), p. 519.

5. *Ibid.*

6. *Ibid.*

7. P. Ham, *Hiroshima Nagasaki* (London: Black Swan, 2011), p. 297.

8. C. Wikstrom, *The Day Hiroshima Turned into Hell* (Doha: Al Jazeera, 2011), www.aljazeera.com/indepth/2011/08/20118514019236497.html (accessed 14 September 2014).

9. K. Ogura, *Surviving Hiroshima* (London: BBC, 2005), http://news.bbc.co.uk/1/hi/world/asia-pacific/4739615.stm (accessed 14 September 2014).

10. D. Smith, *Children of Hiroshima* (London: Guardian, 2005), http://www.theguardian.com/world/2005/jul/24/secondworldwar.japan (accessed 14 September 2014).

11. M. Hastings, *Nemesis: The Battle for Japan, 1944–45* (London: Harper Perennial, 2008), p. 498.

12. *Ibid.*, p. 497.

13. *Ibid.*, pp. 497–8.

14. P. Ham, *Hiroshima Nagasaki* (London: Black Swan, 2011), p. 483.

15. *Ibid.*, p. 487.

16. M. Hastings, *Nemesis: The Battle for Japan, 1944–45* (London: Harper Perennial, 2008), p. 515.

17. *Ibid.*, p. 516.

18. P. Kuznick and O. Stone, *The Untold History of the United States* (New York: Simon & Schuster, 2012), p. 175.

19. *Ibid.*

20. *Ibid.*, p. 173.

21. *Ibid.*

The Rhetorical Significance of *Gojira*: Equipment for Living Through Trauma

SHANNON STEVENS

The first time I watched *Gojira* (*Godzilla*, 1954), immersed as I was that year in my studies of the Atomic Testing Museum in Las Vegas, the film affected me deeply, nearly moving me to tears with its painful images of injured and dying children in overflowing hospital wards, of poisoned wells in small villages, and of mothers trying in vain to shield their children from the fires about to consume them, a clear homage to the suffering brought about by the atomic bombing of Japan. After another screening and some early research into the film, beginning with William M. Tsutsui's 2004 seminal text *Godzilla on My Mind: Fifty Years of the King of Monsters*,[1] it became increasingly clear that *Gojira* exists as an important and unique response to a profound historical-cultural experience. Known to most Americans as "*Godzilla*," a crude phonetic interpretation of the Japanese name for the country's most memorable monster, Japan's 1954 science-fiction blockbuster looms large amid others of its time and genre, not just because of its superior special effects, actors and directors, but more importantly because of its vital therapeutic function for a society traumatized both by atomic bombings and by an oppressive regime that forbade all discussion of that trauma. As a rhetorician, I understand films to exist as equipment for living,[2] and *Gojira* is no exception. In this essay I will show that *Gojira* is equipment for living, but, more importantly, I show that it is equipment for living through trauma.

The method I used to enable the analysis you will read below is based primarily on the work of rhetoricians Martin J. Medhurst and Thomas W. Benson, which called for extensive research of the historical framework in which the film exists. To establish that context, I utilized a depth of rhetorical and historical texts on the time period, including a range of analysis of nuclear culture, the Cold War, World War II, popular culture/science fiction, the monster-movie genre, and *Gojira* itself[3] as well as primary texts (government documents, news reports from the period, and speeches from the period).[4] It was through this extensive analysis that I was able to ascertain several important facts that you will need to know before proceeding to the analysis of the film. First, even prior to the bombings, Japanese society had endured centuries of Empirical domination, a domination ratcheted to new heights when Japan went to war with China in 1937; under such domination every aspect of society was controlled by the empire, from Nazi-inspired schooling to required village meetings for listening to propaganda messages to the sleeve length and fabric of clothes.[5] Second, the U.S.–led occupation of Japan not only profoundly changed the structure of Japanese society, but engaged in absolute censorship of *any negative references* to the bombing of Hiroshima and Nagasaki or anything critical in any way of the nuclear; references to the bombs were only allowed when they focused on the significant (and positive) role nuclear weapons played as an end to the war and a pathway to peace.[6] And, finally, although in 1952 the occupation forces left Japan to its own rule and to decide for itself what would and would not be discussed openly, by that time it was too late for free expression to take hold.[7] After more than a decade of strict Japanese and American governmental controls, and more than five years of legal constraints on freedom of expression about the nuclear, what was once verboten through hegemonic means remained as a cultural taboo that limited open criticism of atomic weapons and weapons testing.[8]

Having established the historical context of *Gojira*, which was released in 1954 just two years after the occupation ended, it was possible to move forward with a close reading of the film. Here I chose to draw my method from a psychoanalytic approach, much like that established by Janice Hocker Rushing and Thomas S. Frentz who use Jungian psychology to explore cultural fears and beliefs as a way to make sense of the dominant motifs in the film. For my analysis I rely upon research in the area of Post Traumatic Stress Disorder (PTSD) to better understand the film's response to the war; as will be discussed in further detail, PTSD research that expands our understanding of trauma and its effect on the individual and cultural psyche makes it a natural fit for examining an artifact that came into being from the wellspring of profound trauma. Further, a primary treatment method for PTSD is that of the guided narrative. At the same time, narrative is a long-recognized tool among critical scholars, understood as a powerful tool for symbol making by all humans.[9] What emerges from close study of the film is three emotional pairings, which align with primary emotions present in PTSD literature. Considering that from a mental health perspective it is vital to talk about the emotions that inevitably surface after a trauma, it is not surprising that *Gojira*, one of the earliest post-occupation/post-censorship public artifacts to be created in Japan, would be rife with relevant emotional themes. In my analysis of the film I explore the representations of those emotional pairings and how they relate to the experience of enduring a nuclear attack. Specifically, *Gojira*, developed simultaneously by its creators to be a blockbuster film and a response to the war, functioned as a safe venue for the Japanese people to gather publically and share their experiences and their memories of the horrors of the war that changed everything for them. By sharing that experience through a creative narrative that ultimately restores Japan's honor, the creators and watchers of the film could use the fiction of *Gojira*, "the coalescing into solid form"[10] of nearly a decade of suppressed thought and feeling, to find some peace in the reality of their existence. As such, the film served a needed function in Japan by helping its people to work through their trauma and create a healthier narrative in which to move forward with their lives.

Analysis

> *Although most films provide avenues for escape and are primarily produced for profit they do much more than that. They pull us into our cultural unconscious to meet our shadows, those disowned aspects of ourselves that we loathe.*[11]

Research into the area of Post Traumatic Stress Disorder (PTSD), which in World War II was called "shell shock," is extensive. That matters here for two reasons: first, it is increasingly apparent that trauma affects humans universally regardless of their cultural setting; and second, when PTSD is ignored the effects on those who have experienced the trauma can be socially and psychologically crippling.[12] The importance of recognizing the emotional and psychological ramifications of trauma in leading a healthy and productive life help make it clear why the emotionality of *Gojira* was so important for the Japanese, many of whom left the theaters in tears after seeing the film the first time.[13] Further, recognition of the grief of others is an important step toward reconstructing the traumatized people's reality positively, as Donna K. Nagata and Wendy J. Y. Chen observed in relation to redress for Japanese Americans put in concentration camps after Pearl Harbor. The American government's admission of wrongdoing in that case opened the door for more open discussion of the experience by the survivors and their offspring, thereby leading to reduced feelings of guilt and shame.[14] A growing body of research also points to the use of narrative as an effective treatment approach for those with PTSD[15]; through guided story telling about the traumatic events—story telling that is encouraged to include metaphor—therapists and social workers can help their clients find avenues to growth as opposed to "chronic interpersonal, societal, and medical problems."[16]

To be clear, although the label PTSD includes the word "post," delayed response is not necessary. It is important to remember that those who suffer from PTSD often get stuck in a heightened emotional state, causing them to relive almost constantly the emotions related to the trauma.

Narrative is especially useful in helping people recover from trauma because it allows them to experience concurrently the trauma of the past in the present, but in a guided and safe way.[17] A film that explores trauma metaphorically allows viewers to revisit their past trauma simultaneously with the characters on the screen, who are fictionally experiencing the emotions for the first time. While it is impossible to return to 1954 and study the audience response to *Gojira*, we do know some things that indicate its powerful effect on viewers. Many left the theater in tears, but their tears did not discourage others from watching the film; rather, *Gojira* became a blockbuster success viewed by millions of Japanese.[18] And while it was certainly the intent of producer Tomoyuki Tanaka and director Ishirō Honda to create a blockbuster film, multiple sources from IMDB to William Tsutsui to the liner notes of the *Gojira* 2004 DVD release tell us that both men also intended the film to be a response to Hiroshima and Nagasaki. As such, it can be reasonably assumed that their intent, at least in part, was to evoke war-related emotion with the film's narrative.[19] By examining the strong emotional themes expressed in the narrative *Gojira* we can begin to understand better the experience of the Japanese survivor of World War II, as well as the part Americans played in the creation of that reality at a most profound intersection of cultures, technologies, and war.

Close reading of *Gojira* reveals three dominant emotional pairings in the film, pairings that are included in mental health literature among the primary responses to a war experience and are prevalent in PTSD. Those pairings are: guilt/anger, pain/suffering, and powerlessness/fear. Although in my own complete analysis of the film, I unpack every scene that contains such a pairing, for this essay I will focus on the scenes where there is overlap of emotional themes. Such overlap creates heightened tensions and drama that, at first viewing, can make it difficult to make sense of the messages being shared in *Gojira's* most powerful scenes. One of the advantages of this type of thematic analysis is that it allows space for moving beyond affect at its blinding core to enable clearer readings of texts.

Guilt/Anger

Guilt and anger are complex emotions that are often intertwined, mixed up as they are in feelings of causality, culpability, and responsibility.[20] It is known from historical accounts that shortly after the war ended in Japan, many of the country's citizens felt some responsibility for bringing upon them the wrath of American technology. At the same time, many of the country's leaders preferred to avoid discussions about the bombs as a means of avoiding a related conversation about Japan's own guilt of committing wartime atrocities.[21] In *Gojira*, while some of that complexity of guilt and anger about the war can be observed from early in the film, here I will begin with the segment of the film that clearly indicates the guilt of the Japanese people for enraging the beast, a segment which spans four chapters: "Godzilla Attacks," "Unstoppable Rampage," "Live from the Scene," and "Air Strike."[22] In this central part of the film—the monster's attack on Tokyo—the retribution response of Godzilla is shockingly severe, yet somewhat understandable, as the Japanese leaders and military enact a plan devised to crush the monster. Instead, their plan merely hurts Godzilla, further enraging it and incurring its wrath just as Japanese military action did to the United States in World War II. With such clear metaphorical representations of guilt and anger experienced by Japanese citizens, the narrative of *Gojira* begins in this pairing its work to allow a guided traversing of these challenging emotions.

As the chapter "Godzilla Attacks" begins, a radio bulletin announces that Godzilla has been spotted and that it is time to power the thirty-meter high, eighty-meter deep electric fence. The fence was built in conjunction by the Coast Guard and the Army at the water's edge in Tokyo, despite the opposition of Professor Yamane, the scientist/archeologist who is the film's "expert" on the monster. The goal of the fence is to have fifty-thousand volts of current run through it in order to electrocute Godzilla when it comes ashore, which the leadership apparently deems an inevitable occurrence. By ignoring Professor Yamane's repeated warnings about bright lights aggravating the monster, the military does in fact drive Godzilla to shore with giant spotlights shone over the ocean. The soldiers also aim cannons at the monster as it lumbers toward land, though they appear as toys in comparison to the towering, fifty-meter high Godzilla; the electric fence comes up only as high as the creature's chest. As the fence is reached, the power is turned on, electrifying it, and the cannons are fired.

However, despite the efficiency of the military in erecting its electric barrier, rather than kill Godzilla the fence merely causes the creature to scream out in pain and rage. The cannon balls exploding earth at its feet further anger the creature as it tears the fence apart with its "hands" and screams its unearthly bellow,[23] tearing more of the fence down with its tail. Now completely outraged by what is happening, Godzilla melts the fence with its breath and its back fins light up the angrier it gets. With those fins aglow it exhales hot wind that instantly ignites, as would an atomic radiation flash, whole blocks at a time, incinerates people to ash where they stand, and burns and melts vehicles both stationary and in motion. It is impossible to watch this scene and not think of atomic blast testing videos and Hiroshima and Nagasaki footage and reports. As the scene progresses, the military's next line of defense opens fire, unloading cannon balls into Godzilla's abdomen and chest. Again, the military's action fails to stop the monster's progress; to the contrary, the monster responds by advancing farther and unleashing more hot breath onto the tanks and then all of Tokyo. Though we are not sure if Godzilla would have advanced on Tokyo anyway, the film makes clear that Japan's military ensured the monster's attack and increased its ferocity many times, which again clearly functions metaphorically for Japanese responsibility for the actions taken by the United States during the war.[24]

The final two chapters of this section, "Live from the Scene" and "Air Strike," are the last two segments that illustrate the guilt of the people in fueling the wrath of Godzilla. In "Live from the Scene," which follows the near-complete destruction of Tokyo, the ever-present reporters are seen in a large radio tower from which they are reporting the entire scene on camera, by radio, and with notebooks as it unfolds. From Godzilla's perspective the tower is a maddening collection of flashing lights—again Professor Yamane's warning about bright lights goes unheeded. It is clear from the audience's perspective that the camera flashes simultaneously disturb and attract the monster. Reporters fall to their deaths in the midst of their reports as the monster melts and tears the tower to the ground. At last, Godzilla heads back toward the sea, though the military still has time for one more hapless attack in "Air Strike." This time the military tries using its planes to shoot guns and rockets at Godzilla, which, like all other attempts to conquer, only causes it to become angry and confused as it bats the planes from the sky. Finally, as Godzilla submerges into the water—seemingly because it is exhausted for now rather than defeated—the sea glows and bubbles and steams as the enraged monster disappears. The scene closes with rays spreading out over the water, not unlike the rays on the flag of the Japanese navy, which had itself been ineffective in keeping America from Japan's shores. At last the viewers of the film, grouped safely together in a theater, can openly experience guilt and anger through this narrative, enabling them to begin facing the shadows in their psyche, an important step toward healing.

The next two dominant references to guilt in the film relate directly to that felt by scientists about creating deadly weapons, a guilt that often erupts into anger. The first scene expressing scientific guilt is in "An Ultimate Weapon," the chapter in which Emiko (Professor Yamane's daughter) has a flashback to an earlier conversation with Professor Serizawa, the scientist and war veteran whom she has known all her life and is expected to marry (although she intends to marry the suave young Ogata, not Serizawa). It is during the flashback that the secret weapon developed by Serizawa is revealed. Dubbed "Oxygen Destroyer," the fictional weapon, initially studied as a source of energy in a clear nuclear parallel, works by splitting oxygen atoms into liquids. Its power is illustrated as a small version (in the form of something resembling a ball bearing) is dropped into a fish tank in the lab. The ball begins to bubble and as Emiko watches the fish are reduced first to skeletons, then to a few pieces of flesh, and finally to nothing in a foreshadowing of another guilt-ridden scene, also to be discussed. After the flashback, the scene continues in the chapters "A Moral Dilemma" and "Never to Be Used Again," when Ogata and Emiko break into the lab and an argument about the use of the weapon against Godzilla ensues.

Serizawa expresses the emotion of guilt in these scenes both verbally and nonverbally. Verbally it is expressed in his conversations first with Emiko and then with Ogata. In the early part of the scene, Emiko functions as an externalization of Serizawa's own conscience when she asks questions such as "Why are you working on such an awful project?" and "What if your discovery is used for some horrible purpose?" While at first he tries to defend his work—in an irritated tone—by claiming to perform it "strictly as a research scientist," he quickly admits that if his discovery were to be used as a weapon, its power would equal a nuclear bomb. "I could totally destroy humankind," he says. Here it is possible not only for viewers to work through their own feelings of guilt and anger about nuclear weapons, but to simultaneously empathize with themselves and with the creators of the bombs, as narrative works again to help heal the psyche so damaged by trauma and decades of silence.

In the very next chapter, "A Moral Dilemma," back in the lab and immediately following a violent altercation between Serizawa and Ogata, Serizawa tries to explain to Ogata why the Oxygen Destroyer must not be used against Godzilla. Serizawa says that if his device could be used for a good purpose, of course he would "announce it to everyone in the world! But in its current form, it is just a weapon of horrible destruction." His guilt about his creation is further expressed verbally as he explains that to use the weapon even once would expose it to politicians worldwide. "Of course they will want to use it as a weapon.... Bombs vs. bombs, missiles vs. missiles. And now a new superweapon to throw upon us all. As a scientist, no, as a human being, I cannot allow that to happen! Am I right?" Serizawa also expresses his anxiety further when he says that "humans are weak animals," and that even if all of his notes were destroyed, so long as the secret exists in his head, humankind would be at risk. "Until I die, how can I be sure that I won't be forced by someone to make the device again?" asks Serizawa before crying out in anguish, "What am I going to do?"

Nonverbally, the scenes just discussed are rife with guilt imagery as well as eruptions of guilt into anger. When Serizawa talks about how the Oxygen Destroyer works, he does so standing up straight, hands behind his back, and head up in a noble but rigid stance as he explains that his intent was to devote his life to the study of oxygen; all the while, Emiko (still in the role as an externalization of Serizawa's conscience) stares at him with a mix of horror, anguish, and accusation. As his story progresses and he discloses his terrifying discovery, the character begins leaning heavily on a work table covered in glass testing equipment, apparently weighed down by this knowledge. He casts his head down as he tells Emiko that he didn't eat for two or three days, so heavy was the guilt about his discovery.

Serizawa's upset and feelings of guilt become even more obvious as he begins pacing. He reaches down and picks up the mortar and pestle that contains his Oxygen Destroyer as he shouts out its destructive ability, holding it chest height and away from his body, in a pose at once reverential and filled with fear and disgust. He pauses, looks at it. Then, weighed down by guilt, he continues at a methodical pace to walk toward the cabinet where he locks up the Oxygen Destroyer. As the flashback ends and the film continues with "A Moral Dilemma" the nonverbal expressions of guilt intensify. First, just after Ogata and Emiko have broken into the lab to find Serizawa burning his notes, the tension that has been building over the weapon erupts into a physical altercation between Serizawa and Ogata which ends with the war-veteran scientist victorious, standing over the younger, wounded Ogata who is bleeding on the floor. Serizawa's expression is one of stunned embarrassment rather than victory, however, and he soon kneels to the floor to help Ogata. As Emiko is wrapping Ogata's head wound, Serizawa looks on in horror, sweat covering his face, and then he turns away and hangs his head as his guilt, shame, and anguish overtake him. Through the painful narrative of the noble Serizawa, viewers can at once witness and remember the many physical and emotional manifestations of a post-traumatic state while empathizing with the characters and, at the same time, with themselves.

After discussing with Ogata his fears that if the weapon is used against Godzilla it will be turned next against all of humankind unless Serizawa himself dies along with all his research, the scientist ends up crying and hunched over in his chair, rocking back and forth with his head in his hands. It is not until the next chapter, "Never to Be Used Again," that we see a physical change in Serizawa as he finds a way to assuage some of his guilt by destroying his research. A televised prayer vigil with children singing a chant for peace finally spurs Serizawa out of his crippling state of guilt and into action. While still appearing to show the manifestations of his guilty conscience with his head down and his shoulders hunched over, the character clearly has an internal change. He steadies himself and stands up, wordlessly moving past Emiko, Ogata, and the television to pick up a stack of papers. As he burns his research notes and so purges the cause of his guilt, for the first time in the film Serizawa looks happy and at peace, smiling serenely as he tells Emiko not to cry. In the final scene of the film the audience learns that his peace comes from his decision to destroy not just his research, but to sacrifice his own life to secure his guilty secret and, at once, restore his honor and that of his country. So, too, can the audience experience through the narrative of Serizawa what it could mean for them to let go of the guilt and anger, to move through the trauma.

The next chapters that express guilt rooted in science are also the last two of the film, "Weapon of Choice" and "Danger of the Deep," the scenes in which the Oxygen Destroyer is used to kill Godzilla. In those final chapters the verbal expressions of guilt come through the words of the old scientist, Professor Yamane. Most of the expressions of guilt are non-verbal as much of the closing chapters take place under water or on deck where Emiko and Ogata appear to be too wracked with guilt and grief to say much. Interestingly, the sorrowful expressions of Professor Yamane are in direct contrast to the exhortations of the throng of reporters present to witness the demise of Godzilla. The reporters shout their news, reporting "exhilaration" and "jubilation" at the victory over Godzilla, a success they attribute to the "young scientist Serizawa," a jubilation reflective of the journalists during World War II who reported on the latest scientific and weapons advancements often with unabashed enthusiasm.[25] Professor Yamane, however, when he realizes that Serizawa has sacrificed his life with Godzilla's on the ocean floor, stands up on deck on the ship that floats above where his friend is dying and removes his hat in respect, his face filled with sorrow, saying only "Serizawa…" Though the actual last words of the film are "Salute!" and "At ease," part of the final farewell to Serizawa, the last meaningful words spoken by a known character are Professor Yamane's. The words hark back to the earlier expressions of guilt as it relates to humankind's role in creating Godzilla, while simultaneously preparing the audience for a sequel. "I can't believe that Godzilla was the only surviving member of its species…," he says, trailing off in sadness at the death of the monster. "But, if we keep on conducting nuclear tests, it's possible that another Godzilla might appear … somewhere in the world, again."

The nonverbal expressions of guilt in those final chapters begin underwater where Serizawa and Ogata have trekked in diving suits to release the Oxygen Destroyer where Godzilla rests. Serizawa tricks Ogata into returning to the surface without him, leaving Serizawa to his planned suicide. He sweats profusely as he watches the monster writhe in pain. Once he is certain his weapon has worked, he releases Ogata and Emiko to one another by wishing them happiness, shouting out "Goodbye…. Farewell!" as his weapon destroys him. It is primarily Emiko and Ogata who physically express guilt in that last chapter. Ogata's head is bowed as he weeps, still wearing his diving suit, as all the guilt about his clandestine relationship with Emiko, his inability to save Serizawa, and his unwillingness to consider another fate for Godzilla coalesce. Emiko is next to him, holding onto his shoulders, sobbing. Ogata picks up his head just long enough to look at Emiko and says of Serizawa, "He wanted us to be happy"; that causes both to bow their heads again and weep in sorrow and guilt. Their eyes are cast away from one another in a nonverbal expression of guilt too great and shameful to allow them to look at each other. Emiko lets go of Ogata and falls to the deck sobbing, she is so overcome. Finally, the secondary character of Professor Tanabe, who has assisted Professor Yamane throughout the film, gives the last indication of scientific guilt after Yamane makes his statement about continued nuclear testing likely to create more monsters. Tanabe, who has been seated behind Yamane, gets up as the words are spoken, pulling his hand through his hair, his face troubled, and he walks slowly away, his shoulders slumped. This profoundly emotional narrative creates space for remembering, for feeling, for contextualizing a decade of guilt and anger, a vital step toward the healing offered in addressing the emotions heightened for those living in a post-traumatic stress state.

Pain/Suffering

There is surely no shortage of information available regarding the pain and suffering experienced by all peoples involved in World War II, or any war for that matter. Pain and suffering are virtually a requirement of warfare and are themes that crop up not only in PTSD research but in narratives of all kinds, including novels, films, documentaries, and even history books. Pain and suffering, common in many narratives both fictional and factual, also have an inherent drama as every human can relate to the emotions on some level. Pain and suffering can also be effective tools for moving a plot forward as those feelings often elicit a response and can lead to growth and change. As illustrated here, however, the pain and suffering themes in *Gojira* are more than effective plot-driving mechanisms; clear metaphors with the war and the bombings throughout the scenes rife with pain and suffering emphasize that the emotions are a post-war expression and purging.

During Godzilla's first urban attack in "Destruction from the Deep" is a scene of emotional overlap where we can experience pain and suffering. In this chapter, Godzilla comes ashore, trampling in its methodical way the massive power lines in its path as it heads toward the railroad tracks that run along the bay. The oblivion of the engineers and the passengers of the train to the danger ahead of them changes abruptly when the monster's foot falls on the tracks just as the train gets there, causing a terrible crash and destruction. People are hurled about the train cars; while some escape from the windows, many do not as Godzilla even chomps on a train car before tossing it aside with his jaws to the sounds of people screaming in pain and fear.

Pain and suffering also are palpable in those key chapters during which Godzilla attacks Tokyo, chapters already discussed in relation to guilt and anger. Here the pain and suffering are not just that of the humans under attack by the monster but also that of the monster itself. First, the pain caused to Godzilla by the electrified fence is clear by its screams and its physical response of tearing at the fence with its "hands" to get the fencing off its body. Its pain and suffering are also clear as it bends and screams when it is being pelted with cannon fire, when it is shocked as it runs into a train station, and again when it swats at the planes that shoot at it as it attempts to return to the sea. However, in the chapters that span the Tokyo attack, it is clearly the humans who suffer most.

First, Godzilla in its rage and pain exhales hot wind that instantly ignites whole blocks at a time and incinerates people where they stand. The people under attack endure not only a painful death by fire, but they get the added suffering of knowing it is coming; they try to run, but they cannot run fast enough. Fire spreads from district to district, burning anything in its path in a scene reminiscent of the fire bombings before the atomic bombs were dropped as well as the aftermath of the atomic bombs themselves. In a particularly emotional vignette, a mother and her two small children cower in an alley while Godzilla continues on its rampage. Huddling in their street corner, the mother says to the children, "We'll be joining your father in just a moment! A little longer, a little longer, and we'll be with your daddy!" The audience endures with the mother the pain of knowing her children are about to die with the simultaneous recognition that she has likely been suffering since her husband's death. Though the film does not show the family dying, their death is clearly implied with the destruction of a massive building like the one beneath which they crouched. The final bit of human pain and suffering in that section of the film is the death of the reporters as their radio tower is torn down and the reporters all die, fully aware of what is about to happen to them. While it may not be possible to put ourselves in a matching psychological state with the viewers, it is a fairly small step to imagine their powerful reliving of pain and suffering permitted here, a reliving made safe through narrative and metaphor.

"The Human Toll," the chapter following the attack on Tokyo, is among the most powerful of the expressions of pain and suffering, which is certainly fueled by the direct allusion to the aftermath of the devastating fire bombings and atomic attacks on Japan. The chapter opens with the camera panning over what is left of Tokyo in the morning—and it is not much. Crumbled buildings, smoking rubble, spots of flame, melted metal—it looks virtually identical to the post-bombing photos of Hiroshima and Nagasaki. The hospital shown next is full of people—nurses, military paramedics, and civilian paramedics all bringing in the wounded in a steady stream. As the camera moves inside the hospital it is clear that it is filled to capacity as the wounded continue to be brought in where they are placed on stretchers on the floor. Even the floor and hallways are filling up to capacity with wounded. Emiko is inside volunteering as a scientist and takes Geiger counter readings on a child who sits on the floor next to her mother and sister. The child looks forlorn and stunned, and the rapid ticking of the Geiger counter tells us that the pain she suffers likely is just the beginning. It is a powerful narrative for anyone, but a particularly important one for expressing pain and suffering by those who had not been permitted to discuss the trauma of radiation poisoning.

In the next chapters, set in Serizawa's lab, there are a few scattered images of pain and suffering, such as Ogata's injuries after his fight with the scientist and the televised report that shows row upon row of wounded being tended by medical personnel as well as family, again including children both as wounded and as tenders. However, for the most intense pain and suffering imagery, it is necessary to move on to the final chapter, "Danger of the Deep." It is Godzilla and Serizawa that best illustrate this emotional pairing in the closing scenes. Serizawa's pain and suffering, of course, also function as his release from the same, which he has endured since discovering the Oxygen Destroyer. Regardless of his resolve, the desperate tone in his voice as he shouts his "Goodbye.... Farewell!" to Emiko and Ogata makes it clear that his death will not be a comfortable one. Witnessing the death of Godzilla drives home that point as well.

Once the Oxygen Destroyer has begun to bubble, almost immediately Godzilla begins to writhe in pain. Soon it is clear that the monster is screaming in pain, though because it is underwater, nothing can yet be heard. However, with the flailing of its arms and its mouth wide open and thrown back as it was when screaming on land, its pain and its suffering are obvious. The death is not a quick one. As the scene progresses the cameras show the boat that holds the scientists and military; the Oxygen Destroyer creates tremendous turbulence in the water next to the boat. Godzilla rises out of the water to its shoulders and utters its familiar scream one long, last time. It falls backwards into the furiously bubbling water soundlessly. As it reaches the ocean floor, it is nearly motionless. Lying face down, it is only able to lift one arm slightly, its last move in a painful death. The pain and suffering end only when the monster is dissolved, first into a skeleton, then into nothing.

As should be clear, both pain and suffering are dominant and important motifs in *Gojira*. Serving as more than plot-moving devices, the emotions give voice to much of the Japanese experience toward the end of and after World War II. The destruction of cities in Japan was a traumatic experience that affected all of its citizens. By separating out the complexities of emotion into individual pairings, it is easier to understand and identify with this one-time enemy. For example, it can be difficult for American World War II veterans to identify with *Hibakusha* in any meaningful way because guilt and anger make it difficult to see past the Japanese atrocities that played a part in bringing the wrath of atomic weapons upon them. By extracting guilt and anger and focusing on pain and suffering, it is possible in this new narrative to relate better to the humanity of the people and to see how profoundly the events of the war affected their group and individual psyches.

Powerlessness/Fear

Powerlessness and fear is the final emotional pairing theme to be addressed. The emotions are rampant in *Gojira* and are most often tied to scenes that evoke wartime occurrences through imagery or allegory. Remembering the importance of narrative in working through PTSD, it can be extremely useful for those who have endured trauma to give voice to their feelings of powerlessness both during and after the event, particularly in story form. Putting powerlessness into a narrative gives the story teller and the listener the ability to rewrite the outcome in beneficial ways. The same goes for fear, which in those with PTSD is an emotional response that is often amplified in reaction to stimulus long after the event has passed. By exploring it in story form, fear can be understood and dealt with and, hopefully, reduced from daily life.

Powerlessness and fear, although the very first emotions expressed in the film in the opening scene, "Attack on the Eiko-Maru," will be discussed here only in places where the pairing overlaps with other emotional pairings. That means revisiting Godzilla's first urban attack in "Destruction from the Deep." In this chapter, Professor Yamane again is powerless to stop the military from making terrible mistakes that exacerbate the situation. He tries to tell them to stop shining bright lights because it angers the monster. A soldier tells him, "We don't have time for that now," in a tone both gruff and disrespectful. At the same time, the military is powerless to stop the monster as it tosses aside bridges, burns emergency vehicles and tanks, and wipes out whole blocks at a time with its tail. The powerlessness of the citizenry is also illustrated in another scene evocative of wartime activities, including evacuations. People are seen running, all their possessions on hand carts, as small children are lifted up by soldiers and put onto military trucks. Clearly frightened, everyone runs at the command of the Army soldiers, trying to flee the approaching footfalls. Their efforts will be largely useless, though there is nothing else for them to do, so powerless are they against the force coming down upon them.

The next scene rife with powerlessness and fear has been touched upon twice, and that is the attack on Tokyo. It does not matter what the military does, what the scientists say, what the journalists report—no one has the power to stop Godzilla. Cannons fail, fighter planes fail, giant electrified fences fail, barricades fail, tanks fail, rifles fail. Firefighters' attempts to quell the damage also fail. Concrete is fallible, children are not exempt, even birds in an aviary are incinerated. The reporters, even as they report blow by blow what is happening, are powerless to stop their own death. As a powerless observer of not one but two attacks, a boy who earlier watched and screamed as his brother Masaji was trampled to death on Ōto Island (the first place Godzilla is sighted) stands next to Professor Yamane during the Tokyo attack. As the monster returns to sea, the boy curses, "Damn it. Damn it." Finally the scene concludes with one more impotent attempt by the military to shoot down Godzilla by plane; though some people cheer as it submerges, it is clearly not a real victory as the monster has gone away—for now—because it is tired, not because of any efforts to force it to leave. That powerlessness is reflected in the clear allegory for the failed efforts of Japan to thwart its enemies as the scene closes with the rays of the sun spread over the water under which Godzilla waits. As mentioned earlier, those rays evoke the Japanese naval flag, and when seen in light of the powerlessness of the navy to actually defeat its enemy, the imagery strengthens that feeling of powerlessness with undertones of irony.

The next expressions of powerlessness arrive in the hospital scenes in "The Human Toll." The scientists who hold the ticking Geiger counter on the children are powerless to do anything about it, as indicated by the grave shaking of heads and downcast eyes. Even Emiko's attempts to comfort a frightened child whose mother has been taken away are useless as she is completely powerless to help the child. As Emiko tells her that her mother will be all right, that is clearly a most unlikely scenario. Interestingly, it is that powerlessness and fear of more of the same that drives the character to break her promise to Serizawa and tell Ogata about the Oxygen Destroyer. In this narrative, the viewers can at once relive their own powerlessness and fear while experiencing what might happen if such emotions were turned into action, an important step toward healing.

In the flashback scene in which Emiko visits Serizawa's lab, the powerlessness and fear expressed is primarily related to scientific discovery. Remember that in the scene, Serizawa talks about his accidental (i.e., without the power of control) discovery of an unknown form of energy, a powerful force that scared him "beyond words." Much as J. Robert Oppenheimer and other scientists involved in the Manhattan Project experienced terrible anxieties about the potential destructive use of their research,[26] Serizawa is terrified that his discovery will be used as a weapon that would "destroy humankind." So powerless is he over the use of his discovery that he keeps it a complete secret, revealing it finally only to his betrothed, whom he has known since they were children. Even so, he swears her to secrecy as he explains further that if anyone finds out about his device he will destroy all of his research so that it cannot be created again, and here he alludes to his death as a necessary outcome if he is to keep the discovery secret. In a strange twist on powerlessness and fear, Serizawa can only conquer both by essentially taking his life as his last act of self will, an act that permanently removes all power at his own hand.

This same discussion continues in "A Moral Dilemma" as Serizawa is forced to explain his reasoning to Ogata. The scientist's terrible dilemma puts him in the unenviable position of being the only human with the power to stop the monster, yet he has the knowledge and understanding that to do so must mean his death or else the end of the world. This complex portrait of a scientist, clearly an allegory for nuclear researchers, is further deepened when the television kicks on and the terrible images of Tokyo destroyed and sick wounded children and families in the hospital brings Serizawa's anxiety to a head. Of course, witnessing such destruction and suffering is too much for the war veteran, and so he internally makes the decision to take action. As he knows he is powerless against the military and government machine, once he has made the decision to use the Oxygen Destroyer, he begins burning his research as Emiko looks on, powerless herself to do anything to stop him for the same reason that he must destroy his work.

At last, the culmination of powerlessness and fear in the film is exhibited in Godzilla itself. It is in "Danger of the Deep" that Godzilla is for the first time shown when it is at rest rather than out on a rampage. It does not look as scary when it is sleeping at the bottom of Tokyo Bay, resting its head on a rock. As it notices the arrival of Serizawa and Ogata in their diving suits, it is slow to move its head around, and as it moves to get up for the first time it is possible to see without distraction that its flesh appears burned and ragged like the body of someone wounded or killed by an atomic bomb. The imagery of burned flesh and a resting sea creature drives home the point that the monster itself was powerless to decide its fate; it was once a peaceful resident of the deep sea. The actions of scientists, the military, and governments without provocation drove Godzilla from its home, burned it, irradiated it, leaving the simple animal few outlets for its rage other than turning it on the humans that changed its world. Here, through this metaphorical narrative, viewers can witness, magnified and expanded to monstrous proportions, their own powerlessness and fear in the face of a nuclear attack.

Godzilla's giant stature is irrelevant once the Oxygen Destroyer is released. The monster is powerless to defend itself, despite the fear it must be experiencing during the attack. In the first stages Godzilla is asphyxiated when all Oxygen is removed from the water. Obviously, Godzilla remains powerless as its flesh is liquefied and finally its skeleton rolls from the rocks to the sandy bottom of the ocean in a last illustration of the monster's complete defeat before its bones disappear as well. Meanwhile, above the water, powerlessness and fear are expressed primarily by Professor Yamane, Emiko and Ogata. For Yamane, the entire execution of Godzilla underscores his inability to affect change in the military despite his arguments that a creature that can survive an H-bomb ought to be studied, not killed. Yamane's powerlessness is further deepened as his dear friend Serizawa—whom he thought to be his future son-in-law—commits suicide at the bottom of the bay. It is Ogata's inability to protect and save Serizawa that illustrates powerlessness from that character, while Emiko is powerless to say or do anything that can help Serizawa nor is she able to comfort her father or Ogata. All she can do is stand by and watch everything unfold before her, as was the case for many Japanese during and after the war: During the war the empire ruled, and after the war, censorship was the law of the land. And, in a darkened theater, viewers had the opportunity to witness powerlessness and fear in others and in themselves, openly and together, moving them through the trauma.

Emotional Overlap

While the scenes discussed thus far illustrate the separate emotional pairings of guilt/ anger, pain/suffering, and powerlessness/fear, it should start to become clear that the most powerful scenes in *Gojira* occur when there is an overlap of these themes, particularly when all three are present. This is important to note for two reasons. First, exploring the pathos of a film in this manner can provide a useful way to understand why a particular film or scene within a film is emotionally impactful on its audience, which in turn gives a deeper understanding of how messages are sent and received through this medium. Secondly, keeping in mind the PTSD literature discussed earlier, it is useful to note that as more and more emotional response is loaded into a narrative, that narrative becomes increasingly evocative to the point that it can hamper the ability to see clearly what is happening in the story and why. In this case, by separating the layers and looking at each distinctly and then together, the critic can more easily see how this film functions as a rhetorical expression of post-war anxiety and why it would have moved audiences at the time to tears.[27]

The first scene in which all three emotional pairings overlap is when Godzilla attacks Tokyo. At first viewing, it might seem that the scene has such emotional resonance because of the obvious allegory for cities that were burned and bombed in Japan during World War II. But that explanation falls short; this scene does feature, after all, a man in a latex suit pretending to be a giant fictional sea monster with glowing fins stomping through a scale model of Tokyo. Regardless of the impressive special effects for the day, by today's standards the scene should be laughable; it is far from it.[28] However, it becomes clear why the scene has such resonance once there is recognition of the post-war trauma that is represented in the combined threads of guilt/anger (the people made this happen and continued to exacerbate the problem), pain/suffering (of innocent bystanders, including children, as well as the monster itself), and powerlessness/fear (nothing can stop Godzilla). Considering that the Japanese were not permitted to discuss any of those emotions after the war, it makes awareness of this scene all the more important as an avenue of understanding into the Japanese psyche at the time, which in turn broadens the perspective on this important time in history.

The second scene with the magical triple pairing occurs in Serizawa's lab when he is joined by Ogata and Emiko.[29] In this scene the guilt/anger (scientific guilt and eruptions of anger of the use of the discovery), pain/suffering (Ogata's injury along with what is shown on television after Godzilla's Tokyo attack), and powerlessness/fear (inability to control the discovery and fear that he'll be forced to reveal it) work together to provide an emotional window into some of what must have been going on with scientists such as Oppenheimer who were so troubled by their work on the atomic bomb.[30] It is also interesting to consider that the outcome in this fictional Japan is quite different from the outcome of the Manhattan Project. While a few of our scientists may have been disturbed by guilt after the fact or concern before the bombs' use, as the research was in the hands of the government even if one had wanted to prevent the use of atomic weapons that would not have been possible. In this narrative, however, the Japanese scientist, recognizing the inherent danger in his discovery, chooses to sacrifice his life's work and, ultimately, his life rather than destroy humankind. It would not be unreasonable to argue that rewriting the narrative in such a way, as is done in PTSD therapy, could have proved quite useful in helping the people cope with what happened to them.

It is, of course, the final chapter, "Danger of the Deep," that brings together all of the emotional pairings for the climax of the film. Guilt/anger (over the creation of Godzilla and the Oxygen Destroyer, the inability to prevent Godzilla's and Serizawa's death, and finally about the clandestine relationship between Ogata and Emiko), pain/suffering (primarily of Godzilla, but also of Serizawa), and powerlessness/fear (of all of the characters, including Godzilla, in various manifestations) combine here to create a devastating end to the film. Again, as with the attack on Tokyo, it is at first surprising to find that the death of a fictional monster with something as, frankly, silly as an Oxygen Destroyer could stir such palpable emotion more than 50 years after the film was made. But by understanding the powerful emotional chords running through the scene and again remembering the importance of narrative in addressing PTSD it becomes clearer why this scene works so well. While they are far from perfect here, as the dire warning from Professor Yamane reminds us (testing is still going on so there could be more monsters/sequels), the Japanese do put an end to the monster and all that it stands for here. That means putting an end to the U.S. as the enemy, an end to the errors that brought about Godzilla's wrath, an end to the threat of radiation and unexpected attacks. That encompasses a great deal of post-war trauma being explored and put to rest.

Conclusion

Gojira is an important cultural artifact that functions rhetorically as a post-war expression of the guilt and anger, pain and suffering, and powerlessness and fear of the Japanese people during and after World War II. In particular, by utilizing a thematic approach and viewing the film through the lenses of PTSD research and narrative criticism, it becomes clear that this blockbuster monster movie functioned not as throw-away entertainment. Rather it functioned as a safe venue through which the Japanese people could for the first time come together publically to experience their shared memories of the horrors of war.[31] In that shared experience, threaded through a narrative that ultimately restores Japan's honor, the creators and watchers of the film could use that fiction to find some peace in the reality of their existence.

As we know, all cultures experience similar emotional responses to trauma, and all cultures use narrative to create social reality. As such, Gojira served a needed function in Japan in 1954 by helping its people work through their trauma and create a healthier narrative in which to move forward with their lives. In essence, Gojira did important work as equipment for living through trauma. Further, critical analysis of the film shows us that it has equal import for us today as a bridge to understanding the consequences of war and nuclear weapons' use. The film is particularly important as a window into post–World War II Japan, as at that time and in that place censorship precluded the existence of more official documents on which to base analysis. Gojira, critically viewed, brings to a conscious level not only some of the darkest shadows of the Japanese people, but also some of the loathed and disowned aspects of self that continue to haunt the American conscience relative to the use of nuclear weapons.

Notes

    1. W. Tsutsui, *Godzilla on My Mind: Fifty Years of the King of Monsters* (New York: Palgrave Macmillan, 2004).
    2. D. Blakesley, ed., *The Terministic Screen: Rhetorical Perspectives on Film* (Carbondale: Southern Illinois University Press, 2003); C. Harold, "The Rhetorical Function of the Abject Body: Transgressive Corporeality in Trainspotting," *JAC: Journal of Advanced Composition* 20 (Fall 2000); M. J. Medhurst, "Temptation as Taboo: A Psychorhetorical Reading of *The Last Temptation of Christ*," in *The Terministic Screen*, ed. Blakesley, pp. 55–69; B. L. Ott, "(Re)Framing Fear: Equipment for Living in a Post–9/11 World," in *Cylons in America: Critical Studies in Battlestar Galactica* (New York: Continuum, 2008); E. Walker Mechling and J. Mechling, "The Atom According to Disney," *Quarterly Journal of Speech* 81 (1995), pp. 436–453; Martin J. Medhurst, "*Hiroshima, Mon Amour*: From Iconography to Rhetoric," *The Quarterly Journal of Speech* 68 (1982), pp. 345–370.
    3. N. Anisfield, "Godzilla/*Gojiro*: Evolution of the Nuclear Metaphor," *Journal of Popular Culture* 29, no. 3 (Winter 1995), pp. 53–62; P. S. Boyer, *By the Bomb's Early Light: American Thought and Culture at the Dawn*

of the Atomic Age (Chapel Hill: University of North Carolina Press, 1994); P. Brophy, "Monster Island: Godzilla and Japanese Sci-Fi/Horror/Fantasy," *Postcolonial Studies* 3, no. 1 (2000), pp. 39–42; J. A. Evans, *Celluloid Mushroom Clouds* (Boulder, CO: Westview Press, 1998); Ishirō Honda, Takeo Murata, and Shigeru Kayama, *Gojira,* DVD. Directed by Ishirō Honda, 1954 (Tokyo: Toho Co., 2004); L. S. Wittner, *The Struggle Against the Bomb: Volume One—One World or None: A History of the World Nuclear Disarmament Movement Through 1953* (Stanford: Stanford University Press, 1993); P. Loeb, *Nuclear Culture* (Philadelphia: New Society, 1986); M. J. Medhurst, "Eisenhower's 'Atoms for Peace' Speech: A Case Study in the Strategic Use of Language," *Communication Monographs* 54 (1987), pp. 204–205; T. Schnellbacher, "Has the Empire Sunk Yet?—The Pacific in Japanese Science Fiction," *Science Fiction Studies* 29, no. 3 (2002), pp. 382–396; C. Noriega, "Godzilla and the Japanese Nightmare: When *Them!* Is U.S.," *Cinema Journal* 27, no. 1 (1987), pp. 63–77; Tsutsui, *Godzilla;* A. M. Winkler, *Life Under a Cloud: American Anxiety About the Atom* (New York: Oxford University Press, 1993); S. R. Weart, *Nuclear Fear: A History of Images* (Cambridge: Harvard University Press, 1988).

    4. T. N. Dupuy, *The Evolution of Weapons and Warfare* (New York: Da Capo Press, 1984); W. W. Epley, ed., *International Cold War Military Records and History: Proceedings of the International Conference* (Washington, D.C.: Office of the Secretary of Defense, 1996); L. Freedman, *The Evolution of Nuclear Strategy,* 2d ed. (New York: St. Martin's Press, 1989); J. Hersey, *Hiroshima* (New York: Vantage, 1989); W. O'Neill, *World War II: A Student Companion,* ed. William H. Chafe (New York: Oxford University Press, 1999); "Principal Wars in Which the United States Participated," Department of Defense, accessed 11/30/2008 at http://siadapp.dmdc. osd.mil/personnel/CASUALTY/WCPRINCIPAL.pdf; "Text of Hirohito's Radio Rescript." *New York Times,* August 15, 1945, p. 3; O. D. Tolischus, "The Savage Code That Rules Japan." *New York Times,* February 6, 1944, p. SM5; Y. Totani, *The Tokyo War Crimes Trial: The Pursuit of Justice in the Wake of World War II* (Cambridge: Harvard University Press, 2008); "The Atomic Bombings of Hiroshima and Nagasaki: Chapter 10—Total Casualties," *The Avalon Project, Documents in Law, History and Diplomacy,* Lillian Goldman Law Library, Yale Law School, accessed 3/1/2008 at http://www.yale.edu/lawweb/avalon/abomb/mp03.htm

    5. *Oxford Companion to World War II,* s.v. "Japan."

    6. L.S. Wittner, *The Struggle Against the Bomb,* p. 46. There was only one attempt, in September of 1945, by the Japanese press agency Domei and a prominent newspaper, *Asahi Shimbun,* to run a story critical of nuclear weapons. The censorship bureau responded swiftly, shutting down both news outlets as punishment. Occupation authorities also aggressively censored literature and the arts, a particularly culturally damaging move as the arts function as an important natural human outlet for coping with emotions rooted in the bombs' destruction and the radiation they left behind.

    7. *Ibid.*

    8. W. Tsutsui, *Godzilla on My Mind.*

    9. K. Burke, "Four Master Tropes," in *A Grammar of Motives* (Berkley: University of California Press, 1969), pp. 503–517; W. R. Fisher, "Narration as a Human Communication Paradigm: The Case of Public Moral Argument," in *Readings in Rhetorical Criticism,* 3d ed., ed. Carl R. Burgchardt (State College, PA: Strata, 1995), pp. 240–262. Please note that while the narrative focus in this essay is primarily drawn from PTSD treatment research, narrative itself crosses disciplinary boundaries. From a rhetorical standpoint, Fisher is the helps contextualize the idea, although Fisher himself argues not that he did not "invent" the concept of narrative as a rhetorical construct, but rather that he built on generations of critical thought to get there.

    10. S. R. Weart, *Nuclear Fear,* p. 191.

    11. J. Hocker Rushing and T. S. Frentz, *Projecting the Shadow: The Cyborg Hero in American Film* (Chicago: University of Chicago Press, 1995), p. 6.

    12. J. C. Beckham, A. A. Roodman, J. C. Barefoot, T. L. Haney, M. J. Helms, J. A. Fairbank, M. A. Hertzberg, and H. S. Kudler, "Interpersonal and Self-Reported Hostility Among Combat Veterans with and Without Posttraumatic Stress Disorder," *Journal of Traumatic Stress* 9, no. 2 (1996), pp. 335–342; D. K. Nagata and W. J.Y. Chen, "Intergenerational Communication of Race-Related Trauma by Japanese American Former Internees," *American Journal of Orthopsychiatry* 73, no. 3 (2003), pp. 266–278; J. Norman, "Constructive Narrative in Arresting the Impact of Post-Traumatic Stress Disorder," *Clinical Social Work Journal* 28, no. 3 (Fall 2000), pp. 303–319; C. L. Park, Carolyn M. Aldwin, Juliane R. Fenster, and Leslie B. Snyder, "Pathways to Posttraumatic Growth Versus Posttraumatic Stress: Coping and Emotional Reactions Following the September 11, 2001, Terrorist Attacks," *American Journal of Orthopsychiatry* 78, no. 3 (2008), pp. 300–312; J. M. Cook, D. S. Riggs, R. Thompson, J. C. Coyne, and J. I. Sheikh, "Posttraumatic Stress Disorder and Current Relationship Functioning Among World War II Ex-Prisoners of War," *Journal of Family Psychology* 18, no. 1 (2004), pp. 36–45.

    13. W. Tsutsui, *Godzilla on My Mind,* p. 33.

    14. Nagata and Chen, *Race-Related Trauma.*

    15. Norman, *Constructive Narrative;* Yeomans, Herbert, and Forman, *Traumatic Event Histories.*

    16. Beckham et al., *Hostility Among Combat Veterans,* p. 341.

    17. Norman, *Constructive Narrative;* Yeomans, Herbert, and Forman, *Traumatic Event Histories.*

    18. The Internet Movie Database, "Trivia for *Gojira,*" retrieved April 24, 2010, from http://www.imdb. com.

19. W. R. Fisher, "Narration as a Human Communication Paradigm: The Case of Public Moral Argument," in *Readings in Rhetorical Criticism*, ed. Burgchardt, pp. 240–262.

20. K. Burke, "The Rhetoric of Hitler's Battle" (1941), in *Readings in Rhetorical Criticism*, ed. Burgchardt, pp. 188–202; Burke, "Master Tropes"; B. Brummett, "Burkean Scapegoating, Mortification and Transcendence in Presidential Campaign Rhetoric," *Central States Journal* 32 (1981), pp. 254–264; B. L. Ott and E. Aoki, "The Politics of Negotiating Public Tragedy: Media Framing of the Matthew Shepard Murder," in *Readings in Rhetorical Criticism*, ed. Burgchardt, pp. 220–237; M. Boor Tonn, V. A. Endress, and J. N. Diamond, "Hunting and Heritage on Trial in Maine: A Dramatistic Debate over Tragedy, Tradition, and Territory," in *Readings in Rhetorical Criticism*, ed. Burgchardt, pp. 203–204.

21. "Calls Enemy Torture Deliberate," *New York Times*, January 30, 1944, p. 28; Weart, *Nuclear Fear*, p. 196. According to Wittner, *The Struggle Against the Bomb* (pp. 45–48), an early poll in Japan asking who was responsible for the atomic bombings found 19 percent blamed the Americans, 35 percent blamed Japan, and 29 percent blamed neither, viewing it rather as an "inevitable consequence of war."

22. Please note that for ease of analysis, the film will be discussed in chapters. While the original film shown in theaters did not have chapter divisions obvious to the audience, the DVD released by Toho Productions does include chapters, which are a useful way to segment the film for discussion.

23. Tsutsui, *Godzilla*, p. 26. Godzilla's roar was created by renowned composer and film-score creator Akira Ifukube by using a leather glove, a contrabass, and an echo chamber.

24. Weart, *Nuclear Fear*, p. 196.

25. P. S. Boyer, *By the Bomb's Early Light*; S. R. Weart, *Nuclear Fear*, pp. 77–78, pp. 80–81.

26. S. R. Weart, *Nuclear Fear*, pp. 101–102; A. M. Winkler, *Life Under a Cloud*, p. 38.

27. Tsutsui, *Godzilla*, pp. 23–24 and p. 33. As an aside, on a first viewing this author was also moved to tears, viewed as it was while in the midst of an in-depth study of nuclear rhetoric and exclusion of the Japanese experience in the Atomic Testing Museum in Las Vegas.

28. Tsutsui, *Godzilla*, pp. 23–24 and p. 33.

29. This happens in the *Gojira* chapter titled "A Moral Dilemma."

30. S. R. Weart, *Nuclear Fear*, pp. 101–102; A. M. Winkler, *Life Under a Cloud*, p. 38.

31. The word "safe" is used here to describe the film because it protects its watchers from too much pain and horror by using science fiction, which as permits us to think about difficult issues from the once-removed safety of metaphor and allegory.

Bibliography

Anisfield, Nancy. "Godzilla/Gojiro: Evolution of the Nuclear Metaphor." *Journal of Popular Culture* 29, no. 3 (Winter 1995): 53–62.

"The Atomic Bombings of Hiroshima and Nagasaki: Chapter 10—Total Casualties." *The Avalon Project, Documents in Law, History and Diplomacy*, Lillian Goldman Law Library, Yale Law School. Accessed 3/1/2008 at http://www.yale.edu/lawweb/avalon/abomb/mp03.htm.

Beckham, Jean C., Allison A. Roodman, John C. Barefoot, Thom L. Haney, Michael J. Helms, John A. Fairbank, Michael A. Hertzberg, and Harold S. Kudler. "Interpersonal and Self-Reported Hostility Among Combat Veterans with and Without Posttraumatic Stress Disorder." *Journal of Traumatic Stress* 9, no. 2 (1996): 335–342.

Blakesley, David, ed. *The Terministic Screen: Rhetorical Perspectives on Film*. Carbondale: Southern Illinois University Press, 2003.

Boyer, Paul S. *By the Bomb's Early Light: American Thought and Culture at the Dawn of the Atomic Age*. Chapel Hill: University of North Carolina Press, 1994.

Brophy, Philip. "Monster Island: Godzilla and Japanese Sci-Fi/Horror/Fantasy." *Postcolonial Studies* 3, no. 1 (2000): 39–42.

Brummett, Barry. "Burkean Scapegoating, Mortification, and Transcendence in Presidential Campaign Rhetoric." *Central States Speech Journal* 32, no. 4 (1981): 254–264.

Burke, Kenneth. "Four Master Tropes." In *A Grammar of Motives*. Berkley: University of California Press, 1969, 503–517.

_____. "The Rhetoric of Hitler's 'Battle.'" In Kenneth Burke, *The Philosophy of Literary Form: Studies in Symbolic Action*, 3d ed. Berkley: University of California Press, 1973.

"Calls Enemy Torture Deliberate." *New York Times*, January 30, 1944: 28.

Cook, Joan M., David S. Riggs, Richard Thompson, James C. Coyne, and Javaid I. Sheikh, "Posttraumatic Stress Disorder and Current Relationship Functioning Among World War II Ex-Prisoners of War." *Journal of Family Psychology* 18, no. 1 (2004): 36–45.

Dupuy, Trevor N. *The Evolution of Weapons and Warfare*. New York: Da Capo Press, 1984.
Epley, William W., ed. *International Cold War Military Records and History: Proceedings of the International Conference*. Washington, DC: Office of the Secretary of Defense, 1996.
Evans, Joyce A. *Celluloid Mushroom Clouds*. Boulder, CO: Westview Press, 1998.
Fisher, Walter R. "Narration as a Human Communication Paradigm: The Case of Public Moral Argument." In *Readings in Rhetorical Criticism*, 3d ed., ed. Carl R. Burgchardt. State College, PA: Strata, 2005.
Freedman, Lawrence. *The Evolution of Nuclear Strategy*, 2d ed. New York: St. Martin's Press, 1989.
Harold, Christine. "The Rhetorical Function of the Abject Body." *JAC: Journal of Advanced Composition* 20, no. 4 (2000): 865–885.
Hersey, John. *Hiroshima*. New York: Vantage, 1989.
Hocker Rushing, Janice, and Thomas S. Frentz. *Projecting the Shadow: The Cyborg Hero in American Film*. Chicago: University of Chicago Press, 1995.
Honda, Ishirō, Takeo Murata, and Shigeru Kayama. *Gojira*. DVD. Directed by Ishirō Honda. 1954. Tokyo: Toho, 2004.
The Internet Movie Database. "Takashi Shimura." Accessed 8/12/2009 at http://www.imdb.com.
Mechling, Elizabeth Walker, and Jay Mechling. "The Atom According to Disney." *Quarterly Journal of Speech* 81 (1995): 436–453.
Medhurst, Martin J. "Eisenhower's 'Atoms for Peace' Speech: A Case Study in the Strategic Use of Language." *Communication Monographs* 54 (1987): 204–205.
_____. "*Hiroshima, Mon Amour*: From Iconography to Rhetoric." *The Quarterly Journal of Speech* 68 (1982): 345–370.
_____. "Temptation as Taboo: A Psychorhetorical Reading of *The Last Temptation of Christ*." In *The Terministic Screen*, ed. David Blakesley. Carbondale: Southern Illinois University Press, 2003.
Mental Health America. "Factsheet: Coping with the War and Terrorism: Tips for College Students." Accessed 11/15/2009 at http://www.nmha.org.
Nagata, Donna K., and Wendy J.Y. Chen. "Intergenerational Communication of Race-Related Trauma by Japanese American Former Internees." *American Journal of Orthopsychiatry* 73, no. 3 (2003): 266–278.
Noriega, Chon. "Godzilla and the Japanese Nightmare: When *Them!* Is U.S." *Cinema Journal* 27, no. 1 (1987): 63–77.
Norman, Judith. "Constructive Narrative in Arresting the Impact of Post-Traumatic Stress Disorder." *Clinical Social Work Journal* 28, no. 3 (Fall 2000): 303–319.
O'Neill, William. *World War II: A Student Companion*. Ed. William H. Chafe. New York: Oxford University Press, 1999.
Ott, Brian L. "(Re)Framing Fear: Equipment for Living in a Post–9/11 World." In *Cylons in America: Critical Studies in Battlestar Galactica*." New York: Continuum, 2008: 13–26.
_____, and Eric Aoki. "The Politics of Negotiating Public Tragedy: Media Framing of the Matthew Shepard Murder." *Rhetoric & Public Affairs* 5, no. 3 (2002): 483–505.
Oxford Companion to World War II. s.v. "Japan: Domestic Life, Economy, and War Effort." By Gordon Daniels. Available online at http://www.oxfordreference.com (accessed 9/7/2009).
Park, Crystal L., Carolyn M. Aldwin, Juliane R. Fenster, and Leslie B. Snyder. "Pathways to Posttraumatic Growth Versus Posttraumatic Stress: Coping and Emotional Reactions Following the September 11, 2001, Terrorist Attacks." *American Journal of Orthopsychiatry* 78, no. 3 (2008): 300–312.
"Principal Wars in Which the United States Participated." Department of Defense. Accessed 11/30/2008 at http://siadapp.dmdc.osd.mil/personnel/CASUALTY/WCPRINCIPAL.pdf.
Schnellbacher, Thomas. "Has the Empire Sunk Yet?—The Pacific in Japanese Science Fiction." *Science Fiction Studies* 29, no. 3 (2002): 382–396.
"Text of Hirohito's Radio Rescript." *New York Times*, August 15, 1945: 3.
Tolischus, Otto D. "The Savage Code That Rules Japan." *New York Times*, February 6, 1944: SM5.
Tonn, Mari Boor, Valerie A. Endress, and John N. Diamond. "Hunting and Heritage on Trial in Maine: A Dramatistic Debate Over Tragedy, Tradition, and Territory." *Quarterly Journal of Speech* 79 (1993): 165–181.
Totani, Yuma. *The Tokyo War Crimes Trial: The Pursuit of Justice in the Wake of World War II*. Cambridge: Harvard University Press, 2008.
Tsutsui, William. *Godzilla on My Mind: Fifty Years of the King of Monsters*. New York: Palgrave Macmillan, 2004.
Weart, Spencer R. *Nuclear Fear: A History of Images*. Cambridge: Harvard University Press, 1988.
Winkler, Allan M. *Life Under a Cloud: American Anxiety About the Atom*. New York: Oxford University Press, 1993.
Wittner, Lawrence S. *The Struggle Against the Bomb: Volume One—One World or None: A History of the World Nuclear Disarmament Movement Through 1953*. Stanford: Stanford University Press, 1993.
Yeomans, Peter D., James D. Herbert, and Evan M. Forman. "Symptom Comparison Across Multiple Solicitation Methods Among Burundians with Traumatic Event Histories." *Journal of Traumatic Stress* 21, no. 2 (April 2008): 232–234.

Japan Removed: *Godzilla* Adaptations and Erasure of the Politics of Nuclear Experience

Jason C. Jones

The timelessness of *Gojira* remains bound with the monster's serving as a metaphor for war and nuclear destruction, particularly that experienced by Japan during World War II, considering that Godzilla's path of destruction in the original 1954 film followed the lines of devastation and death wrought by the firebombing of Tokyo by American forces. As has been argued by a battalion of researchers, *Gojira*, therefore, serves not only as a moral tale, recalling the destructive capacity of nuclear weapons, but also as an allegory of regression and repression, threatening to return a quickly developing Japan into a postwar state defined by death, destruction, displacement, and military occupation. In a world that has since the conclusion of World War II seen the number of nuclear states increase by a factor of eight throughout multiple nuclear arms races and a Cold War that gave birth to such fear-inducing terms as "nuclear winter," the idea of Godzilla has the potential to serve as a fearful reminder of human behavior at its worst and political failure at its lowest point of depravity. In a world in which wars of nuclear annihilation remain a possibility, Godzilla can serve as the mirror into which humans must stare and come to terms with what stares back. The larger, clearer, and more refined Godzilla's physical image, however, the less significant he becomes. With the Olympic Games ushering into Japan an age in which families "rushed to acquire television sets,"[1] Godzilla would become that much smaller in stature and significance.

Perhaps it is partially the result of an aversion to looking into the mirror that we see not the asymmetrical, war-torn, googly-eyed, imperfect face of the original Godzilla, but the highly-stylized, consumer-friendly, even child-friendly monster. It should come as no surprise then, that the internationalization of Godzilla—his introduction to a world characterized by "increasing fluidity of national and cultural boundaries"[2]—has involved the monster's trivialization, and there is no greater trivialization of Godzilla as that caused by making it huggable. As the Godzilla of the 1954 film with all of its physical imperfections disappeared to be replaced by modern versions, the creature's significance within the context of war and nuclear weaponry has adversely mutated.

It is the Godzilla of popular culture that adorns the fireplace mantles in television shows such as *Roseanne* and *The Simpsons*. In 2008, the U.S.–based sandwich chain Subway released what would become a viral advertising campaign, one commercial of which featured a Godzilla-like monster stomping through the high-rise buildings protruding upward to form a Tokyo-esque landscape. The monster—in a display of upper-body dexterity unconceivable in the original Godzilla suit—positions his arms in a manner showing the size of a "foot long" sandwich as an onlooker stands mouth agape in shock, not at the monster, but at the size of the sandwich. In the 1995 airing of the annual "Treehouse of Horror" Halloween special on *The Simpsons*, Lard Lad—mascot of the eponymous fast-food restaurant chain—came alive after having been struck by a lightning bolt. Ripping his feet from the iron tie rods that secure his towering figure to the ground, Lard Lad opens his mouth to release Godzilla's unmistakable roar. Tina's dinosaur tattoo is revealed with the same yell in the Season 2 "Bad Tina" episode of Bob's Burgers. *South Park*'s first take on Godzilla occurred in the Season 3 episode "Mechastreisand," in which a Barbra Streisand endowed with mystical powers morphs into a mechanical form reminiscent of Mechagodzilla and proceeds to destroy the town of South Park. *Rugrats: Runaway Reptar* sees the group of infants travel to Japan to settle the question of whether Reptar stands for the good of human civilization or wishes to aid in its destruction. The image of Godzilla has been used in newspaper ads for everything from real estate to cars. The name "Godzilla" has been bestowed upon former Tokyo Giants slugger Hideki Matsui for both his power and visage, Nissan's GTR sports car, brides-to-be, and partly to films such as *Croczilla* (2012).

The dissonance created between the original Godzilla and the aforementioned pop culture iterations of the icon is jarring. Stricken from post–1954 Godzilla discourse, particularly in its international presence, is the idea of human self-reflection. Absent from these images is commentary on the scientific conundrum so embodied by Serizawa (Akihiko Hirata) in his wish to harness the power of energy for constructive purposes while keeping his discoveries a secret lest they fall into misuse, i.e., any government-endorsed action against humans. Gone is any hint of moral implication. Gone is the opportunity to question ourselves as individuals.[3] Our new internationalized Godzilla attempts to sell us sandwiches and real estate. His yell is a sound bite no longer instilling the panic and fear of ensuing destruction and the chains of an inescapable past, but laughter. "Godzilla" now refers to anything the chief characteristics of which are massive size and strength. Godzilla the metaphor has been neutralized, and through this neutralization the idea of Godzilla has become safe for international consumption. Such neutralization has been long in the making, running parallel with the attitude toward Hiroshima held by American officials shortly after the war, an attitude seeking to maintain "an official version of Hiroshima that discouraged genuine reflection."[4] This essay examines Hollywood's role in the severing of Godzilla and the Godzilla narrative from Tokyo's firebombing and the nuclear bombing of Hiroshima and Nagasaki, through the excision of Japan itself.

The Significance of Gojira, Godzilla 1984 *and* Godzilla 1998

Research on Godzilla spans the life of the entire series from its first release as *Gojira* in Japan to Toho's efforts to reinstate the original image of the monster upon its 50th anniversary in *Godzilla: Final Wars (Gojira: fainaru wōzu*, 2004). The years between 1954 and 2013 have seen Godzilla star in approximately 30 films and appear in countless cartoons, video games, film shorts, and parodies. However, *Gojira* and *Godzilla 1984 (Gojira: 1984)* reserve a special place within the film canon. Amongst a collection of films the majority of which have been reimagined and repurposed into children's fodder, *Gojira* and *Godzilla*

1984 remain decidedly adult in nature. These are films that matter. Their narratives are primarily woven around Godzilla's presence serving as punishment against human transgression in the form of testing and proliferation of nuclear weapons. As Mark Anderson states of the 1954 original, "*Gojira* implicitly raises questions about the ethics of the United States and U.S. Scientists in pursuing the Manhattan Project and enabling the subsequent arms race that awakens *Gojira*."[5] *Godzilla 1984*, meanwhile, introduces us to a Japan willing to take a stance directly opposed to the intentions of the two other leading international powers—the U.S. and USSR—who have no qualms with nuking Godzilla and sacrificing Japan in the process. Thus both films serve as commentary reflecting the sociopolitical landscape of the eras to which they were conceived, while also illustrating a clear, deliberate warning. *Gojira* and *Godzilla 1984* are thus Godzilla as philosophy and political statement. It is of no little significance that in Japan, both films are simply titled *Gojira*.

The formula for the Godzilla film saw substantial deviation as the number of films increased, with *Godzilla vs. Mothra* (*Mosura tai Gojira*, 1964) being viewed as the fork in the road at which Godzilla completely lost his connection with humanity through his turn toward juvenility and the establishment of Godzilla as the "good guy."[6] It is the existential crisis caused by this turning point and the resulting juxtaposition of Godzilla as allegory and Godzilla as children's entertainment that is exemplified in the aforementioned *Rugrats: Runaway Reptar* episode. At the local drive-in theater, the Rugrats watch in horror as Reptar, a parody of Godzilla, aids a pterodactyl named "Dactar" in the destruction of a large city, presumably a futuristic Tokyo. Watching the destruction from a safehaven, a character in the film states: "How can this be? Reptar has always been our friend! He protected us from the mole people, the aliens…. Yet now he seems to have turned evil. Has the world gone mad?" Rugrat Tommy Pickles concurs, responding, "But Reptar's not apposed [*sic*] to help the bad guy. He's a hero!" As Jan Susina states in his treatment of the episode, "For the Rugrats, Reptar is a hero, not a villain."[7]

That Godzilla's nature should at all be brought to question illustrates the rift within the Godzilla film body. On one hand, we have the original *Gojira* and Kōji Hashimoto's 1984 reboot of the monster. Both of these films have in common the implication of human behavior in the awakening of Godzilla and ask questions about the socio-political landscape allowing for the disturbance of a force that once awakened, cannot easily be stopped. But Godzilla in these films simply serves as the sum of human choices. It can be categorized neither as good nor evil, but exists as a fact of life that reflects human progress or lack thereof. As paleontologist Yamane (Takashi Shimura) alludes, Godzilla's having all but destroyed Ōto Island and the immense threat he poses to Tokyo does not necessarily mean that the monster is "bad" anymore than the application of scientific knowledge to the purpose of destruction makes human beings "bad."[8] Much more difficult is the task of eking out similar meaning from much of the remainder of the Godzilla film body. Replacing the socio-political commentary made possible through the reflection of major nuclear events within specific time periods is the imposition of a "hero" narrative in which "Godzilla acts as a free agent, who battles monster foes for his own reasons."[9] The result is a film narrative in the center of which is placed not a socio-political commentary that prompts self-reflection, but a battle, or even "battle royale" amongst beasts of a mutated, extraterrestrial, or mechanical nature. Godzilla thus becomes something to root for, not think about, making the world (or the market, at least) safe for the mass production of Godzilla-themed t-shirts, toys, video games, cartoons, and comics.

That both *Gojira* and *Godzilla 1984* have seen Hollywood remakes is thus of great significance, as it affords an opportunity to disarm the films, removing the metaphoric. Onto a narrative interlaced with events specific to Japan, Hollywood superimposes its own interpretation that operates along considerations made for a new, "international" audience. Making the monster consumable as part of a larger body of popular culture necessitates the removal of the moral element—a moral element specific to Japan. The Hollywood remake of *Gojira*, *Godzilla, King of the Monsters!* (1956) begins the procedure through which Godzilla is globalized through the surgical excision of Japan from the Godzilla "incident," paralleling the process through which the remake was made—the dismembering and discarding of particular portions of the original film, the insertion of locally-filmed segments, and the stitching together of these to form a film that at first glance appears to retain the significance of the original, but actually accomplishes the opposite.

Gojira: *Japan's Godzilla Problem*

Gojira's critical reception upon arrival in the U.S. was anything but stellar. In his oft-quoted scathing condemnation of *Godzilla, King of the Monsters!* Bosley Crowther wrote for the *New York Times*:

> As though there are not enough monsters coming from Hollywood, an organization that calls itself Jewell Enterprises had to import one from Japan. It is a great scaly prehistoric creature, reactivated by H-bomb tests, and it goes by the name of "Godzilla…"
>
> To say that this Oriental monster is fantastic is to state but half the case. "Godzilla," produced in a Japanese studio, is an incredibly awful film. It looks as though its Japanese producers, assisted by a stray American—a fellow named Terry Morse, who is an alumnus of Hollywood's Poverty Row—made a close study of the old film "King Kong," then tried to do substantially the same thing with a miniature of a dinosaur made of gum-shoes and about $20 worth of toy buildings and electric trains.
>
> Their idea, is that this monster, which exhales atomic breath, much as the cigarette billboard in Times Square blows out puffs of smoke, takes it upon itself, for no clear reason, to destroy Tokyo.[10]

The review exemplifies not only the sense of derision with which this particular critic welcomed Godzilla in the U.S., but also the success with which the significance of Tokyo's destruction has been stricken from the film—there was, after all, palpable reason for Tokyo's being the object of annihilation—while also illustrating a lack of imagination toward a Japan that had only one decade earlier capitulated after the atomic bombing of Hiroshima and Nagasaki and the firebombing of Tokyo.[11] At least for this critic, there was little room for empathy, reflecting what Sheila Johnson notes as an American curiosity leaning heavily toward "the bomb's secret development and how it had been dropped than about its effect on Japan."[12]

Godzilla was destined to become a ubiquitously known, international icon nonetheless. More than half a century later, as Susan Napier writes, Godzilla has become as American as he is Japanese.[13] The Godzillas featured in *Gojira* and *Godzilla 1984*, however, remain a problem peculiar to Japan. As researchers have pointed out, positioning Godzilla as a force with which to be dealt by Japan and Japan alone in the 1954 film flies in the face of the reality that American troops were stationed in Japan at the time in which the film takes place.[14] Consideration must also be given to a general hesitance to have America or the American military increase its activity during a time that marked greater post-occupation autonomy. As Lapp writes on why the crew of the Lucky Dragon was hesitant to draw atten-tion to itself after having been covered in radioactive ash, there was a fear of Americans and American military men: "Things could have been worse; [the ship and its crew] could have been picked up by the Americans and anything could have happened then. This fear of what American authorities might do was primarily responsible for the men not asking for outside assistance."[15] The omission of foreign military power goes far in lending the film its sense of absolute isolation. Japan alone is the victim of Godzilla, and Japan must save itself independently.

Here, we should note that *Gojira* is not an all out condemnation of violence itself, nor is it necessarily a complete condemnation of the creation of advanced weaponry per se, either of which would dramatically widen the scope of the film, resulting in removal of the Godzilla problem from the confines of Japan. As William Tsutsui notes, "One might under-standably be surprised to find this focus on the military—indeed, the glorification of sol-diers, weaponry, and the thrill of combat—in postwar Japanese cinema."[16] While aggrandizing, glorifying, and simultaneously illustrating the futility of the weaponry desperately hurled against Tokyo's destroyer—mortar shells fired from tanks, machine guns emptying their magazines, an onslaught of missiles propelling their way toward Godzilla from fighter planes as they maneuver around the beast— it rather openly criticizes nuclear weaponry. This criticism is given both scientific and political frameworks within the film. For instance, Yamane and Tanabe (Fuyuki Murakami)—representing science in the form of paleontology and nuclear physics[17]—standing inside Godzilla's radioactive footprint, allude to the proven long-lasting destructive properties of nuclear fallout by urging the local islanders to stay away. Such criticism is even more recognizable in its political form connected to the history of nuclear weapons use, as alluded to within parliamentary discussions over whether or not to make public the "discovery" of Godzilla.

Nonetheless, the assault weapons used to deter Godzilla are of great importance. Although this is not made clear within the film, much of the arsenal consists of American military equipment, most notably the M24 "Chaffee" tanks and F-86 "Sabre" jet fighters.[18] Though the ship conducting the examination of Ōto Island as well as that used during the deployment of the Oxygen Destroyer is a Japanese "shikine" ship, the destroyers used to release depth charges against Godzilla are American frigates.[19] The onslaught of shells, mis-siles, and depth charges launched from this American military equipment prove only an ineffective annoyance against the wrath of Godzilla. Amidst a slew of economic, political, and military treaties concluded between the United States and Japan—for instance the Japan–U.S. Security Treaty in 1951, Friendship, Commerce and Navigation Treaty in 1953, and Mutual Defense Assistance Agreement in 1954—weapons produced by the U.S. military so integral to maintaining any advantage in the Korean War prove powerless in the face of what American nuclear weapons testing has awakened.[20] In the end, Godzilla is quelled with Japanese technology developed by a Japanese chemist deployed from a Japanese ship. Japan solves its own problem.

Gojira *Remade: Displacing Japan, Placing Hollywood*

Gojira and the monster therein are a media event.[21] The film is filled with Yutaka-brand television sets and Onkyo radios. Newspapers keep the film-watcher in sync with the denizens of Tokyo, with headlines of the sinking of ships, the coming of Godzilla, and government response to it all filling the screen. Serizawa, who is otherwise cut off from the world, is only convinced to use his Oxygen Destroyer after having confirmed through television the death and destruction being caused by the monster.[22] A crew of news announcers dies in order to fulfill their mission to bring news of Godzilla to Japan, bidding the country farewell as Godzilla topples the news tower on which the reporters and photographers stand. Mark Anderson summarizes the role of the media in *Gojira* as such: "Thus, media in the film serve as a platform on which events staged within the film and for us as viewers become national Japanese events."[23] Tsutsui, meanwhile, extrapolates on the importance of the reporters and journalists whose presence has been constant throughout the Godzilla film canon, stating, "To a large extent… journalists hold on to their reputations because they remain firmly on the sidelines, observing, commenting, and facilitating rather than taking responsibility for decisive action themselves."[24] There can be no doubt that the reporter and the press remain central elements and alterations made to these central elements have the potential to reverberate throughout the film. It stands that if the role of the Japanese reporter has been completely hijacked by an American reporter in *Godzilla, King of the Monsters!*, the "national" nature of events is replaced by an international—or more specifically American—character who tells us to see events as he sees them and hear things as he hears them. Japan has been displaced.

This displacement of Japan is firmly symbolized through the relegation of the Japanese news media and its central members to insignificant roles, and even this with inconsistency. Hagiwara (Sachio Sakai), the Maiasa Shimbun reporter, plays a central role in the original film. Hagiwara's visitation to Serizawa's laboratory also serves as the device through which Emiko is introduced to Serizawa's Oxygen Destroyer—a secret that she fails to keep when she tells Ogata of its existence. Hagiwara is thus central to the extermination of Godzilla. It is no surprise that he should hold a place beside Ogata, Serizawa, Emiko, and Yamane aboard the ship overseeing Godzilla's extinction. With the introduction of Steve Martin (Raymond Burr), an American reporter for United World News based in Chicago, Hagiwara disappears from the film, his only presence being residual and arbitrary, and remaining only because his central role in the original precludes his being entirely erased. When Hagiwara does make an appearance, the film desperately redefines him so as not to interfere with Martin's role as reporter. The first verbal introduction he receives occurs upon the crew's arrival to Ōto Island. Martin refers to Hagiwara as one of many government officials by whom the islanders were "interrogated." Martin, meanwhile, conducts the real work of a reporter, asking the natives what they have seen.

One of the most comical, yet significant scenes in which the displacement of Hagiwara by Martin serves to place Japan in a more subjective context as it might be seen from the eyes of an outsider, occurs during this examination of Ōto Island. Replacing the conversation held directly between Hagiwara and the elderly fisherman who dubs the hitherto unnamed assailant "Godzilla," the remake introduces a third party, Martin's Japanese guide security officer, Iwanaga (Frank Iwanaga), who must explain the ceremony to Martin. That the scene is being explained to Martin by Iwanaga lends authenticity to the scene, convincing viewers that what they are seeing is indeed the real Japan, as opposed to a Japan reconstructed within the walls of a Hollywood studio. The audience is forced to share the perspective of the foreign onlooker with Martin through the use of point-of-view camerawork, allowing the audience to see the spectacle as Martin sees it. Adding insult to injury, one of the "native" islanders in the added scene dons a happi coat on which is written "Lucille Anderson"—a name which could have very little to do with staving off another attack by the giant monster. The name *"Gojira"* comes to Martin and Iwanaga only through eaves-dropping on the conversation being held between Hagiwara and the elderly fisherman. The role that had been held by Hagiwara in the original—that of divulging the name of that which cannot be named—is thereby bequeathed to Martin. The scene is more decoration than objective observation. Japan is no longer in charge of defining itself, but is instead being defined, placed into the role of keeper of legends.

The next time we see Hagiwara is at the Japanese Diet debriefing. Here, despite a plethora of hints showing us otherwise—his having already been introduced as a government official, his donning an armband identifying him as anything but a resident of Ōto Island, and his having been holding a camera in the previous scene—he is reintroduced as a native of Ōto Island, providing testimony after Inada, the island's mayor, and Shinkichi, the younger brother of one of the few survivors of Godzilla's attacks on fishing vessels in the area.[25] This alteration not only represents a displacement of the character within the narrative, but a replacement of the character within the minds of American viewers in the 1950s, thus allowing the same character to be used as both bureaucrat and villager without raising a red flag for an undiscerning audience. Kalat refers to this as one of a number of condescending attitudes toward Japan, stating that "the editors of the Embassy Pictures version evidently do not expect American viewers to be able to recognize Japanese faces with ease, a racist assumption that justifies sloppy editing."[26]

The involvement of Hagiwara as well as that of the Maiasa newspaper office in the discovery of Serizawa's secret research has been completely preempted at the outset of the remake. Martin's reason for being in Japan is not to report on Godzilla. That he was able to do so is only a matter of coincidence. Martin's original purpose in flying to Japan is to visit his old college friend—Daisuke Serizawa. Not only does Serizawa have a college friend, but he also has an assistant who meets Martin at the airport in Serizawa's place, due to the chemist's being preoccupied with "field experiments." The change of events represents a dramatic, almost contradictory alteration in the character of Serizawa thereby eliminating the meaning behind his actions. As Kanahara tells us in her essay on Serizawa's role in *Gojira*, Serizawa represents a tact antithetical to that of Godzilla. He is the anti–Godzilla not because he invents the Oxygen Destroyer, but because attempts to hide his past action of having invented it.[27] Whereas Godzilla is a forced remembrance of the past, Serizawa is the forced repression of it. We know that Serizawa suffered an injury that permanently damaged his right eye, but we are left to guess that it is a war injury, as he never discusses it.[28] Serizawa is a recluse, spending his days inside an underground laboratory instead of in the open air and light of day as does his counterpart, Hideto Ogata (Akira Takarada). It is for this reason perhaps that Emiko, originally to be married to Serizawa, falls in love with Ogata. For Serizawa, the hiding of the Oxygen Destroyer is synonymous with the preservation of life. The breaking of this silence, which occurs when he shows Emiko his life's work, means the death of many, which is only circumnavigated by Serizawa's destruction of his knowledge of the past (his blueprints and research writings) and finally himself. Serizawa's silence thus becomes eternal, dragging with him the possibility of the past repeating itself.

Steve Martin's replacement of Hagiwara—replacing Japan with the foreign—thus irreparably severs the relationship between the past and present, destroys the juxtaposition between Godzilla and Serizawa, and relegates an important character to a mere ornament. The Japanese reporter no longer serves as the carrier of the narrative, discovering and uncovering the relationships between Godzilla, Godzilla's adversaries, the government, and other protagonists and antagonists. Instead, we are left to take Steve Martin's word for it.[29] If the replacement of Hagiwara works to globalize the Godzilla problem by introducing Martin as the character through which the audience would understand and interpret it, then the replacement of Japanese with English and its use by Japanese characters works to globalize the problem by providing other countries direct access to it and by denying access when convenient.

Martin opens the film by way of narration: "Tokyo…. A smoldering memorial to the unknown. An unknown which at this very moment still prevails and could at any time lash out with its terrible destruction anywhere else in the world." He continues, "An incident was about to take place that would shake the foundations of the civilized world." The film thus begins by looking back. Martin's recollection of events already betrays most of the story. Whereas the emotional current underlying *Gojira* is the feeling that Tokyo's destruction is imminent, the remake does not allow us this feeling of suspense, thus undercutting one of the most important properties of the original—the threat of destruction, as opposed to the fact of it. Of great significance, however, is not that Tokyo has been destroyed, but that the beast responsible for it could appear anywhere else in the world. Martin's narration reminds us of the international nature of the threat throughout the film. That it is a threat to the civilized world places Godzilla in the shadow of King Kong, well known for its allegorical treatment of the "civilized world" versus the "world of beasts," and defines Godzilla as nothing more than a monster, from the very beginning stripping its existence of any meaning not already established by previous Hollywood monster films. Thus, the Godzilla problem is globalized both intrinsically, in terms of the monster being a threat to the world within the film, and extrinsically, in that the monster and its existence are being adjusted to fit into the confines of the Hollywood monster movie outside of the film. While *Gojira* stirs up imagery of people not long ago devastated by war, and undergoing crises on a level of destruction that is if not comparable, then at least reminiscent, what we see in the 1956 version is simply a people in panic, running from an ensuing monster. The political aspects of these scenes are removed, and together with them any moral questions, thus again aligning Godzilla with the preexisting body of monster films. What is at stake here is the destruction of a large city by a monster from the depths of the earth, not the reincarnation and diffusing of a history that would implicate American audiences.

The use of language—or lack thereof—plays a key role in hiding the political undertones of the 1956 film. Perhaps the scene most illustrative of such undertones and allegorical meaning of the monster is that in which a mother (Teruko Mita) under the ensuing shadow of Godzilla as he ravages Tokyo, tells her children that they will soon be joining their father. We can safely assume that considering the context of the original, this woman was left a widow, having been bereaved of her husband in World War II.[30] Although the scene remains in *Godzilla, King of the Monsters!*, the mother's voice cannot be heard over the music and sounds of destruction accompanying the wrecking of Tokyo, and although it is obvious that she is saying something, her exact words are left to the imagination of the audience.

A similar tactic is used when Mayor Inada of Ōto Island testifies in front of the Diet and is questioned by conservative Diet member Ōyama concerning the details of how much livestock has been lost in the wake of Godzilla's decimation of the island. Inada apologetically admits that he forgot to include in his report a breakdown of exactly how much livestock has been lost, updating the Diet with the figures of 12 cows and eight pigs. The scene is shortened in *Godzilla, King of the Monsters!* as Inada becomes one of the many referred to simply as an island native. A cynical view would have it that Ōyama's questioning represents government nitpicking at its finest. Seventeen houses have been swept away while nine people have died. Yet, Ōyama challenges Inada to recall specific numbers of livestock that perished in the event. *Gojira*, however, does not invite such a cynical viewpoint. Kanahara interprets the mayor's forgetting as a metaphor that functions antithetically to Godzilla itself. Inada may unwittingly forget to include details of damage in his report, but his recollection of these details will be forced upon him in the same way that Godzilla's presence represents a forced remembrance of the past.[31] There is also, however, the possibility that the scene simply wishes to remind us of yet another measure of stability being violently trampled over—that of food (including milk), thus placing into jeopardy the health and vitality of the people of Ōto Island, presaging the same fate for Tokyo and the larger population should Godzilla ever set foot there. As Katarzyna Cwiertka points out in her monograph on modern Japanese cuisine, considering the food shortages that plagued Japan after World War II, there "can be no doubt that the 1940s constituted the most tragic episode in modern Japanese history."[32] Japan's postwar years were characterized by malnutrition and starvation, and it wasn't until 1949 that meat was removed from the list of rationed goods.[33] Ōyama's questioning, therefore, is not a trifling matter. It is nonetheless glossed over in *Godzilla, King of the Monsters!*, thereby denying the audience a glimpse into the horrific nature of post-war life in Japan. It is symbolic that Martin's own voice keeps us from hearing Inada's answer.[34]

In other scenes, however, the effect of globalizing Godzilla is achieved through opposite means—the addition of English. The addition of language in *Godzilla, King of the Monsters!* stands out not so much because of the information that it provides in presenting the narrative, but because of when and how it presents that information. When Yamane returns from conducting a scientific study of the destruction caused by Godzilla, he addresses Japan's national Diet in English. Naturally, it makes much more sense for Yamane to present his findings in Japanese, considering that he is addressing the Japanese Diet. Perhaps this is the point. Yamane's testimony in *Godzilla, King of the Monsters!* has gone global. It transcends the Japanese Diet, addressing the world's Diets, Parliaments, Congresses and other governmental bodies. That the world has been clued in to events happening in Japan remains the pretext for the entire film, despite the unfeasibility of the sinking of Japanese ships garnering much attention outside Japan. Nonetheless, the film begins with scenes of Martin reporting on the events for Chicago's United World News from a newsroom in Japan. Not only do we hear reports being conducted in English, but a number of other languages as well. Martin's superior at United World News goes so far as to mention that Martin's story has made front page all over the country. Note that no such pretext existed for the original, in which whether or not to even tell the people of Japan was the issue of great contention at the Diet. Telling Japan is questionable. Telling the world is unfathomable.

By the same device, what was originally framed as a problem exclusive to Japan, becomes reframed as a problem for the world. The overcoming of that problem represents not a victory for Japan, but one for the world. This reframing of the Godzilla problem is emphasized at key points throughout the film. When Serizawa and Ogata begin their dive to plant the "Oxygen Destroyer" near Godzilla's lair, Martin stands onboard the vessel, reporting live: "And now, the divers are descending. We ask the whole world to stand by." Soon afterward, when Godzilla succumbs to the destructive power of Serizawa's secret weapon Martin releases a sigh of relief, telling us, "People of the world, Godzilla is dead," referring to the monster as a menace, separate from man. From the opening title to the very end of the film, in the mind of Martin, Godzilla represents nothing but a ravenous monster, antithetical to man, and born by chance, while the original treated Godzilla as the product of man, the two being inseparable. Martin finally leaves us, stating that "the whole world could wake up and live again." And it would wake up to another nominal Godzilla.

Godzilla 1984: *Japan's Godzilla Problem Expanded*

Godzilla 1984 appears to take more of an international stance due to its inclusion of the U.S. and USSR; however, it clearly proceeds from a perspective that again locates the Godzilla problem within Japan. It begins where the 1954 film leaves us—the Cold War. With tensions between the Soviet Union and the United States escalating in the midst of the Cold War,[35] the writers of *Godzilla 1984* were presented with the perfect opportunity to reintroduce the nuclear issue in all of the seriousness with which it was presented in *Gojira*, but in a modern context that described the nuclear issue as one that could bring death and destruction not only to Japan (with the fictional "Ihama" power plant in Shizuoka playing host to one of Godzilla's feeding frenzies), but to the world. As David Kalat says of the film, "With such serious intentions underlying the drama, Shūichi Nagahara's screenplay rises to a level of mature drama not seen in the series since 1954."[36]

The resulting film capitalizes on the antagonism defining the U.S. and Soviet relations of the period and thus implicates two of the world's most politically active and mutually antagonistic states, but nonetheless assumes a stance similar to its 1954 predecessor in that Japan remains alone in defending itself against Godzilla. In fact, Japan must not only defend itself against Godzilla, but also against a belligerent United States and Soviet Union that seek to eliminate Godzilla through the use of nuclear weaponry in utter disregard for what the nuclear fallout would entail for Japan. After all, neither the United States nor the Soviet Union had ever had nuclear weapons used against them, although the former had experienced nuclear panic with the Three-Mile Island incident and the latter would within two years be evacuating Chernobyl.

The most telling scene involves a trilateral meeting between Japan's prime minister and ambassadors for the U.S. and USSR. The reactions of the Soviet Union and the United States toward Godzilla greatly mirror the mood of the Cold War. Their responses are not to a direct, physical attack upon the land of either power but to the perception of a threat—the possibility of Godzilla's traversing international borders to siphon energy from Vladivostok's nuclear power plants. Such is the assumption of Soviet ambassador Chevsky (Walter Nichols) who expresses to Japanese prime minister Mitamura (Keiju Kobayashi) his belief that once Godzilla has trampled Japan, its next destination will be Vladivostok, placing its destruction on par with that of Tokyo should Godzilla decide to again destroy the Japanese capital. Meanwhile, American ambassador Rosenberg requests that Mitamura allow the U.S. to use nuclear weaponry against Godzilla as the only effective means of stopping the annihilation of Japan. Chevsky remains the more aggressive of the two because Godzilla, in seeking to devour nuclear power sources has attacked a soviet nuclear-powered submarine. The choice for Japan is thus to be eviscerated by Godzilla or suffer the long-term disaster of nuclear fallout, and in the worst case, both.

Japan's solitude in the world is further emphasized by the fact that despite Soviet and U.S. relations being strained within the Cold War, they are in agreement about using nuclear weapons against Godzilla. That two bitter rivals could agree on this should immediately raise eyebrows. Not only must Japan protect itself against Godzilla, but also against the intentions of two Cold War powers, unwaveringly aiming to prove the utility of their arsenals. The sense of isolation and pressure of the situation are well expressed through the camerawork, which alternates between point-of-view shots of Mitamura and Chevsky, and Mitamura and Rosenberg, producing the effect of squeezing Mitamura between two military and political powers. For all of Professor Hayashida's (Natsuki Yōsuke) claims that Godzilla plans to destroy mankind, it all begins and ends with Japan.

Not only is Japan portrayed as the only country morally and technologically equipped to vanquish Godzilla, but in the case of *Godzilla 1984*, the pro-nuclear countries are portrayed as irritants, only exacerbating Japan's problems and bringing even further destruction to Japan through the smuggling of nuclear weapons launch devices. Upon passing through Tokyo Bay, Godzilla damages a Soviet container ship carrying a nuclear missile launch trigger, which is accidentally activated when the ship is damaged literally in the wake of Godzilla, violently colliding against the pier at which it sits docked. The scene acts as a mechanism to implicate the Soviet Union in the further destruction of Japan, welcoming the Secretary of Defense to quip, "How could they bring such a thing into Japan!?"[37]

While the Soviets are busy fanning political flames and exponentially increasing the possible damage to be done to Japan, the futility of American weapons technology is evinced by an American interceptor missile that upon successfully colliding with the Soviet nuclear missile causes a nuclear explosion the fallout of which feeds a Godzilla whose rage had just minutes earlier been successfully quelled by the cadmium missile-equipped Super X. Japan has foreseen its own problems—i.e., the arrival of Godzilla—and has acted accordingly in creating the Super X, outfitting it with perhaps the only weapon that could be effective against Godzilla. What Japan conveniently lacks, however, is the weapons technology to intercept a missile, a technology which we can infer is inferior to the Super X. What we see here is a series of dualisms that consistently work to stress Japan's uniqueness and aloneness in tackling the Godzilla problem. With the Super X, Japan not only displays its technological superiority and economic development to the United States and Soviet Union, but also that it has come to terms with the production of weapons technology. Serizawa's fear that his Oxygen Destroyer could be put to ill use has been addressed as has distrust in the moral compass of politicians.

Godzilla 1985: *Erasing Japan's Perspective*

Considering the high stakes of the Cold War and entertainment therewith, Godzilla could not be remade unscathed. *Godzilla 1985* would be born in a tumultuous decade, characterized by such films as *Red Dawn* (1984), *Rocky IV* (1985), *Rambo III* (1988), *Red Heat* (1988), and *Red Scorpion* (1988). As Harlow Robinson writes in his treatise on representations of Russians in Hollywood: "The 1980s were a very confusing decade in Soviet-American relations, beginning in tense hostility but ending with the euphoria of glasnost and the melting of the Iron Curtain.... Especially in the early years of his new presidency, the longtime anti–Communist Reagan led a virtual crusade against the 'evil empire' of Communist states controlled by the Soviet Union."[38] Robinson then describes the state of the arms race: "Reagan also promoted the development of a new system of satellite-based missiles (Star Wars) that would further escalate the arms race."[39] March 1983 marked Reagan's announcement that the U.S. would intensify antimissile technological research in the form of the Strategic Defense Initiative.[40] An idealized representation of it would gain screen time in *Godzilla 1984*. In fact *Godzilla 1984* may be read as a commentary on the ability of world powers to wage war from afar using tools that have been strategically placed so as to keep war an arm's length away. It is within this scenario of potential world destruction that Japan gains its legs to become a country that will not be intimidated into the use of nuclear weapons.

Godzilla 1985 denies Japan this privilege, rejecting the premise that Japan serves as the only moral actor in a scenario that sees U.S. and Soviet trigger-happiness as occurring at equal levels. Kalat notes that "by depicting the Americans and the Soviets as moral equals, and the Japanese as principled victims caught in the cross fire, Toho's version was unlikely to find a sympathetic audience in Ronald Reagan's America."[41] Thus American patriotism and Cold War ideology serve to displace Japan, if not denying it its place in the world, then denying the route through which it arrives at the decision not to allow the use of nuclear weaponry.

Here, we return to the previously mentioned scene of the trilateral meeting between the Japanese prime minister and U.S. and Soviet ambassadors. Only the very beginning of this scene remains intact. The rest of it has been cut, including the entirety of Mitamura's leaving the meeting room to discuss options with his advisors and cabinet members. The more interesting story is told by what is cut rather than what remains. In the original film, ambassadors Rosenberg and Chevsky unequivocally agree that the nuclear option is the only one, and both attempt to coerce Japan into the use of these weapons, which both countries hold on standby. Rosenberg invokes the ruling of the National Security Council with the implication that the word of the Council is the final word, stating, "Mr. Prime Minister, our National Security Council has already made its decision." The Japanese subtitles make it clear that by "our," Rosenberg means an American council making decisions unilaterally—decisions that Japan is expected to obey. Rosenberg continues, "The only way we can be absolutely certain of destroying Godzilla is by using nuclear weapons." This is followed by ambassador Chevsky similarly stating that the Soviet Union has come to a decision to use nuclear weapons against Godzilla. Rosenberg then utilizes an appeal to higher authority in stating that allowing the use of nuclear weapons should Godzilla resurface in Japan or in Japan's coastal waters is "a direct request from our president to the prime minister of Japan." Thus Mitamura is squeezed between two countries that wish to circumvent any Japanese autonomy in the decision-making process.

This process, however, is stricken from *Godzilla 1985*. Mitamura is goaded by the Soviet Ambassador—in a threatening close-up—to make an immediate decision in favor of the use of nuclear weapons by the Soviet Union. The effect is one that produces an image of one-sided Soviet aggression, to which Mitamura responds by stating that he will not deviate from Japan's policy of strictly forbidding the production, possession, or importation of nuclear weapons. While this marks the end of the scene in *Godzilla 1985*, it continues in *Godzilla 1984*, and it is in this continuation that we learn details central to the narrative progression. The first is that the Soviet ambassador forces Mitamura—and thus the audience as well—to make the distinction between tactical and strategic nuclear weapons, the former having lower yields and thus "suitable" for use in situations in which the destruction of an entire population is deemed undesirable. Chevsky is pleading that Japan allow the use of tactical nuclear weapons, a suggestion to which Rosenberg overtly agrees, emphatically stating, "He's right!" Chevsky removes his spectacles to impart an air of increased urgency and seriousness as he presses the point that only a small area will be affected by the blast—

though he fails to mention the ensuing fallout—and that missile guidance systems will guarantee that the missile hits and extinguishes Godzilla. Chevsky finally prognosticates that if Godzilla attacks Japan, he will next attack Vladivostok and other nuclear and military installations operating in the Pacific. The meeting is thus not only dominated by the Russian ambassador, but also hints at U.S.–Soviet cooperation in burying Godzilla under an umbrella of nuclear smoke.

Unlike *Godzilla 1985*, the Mitamura of *Godzilla 1984* does not come to an immediate decision. During a brief interlude, Mitamura and his advisors adjourn to a separate room to discuss the options. This meeting, which does not appear in the remake, serves as a dense, compressed representation of the moral issues surrounding the use of nuclear weapons. It is no coincidence that the U.S. and USSR, who appear at best apathetic toward any humanistic issues that would inevitably arise as the result of their use of nuclear weapons, have no place in this meeting, at which we learn that (1) The yield of the weapons proposed for use are 10 kilotons each, quoted as being approximately half the yield of the bomb dropped on Hiroshima; (2) the amount of damage that Godzilla could do to Tokyo is immeasurable; (3) the area in which the nuclear blast occurs will incur great, but measurable damage; (4) there is no strategy to address the fallout that would occur after the blast; and (5) there is no guarantee that a nuclear weapon would be effective against Godzilla. The sixth point is perhaps the most incriminating: tactical nuclear weapons are a new technology, the effectiveness of which has yet to be measured on the battlefield, despite the U.S. and USSR having had multiple opportunities to conduct such tests. The conclusion is thus that the U.S. and USSR simply seek to use Japan as a testing ground for the effectiveness of their nuclear arsenal. For these world powers, Godzilla's appearance is incidental.

Mitamura's private meeting, therefore, serves to illustrate the politics of nuclear weapons use in addition to Japan-U.S.-USSR power relations. Whatever happens, the U.S. and Soviet Union come away from the Godzilla incident victorious, having accomplished the successful testing of tactical nuclear weapons, having blown apart Godzilla, or both. Japan, conversely, is denied the possibility of escape without massive loss, a situation which arguably mirrors the inevitability that nuclear weapons would be used against Japan—twice—in World War II. Death is presented as inescapable, Japan's best option being whatever stems the tide of destruction. The inevitability of destruction and the resulting radiation poisoning is further reflected in the trajectory of the Soviet nuclear missile and its projected time of arrival—the heavily populated district of Shinjuku in 30 minutes. Both Rosenberg and Chevsky have been exposed as "dishonest" politicians, simply following orders issued from the highest authority. Their wanting to take the nuclear option thus becomes a matter of incidental collusion for the purpose of experimentation that will only help further entrench both sides in the bitterness of the Cold War as they continue efforts of one-upmanship that began with the atom bomb, but persisted in the form of the hydrogen bomb, Intercontinental Ballistic Missiles, Anti-Ballistic Missiles, Multiple Independently Targetable Reentry Vehicles, antisatellite weapons, and various missile defense systems deployed by both the Soviet Union and the U.S. Moreover, the idea that the use of tactical nuclear weapons is more about experimentation than problem-solving recalls the debate following the dropping of the bombs on Hiroshima and Nagasaki. Dennis Wainstock reminds us of the experimental factors contributing to the decision to deploy Little Boy over Hiroshima: "Because an untouched city was necessary to measure more accurately the effects of the atomic bomb, orders came down for the Air Force to bypass [Kyoto, Hiroshima, Kokura, and Niigata]."[42] *Godzilla 1984* posits that Tokyo has become the new testing ground for the effects of experimental tactical nuclear weapons. The film also clearly displays and labels the antimissile devices orbiting the earth, held by both the U.S. and Soviet Union, thus further illustrating the parity of their positions. *Godzilla 1985* eliminates this parity through cutting the display of the antimissile system thereby also eliminating the attendant labels.

Godzilla 1984, then, places the U.S. on equal footing with the USSR in its nuclear ambitions and recalls the faults of a political process built into which is the inexorable and gratuitous use of violence. It should come as no surprise that its Hollywood remake—a remake made in the "editing room floor" fashion of the 1956 remake of *Gojira*—would seek to exclude any messages of U.S.–USSR similarity and instead reinforce an already common narrative of U.S. innocence under Soviet aggression. The full significance of Japan's perspective has been carefully removed, to be replaced by unarguably minimally inspired scenes featuring Raymond Burr—who had by this time become synonymous with Perry Mason—and a crew of heavily typecast military personalities.

Other representations of Japanese experience would naturally become inconsequential and imperceptible within the remake process, with the new audience lacking the cultural and historical background to add meaning to the events. For instance, the cadmium-loaded missiles of the Super X bring back a painful chapter in Japan's history during which cadmium poisoning resulting in what would be called "itaiitai disease" became prevalent in areas such as Toyama Prefecture's Jinzū River. Particularly during the increased militarization seen throughout World War II, the mines nearby would be utilized for munitions production, with chemical runoff entering the Jinzū River, poisoning the rice and vegetables grown with the river water.[43] The development of cadmium missiles represents Japan's ability to turn atrocity into advantage, much as Serizawa's Oxygen Destroyer saw use only in as much as it would be beneficial to Japan.

Similarly, the volcanic mountain into which Godzilla falls at the film's conclusion is not a mere volcanic mountain. To stand at the edge of Miharayama, or Mount Mihara, was to stand on the precipice of death. The volcano gained a permanent place in Japan's cultural iconography when early in 1933 two schoolgirls visited the mountain to commit what was sensationally reported as an attempted double-suicide, one of the girls surviving, having been found in a confused state. However, it was later discovered that the survivor—Tomita Shōko—was not attempting to commit suicide, but only served as a guide and lookout while the other schoolgirl threw herself into the volcano. The investigation also uncovered that Tomita had done this before, thus earning her the title of "the woman who brings death."[44] Miharayama, which had already been known as a venue for suicide, became even more connected with death as the island saw an uptick in visitors contemplating suicide, with over 940 people either successfully or unsuccessfully attempting suicide in 1933 alone. As Kon Sakimori describes in his paper on the prevalence of suicide at Izu Ōshima—the island home of the volcano—by 1933 Miharayama had already become a "mecca" for suicide. It is no coincidence that this is where Godzilla would meet his demise.[45]

Neither *Godzilla 1984* nor its remake ever received the credence or critical acclaim that *Gojira* and *Godzilla, King of the Monsters!* would eventually receive. Perhaps this is partially the result of Godzilla having lost its resonance through serialization. Once the Godzilla franchise became centered on Godzilla, the monster lost his significance. As Nakamoto Ryō observes, we rarely get a clear glimpse of Godzilla in the original film.[46] Instead, *Gojira* focuses on the lives of the people living and dying in the wake of destruction and psychological torment brought about by the knowledge of imminent destruction. In other words, despite its title, Gojira is not about Godzilla, but about the lives of the humans affected by an unknown, unknowable monster that threatens to reintroduce the familiar. With the introduction of *Godzilla 1984*, we see a Godzilla that is completely knowable, its behavior scientifically explainable, and thus mortal, as flawed as the humans surrounding it. The threat is no longer Godzilla's ability to resurrect the past, but instead human ability to wreck the future in the form of Mutually Assured Destruction. Godzilla's mortality would only grow with Hollywood's 1998 reboot, *Godzilla*.

Godzilla *1998: Godzilla Without Question*

The 1998 Hollywood film, *Godzilla*, marks the complete excision of Japan from Godzilla. *Godzilla* is a significant title in a number of respects. First, it marks a watershed moment for relations between Hollywood and the Japanese film industry, beginning the slew of Japanese films that would be either remade or rebooted by Hollywood from the late 1990s and continue throughout the first decade of the 21st century. It simultaneously represents a crossroads—at least temporarily—in Hollywood's approach to Japanese adaptations that would see producers and motion picture studios steer shy of well-known properties the production budgets of which could possibly run in the hundreds of millions of dollars. Instead, Hollywood would move toward lesser-known properties the rights to which could be bought without incurring extravagant financial risk. Second, it represents an evolution of the Godzilla series in that Toho's "suitmation" techniques would take a back seat to computer generated graphics in reproducing the green monster.[47] The Hollywood version, instead, aligns itself with the popular Hollywood films of the 1990s, in particular *Independence Day* (1996)—the creation of a spectacle through highly destructive, fast-paced action sequences—and *The Lost World: Jurassic Park* (1997)—the creation of a spectacle through the sheer size of the creatures on the screen, and the ability to lend to them smooth, lifelike movement. Shinichirō Kobayashi in his work on realism and the morphology of Japanese and American iterations of Godzilla recognizes the focus on size in Emmerich's Godzilla as a telling hint toward the director's aim—to destroy Manhattan in spectacular fashion.[48] Hollywood has always been infatuated with Godzilla's size, having changed the 164-foot monster in *Gojira* to one over 400 feet tall in *Godzilla, King of the Monsters!*[49] It would continue to take great creative liberties with every aspect of the monster in adapting it for an American audience that has heretofore been trained to think of Godzilla as spectacle instead of allegory, creating something that in the end was indeed a giant green organism, but still far from a monster, and arguably not Godzilla beyond the forced name.[50]

Steve Ryfle, in his biography of Godzilla, states that Toho originally held tight control over not only the Godzilla name, but also the Godzilla aesthetic and the principles governing the monster's behavior. Toho's writ to TriStar pictures would include the following stipulations: "Godzilla's birth must be the result of a nuclear explosion; Godzilla must have four claws on its hands and feet; Godzilla must have three rows of dorsal fins along its spine; Godzilla does not eat people; Godzilla cannot die."[51] The Godzilla that was eventually born, nonetheless broke almost all of these tenets, causing an ideological break with any of the other "serious" Godzilla films. A Godzilla as mortal as the humans trying to kill him cannot begin to approach the sense of dread imparted by the original monster, his mysteriousness magnified as the result of his being born of the ocean.

Though the 1998 film diverges from the 1954 and 1984 films aesthetically, in the method through which it is globalized and made fit for American consumption it retains similarity with its predecessors. Godzilla lives in the intertextual shadow of previous Hollywood efforts, and is denied access to representation of the issues presented in *Gojira* and re-presented and re-contextualized in *Godzilla 1984*. The film begins with an homage to and reconstruction of the nuclear issue. As previously stated, *Godzilla, King of the Monsters!* only briefly mentions atomic weapons testing in comparison with the original. The film discards the nuclear issue entirely once the audience has been made aware that nuclear testing resulted in the monster's awakening. As previously stated, it is the author's assertion that this has the effect of aligning the Godzilla origin story with that of the other giant beasts prevalent in the monster movie era, while simultaneously stripping the political aspects of nuclear testing from the film. An understanding of nuclear weapons use during the end of World War II and continued testing in the post-war world thus becomes unnec-essary, as the narrative has been made to function without the political and historical back-drop which provided the original its allegorical rooting.

By design, Godzilla shows from its opening not only that Godzilla's origin is in nuclear testing, but that it is in French nuclear testing. Godzilla resets the nuclear narrative, impli-cating the French in the creation of a giant iguana. French nuclear testing lends the film its impetus for tracing the origin of Godzilla back to subsequent underground testing of the atomic bomb in French Polynesia.[52] Much of the film spends time making traversing shots of land, including Tahiti, Panama, Jamaica (where a wrecked Japanese ship runs aground), then eastern U.S. waters, and on to New Jersey, and New York. Whereas we are aware that Godzilla ravaged Tokyo in 1954 as a kind of recollection device to vividly bring back mem-ories of firebombing and nuclear annihilation,[53] Godzilla never provides a satisfactory answer to the question of why Godzilla would choose New York as a nesting ground. Dr. Nick Tatopoulos (Matthew Broderick) attempts to justify this by explaining that New York is an island at which Godzilla might feel at home, but like no other island there are places to hide. In other words, somehow Godzilla's animal instincts led it to New York. Again, this is Godzilla by chance. In both shifting responsibility for the creation of Godzilla to the French and bringing Godzilla's destruction to Manhattan, the Godzilla problem has been globalized—or at least Americanized—to a level unattainable through the editing tech-niques used in the 1956 and 1985 remakes. Again, the result of this globalization is a lack of material that promotes introspection concerning how America fits into the world's nuclear puzzle. Moreover, the film avoids asking any serious questions concerning France's role either. For instance, as former French defense minister Pierre Messmer states in director Ben Lewis' film on French nuclear testing in the South Pacific titled *Blowing Up Paradise*, France could not conduct nuclear tests in Algeria after the country won independence in 1962 and was thus forced to look for another test site.[54] The political implication here is that nuclear testing is abetted by colonization. The aftereffects of this testing are conse-quently bequeathed to "other people" instead of the testers and colonizers. The failure to ask any questions of anyone represents a missed opportunity to give the film relevance beyond its own perceived self-importance as a spectacle.

Japan also remains absent from the film. The significance of the Godzilla-Japan con-nection is stripped away through giving the monster a biological, overseas origin. The Japa-nese elements that appear sporadically throughout the film serve merely as superficial tributes. For instance, the film begins with Godzilla sinking a Japanese cannery ship, an event robbed of meaning through its coincidental nature. It serves only the purpose of introducing a Japanese fishing veteran who survives the incident and gives the monster its name. Additionally, one of the newscasters reporting on Godzilla's appearance in New York City happens to be named Rob Fukuzaki—an obvious attempt to invoke "Japanese" elements.

The ignoring of Toho's Godzilla tenets, refusal to find any questions worth asking, and removal of Japan from the foreground combine to alter the meaning and significance of the major players in the film. The military in particular enjoys a role and powers undesignated in *Gojira* and *Godzilla 1984*. Both *Gojira* and *Godzilla 1984* directly and indirectly comment on the involvement of the American military as an aggressor, either having used nuclear weaponry against Japan, or anxious to use nuclear weaponry within Japan for the purpose of testing its efficacy. Militarism and the eagerness to use destructive weapons are portrayed as morally flawed approaches to monster diplomacy, placing Japan in the position of having to uphold an ethical obligation to disallow the use of any such weaponry. American flags abound in *Godzilla* (1998), however, with America solving the world's problems through a military that is no longer an aggressor, but a savior, mimicking a formula often repeated in the Hollywood blockbuster, including the previously mentioned *Independence Day*, as well as *Armageddon* (1998).

Military efficacy against Godzilla points to a decidedly different beast. Perhaps one of the most important distinctions to be made is that the hydrogen bomb did not create the original Godzilla, but awakened or disturbed him. Godzilla is thus a highly confused product. In its effort to rationalize the massive growth of a life form much larger than the *Jurassic Park* dinosaurs with which the film compares Godzilla, the film loses Godzilla's extraordinary meaning. Here again, Godzilla no longer represents the past, but the future. In this future, Manhattan becomes the incubator and coincidentally the center of the human race's supplanting. The premise is that America serves not only as the center of everything good in the world, but also as the center of world destruction—at the fault of the French. Godzilla thus becomes a reflection of insularity, while the military serves as the scalpel that removes from this insular body its external threat—Godzilla.

Following the repositioning of the American military and its function within the film is the repositioning of modern weaponry. The secret weapons that disposed of Godzilla in the Japanese versions were always triumphs of ethical technology over extravagant displays of violent brute force. As mentioned above, the *Gojira* films attempt to illustrate the futility of using modern weaponry to rectify a problem brought about by the use of modern weaponry. Not one in the barrage of missiles fired at Godzilla from Japanese warplanes manages to cause it any harm. The sole weapon in existence that can do Godzilla any harm is the Oxygen Destroyer, even that coming with the greater price of the destruction of all life within the active radius of the weapon. Similarly, the Super X in *Godzilla 1984* placates Godzilla through cadmium missiles, weakening the energizing effect that nuclear power has on the monster. Notice that none of these weapons cause any dramatic explosions. Both weapons are highly contextualized, with the former introducing an ethical dilemma, and the latter constructed in such a manner that the ethical connotations are not paralyzing. *Godzilla* on the other hand, brings mortality to its giant lizard, seeing that it succumbs to missiles, and that large explosions bring an end to its offspring tucked away in Madison Square Garden, all for the purpose of allowing the French secret service to "protect the world from mistakes" about which it does not want the world to know and to prove the efficacy of American military might. *Godzilla* thereby effectively eliminates both the physical and psychological characteristics once represented by Godzilla. It leaves no room for the concept that, despite the resultant destruction or even because of it, Godzilla is a hero the killing of which deserves mourning. There are no happy endings, because Godzilla is survived by the human capacity to destroy and a penchant for realizing it.

Conclusion

The Godzilla series is one that will forever live in the hearts and minds of its fans, if not revered within the annals of film history. That it has become the object of several Hollywood remakes as well as countless parodies and representations illustrates just how powerful an influence Godzilla has proven. What we must take care to consider however, is that it is Godzilla the character, not *Gojira* the narrative that has received attention from American media. The globalization of the *Gojira* narrative represents the expansion of the Godzilla problem beyond the borders of Japan, and thus the removal of the political and historical issues particular to Japan. In an age in which nuclear weapons proliferation, the threat of subsequent cold wars, and issues of government accountability remain all the more relevant, it is important that Godzilla remain immortal, unstoppable, fearsome, and unsilenced.

Notes

1. N. Sawaragi, "On the Battlefield of 'Superflat': Subculture and Art in Postwar Japan," in *Little Boy: The Arts of Japan's Exploding Subculture*, trans. Linda Hoaglund (New Haven: Yale University Press, 2005), p. 188.

2. C.A. Durham, *Double Takes: Culture and Gender in French Films and Their American Remakes* (Hanover, NH: Dartmouth, 1998), p. 89.

3. Richard Hudson challenges us to question ourselves concerning the death of Kuboyama Aikichi within the context of the Lucky Dragon: "Why did Kuboyama die? This is a personal question, a question for each individual to ponder after hearing Kuboyama's simple tragedy." In remaking Godzilla, the tragedy is deemphasized, preempting any self-inquiry. See Hudson, *Kuboyama and the Saga of the Lucky Dragon*, p. 7.

4. R.J. Lifton and G. Mitchell, *Hiroshima in America* (New York: Harper Perennial, 1996), p. 95.

5. M. Anderson, "Mobilizing Gojira," in *In Godzilla's Footsteps: Japanese Pop Culture Icons on the Global Stage* (New York: Palgrave Macmillan, 2006), p. 22.

6. S. Guthrie-Shimizu, "Godzilla in Cold War America," in *In Godzilla's Footsteps: Japanese Pop Culture Icons on the Global Stage* (New York: Palgrave Macmillan, 2006), p. 59.

7. J. Susina, "Reptar: The Rugrats Meet Godzilla," in *The Japanification of Children's Popular Culture: From Godzilla to Miyazaki* (Lanham, MD: Scarecrow Press, 2008), p. 11.

8. Also often given as "Ōdo Island," here the name of the island as given in the original script and novelization—Ōto Island—will be used.

9. D. Kalat, *A Critical History and Filmography of Toho's Godzilla Series* (Jefferson, NC: McFarland, 2007), p. 110.

10. B. Crowther, "Godzilla a Japanese Film, Is at State," *New York Times*, April 28, 1956, p. 11.

11. The death and destruction wrought by the latter is often overshadowed by Hiroshima and Nagasaki. The firebombing of Tokyo, however, is intimately linked with use of the atomic bomb. Conrad Crane allows us to vividly resurrect the moment: "Before [the first full-scale fire raid] was over, between 90,000 and 100,000 people had been killed. Most died horribly as intense heat from the firestorm consumed the oxygen, boiled water in canals, and sent liquid glass rolling down the streets. Thousands suffocated in shelters or parks; panicked crowds crushed victims who had fallen in the streets as they surged toward waterways to escape the flames." See *Crane, Bombs, Cities, and Civilians: American Airpower Strategy in World War II*, p. 132. The mass, indiscriminate havoc brought about by using incendiary devices on a country the infrastructure of which depended largely on highly flammable materials made the operations to bomb Hiroshima and Nagasaki seem precise. As Conrad concludes, "If an atomic bomb dropped on a city could be construed as a method of precision bombing, then that doctrine [concerning the most effective way to destroy Japan's capacity for war] had evolved to the point where civilian casualties were no longer taken into consideration at all." See *Crane, Bombs, Cities, and Civilians: American Airpower Strategy in World War II*, p. 142. Godzilla not only embodies this past destruction and indiscriminate death, but re-realizes it.

12. S. Johnson: *The Japanese Through American Eyes* (Stanford: Stanford University Press, 1991), p. 41. In all fairness to Crowther, it should also be noted that his critical reviews of *The Beginning or the End* as well as *Above and Beyond*—two of the first films that attempted a cathartic documentation of the development and deployment of the atomic bomb for American audiences—were lined with a characteristic unwillingness to mince words. Of the former, Crowther writes about the film's romance element, "despite its generally able reenactments, this film is so laced with sentiment of the silliest and most theatrical nature that much of its impressiveness is marred." Though the latter received a less scathing review, Crowther nonetheless comments on a similar romantic element: "As a consequence of the necessity to act out this meretricious sham of painful domestic tensions, Mr. Taylor does not come off in the whole film as fairly and forcefully as he does in the strictly military scenes." See Crowther, "Beginning or the End, Metro Study of Historic Weapon," *New York Times*, February 21, 1947, and Crowther, "Domestic Trials of Atom Bomb Pilot Portrayed in Above and Beyond," in *New York Times*, January 31, 1953, both available through the *New York Times* online archives.

13. S. Napier, "When Godzilla Speaks," in *In Godzilla's Footsteps: Japanese Pop Culture Icons on the Global Stage* (New York: Palgrave Macmillan, 2006), p. 18.

14. W. Tsutsui, *Godzilla on My Mind: Fifty Years of the King of Monsters* (New York: Palgrave Macmillan, 2004), p. 99.

15. R.E. Lapp, *The Voyage of the Lucky Dragon* (New York: Harper & Brothers, 1957), p. 50.

16. W. Tsutsui, *Godzilla on My Mind: Fifty Years of the King of Monsters* (New York: Palgrave Macmillan, 2004), p. 95.

17. T. Iwahata, *Terebi Magajin Tokubetsu Henshū Supesharu: Gojira* (Tokyo: Kōdansha, 2007), p. 40.

18. The M24, though underpowered, was one of the few U.S. military tanks that Japan could accommodate. As Oscar Gilbert writes about U.S. forces stationed in Japan leading up to the Korean War: "Exactly how the United States would defend the South Koreans was problematical. Four soft, under-strength, and ill-equipped divisions were maintained on occupation duty in Japan. Each was short of weapons and lacked the spare parts necessary to maintain what little equipment they possessed.... The only forces available to counter the NKPA's mechanized onslaught were the "tank battalions" of the infantry divisions. Each of the tank battalions was in reality a company equipped with M24 light scout tanks. These small vehicles were the heaviest the frail bridges and roads of Japan could accommodate." It is no wonder that these tanks held no sway against Godzilla. See Gilbert, *Marine Corps Tank Battles in Korea*, p. 10.

19. *Ibid.*, p. 44.

20. Here, it should also be noted that the Korean War played a great role in accelerating Japan's moribund post–World War II economy. John Dower provides an exhaustive list of those industrial sectors stimulated by the outbreak of war. These would include metal products, fossil fuels, vehicles, and electronics, but perhaps more importantly, "the Americans turned to Japan for Ammunition, light weapons, and napalm bombs, although in theory such manufactures were still proscribed." See Dower, *Embracing Defeat: Japan in the Wake of World War II*, pp. 641–642. The destruction brought to Tokyo by Godzilla thus revokes any economic advantages gained through even indirect participation in a proxy war.

21. B. Kushner, "Japan's First Postwar Media Event," in *In Godzilla's Footsteps: Japanese Pop Culture Icons on the Global Stage* (New York: Palgrave Macmillan, 2006), p. 41.

22. C. Kanahara, "Serizawahakase wa nankai Gojira no na wo yonda ka," in *Nichibei Gojira Taisen* (Tokyo: Seikyūsha, 1998), pp. 90–91.

23. M. Anderson, "Mobilizing Gojira" in *In Godzilla's Footsteps: Japanese Pop Culture Icons on the Global Stage* (New York: Palgrave Macmillan, 2006), p. 24.

24. W. Tsutsui, *Godzilla on My Mind: Fifty Years of the King of Monsters* (New York: Palgrave Macmillan, 2004), p. 90.

25. It should be noted someplace that Shinkichi and Masaji live with their mother. There is no man in the house.

26. D. Kalat, *A Critical History and Filmography of Toho's Godzilla Series* (Jefferson, NC: McFarland, 2007), p. 27.

27. C. Kanahara, "Serizawahakase wa nankai Gojira no na wo yonda ka" in *Nichibei Gojira Taisen* (Tokyo: Seikyūsha, 1998), p. 88.

28. In the novelization of *Gojira*, Serizawa's eye patch is the result of a war injury, while in one version of the *Gojira* script, Serizawa's eye injury was the result of being attacked by a wolf during an excavation. His relationship with Yamane was solidified when Yamane rescued him from this wolf. Stills that never made the final cut of the original *Gojira* betray a Serizawa with not only an eye patch, but also a face half covered in scar tissue. See Kayama, *Gojira*, p. 53 and p. 335.

29. As if matters could not get worse for Hagiwara in *Godzilla, King of the Monsters!*, even Yamane gets his name wrong, referring to him not as Hagiwara but "Mr. Ojihara." Anything goes as long as it sounds Japanese.

30. D. Kalat, *A Critical History and Filmography of Toho's Godzilla Series* (Jefferson, NC: McFarland, 2007), p. 27.

31. C. Kanahara, "Serizawahakase wa nankai Gojira no na wo yonda ka" in *Nichibei Gojira Taisen* (Tokyo: Seikyūsha, 1998), p. 86.
32. K. Cwiertka, *Modern Japanese Cuisine: Food, Power and National Identity* (London: Reaktion Books, 2007), p. 134.
33. *Ibid.*, 150. Postwar food conditions have often been a subject of commentary in Japanese Yakuza film, with gangs having gained power through the black markets that rose as the result of severe rationing and food shortages.
34. Of course, entire scenes have been left out of the film, most famously the scene that takes place between commuter train passengers making references to Nagasaki and shelters. See Kalat, *A Critical History and Filmography of Toho's Godzilla Series*, p. 27.
35. Stephen Whitfield describes the pervasive nature of these tensions in their post–World War II origins: "In this era, a specter was haunting America—the specter of Communism. Trying to exorcise it were legislators and judges, union officials and movie studio bosses, policemen and generals, university presidents and corporation executives, clergymen and journalists, Republicans and Democrats, conservatives and liberals." See Whitfield, *The Culture of the Cold War*, p. 1.
36. D. Kalat, *A Critical History and Filmography of Toho's Godzilla Series* (Jefferson, NC: McFarland, 2007), p. 162.
37. Author's translation.
38. H. Robinson, *Russians in Hollywood, Hollywood's Russians: Biography of an Image* (Boston: Northeastern University Press, 2007), p. 242.
39. *Ibid.*
40. L. Pressler, *Star Wars: The Strategic Defense Initiative Debates in Congress* (Westport, CT: Praeger, 1986), p. 156.
41. D. Kalat, *A Critical History and Filmography of Toho's Godzilla Series* (Jefferson, NC: McFarland, 2007), p. 169.
42. D.D. Wainstock, *The Decision to Drop the Atomic Bomb* (Westport, CT: Praeger, 1996), p. 83.
43. N. Iijima, K. Fujikawa, and S. Watanabe, *Environmental Sociology of Itai-itai Disease and Cadmium Pollution Problem* (Tokyo: Tōshindō, 2008), pp. 42–43.
44. Rekishizatsugakutanteidan, ed., *Hakken! Igai ni shiranai Showa-shi 1924–1989* (Tokyo: Tokyoshoten, 2007), p. 24.
45. S. Kon, "Kankōchi to Jisatsu: Shōwa Hachi Nen, Izu Ōshima · Miharayama ni okeru Tōshin Jisatsu no Ryūkō wo Chūshin ni," in *Ryūtsu Mondai Kenkyū 23* (1994), A1–A51, p. 10.
46. R. Nakamoto, "Gojira wa kakujikken ga umidashita kaijū de areba, sore de ii no ka?," in *Nichibei Gojira Taisen* (Tokyo: Seikyūsha, 1998), p. 33.
47. S. Ryfle, *Japan's Favorite Mon-Star: The Unauthorized Biography of "The Big G"* (Toronto: ECW Press, 1998), p. 337.
48. S. Kobayashi, "Keitaigakuteki nichibeigojiraron: Riarizumu no chihei," in *Nichibei Gojira Taisen* (Tokyo: Seikyūsha, 1998), p. 26.
49. For specifics concerning the sizes of the various Godzilla iterations, see Kashiwagi, *Gojira gahō: Toho gensō eiga hanseiki no ayumi*, pp. 22–40. Concerning the size of Godzilla in *Godzilla, King of the Monsters!*, Yamane tells us himself.
50. In his chapter on "truth, good, beauty" and ethics in Japanese narratives, Isayama Yōtarō points out that Kaneko Shūsuke's 2001 continuation of the Godzilla series serves as a disavowal of Hollywood's 1998 version of the monster, with characters conversing in the Japanese Ministry of Defense stating that Japanese scientists do not consider the "Godzilla" that appeared on America's shores a real Godzilla. "In other words, the American Godzilla is a fake, and the Godzilla soon to make its appearance is the real Godzilla" (author's translation). See Isayama, *Manga · Tokusatsu Hirō no Ronrigaku: Monogatariteikoku Nihon no gunzō*, pp. 89–90.
51. *Ibid.*, p. 322.
52. G.J. DeGroot, *The Bomb: A Life* (Cambridge: Harvard University Press, 2006), p. 233.
53. H. Yoshii, *GojiraMosura · Gensuibaku: Tokusatsueiga no Shakaigaku* (Tokyo: Serika Shobō, 2007), pp. 48–49.
54. Pierre Messmer in *Blowing Up Paradise: French Nuclear Testing in the Pacific*, DVD, directed by Ben Lewis (Bergmann Pictures, 2005).

Bibliography

Brothers, Peter H. *Mushroom Clouds and Mushroom Men: The Fantastic Cinema of Ishiro Honda*. Bloomington: AuthorHouse, 2009.

Brower, Charles F. *Defeating Japan: The Joint Chiefs of Staff and Strategy in the Pacific War, 1943–1945.* New York: Palgrave Macmillan, 2012.

Crane, Conrad C. *Bombs, Cities, and Civilians: American Airpower Strategy in World War II.* Lawrence: University Press of Kansas, 1993.

Crowther, Bosley. "*Beginning or the End,* Metro Study of Historic Weapon." *New York Times,* February 21, 1947 (online).

_____. "Domestic Trials of Atom Bomb Pilot Portrayed in *Above and Beyond.*" *New York Times,* January 31, 1953 (online).

_____. "*Godzilla* a Japanese Film, Is at State." *New York Times,* April 28, 1956, p. 11.

Cwiertka, Katarzyna J. *Modern Japanese Cuisine: Food, Power and National Identity.* London: Reaktion Books, 2007.

Dower, John W. *Embracing Defeat: Japan in the Wake of World War II.* New York: W.W. Norton, 2000.

Durham, Carolyn A. *Double Takes: Culture and Gender in French Films and Their American Remakes.* Hanover, NH: Dartmouth, 1998.

Feis, Herbert. *The Atomic Bomb and the End of World War II.* Princeton: Princeton University Press, 1966.

Gilbert, Oscar. *Marine Corps Tank Battles in Korea.* Havertown: Casemate, 2003.

Honda, Ishirō. *Gojira to Waga Eigajinsei.* Tokyo: Wani Bukkusu, 2010.

Hudson, Richard. *Kuboyama and the Saga of the Lucky Dragon.* New York: Thomas Yoseloff, 1965.

Iijima, Nobuko, Ken Fujikawa, and Shinichi Watanabe. *Environmental Sociology of Itai-itai Disease and Cadmium Pollution Problem.* Tokyo: Tōshindō, 2008.

Isayama, Yōtarō. *Manga · Tokusatsu Hīrō no Ronrigaku: Monogatariteikoku Nihon no gunzō.* Tokyo: Chōeisha, 2006.

Iwahata, Toshiaki. *Terebi Magajin Tokubetsu Henshū Supesharu: Gojira.* Tokyo: Kōdansha, 2007.

Johnson, Sheila, *The Japanese Through American Eyes.* Stanford: Stanford University Press, 1991.

Kalat, David. *A Critical History and Filmography of Toho's Godzilla Series.* Jefferson, NC: McFarland, 2007.

Kashiwagi, Makoto, ed. *Gojira gahō: Toho gensō eiga hanseiki no ayumi.* Tokyo: Takeshobō, 1999.

Kayama, Shigeru. *Gojira.* Tokyo: Chikuma Shobō, 2004.

Kiridōshi, Risaku. *Nichibei Gojira Taisen.* Tokyo: Seikyūsha, 1998.

Kon, Sakamori. "Kankōchi to Jisatsu: Shōwa Hachi Nen, Izu Ōshima · Miharayama ni okeru Tōshin Jisatsu no Ryūkō wo Chūshin ni." *Ryūtsu Mondai Kenkyū* 23 (1994): A1–A51.

Lapp, Ralph E. *The Voyage of the Lucky Dragon.* New York: Harper & Brothers, 1957.

Lifton, Robert J., and Greg Mitchell. *Hiroshima in America.* New York: Harper Perennial, 1996.

Murakami, Takashi. *Little Boy: The Arts of Japan's Exploding Subculture.* New Haven: Yale University Press, 2005.

Nakajima, Haruo. *Kaijū jinsei: Ganso Gojira haiyū Nakajima Haruo.* Tokyo: Yōsensha, 2010.

Polmar, Norman, and Robert S. Norris. *U.S. Nuclear Arsenal: A History of Weapons and Delivery Systems Since 1945.* Annapolis: Naval Institute Press, 2009.

Pressler, Larry. *Star Wars: The Strategic Defense Initiative Debates in Congress.* Westport, CT: Praeger, 1986.

Rekishizatsugakutanteidan, ed. *Hakken! Igai ni shiranai Showa-shi 1924–1989.* Tokyo: Tokyoshoten, 2007.

Robinson, Harlow. *Russians in Hollywood, Hollywood's Russians: Biography of an Image.* Boston: Northeastern University Press, 2007.

Ryfle, Steve. *Japan's Favorite Mon-Star: The Unauthorized Biography of "The Big G."* Toronto: ECW Press, 1998.

Skal, David J. *The Monster Show: A Cultural History of Horror; Revised Edition with a New Afterword.* New York: Faber & Faber, 2001.

Tsutsui, William. *Godzilla on My Mind: Fifty Years of the King of Monsters.* New York: Palgrave Macmillan, 2004.

_____. "Godzilla and Postwar Japan Lunch Keynote Address 2004 National Meeting Asian Studies Development Program." *East-West Connections* (2004).

_____, and Michiko Ito, eds. *In Godzilla's Footsteps: Japanese Pop Culture Icons on the Global Stage.* New York: Palgrave Macmillan, 2006.

Wainstock, Dennis D. *The Decision to Drop the Atomic Bomb.* Westport, CT: Praeger, 1996.

West, Mark, ed. *The Japanification of Children's Popular Culture: From Godzilla to Miyazaki.* Lanham, MD: Scarecrow Press, 2008.

Whitfield, Stephen J. *The Culture of the Cold War.* Baltimore: Johns Hopkins University Press, 1996.

Yoshii, Hiroaki. *Gojira · Mosura · Gensuibaku: Tokusatsueiga no Shakaigaku.* Tokyo: Serika Shobō, 2007.

Filmography

Gojira. Dir. Ishirō Honda. Perf. Akira Takarada, Akihiko Hirata, Kōchi Momoko, and Takashi Shimura. *Gojira,* DVD. Toho Video, 1954.

Godzilla, King of the Monsters!. Dir. Ishirō Honda and Terry Morse. Perf. Raymond Burr, Akira Takarada, Akihiko Hirata, Kōchi Momoko, and Takashi Shimura. DVD. Embassy Pictures, 1956.

Gojira 1984. Dir. Kōji Hashimoto. Perf. Ken Tanaka, Keijū Kobayashi, Yasuko Sawaguchi, and Yōsuke Natsuki. DVD. Toho Video, 1984.

Gojira 1985. Dir. Kōji Hashimoto and R.J. Kizer. Perf. Raymond Burr, Ken Tanaka, Keijū Kobayashi, Yasuko Sawaguchi, and Yōsuke Natsuki. VHS. Anchor Bay, 1985.

Godzilla. Dir. Roland Emmerich. Perf. Matthew Broderick, Jean Reno, Maria Pitillo, Hank Azaria, and Kevin Dunn. DVD. Sony Pictures Home Entertainment, 1998.

Rugrats—Runaway Reptar. Dir. Anthony, Barry Vodos, Celia Kendrick, Chris Hermans, and Craig Bartlett. Perf. Elizabeth Daily, Christine Cavanaugh, Nancy Cartwright, Kath Soucie, Melanie Chartoff. VHS. Paramount Pictures, 1999.

Blowing Up Paradise: French Nuclear Testing in the Pacific. Dir. Ben Lewis. Nar. Crispin Redman. DVD. Bergmann Pictures, 2005.

Atomic Reaction: Godzilla as Metaphor for Generational Attitudes Toward the United States and the Bomb

John Vohlidka

At the finale of Akira Kurosawa's *Rhapsody in August* (*Hachigatsu no kyoshikyoku*, 1991), the elderly grandmother, a survivor (*Hibakusha*) of the bombing of Nagasaki, rushes out into the storm followed by her grandchildren and children. Neither group is able to catch the old woman, symbolically representing that they are unable to understand her experience. What is telling is that the grandchildren, while unable to catch their grandmother, are able to come much closer to her through their efforts, as opposed to their parents, who lag behind miserably. Kurosawa's comment about generational reaction to the atomic bomb is important. Throughout much of the film, the grandchildren demonstrate a curiosity about their family history and their grandmother's experience with the bomb, even if they could not fully understand it. Their parents, on the other hand, were caught up in their own problems, demonstrating a lack of knowledge, denial, greed and self-centeredness. They tended to avoid the subject and were even afraid to discuss it with their newly discovered American relative, worried they might anger or offend him. In a 1991 interview, Kurosawa stated, "the worst part is that the Japanese have already cast [the bombing] into oblivion."[1]

Kurosawa's film was a comment on how different generations dealt with the atomic blast: the elderly grandmother felt shame, her spoiled children avoided the subject, and her grandchildren, while curious, were too far removed from the event to truly understand it. How Japanese society reacted to the atomic bombing of Japan, the Nuclear Age, and the United States changed with the coming of new generations.

Assisting Kurosawa on *Rhapsody in August* was his friend and colleague Ishirō Honda. Honda is best known for directing one of Japan's most internationally known films, *Godzilla* (released as *Gojira* in Japan), in 1954. Honda directed a number of films in what became a Godzilla franchise, a franchise which outlived him, with the last film to date being *Godzilla Final Wars* (*Gojira fainaru wōzu*) released in 2004. This essay will look at Toho Studio's giant monster (*kaiju eiga*) films with particular focus on their main star: Godzilla. It is generally acknowledged among scholars today that the original 1954 *Gojira* was a multi-layered thematic comment on the bombing of Japan. The later films in the franchise, while deeply loved, hated and debated by fans, are less regarded among scholarly critics, yet they too are deserving of some analysis and historical context.

In the original *Gojira*, the monster represented both the atomic bomb and the United States. As a result of the film's popularity, Toho Studios turned Godzilla into a franchise with a slew of sequels producing films in every decade until 2004. As the times changed, so did the films, and the representational nature of the monster himself changed as well. This essay will argue that, with some cinematic exceptions, Godzilla reflected Japan's changing attitudes regarding the atomic bomb, the Nuclear Age, and the United States through the 1950s to 1970s (the original run), the late 1980s and 1990s (the Heisei era), and into the new millennium. Further, the changing attitudes are a result not just of economic turns and international tensions, but the birth and coming of age of new generations of young people in Japan. In the 1950s, with the war just over, Godzilla became a symbol of the destruction of the atomic bomb and the unstoppable military power of the United States. As a new generation matured in the 1960s, accompanied by the "economic miracle," a new sense of optimism permeated society and Godzilla transitioned into a tamer and friendlier character. In the 1980s, new international tensions over nuclear war led to a more violent, destructive Godzilla. The 1990s saw a new generation more interested in Japan's past, so the monster remained unfriendly as a reminder of the dangers of the nuclear age and a threat to the Earth as a whole. With the millennium series of films, over sixty years had passed since World War II and nearly fifty years since the release of the first Godzilla film. The films demonstrate a certain lack of direction, mirroring Japan's economic troubles, combined with the distance of years from the event that made Godzilla the most relevant.

The Birth of Godzilla

In August of 1945, the United States dropped two atomic bombs on the cities of Hiroshima and Nagasaki, respectively, forcing Japan to surrender. American occupying forces expected to deal with a great amount of resentment over those bombings, as well as from other aspects of the war. They were surprised to find little resentment among the Japanese who had adopted a traditional attitude of "It can't be helped." In fact, Donald Richie has argued that the narrative of suffering and tragedy in connection with the atomic bombing was largely appropriated from the guilt felt by the occupying forces.[2]

The American occupation of Japan lasted from 1945 to 1952. The overall purpose of the occupation was to promote democratic tendencies over the imperialistic goals of Japan during the war. Specifically, part of the surrender demanded that Japan require the democratization of society, as well as the establishment of freedoms of speech and religion.[3] Nevertheless, the cultural policy of American officials focused on censorship of films to paradoxically promote those freedoms. Depictions of militaristic, xenophobic, and antisocial behaviors, along with depictions of the occupation, were prohibited.[4] In such an environment, depictions of the atomic bombings of Hiroshima and Nagasaki were problematic. The official position of the censors (the Civil Information and Education Section and the Civil Censorship Detachment) was that the bombing was justified in order to end the war, and they were therefore uncomfortable with portrayals of the bombing and the impact on its victims.[5] So, while some films about the atomic bombings were made, they tended to be strictly factual and avoided issues of suffering. As a result, U.S. censors effectively pushed Japanese filmmakers into thinking that depictions of the suffering were important by the banning of them. It would not be until after the occupation ended in 1952 that such depictions would inevitably be shown.

The most powerful depiction was *Gojira* in 1954. With the occupation over, the long expected feeling of resentment regarding the bombings appeared.[6] This feeling was buttressed by the awareness of two factors: one, Japan being caught up in the Cold War between the United States and the Soviet Union, and two, the U.S.'s ongoing nuclear bomb tests in the Pacific. This second factor turned into heated debate in early 1954, when the U.S. tested a hydrogen bomb in the Marshall Islands. While the U.S. had warned Americans about the test, they did not warn Japan. A tuna boat, *The Lucky Dragon 5* (*Daigo fukuryū maru*), was close enough to see the blast and be hit by radioactive fall-out.[7] Several sailors slowly died from radiation sickness.[8] The entire incident created an uproar in the newspapers.

A producer at Toho Studios, Tomoyuki Tanaka, decided to use this public outcry as inspiration for a film, which eventually became *Gojira*. Directed by Ishirō Honda, with a screenplay by Takeo Murata and Honda (which was in part based on the story by Shigeru Kayama), the film was a direct commentary on the aftermath of Hiroshima and Nagasaki, as well as a moral discussion on the use of atomic weapons. In the film, Godzilla is both the atomic bomb and the strength of the U.S. military as witnessed by his destructive behavior and unstoppable onslaught. Arriving in Tokyo, the monster does not go around buildings, but steps right through them creating the maximum amount of destruction. In his wake are deserted, desolate streets, crumbled buildings, and the dead and wounded who also suffer from radiation burns. The radioactive monster was the bomb, and the scenes of his destruction and the suffering he caused would have resonated with a movie going audience who had lived through the end of the war.[9]

Some critics and fans have argued whether the 1954 *Gojira* was a rip-off of the 1953 American film *The Beast from 20,000 Fathoms*.[10] In the context here, the controversy is irrelevant, but the comparison is useful. While both have similar devices (nuclear testing wakes a pre-historic monster), the Japanese film has a completely different take on the subject. In the American film, the monster is dispatched with an atomic bomb. Atomic science solves the problems it creates.[11] This is a useful mindset to have in a country that felt it needed its nuclear advantage to fight the Cold War. Japan, however, viewed it differently. Japan saw itself as the victim of a nuclear attack and caught in the middle of the Cold War. *Gojira* was then a moral discussion on the rights and wrongs of ultimate weapons, mostly arguing that they were wrong. When the character Serizawa uses the ultimate weapon he had accidently discovered (the Oxygen Destroyer), he destroys himself along with Godzilla to prevent unleashing an even greater horror on the world than the monster. The paradox was clear in the film, the only way to destroy an ultimate weapon (Godzilla) was through the use of another ultimate weapon (the Oxygen Destroyer); but the film demonstrates that there was a moral way out. By killing himself with his own device, Serizawa was taking the ultimate responsibility for his invention.

In this movie, science trumps politics. While politicians in the film argued fruitlessly throughout the story (mainly about whether to cover up information regarding Godzilla), it is the scientists, in the form of Dr. Yamane and Serizawa, who lead the moral way. By destroying himself with his creation, Serizawa takes a symbolic responsibility for Japan's guilt in starting the war, which is what ultimately led to the dropping of the bomb. Only by accepting his guilt (over creating the Oxygen Destroyer), can he find peace. At the end of the film, Dr. Yamane warns of the dangers of continuing nuclear tests awakening more monsters, meaning that unless the world abandoned nuclear weapons, the world would destroy itself.

The movie's popularity spawned an entire series, as well as imitators. Toho's output in the 1950s consisted of a Godzilla sequel, *Godzilla Raids Again* (*Gojira no gyakushū*, 1955), and *Rodan* (*Sora no daikaijū Radon*, 1956), and *Mothra* (*Mosura*, 1961), also focusing on nuclear issues. Rodan was hatched by hydrogen bomb tests and destroyed the city of Fukuoka. Mothra's Infant Island was ravaged by nuclear bomb tests and she in turn ravaged parts of Japan and Rolisica (a stand-in for the U.S. and Russia). Throughout the fifties, Toho produced a number of atomic inspired thrillers, such as *The H-Man* (*Bijo to ekitainingen*, 1958) and *Varan the Unbelievable* (*Daikaijū Varan*, 1958). Some of these, like Rodan and Mothra, made appearances in later Godzilla films. Other studios copied Toho's success as Daiei Studios did with Gamera.

The Sequels

The 1960s saw continuous prosperity for Japan. The economic recovery that began in the 1950s was now in full swing. Average incomes were doubling every seven years and consumerism was on the rise.[12] The country remained politically stable through the late 1970s. Public opinion toward the United States tended to go up and down. There was tension in 1960 and demonstrations in the streets over the revision of the security treaty between the U.S. and Japan which determined their political and military relationship. This mood was fueled by Japanese economic strength and a growing sense of confidence in the nation.[13] After the treaty's renewal, public sentiment calmed once again, only becoming negative with the United States' involvement in Vietnam. This culminated in student protests in 1968. The mood reverted once again in 1969 with the announcement that Okinawa would be returned to Japan.

Children in the 1960s grew up in a time of increasing prosperity, consumerism and national confidence. In a way, these were new threats, as commercialism and capitalism threatened the traditional way of life. In such an environment, there was little need to dwell on the horrors of the past, and less sense of responsibility for past conflict. If you were 10 in 1961, you were not even alive during the war and could share no collective responsibility for that conflict or its aftermath. A change in attitude occurred.

This change in attitude is reflected in the Godzilla films. In *King Kong vs. Godzilla* (*Kingu Kongu tai Gojira*, 1962), Godzilla remains the villain, but Japan's growing confidence is seen in the solution to the story. Definitely ruling out a nuclear strike, General Shinzo opts instead to accept a plan to manipulate Kong into battling the mutated dinosaur. This pattern is repeated in *Mothra vs. Godzilla* (*Mosura tai Gojira*, 1964), in which a Japanese reporter, Sakai, a photographer, Junko, and a scientist, Professor Miura, travel to Infant Island to convince Mothra to battle Godzilla. The natives of the island are dead set against helping Japan against the monster. Their island was once green and flourishing; now most of it is dead thanks to nuclear testing in the outside world. Both Sakai and Miura, acknowledge that, as outsiders, they have no right to ask for help, accepting a communal guilt for the nuclear testing. Junko, the photographer, is not as accepting. She points out if Mothra does not help, many innocent people will die. In this speech, she is speaking female-to-female to Mothra who is the mother-figure on the island, attempting to invoke a motherly-like compassion from Mothra (who is also clearly designed to be a mother-deity). Junko is also clearly absolving Japan of the guilt of nuclear testing. Japan, like Infant Island, is caught between outside powers and was also the victim of a nuclear attack. This displacement of responsibility is a demonstration of Japan's self-image and confidence. It is also an interesting avoidance of the same message from the original film where Serizawa takes responsibility for the war. Japan might be more confident, but it was not willing to take responsibility for its past actions in the war. Taking responsibility or feeling guilt over the war is a rare trait overall in the Godzilla films and happens only a few times, the major two instances being the original *Godzilla* and 2001's *Godzilla, Mothra, and King Ghidorah: Giant Monsters All-Out Attack (Gojira, Mosura, Kingu Ghidorah: Daikaijū Sōkōgeki)*.

These films are also a comment on the now firmly entrenched capitalist, consumerist society the country had become.[14] They also can be seen as a comment on Western capitalism since it could be argued the West brought those attitudes to Japan. Kong is brought to Japan to be part of an advertising campaign. Only greed could inspire such a misguided plan. *Mothra vs. Godzilla* goes even further exploring the darker side of capitalism and pure greed. A businessman and his backer take control of Mothra's egg which has washed ashore. They plan to use it as an attraction in a theme park where everyone, even scientists wanting to study the egg, would have to pay to view it. In capitalism, everything is a commodity and everything has a price, even Mothra's egg.[15] They even try to trap and then buy the Tiny Fairies of Infant Island. The dangers of greed reach their height when the men squabble over money as Godzilla is seen approaching. They value money more than life as one man kills the other and grabs as much cash as possible before dying in Godzilla's rampage. Their destruction by Godzilla could have been avoided, but for their greed. Godzilla, for his part, represents the dark side of western capitalism (which will crush you if you are not careful) as he rises up from out of the ground in the heart of an industrial district. He is defeated by Mothra, a figure from the South Seas (a part of Japan's romantic pre-capitalist past).

In both the original *Godzilla* and *Mothra*, both beasts came from the south, essentially coming from the same direction as American bombers.[16] With the new generation of audiences, there was less connection with the war. Although the south was far from forgotten, its relevance changed as the south came to symbolize, for consumerist Japan, a nostalgic and counter-commercial past.[17] Also, monsters started coming from different directions. From this point on, more and more monsters would start arriving from outer space. The arrival of monsters such as Ghidrah, Gigan and Mechagodzilla, along with American actors such as Nick Adams, showed that Japan saw itself as an important player on the global stage. Japan had come out of its global isolation.

While welcoming the world for the Tokyo Olympics, this decade also saw Japanese tourists venture out to travel the world. The shadows of war, the bomb, and the occupation barely reached this generation. Godzilla himself changes dramatically during this decade, responding to the need to relate to the new emerging audience. In 1964's *Mothra vs. Godzilla*, Godzilla is clearly the destructive enemy. That same year in *Ghidrah, The Three-Headed Monster (San daikaiju chikyu saidai no kessen)*, Mothra convinces Godzilla and Rodan to join forces against Ghidrah. In this film, as in *Invasion of Astro-Monster (Kaijū daisensō, 1965)*, Godzilla becomes the reluctant hero. Now secure in their place in the world, the Japanese could focus on domestic issues, and the movies reflected this shift in values and attitudes. Godzilla transformed into a benevolent guardian spirit and the friend to all children. Societal problems, as in *All Monsters Attack (Oru kaijū daishingek, 1969)*, and environmental issues, as in *Godzilla vs. Hedorah (Gojira tai hedorah, 1971)*, became the foes with Godzilla assuming the role of "protector."

The Godzilla films of this time are generally seen as the culmination of the trend toward the kiddification of the franchise. It would be foolish to argue that these later films have the same sort of complexity as the earlier ones. Goro from *Godzilla vs. Megalon* (*Gojira tai Megaro*, 1973) comes across as flat and two-dimensional compared to Serizawa from *Gojira*. A more important point to consider is, whether they needed to be as complex. As a franchise targeting a younger audience, a certain level of complexity might be removed, or their textuality might be replaced with something more visual. This does not mean that the films do not retain a certain amount of nuanced storytelling.

All Monsters Attack is a good example of this. On the surface, the story seems simple. A latchkey kid, Ichirō, is bullied by other boys. He takes refuge in fantasy, specifically on Monster Island where he forms a friendship with Godzilla's son, Minilla, who is also being bullied. As Minilla eventually stands up to his bully (among shots of Godzilla battling other monsters), Ichirō learns to stand up to the bank robbers who have kidnapped him and then to his own bullying peers. At the end of the film, Ichirō now bullies others, particularly targeting a sign painter. What seems like a simple story takes a complex turn at the end. Instead of being virtuous, Ichirō becomes villainous himself. He has learned to survive the urban jungle. Honda's film shows the dark side of the economic miracle.

While Ichirō's parents might not be around much, he does have two parents. As the country needed to rebuild and recover after the war, so too did the family structure. By the mid-sixties, the family unit had restabilized.[18] With the appearance of Minilla, Godzilla's "son" or protégé, the movies started to reflect this as well. The monsters now all live on an island together where they form a sort of community. Frequently, they battle and do not always get along, as being a family is not easy. Godzilla teaches Minilla to stand on his own. Godzilla is a father figure and protector to Japan, but at the same time he is kept outside of Japan itself, at a safe distance. Godzilla, like America, remains an outsider. The United States was still a protector of Japan, but the two nations would not always see eye to eye.

This protector theme carries on in *Godzilla vs. Megalon*. In this film, the undersea people of Seatopia unleash their god, Megalon, on the surface world in anger over continued nuclear testing. To aid and direct Megalon, Seatopian agents steal a robot named Jet Jaguar from an inventor. Once Jet Jaguar is freed from the Seatopians' influence, he programs himself to fly to Monster Island where he enlists the aid of Godzilla in defending Japan against Megalon (who is soon aided by the monster Gigan). Tellingly, Jet Jaguar returns to Japan first to fight the monsters until Godzilla arrives. Together they fight off the attackers threatening Japan.

Jet Jaguar, while clearly an Ultraman clone, was just as clearly meant to represent Japan and its Self-Defense Forces while Godzilla again represented U.S. military might. The Tokyo *Yomiuri Shimbun* recently summed up the difference between Japanese and American forces. The SDF is the "shield, engaging only in defense" while the U.S. is the "pike, entirely responsible for retaliatory attacks."[19] In *Godzilla vs. Megalon*, it is Jet Jaguar who fights the two monsters, keeping them at bay, until Godzilla arrives and the two work together in a spirit of cooperation and harmony to counter-attack.

This kind of fighting was part of a larger context. Wrestling was a popular sport in Japan.[20] Like a wrestling bout, spectators know that it is fake and the audience must participate in pretending it is real. This film required the audience to actively accept what is going on, to actively suspend their disbelief. The antics of Jet Jaguar and Godzilla serve to illustrate a message of friendship between Japan and the United States, but a friendship that is carefully constructed. Godzilla is summoned, but once he is done he must leave. This is an unspoken contract that is implied in the film and is an integral aspect to Godzilla's role as defender.

Godzilla was not so much the "friend to all children" as he was a message to all children, and, for that matter, all moviegoers. Yes, Godzilla (the U.S.) is your friend, and a very powerful friend at that. He is also a dangerous friend (a big brother) you should not trust completely.[21] Yes, he will protect you, but he is dangerous; he destroys things. The message is continued in *Godzilla vs. Mechagodzilla* (*Gojira tai Mekagojira*, 1974). When "Godzilla" first appears, he is destructive and fights his friend Anguirus. Later, it is revealed that this is Mechagodzilla made up to look like the real Godzilla, but it illustrated an important point: be wary of this dangerous friend. This theme was continued in the next film, *Terror of Mechagodzilla* (*Mechagojira no gyakushū*, 1975). This was the last film in the original run. Poor box office returns over the past several films did what nothing else could: defeat the unstoppable beast.

The Heisei Period

The iconic monster was awakened by rising international tensions in the mid–1980s. The arms race had reached a point where nuclear missiles could wipe out all human life on Earth. Once again, the nuclear threat became a serious concern in the popular consciousness of a new generation, making the atomic monster relevant once more. Godzilla returned in 1984's *Gojira*, which came out the following year in the United States as *Godzilla 1985*.

In *Godzilla 1985*, Japan is caught both politically and geographically between two dominant superpowers, the United States and the Soviet Union (a computer map in the film illustrated Japan's location between the two superpowers, demonstrating that they were literally caught in the middle of the Cold War yet again). When Godzilla reappears and destroys a Soviet submarine, nearly triggering a nuclear war, Japan is put under pressure by the United States and the Soviet Union to allow a nuclear strike against the monster. Despite the bullying attitudes of both ambassadors, the Japanese prime minster refuses, re-affirming Japan's anti-nuclear weapons policy. The Soviets accidentally fire a nuke, showing the lax attitudes toward nuclear weapons by the superpowers. The nuclear missile is aimed at Tokyo and once again the nation of Japan is under the threat of an atomic attack on their soil. While Japan was able to stand strong and risk isolation over not allowing the superpowers to strike, when this accident occurs, they must rely on the United States to save them. The tension is eased when Godzilla is lured into an active volcano. The specter of nuclear annihilation is encapsulated in Godzilla.[22]

In the film, director Kōji Hashimoto makes a sustained effort to make the monster frightening once again. To underline this, and to demonstrate that Godzilla once again represented the atomic threat, Godzilla's rampage through Tokyo resembled the rampage from the 1954 film: he lumbers into buildings, he picks up a train, even certain head shots of the monster seem eerily familiar. This is deliberate and serves two purposes: one, to clearly differentiate Godzilla from his 1970s incarnation which was now considered too light, too goofy and designed to appeal mainly to children, and two, to clearly show that this Godzilla is the same as the first one, in that he is the embodiment of nuclear destruction.[23]

For example, the military response to Godzilla was to fire cadmium shells into his mouth. Cadmium, a substance used to contain radiation in nuclear power plants, represents the folly of trying to control atomic energy (either as a weapon or as a power source). It should be noted that Godzilla's first acts were to attack objects that were nuclear: a Soviet submarine and a nuclear power plant in Japan. This was to illustrate the unstable nature of such devices and to illustrate the dangers of "clean" energy.[24] When the American and Soviet nuclear missiles collide above Tokyo, the resulting electromagnetic radiation revives Godzilla who then continues his destruction and his battle with the Japanese secret weapon, the Super X. The monster, as strong as ever, remains a specter of the nuclear threat, a much more imminent threat than it was in the 1950s.

In the 1954 *Gojira*, the monster comes across as a somewhat sympathetic creature, one that is also a victim of the bomb. Hashimoto plays this theme even stronger in *Godzilla 1985*. On the verge of his destruction, Godzilla stands quietly, seeming at peace, even helpless, before his end. Indeed, it is interesting to note that the two characters (the prime minister and Professor Hayashida) who are identified as victims of the past (rampage and bombing) show the most remorse at the "demise" of the monster. Professor Hayashida refers to the monster as "a warning" and does not hate Godzilla, despite having lost his parents in the monster's rampage thirty years before.

This period in the franchise's history, which lasted until 1995's *Godzilla vs. Destoroyah* (*Gojira tai Desutoroia*), is marked by a consistent effort to make Godzilla a deadly monster once again. This should not be surprising considering that tensions between Japan and the U.S. were on the rise in the late eighties as the fiftieth anniversary of the bombing of Pearl Harbor approached, and through the early nineties as Japanese economic strength grew (although its economic bubble burst in 1992, the Japanese remained convinced their basic economic strategies were sound). There was increasing anti–American sentiment in Japan during this period which was reflected in the Godzilla movies of this time. This was also tied into two other related factors: a growing interest in *Hibakusha* as the fiftieth anniversary of the end of the war was approaching, and a growing critical reaction to the use of nuclear power in Japan (note that in several of the films from this period, Godzilla seems drawn to nuclear power plants, emphasizing the vulnerability of these controversial sources of energy).

Anti-American sentiment is more prominent in *Godzilla vs. Biolante* (*Gojira tai Beorante*, 1989). In this film, international tensions grow as Japanese, Middle Eastern, and American companies all vie for possession of "Godzilla cells" left behind from the monster's rampage in *Godzilla 1985*. All three groups, representing the greed of capitalism, hope to use the cells to create an ultimate weapon making this a comment on the international arms race of the 1980s. In the battle over possession of these cells, American-style soldiers shoot their competitors and a Middle Eastern lab is destroyed, ostensibly by American rivals. Godzilla being released from a volcano in Japan shows that, as in *Mothra Versus Godzilla*, Japan is playing with fire. Their own attempt to monopolize the Godzilla cells shows that they face destruction if things get out of control. The absurdity of the arms race is demonstrated at the end of the film, when after all the destruction, a Middle Eastern agent continues to make things difficult.[25]

This film also makes a critique about looking towards the past. The hotel in *Godzilla vs. Biolante* has a memorial to a past Godzilla attack, but no one is looking at it. They are all going on about their busy lives with no regard to the past. It is best to ignore it and move on. In a rather surreal scene, diners at a hotel lounge are viewed through a hole in the ceiling in the shape of Godzilla's footprint, literally living in the shadow of Godzilla (the bomb). Godzilla's attack had been incorporated into daily life so much that no one seems to notice. This is a comment on how society was ignoring the pain and destruction in their own past, mirroring the "It can't be helped attitude" from the occupation period. Godzilla might crush their buildings, but not their resolve or spirit.

As the 1990s continued, Japan began to feel the effects of a poor economy. By 1993, the bursting of the economic bubble had a negative effect as industrial output slowed and unemployment rose. The economic promise of the 1960s and 1970s came to an end. The younger generations of workers were starting to choose family life over work life, a definite split with the past.[26] In the nineties, problems facing Japan were no longer the Cold War, but corruption in government, the economy, consumerism and the environment. Like the grandchildren in Kurosawa's *Rhapsody in August*, the younger generation was more family oriented and more open to explore their past. As such, Godzilla remains the threatening monster through this cycle of films, although touched with a family aspect. The arrival of Little Godzilla ("Baby") in *Godzilla vs. Mechagodzilla II* (*Gojira tai Mekagojira*, 1993) became a draw for the older monster. Godzilla came to find "Baby" and the two leave together at the end of the film, joined together by some innate bond of family. The older monster protects him against Space Godzilla in *Godzilla vs. Space Godzilla* (*Gojira tai Sueesu Gojira*, 1994). The death of Little Godzilla in *Godzilla vs. Destoroyah* is a poignant moment with the realization that Godzilla is alone, having lost his only family.

Godzilla remains the symbol of the atomic bomb in the nineties, but with a new nuance. By the eighties and nineties, the nuclear military power of America reached the point where its missiles easily could wipe out all human life on Earth. Likewise, Godzilla gets larger and his potential threat gets larger as well. In *Godzilla vs. Destoroyah*, his imminent meltdown is defined as something that could wipe out all life on Earth. Godzilla, like the nuclear threat, has gotten larger.

The New Millennium Series

The new millennium series, which began with *Godzilla 2000* (*Gojira ni-sen mireniamu*, 1999), was a reaction to the Tri-Star American production of *Godzilla* in 1998. This series of films lacked any coherent and consistent direction for two reasons: one, the movies' main purpose was to show that Toho did its own monster "better" and two, a lack of cultural "angst" over what Godzilla traditionally represented. Tensions with the United States had receded. By this time many survivors of the bomb had passed away, taking with them any direct link between the younger generation and the experience of their forebears. In other words, Godzilla as metaphor now lacked any heightened relevance.

This can be seen in *Godzilla 2000*. In this case, Godzilla represents Japan. He is battling the American version of himself which represents the pop culture Godzilla who was adopted by the rest of the world. The real Godzilla is the Japanese version. He is the only successful, true version because only Japan has lived through the horrors of the atomic bomb. The past and the bomb (both symbolized by Godzilla) were being forgotten by the characters in the film. The battle between the two Godzillas symbolizes the internal struggle in Japan over the bomb and their history. In this film, it is a grass roots group, rather than scientists, who want to preserve, study and learn from Godzilla. They symbolize the peace promoting and survivor groups of the period who want that part of their history kept alive. The government wants to wipe out Godzilla, thus erasing the past. It is the government representative who is destroyed by his ignorance and arrogance. He is overwhelmed when he comes face to face with Godzilla (the truth about the past) before he is destroyed by it. They must come to terms with the past because that past makes them who they are.

The rise of nationalism in Japan changed attitudes and teaching of the past. The government encouraged the teaching of patriotic indoctrination and the visiting of older shrines rather than the museums and memorials of Hiroshima. They stressed nationalism over peace. The stories and lessons of history were being forgotten and ignored. Many *Hibakusha* did not tell their children about what they went through because they did not want them to know the horrors of the truth and for fear of prejudice against the children of survivors.[27] An example of not wanting to burden younger generations with the stories of the past can be seen in *Godzilla Final Wars*. When the young grandson asks his elderly grandfather about Godzilla, the grandfather will only say that long ago they did something to make the monster mad. He goes into no further detail and makes it sound as if it is so distant in the past that it has no relevance to the boy and could not be comprehended by him.

The movies of this period took a "Do not mess with history or it will come back and stomp on you" type of attitude. This is clearly seen in *Godzilla Against Mechagodzilla* (*Gojira tai Mekagojira*, 2002), *Godzilla: Tokyo S.O.S* (*Gojira x Mosura x Mekagojira: Tokyo S.O.S.*, 2003) and *Godzilla Final Wars*. In *Godzilla Against Mechagodzilla* and *Godzilla: Tokyo S.O.S.*, it is messing with Godzilla's remains that creates problems. In these two films, politicians and scientists use the bones of the original Godzilla, who had been killed by the Oxygen Destroyer in 1954, to create their salvation, a robotic version of Godzilla.[28] This mechanical nightmare was then used against the new Godzilla. In that respect, *Godzilla Against Mechagodzilla* can be seen as a warning about nuclear energy and relying on it too much. They may think it is safe, useful and under their control, but it is still part of a larger more menacing atomic world which created the bomb and things could go horribly wrong. The inherent instinct in Godzilla's bones (the dangers of the atom bomb) takes over and their robot becomes a source of destruction. If they had let the dead rest in peace, problems could have been averted. The message is heightened at the end of *Godzilla: Tokyo S.O.S.*, where Mechagodzilla lifts its wounded "brother" and flies him out over the ocean for their shared final resting place. Yet *Godzilla: Tokyo S.O.S.*'s larger meaning was also about the past as a whole. The mechanic, Yoshito, who is trapped on board Mechagodzilla, is saved when the huge machine turns over so he can fall out to be caught by another pilot. Before he lets go, Mechagodzilla says, "Sayonara, Yoshito." It was time to let go of the past.

In *Godzilla Final Wars*, the oldest generation (Godzilla and the grandfather representing the past) and the youngest generation (Minilla and the grandson representing the future) unite to bring an end to the struggle. Enough is enough. Both sides, Japan and the United States, must put the past (Hiroshima and Pearl Harbor) behind them. It is time to move on. The two former foes will always be linked, but each must take its own path. It is time for Japan to stand alone without Uncle Sam looking over its shoulder. They must fight their own battles. Symbolizing the dawn of a new era, Godzilla and Minilla walk off into the rising sun. This imagery cements the link between the monster and the nation.

Godzilla remained a useful and malleable metaphor for the atomic bombing of Japan. At first in the 1950s, he was clearly a symbol of the bomb's devastating and long-lasting destruction as well as a symbol of the nation which had dropped those bombs. As Japan's economic might grew in the 1960s, a more confident nation decided to focus more on its future. Godzilla went from villain to champion in a relatively short period of time. As such, what he came to symbolize was varied and complex, but so too was the United States. By the 1970s, both Godzilla and the United States were powerful yet potentially dangerous protectors of Japan. When the films began again in the 1980s and 1990s, the prevailing international tensions, and the tremendous military power of the United States led to a more dangerous and darker Godzilla; the films and the monsters became a useful critique of Japan's powerful ally. After 2000, the films seemed to lose direction, many of the survivors had passed on, and what Godzilla symbolized almost became a non-issue.

Notes

1. J. Goodwin, "Akira Kurosawa and the Atomic Age," in *Hibakusha Cinema: Hiroshima, Nagasaki and the Nuclear Image in Japanese Film*, ed. Mick Broderick (London: Kegan Paul International, 1996), p. 196.

2. D. Richie, "'Mono no aware': Hiroshima in Film," in *Hibakusha Cinema: Hiroshima, Nagasaki and the Nuclear Image in Japanese Film*, ed. Mick Broderick (London: Kegan Paul International, 1996), p. 24.

3. R. Dallek, *The American Style of Foreign Policy: Cultural Politics and Foreign Affairs* (New York: Alfred A. Knopf, 1983), p. 148.

4. K. Hirano, "Depiction of the Atomic Bombings in Japanese Cinema During the U.S. Occupation Period," in *Hibakusha Cinema: Hiroshima, Nagasaki and the Nuclear Image in Japanese Film*, ed. Mick Broderick (London: Kegan Paul International, 1996), p. 103.

5. *Ibid.*, p. 116.

6. D. Richie, "'Mono no aware': Hiroshima in Film," in *Hibakusha Cinema: Hiroshima, Nagasaki and the Nuclear Image in Japanese Film*, ed. Mick Broderick (London: Kegan Paul International, 1996), p. 24.

7. V. Schwartzman, "How Gojira became Godzilla," *Canadian Dimension* 41.5 (Sept./Oct. 2007), p. 45.

8. S. Ryfle, "Godzilla's Footprint," *Virginia Quarterly Review* 81.1 (Winter 2005), p. 49.

9. I. Vartanian, *Killer Kaiju Monsters: Strange Beasts of Japanese Film* (New York: Cottins Design, 2009), p. 20.

10. W. Tsutsui, *Godzilla on my Mind: Fifty Years of the King of Monsters* (New York: Palgrave Macmillan, 2004), p. 20.

11. C. Noriega, "Godzilla and the Japanese Nightmare: When Them! Is U.S.," in *Hibakusha Cinema: Hiroshima, Nagasaki and the Nuclear Image in Japanese Film*, ed. Mick Broderick (London: Kegan Paul International, 1996), p. 59.

12. E. Reischauer and M. Jansen, *The Japanese Today: Change and Continuity* (Cambridge: Belknap Press of Harvard University Press, 1995), p. 115.

13. *Ibid.*, p. 113.

14. Y. Igarashi, "Mothra's Gigantic Egg: Consuming the South Pacific in 1960s Japan," in *In Godzilla's Footsteps: Japanese Pop Culture Icons on the Global Stage*, eds. William M. Tsutsui and Michiko Ito (New York: Palgrave Macmillan, 2006), p. 94.

15. *Ibid.*

16. Y. Inuhiko, "The Menace from the South Seas: Honda Ishiro's Godzilla (1954)," in *Japanese Cinema: Texts and Contexts*, eds. Alastair Phillips and Julian Stringer (New York: Routledge, 2007), p. 105.

17. Y. Igarashi, "Mothra's Gigantic Egg: Consuming the South Pacific in 1960s Japan," in *In Godzilla's Footsteps: Japanese Pop Culture Icons on the Global Stage*, eds. William M. Tsutsui and Michiko Ito (New York: Palgrave Macmillan, 2006), p. 84.

18. C. Noriega, "Godzilla and the Japanese Nightmare: When Them! Is U.S.," in *Hibakusha Cinema: Hiroshima, Nagasaki and the Nuclear Image in Japanese Film*, ed. Mick Broderick (London: Kegan Paul International, 1996), p. 65.

19. The Yomiuri Shimbun, "The time has come to consider enabling SDF to attack enemy Bases," http://the-japan-news.com/news/article/0000238197.

20. A. Gerow, "Wrestling with Godzilla: Intertextuality, Childish Spectatorship, and the National Body," in *In Godzilla's Footsteps: Japanese Pop Culture Icons on the Global Stage*, eds. William M. Tsutsui and Michiko Ito (New York: Palgrave Macmillan, 2006), p. 68.

21. E. Reischauer, *Japan: The Story of a Nation* (New York: McGraw-Hill, 1990), p. 268.

22. C. Noriega, "Godzilla and the Japanese Nightmare: When Them! Is U.S.," in *Hibakusha Cinema: Hiroshima, Nagasaki and the Nuclear Image in Japanese Film*, ed. Mick Broderick (London: Kegan Paul International, 1996), p. 68.

23. D. Kalat, *A Critical History and Filmography of Toho's Godzilla Series* (Jefferson, North Carolina and London: McFarland & Company, Inc.), p. 157.

24. *Ibid.*, p. 158.

25. *Ibid.*, p. 171.

26. G. Church and A. Blackman, "Goodbye to the Godzilla Myth," *Time* 141.16 (1993), pp. 42–45.

27. L. Cameron and M. Miyoshi, "Hiroshima, Nagasaki, and the World Sixty Years Later," *Virginia Quarterly Review* 81.4 (Fall 2005), pp. 32–33.

28. This message of letting the dead rest in peace echoes some of the interpretations of the original 1954 *Gojira*, that the monster represented the fallen warriors of the Second World War. See J. Bailey: "Your City Could be Next: Now, Godzilla Takes on the World," *Asiaweek* 20.51 (December 1994), p. 40.

Bibliography

Bailey, Jim. "Your City Could Be Next: Now, Godzilla Takes on the World." *Asiaweek* 20 (December 1994): 38–43.

Cameron, Lindsley, and Masao Miyoshi. "Hiroshima, Nagasaki, and the World Sixty Years Later." *Virginia Quarterly Review* 81 (Fall 2005): 27–47.

Church, George J., and Ann Blackman. "Goodbye to the Godzilla Myth." *Time* 141 (April 19, 1993): 42–45.

Dallek, Robert. *The American Style of Foreign Policy: Cultural Politics and Foreign Affairs*. New York: Alfred A. Knopf, 1983.

Gerow, Aaron. "Wrestling with Godzilla: Intertextuality, Childish Spectatorship, and the National Body," in *In Godzilla's Footsteps: Japanese Pop Culture Icons on the Global Stage*, eds. William M. Tsutsui and Michiko Ito. New York: Palgrave Macmillan, 2006.

Goodwin, James. "Akira Kurosawa and the Atomic Age," in *Hibakusha Cinema: Hiroshima, Nagasaki and the Nuclear Image in Japanese Film*, ed. Mick Broderick. London: Kegan Paul International, 1996.

Hirano, Kyoko. "Depiction of the Atomic Bombings in Japanese Cinema During the U.S. Occupation Period," in *Hibakusha Cinema: Hiroshima, Nagasaki and the Nuclear Image in Japanese Film*, ed. Mick Broderick. London: Kegan Paul International, 1996.

Igarashi, Yoshikuni. "Mothra's Gigantic Egg: Consuming the South Pacific in 1960s Japan," in *In Godzilla's Footsteps: Japanese Pop Culture Icons on the Global Stage*, eds. William M. Tsutsui and Michiko Ito. New York: Palgrave Macmillan, 2006.

Inuhiko, Yomota. "The Menace from the South Seas: Honda Ishiro's *Godzilla* (1954)," in *Japanese Cinema: Texts and Contexts*, eds. Alastair Phillips and Julian Stringer. New York: Routledge, 2007.

Kalat, David. *A Critical History and Filmography of Toho's Godzilla Series*, 2d ed. Jefferson, NC: McFarland, 2010.

Noriega, Chon A. "Godzilla and the Japanese Nightmare: When *Them!* Is U.S.," in *Hibakusha Cinema: Hiroshima, Nagasaki and the Nuclear Image in Japanese Film*, ed. Mick Broderick. London: Kegan Paul International, 1996.

Reischauer, Edwin O. *Japan: The Story of a Nation*, 4th ed. New York: McGraw-Hill, 1990.

_____, and Marius B. Jansen. *The Japanese Today: Change and Continuity*. Cambridge: Belknap Press of Harvard University Press, 1995.

Richards, Andy. *Asian Horror*. Harpenden: Kamera Books, 2010.

Richie, Donald. "'Mono no aware': Hiroshima in Film," in *Hibakusha Cinema: Hiroshima, Nagasaki and the Nuclear Image in Japanese Film*, ed. Mick Broderick. London: Kegan Paul International, 1996.

Ryfle, Steve. "Godzilla's Footprint." *Virginia Quarterly Review* 81 (Winter 2005): 44–63.

Schwartzman, Victor. "How Gojira became Godzilla." *Canadian Dimension* 41 (September-October 2007): 44–45.

Shapiro, Jerome F. "When a God Awakens." *World & I* 13 (May 1998): 182–192.

Tsutsui, William. *Godzilla on My Mind: Fifty Years of the King of Monsters*. New York: Palgrave Macmillan, 2004.

Vartanian, Ivan. *Killer Kaiju Monsters: Strange Beasts of Japanese Film*. New York: Cottins Design, 2009.

Vogel, Ezra F. "Japanese-American Relations After the Cold War." *Daedalus* 121 (Fall 1992): 35–60.

The Yomiuri Shimbun. "The time has come to consider enabling SDF to attack enemy Bases." *The Yomiuri Shimbun*, May 19, 2013.

Suppression and Censorship: Japanese Cinema During the Occupation

MATTHEW EDWARDS

That in the immediate aftermath of Japan's defeat during the Second World War and the use of atomic bombs on their cities the Japanese did not immediately view Hiroshima and Nagasaki as an atrocity comes as little surprise for those who have lived among its people. The late Japanese scholar Donald Ritchie accurately acknowledges this, and perfectly captures Japan's pragmatism and general view of the atomic bombings, in his highly respected essay "*Mono no aware: Hiroshima in Film*":

> The West was quick to identify the bomb-dropping as an atrocity. That the Japanese did not was due in part to the fact that it occurred in wartime, when anything might be expected; in part because, though the destruction had been more spectacular, Hiroshima and Nagasaki were just two of the many totally destroyed Japanese cities; and also, in part, because the Japanese mind does not, unless so directed, tend to think in such terms.
>
> Had the war continued, the Japanese themselves would have been told of the atrocity of the act and this would have made excellent propaganda, something which the bomb-droppers themselves feared. But the war ended and the bomb became an "act of God," one among many.[1]

Japan's failure to see this as an atrocity or a war crime can be attributed to the blanket censorship imposed by the occupying forces on the Arts and media, the result of which meant that any discussion of the bombings were strictly forbidden for fear, as Ritchie points out, that it would serve as useful propaganda in stoking anger towards their occupiers.[2] In truth, in the immediate aftermath of the war the Japanese were less concerned with the dead but the daily reality of survival and rebuilding their decimated landscapes and infrastructures. Aside from pro-nationalistic groups rallying against the occupation, the average Japanese person had little desire to contemplate the issue. Their rationale was that they had to serve their basic primal needs and not to drag up the atrocities of the not-so-distant past. All they wanted to extract was a lasting peace free from the horrors that their homeland had been subjected to.

The American occupying forces were keen to keep it this way and through strict guidelines and supervision the authorities sought to suppress all forms of artistic expression by means of ensuring that Japan did not fall back into a militaristic and fascist state, but one that could be steered towards democracy and a key Pan-Pacific ally for the U.S. and the British. Journalists, writers and filmmakers were under scrutiny, for any depiction of the occupying forces in a negative light and all references to the war or "bad themes" concerning anti-social behavior, suicide or violence were strictly prohibited. Such censorship and suppression was sold to the Japanese as a means of re-educating the masses with worthy principles that could be instilled into them as a means of ridding them of the "blight" that had consumed them during the war years, which had seen the Japanese army commit awful atrocities throughout Asia. In truth, the U.S. authorities wanted to stamp down on dissenting voices within the arts so they wouldn't inflame the masses to rise up against their occupiers. Therefore, censorship of the arts and Japanese ideology saw many artists' freedom of expression suppressed and violated by the political will of the occupiers as a means to quieten ultra-nationalistic voices and to facilitate a safe passage for Japan into the realms of democracy. Kirsten Cather notes in her book on censorship in post-war Japan "that censorship is often used to write political, rather than artistic, history."[3] In this instance, the use of censorship as a political tool was designed to promote the positive values that come with a peaceful democratic society, which America and its allies were laying the foundations down for in Japan. The enforced suppression was also designed to quash negative views that might spread easily through the Arts and undo this work and see Japan slip back into its aggressive wartime ideologies.

Adopting such an approach provoked differing opinions in Japan. Japanese author Jun Etō[4] argues that the Occupation's severe censorship had a fundamental impact on Japan, to which its legacy is still being felt today. He writes: "[Its] censorship and propaganda plan became entrenched in our media and education systems so that even when the CCD (Civil Censorship Detachment) was disbanded and the Occupation ended, the internal destruction of the identity of Japanese people and trust in our history continues, making us permanently exposed to threats of foreign censorship."[5]

In a way, Etō's fears were justified. Ironically, like the U.S. with its suppression and censorship of Hiroshima and Nagasaki, the Japanese learned that it too could hide elements of its shameful past through suppression of information on its own subjects. This has resulted in post-war Japan censoring and suppressing Japanese culpability in wartime atrocities from all state approved education textbooks. Professors such as the nationalistic Nobukatsu Fujioka have been particularly guilty of censoring all anti–Japanese or anti–Japanese ideology from textbooks. This has created a vacuum where large swaths of the Japanese public is ignorant or has little understanding of its colonial past and its use of comfort women in Asia, of massacres in Nanjing and its use of experiments on victims with biological and chemical weapons is partly down to the Japanese trying to hide this brutal phase in their history. Worryingly, such an approach to history has seen some younger generations of Japanese people identifying themselves as the victim and Hiroshima and Nagasaki as an unprovoked atrocity. Such a viewpoint was one I encountered time and time again by students and friends while living in Japan. Japan's failure to own up to and present its own history accurately has created this falsehood. Many Japanese are simply unaware that they committed crimes and atrocities that some perceive to be on par with that of the Nazis. Even more distressing is Japan's denial of its crimes; Japan continually adopts an aggressive defiance to accusations it deems are lies and fabrications and are part of a grand scheme or conspiracy by foreign countries to destroy Japan. As such, Japan's wartime past is not included in textbooks for fear of wrongly portraying themselves in a light that would be deemed barbaric (there is no mention of the sex-slaves, Unit 731 or the death marches and mistreatment of POWs). As a Western ally, and important friend to the U.S and Britain, Japan has to cease in its delusions of victimhood and look hard in the mirror at its own wrongdoings and make amendments and apologize for its previous actions, for otherwise, as novelist and prisoner of war Shōhei Ōoka aptly stated in 1948, "nothing is more idiotic than to deny today the truth of what one did yesterday."[6]

In contrast, other prominent editors saw that censorship was necessary in post-war Japan and that any notions of a legacy of damage are widely exaggerated. Kazuro Kawai, editor of the *Japan Times* in the years after the war supports this viewpoint when he wrote:

> Actually, [the censorship] left few serious ill effects. Practically, all Japanese recognized that censorship was unavoidable in any military occupation; and … the censorship probably was continued longer than was really necessary.… Before any serious harm could be done, as the Occupation neared its end the censorship was sharply curtailed and then abolished altogether.[7]

The occupying forces used censorship of the arts and newspapers as a way to control negative propaganda about the war and in particular the bombings of Hiroshima and Nagasaki. Resultantly, discourse on the matter in Japanese film was censored and forbidden in post-occupied Japan. Kyoko Hirano agrees when she writes: "Cinematic portrayal of the atomic bombings on Hiroshima on 6 August and Nagasaki on 9 August 1945, and their aftermath, was handled with utmost care by the American censors. The censors were afraid that such portrayal was potentially critical of the Allied forces and, thus, the occupational government."[8] This was a deep concern for Lt. Douglas MacArthur. Stabilizing the general public and maintaining overall tranquility was his prime objective in post-war Japan and he wanted to keep the Japanese view that what happened during the war was an "act of God." Placating the Japanese was crucial for the occupation forces and any inflammatory propaganda that could disturb the masses needed silencing. The occupying forces foresaw the problems the bombings of Hiroshima and Nagasaki could have on the Japanese, if the true horrors became public knowledge. Immediately, all discussion of the bombings of Hiroshima and Nagasaki became taboo, with the occupying forces enforcing the strict oppression of all reports and articles pertaining to the damage caused by the atomic blasts. Such a carpet ban included medical and scientific studies which had a detrimental effect on the treatment of *Hibakusha*. In the media, any mention of the atomic bombings in Japanese print was strictly forbidden. This prohibition was issued on September 19, 1945. A month later, a new directive was issued on October 15, 1945, that prohibited all photographic imagery and film of the destruction caused by the bombings both inside and outside of Japan. Photographers such as Australian Wilfred Burchett and the Japanese photographer Yoshito Matsushige from the *Chugoku Shimbun* had their cameras and photos confiscated by the U.S Army. Luckily, Matsushige had the foresight to keep a copy of the negatives and his imagery was published after the end of the Occupation. Even more troubling, the occupying forces put enormous pressure on the surviving *Hibakusha* to keep silent about their injuries and their experiences. They were discouraged from telling others about their personal stories, at once denying them an outlet and voice about their ordeal and the tragedy they had been subjected to. This suppression naturally fed from the *Hibakusha* to writers, journalists, poets and filmmakers who wanted to try and express the national trauma that had been inflicted on the Japanese. Yet they were met with fierce resistance and all work had to be approved before it could reach the public domain. Specifically to film, all mention of the atomic bombings was curtailed and severely dealt with by the censors to the point where all film scripts had to be approved by the occupying authorities before being green-lit for production. This proved to be a major headache for filmmakers, film studios and educational bodies who wanted to promote discourse on the atomic question.

Despite the severe censorship and suppression of the atomic question in Japan, Japanese filmmakers and bodies did attempt to resist the carpet ban on the Hiroshima question. One enterprising young filmmaker did set out to document the aftereffects of the bombing of Hiroshima and the impact it had on both the topography of the city and the natives of Nagasaki and Hiroshima. Sueo Itō assembled a crew from the Japanese Film Company (*Nippon Eigasha*).[9] On September 7, Itō sent his crew to Nagasaki to film the destruction at ground zero and to film the survivors at the hospital and the grim reality of the injuries they had suffered. On September 15, a news crew was dispatched to Hiroshima. When the footage returned, the producer, Akira Iwasaki, was so overcome with horror he described the imagery as so haunting that "every frame was burned into his brain."[10] Iwasaki was a known dissenter who had been arrested during the war for anti-militaristic views and imprisoned by the authorities. On October 24, 1945, while filming in Nagasaki, the film unit was stopped by the occupational forces. Iwasaki was subsequently arrested and his footage confiscated. The rest of the *Nippon Eigasha* footage was confiscated under the orders of Lt. Daniel McGovern and sent to the pentagon, where it remained until "a 16mm print made of the original film was returned to the Education Ministry in 1967."[11] Jasper Sharp writes that the footage filmed by Itō's team was "an exhaustive five-hour record"[12] entitled *The Effects of the Atomic Bomb on Hiroshima and* Nagasaki (*Hiroshima, Nagasaki saki ni okeru genshibakudan no kōka*). Sharp goes on to suggest that the film was "assembled under supervision of the General Headquarters Supreme Commander for the Allied Powers (GHQ SCAP),"[13] until its suppression by the U.S. Although Itō's and *Nippon Eigasha* feared their films would be lost forever their vital cinematic footage has since become a regular feature in documentaries relating to the bombings of Hiroshima and Nagasaki and one of the most important recordings of the devastation and impact of nuclear bombs on topography and mankind.

Further attempts by Japanese filmmakers to disseminate the atomic bomb and the consequences and dangers of nuclear warfare were quickly suppressed by the occupying forces. Shochiku Studios in 1948 submitted a treatment for a film entitled *Hiroshima*, written by Ernest Hoberect, but due to meddling and censorship by the Civil Information and Education Section (CIE) the project was abandoned. The film *No More Hiroshimas*, which was to be commissioned as an educational film by the Hiroshima Chamber of Commerce and Hiroshima Municipal Government, succumbed to the same fate.[14] On both occasions, the censors found the destruction of Hiroshima objectionable and used all its powers to stop the film being made. It highlighted the paranoia and fear the occupying government held with regard to publicizing to the Japanese the damage and misery the atomic bombing had caused, for fear it would sway public opinion against the U.S.

With suppression so tight by the occupying forces, it is curious that one scene escaped the scissors of the Civil Information and Education Section. The film in question is Hiroshi Shimizu's *Children of the Beehive* (*Hachi no su no kodomotachi*) which is partly filmed in the crumbled ruins of the city, albeit a graveyard, as a group of orphans scavenging in the city try to find a connectivity with a soldier (an orphan himself) and townspeople left rootless as a result of a devastating war. The images of Hiroshima speak for themselves in the film and it is shown without any dramatic dialogue or dramatic narrative purpose and Shimizu's use of real life war orphans in the role of the children. One could argue that Shimizu deliberately allowed his visuals to speak louder than mere words; that the visceral horror of the post-atomic landscape would haunt the viewer more profoundly. The film's production tells a more familiar story in that the film *was* subjected to interference and censorship from the CIE. The initial script treatment saw the film opening with the nuclear attack on

Hiroshi Shimizu's beautifully haunting *Children of the Beehive*. Shimizu's film featured a scene shot in the devastated ruins of Hiroshima (courtesy Beehive Films).

Hiroshima before focusing its tale on the orphan survivors of story. The CIE rejected this idea and called for any references of the bomb to be eliminated before they would sanction a working script. They also insisted that any dialogue relating to the orphans experience of Hiroshima be censored as this was deemed irrelevant and unnecessary to the script. Such revelations were discovered by film historian Joseph L. Anderson who when analyzing the original script discovered that the censors only conceded to allow Shimizu to film in the bomb-affected areas of Hiroshima on the pretext that they did not film beyond the cemetery.[15] Images of the bombed out city were a no-no for the censors and occupiers, yet Shimizu's still manages to capture a flavor of the decimated city even in the restricted confines he was allowed to film in. *Children of the Beehive* was produced by Shimizu's own independent company *Hachi no Su Eigaba* (Beehive Films)[16] and domestically fared well at the box office which prompted a sequel in 1951 entitled *Children of the Beehive: What Happened Next* (*Sono ato no hachi no su no kodomatachi*). In his *Historical Dictionary of Japanese Cinema*, Jasper Sharp states that the film was inspired and partly based on "Shimizu's own experiences having taken a group of parentless children into his own home after the war."[17]

The Bells of Nagasaki (*Nagasaki no kane*, 1950) was another Japanese film to deal indirectly with the bombings of Hiroshima and Nagasaki and directed by respected filmmaker Hideo Ōba and scripted by Kaneto Shindō, who would later direct *Children of Hiroshima*. The film was loosely based on the life of Dr. Nagai, a Japanese physician who tended to the atomic bomb survivors in Nagasaki and his story became an instant bestseller in Japan.[18] The film stars Masao Wakahara as Takashi Nagai and Yumeji Tsukioka as his wife Midori, who was killed during the bombing of Nagasaki.

Released a year after the publication of Dr. Nagai's book of the same title, the film was threatened with censorship by the occupying U.S. forces. Pre-production proved to be problematic for Ōba, who was forced to submit a number of treatments to the CIE. Rejecting two synopses, the third was finally green-lit, though at a cost. Many crucial scenes were exorcized from the plot which served to hamper the effectiveness of the film.[19] A precondition for getting the script accepted was that Shindō had to include a statement at the beginning of the film that made clear that the bombings had been a clear result of Japanese militarism and colonialism. This statement served to explicitly imply that Japanese aggression had forced the U.S. and its allies in dropping the atomic bombs. Further omissions instructed by the government board included Dr. Nagai's attempt to save his wife after the bombing and any scenes relating explicitly to her suffering and death. As such, although recognized as the first feature to deal partially with the atomic bombings, the film slides into the realms of the sentimental melodrama as a result of being bound by U.S. government interference and censorship.

Shindō's script, a dramatization of Nagai's career as a radiologist during the 15-year war, his subsequent conversion to Catholicism and finally the destruction of Nagasaki, is a tale of love, science and faith. The CIE had no objection with the story per se. Their objections were to the film's references to the nuclear attacks which they tried to argue served no constructive purpose to the film.[20] The CIE were clearly concerned that unless the film's nuclear message was suppressed, public opinion may be turned against the occupying U.S. forces and could give rise to dissent voices against the bombings, especially from the Japanese far right. Keeping any significant, or politicized, reference of the nuclear attacks out of the arts was imperative, not only for the U.S. but also for the Japanese government who sought bi-literal partnership as a means of prosperity and security, especially from Russian aggression.

Despite this censorship, Ōba, clearly under strict scrutiny from CIE, did succeed in slipping in images of the bombing of Nagasaki indirectly into the final film. In a key sequence in the film, Ōba films Midori praying at her shrine which is surrounded by artifacts of Christ. He intercuts this scene with a close up of a rosary dangling from Midori's hands before a messy zoom captures the date of August 9 on her calendar. Next Ōba cuts to a scene where Nagai's two small children are out picking fruit near a river stream. Evacuated from the city, they are suddenly drawn to a huge explosion behind them. Turning they see a huge pillar of smoke rising into the skies above the mountains. The billowing mushroom cloud covers the frame and is shot from three differing angles. The mood of the film suddenly darkens as Ōba follows this scene with Dr. Nagai frantically searching for Midori through the scorched remains of his family home and the black charred debris. Amongst the smoldering rubble and ash, he locates Midori's sacred rosary, the symbol of her faith. Anguish soon dissipates and he is consumed with horror as the realization hits Nagai that his beloved wife is dead. While this scene does not explicitly deal with the bombing, the viewer can surmise that Midori has perished in the blast.

Nineteen eighty-three saw Keisuke Kinoshita's *Children of Nagasaki*, a new adaptation of Nagai's book. In this re-telling, the film centers on Nagai's own life and his devotion to helping survivors of the atomic blast. The film has been rarely seen outside of Japan, which has further accentuated the lack of knowledge and understanding of Nagai's life here in the West. Both films have drifted into obscurity outside of its native Japan and despite a few translations of his work/books into English, Dr. Nagai still remains relatively unknown to Westerners despite being a well-known figure in Japan.

The Bells of Nagasaki, though viewed as problematic by the occupying forces, was released in cinemas on September 22, 1950. A commercial success for Shochiku, the film received plaudits from reviewers and featured in *Kinema Junpō*'s top sixteen films of the year.[21] Shindō went on to direct *Children of Hiroshima* in 1953 and the cult favorites *Onibaba* (1964) and *Kwaidan* (1964), a film that would deal more specifically with the bombings and without American interference. Despite the suppression and interference into the arts by the occupational forces, the Hiroshima and Nagasaki question was not to remain hidden, as exemplified by the relaxation in censorship once the occupying forces left Japan. Educational bodies and filmmakers like Shindō were anxious that their voices would be heard so that no more Hiroshima's and Nagasaki's would be allowed to be repeated.

Conclusion

No sooner had the U.S. left its shores Japan was free from censorship and suppression. Post-Occupation Japan saw the Japanese free to explore *Genbakudan* cinema and its national cinema was now free to tackle the complex issue of the atomic bombings; it now had the means of tackling a magnitude of subjects from feats of heroism during the bombings, the dangers of nuclear warfare to the plight of *Hibakusha*. Japan wasted no time in exploiting this.

The first wave of films saw the production of *Children of Hiroshima* (*Genbaku no ko*, 1952), which was more direct in its portrayal of the bombings and directed by Kaneto Shindō. Shindō in fact "used the city of his birth as inspiration for a fictional narrative based on a series of short stories written by young survivors of the atomic bombing."[22] *Children of Hiroshima* competed at the 1953 Cannes festival and was co-funded by the Japanese Teachers Union (JTU). So dissatisfied were they with the final result that they produced and funded Hideo Sekigawa's more harrowing *Hiroshima* in 1953. Kaneto Shindō's *Children of Hiroshima* is not without merit, despite its sentimental gloss, as it is beautifully shot and one of the most poignant examples of Japanese atomic cinema and based on the first hand stories of survivors of the bombing. One should not overlook the fact that Shindō wasn't merely cashing in on emotive subject that was still fresh in the minds of the Japanese. A native of Hiroshima, the destruction of his home town and the aftermath had a profound effect on his cinematic output. His films *Mother* (*Hana*, 1963) *Sakuratai 8.6* (*Sakura-tai chiru*, 1988) and *Lucky Dragon No. 5* (*Daigo Fukuryu-Maru*, 1959) all explicitly deal with the nuclear issue. Visiting his home town shortly after the bombings, Shindō was so moved when he stood in front of the obliterated Hiroshima train station, he observed the devastation inflicted on his home town he "felt that he himself was struck by the bomb."[23] The bombings of Hiroshima had a profound effect on his cinematic overture.

The Japanese have returned to the subject of Hiroshima and Nagasaki in their national cinema in the intervening years since the end of the World War II and the Allied Occupation of Japan. While attempting to silence and censor their own past, they have on the flip side tried to reconcile the trauma of Hiroshima and Nagasaki through film, literature and Art. That the Japanese are still trying to come to terms with the bombings is systematic of the scars left on their national psyche. It is a theme that preoccupies Japanese society and it unsurprising that with passing year, new generation of filmmakers try to make sense of what happened on those fateful days. While the Americans initially succeeded in silencing images and cinematic works on the atomic bombings, Japan's national cinema has ensured that the nuclear question is still at the front of the agenda and that Kaneto Shindō's plea of "No more Hiroshimas"[24] is continued to be preached and a world free of nuclear weapons and arsenals.

Notes

1. D. Ritchie, "Mono no aware," in Mick Broderick, ed., *Hibakusha Cinema: Hiroshima, Nagasaki and the Nuclear Image in Japanese Film* (London: Kegan Paul International, 1993), p. 21.
2. *Ibid.*
3. K. Cather, *The Art of Censorship in Postwar Japan* (Honolulu: University of Hawai'i Press, 2012), p. 2.
4. Jun Eto was a Japanese literary critic.
5. H. Passin, "The Occupation—Some Reflections," in Ellis Krauss and Benjamin Nyblade, eds., *Japan and North America Volume II: Post War* (London: Routledge, 2004) p. 27.
6. S. Ōoka, *Taken Captive: A Japanese POW's Story* (New York: J. Wiley & Sons, 1996). The original Japanese title *Furyoki* is based on his own experiences in an American prisoner of war camp.
7. H. Passin: "The Occupation—Some Reflections" in Ellis Krauss and Benjamin Nyblade, eds., *Japan and North America Volume II: Post War* (London: Routledge, 2004) p. 28.
8. K. Hirano, "'Depictions of the Atomic Bombings in Japanese Cinema During the U.S. Occupation Period," in Mick Broderick, ed., *Hibakusha Cinema: Hiroshima, Nagasaki and the Nuclear Image in Japanese Film* (London: Kegan Paul International, 1993) p. 103.
9. J. Sharp, *The Historical Dictionary of Japanese Cinema* (Lanham, MD: Scarecrow Press, 2011), p. 29.
10. G. Mitchell, "For 64th Anniversary: The Great Hiroshima Cover-Up—And the Nuclear Fallout for All of Us Today," *The Huffington Post*, 9 June 2009, http://www.huffingtonpost.com/greg-mitchell/for-64th-anniversary-the_b_252752.html (accessed September 5, 2014).
11. J. Sharp, *The Historical Dictionary of Japanese Cinema* (Lanham, MD: Scarecrow Press, 2011), p. 29.
12. *Ibid.*
13. *Ibid.*
14. K. Hirano, "Depictions of the Atomic Bombings in Japanese Cinema During the U.S. Occupation Period," in Mick Broderick, ed., *Hibakusha Cinema: Hiroshima, Nagasaki and the Nuclear Image in Japanese Film* (London: Kegan Paul International, 1993) p. 110.
15. *Ibid.*, p. 111.
16. J. Sharp. *The Historical Dictionary of Japanese Cinema* (Lanham, MD: Scarecrow Press, 2011), p. 215.
17. *Ibid.*
18. Dr. Nagai's book *The Bells of Nagasaki* was first published in 1949. An English language version was published in 1994 by Kōdansha International. During the Occupation, Dr. Nagai's book was initially prohibited and censored by the Americans for six months as they were worried its contents would inflame reactions towards the Americans and that the use of the bomb would be deemed inhuman. The occupiers later retracted their opposition to the book's publication on the condition that Dr. Nagai included an appendix that clearly detailed Japanese atrocities in the Philippines. (The appendix was named *The Tragedy in Manila* [*Manira no higeki*]). The appendix, not authorized by Dr. Nagai, was written by MacArthur's Military Intelligence Division, and made explicit reference to Japan's brutal and barbaric crimes during the war.) Reluctantly, Dr. Nagai agreed. Interestingly, after the Occupation, the book, which was a bestseller in Japan, was re-released, this time with the appendix omitted from future editions.
19. H. Kitamura, *Screening Enlightenment: Hollywood and the Cultural Reconstruction of Defeated Japan* (Ithaca: Cornell University Press, 2010), pp. 55–57.
20. *Ibid.*, p. 56.
21. *Ibid.*, p. 57.
22. J. Sharp, *The Historical Dictionary of Japanese Cinema* (Lanham, MD: Scarecrow Press, 2011), p. 217.
23. H. Kitamura, *Screening Enlightenment: Hollywood and the Cultural Reconstruction of Defeated Japan* (Ithaca: Cornell University Press, 2010), p. 57.
24. *Ibid.*

Bibliography

Broderick, Mick. *Hibakusha Cinema: Hiroshima, Nagasaki and the Nuclear Image in Japanese Film*. London: Kegan Paul International, 1993.

Brothers, Peter H. *Mushroom Clouds and Mushroom Men: The Fantastic Cinema of Ishirō Honda*. Bloominton: AuthorHouse, 2009.

Cather, Kirsten. *The Art of Censorship in Postwar Japan*. Honolulu: University of Hawai'i Press, 2012.

Kitamura, Hiroshi. *Screening Enlightenment: Hollywood and the Cultural Reconstruction of Defeated Japan*. Ithaca: Cornell University Press, 2010.

Krauss, Ellis, and Benjamin Nyblade, eds. *Japan and North America Volume II: Post War*. London: Routledge, 2004.

Ōoka, Shōhei. *Taken Captive: A Japanese POW's Story*. New York: J. Wiley & Sons, 1996.

Sharp, Jasper. *The Historical Dictionary of Japanese Cinema*. Lanham, MD: Scarecrow Press, 2011.

Pica-don: Japanese and American Reception and Promotion of Hideo Sekigawa's *Hiroshima*

Mick Broderick *and* Junko Hatori

Few films concerning major historical events have received as little attention in the West as Hideo Sekigawa's 1953 production *Hiroshima*. This essay draws from Japanese accounts of the initial release that are translated here for the first time. We situate *Hiroshima* within its national and international context, suggesting that Sekigawa's film remains an important and landmark contribution to the sub-genre of Japanese film that can loosely be defined as *Hibakusha* cinema.[1] Contrasting the film's domestic and American critical reception, we examine the promotion strategies and how the work was re-edited for distribution in the U.S. Given the limited exposure of *Hiroshima* in Japan and abroad, it is prudent to first touch on some key plot points and thematic concerns while noting the differing release versions in Japan (7 October 1953, 104 min) and the U.S. (16 May 1955, 85 min).

The Film Text

Hiroshima was created in response to the poor reception of Kaneto Shindō's 1952 feature *Children of Hiroshima* (*Genbaku no ko*). Derisively described as a "tear-jerker" and "sentimental," Shindō's elegiac feature was promptly dismissed by its commissioning organization, the Japan Teachers' Union (JTU), as largely ineffectual. *Children of Hiroshima* was considered by many a somewhat indulgent art film that did little to satisfy the Union's anti-war political affiliations or the *Hibakusha* community that had greatly anticipated an unadulterated treatment of the subject once the Allied Occupation censorship was lifted by mid–1952.

After the exhibition and distribution of Shindō's film the JTU quickly commissioned director Hideo Sekigawa to craft a new film as a rejoinder that better addressed the Union's agenda to educate contemporary Japanese as to the plight of the atom bomb survivors and the dangers of possible future use of nuclear weapons. During the postwar Occupation (1945–52) Japan was an American strategic base and a staging ground for UN military operations throughout the Korean War. At the time American presidents Truman and Eisenhower threatened the use of atomic weapons against North Korean and Communist Chinese forces.[2] The era was also one of accelerated American atmospheric nuclear testing in the region, with the first thermonuclear detonations occurring in the mid–Pacific throughout 1952–54, including the irradiation of the *Lucky Dragon No. 5* Japanese fishing crew.[3] Given these circumstances, it remains curious that *Hiroshima* has not reached a broader audience both within Japan and internationally.

Surprisingly, no Japanese critic at the time pointed to the film's strident presentation of dogmatic military and political culpability in pursuing the emperor's war of aggression across Asia and the Pacific. Indeed, those soldiers depicted in the film parroting patriotic slogans or battle cries—from the home guard martinets to senior military chiefs of staff—are ultimately shown to be deluded, contemptible or sadistic bullies. Furthermore, the film demonstrates the insensitivity, if not obscenity, of "dark tourism" flourishing in Japan almost immediately after the atomic bombings, where visiting occupation forces (often with female Japanese escorts) are solicited by orphans, street kids and the visibly maimed *Hibakusha*. The harsh privations of post-war life for Hiroshima disabled and abandoned are suggested as the economic motivators for the exploitation of these *Hibakusha*. Yet Sekigawa is careful not to point the finger, interspersing documentary location footage at memorial sites, with the more refined 35mm narrative drama sequences shot in studios or on controlled locations. Apart from the character discourse, didactic or otherwise, implicating Japan's continued production of armaments so soon after World War II (feeding the new Cold War), Japanese authorities and industry—are certainly portrayed as reproachable.

The truncated print released exported to the U.S. and other territories re-arranged the narrative sequences and imposed a new linear chronology. The film opens with the same title sequence as the Japanese original but drastically clips the narration. In the foreign release print the lengthy then-contemporary school scenes are excised, with the film unfolding on the day before the A-bombing. However, much of the film's imagery of graphic destruction and its human consequences are retained. Also included is the post-attack gathering of scientists and the military commanders who berate them as defeatist. Scenes and dialogue featuring the two high school students prominent in the film, one suffering from leukemia (Michiko), the other an orphan drop-out and juvenile delinquent (Hideo), are either diminished or excised, including their listening to a radio broadcast recreating the Hiroshima bombing, and the bedside reading of German philosophy. However, lengthy documentary sequences, potentially hostile to foreign audiences, depicting the tourist exploitation of *Hibakusha*, the prominent display of post-occupation Christianity, and the remilitarization of Japan remain.

Japanese Critical Reception and Suppression

Many scholars have revealed how images of the Atom bombings of Japan were strictly controlled and suppressed by the occupying forces (1945–52) as well as throughout the cold war. As Kyoko Hirano has demonstrated:"While the censors allowed no sympathetic, indeed no noncondemnatory, mention of the Japanese militarism, they wanted to make sure that the Japanese people's anger toward the American atomic bombings received no encouragement."[4] Hence, post-war censorship not only led to a distorted view of life in Hiroshima, but for seven years it suppressed the expression of Japanese sentiments on the subject.[5]

In Japan, early newspaper reports concerning the production and release of *Hiroshima* emphasized the collaborative nature of the work and contrasted the film with the preceding

1952 production, Kaneto Shindō's *Children of Hiroshima*. On the anniversary date of August 6, 1953, the *Mainichi Shimbun* reported that the as-yet unreleased *Hiroshima* had been co-produced by Arata Osada (the author-editor of the source anthology of high-school student stories), the Japan Teachers' Union and the scriptwriter (Yasutarō Yagi) and the director (Sekigawa). According to the *Mainichi*: "Filming started on location in late May. Local labor union members totaling 30,000 cooperated in the production alongside ordinary Hiroshima residents. The extra's participation was the most enthusiastic ever seen in a Japanese film."[6]

The *Mainichi* also described how Shindō's 1952 film was widely derided as a "sightseeing film" that had provoked "intense debate" about whether is should have been entered in the Cannes Film Festival. However, the newspaper noted that Sekigawa's film was anticipated to "bring about a commotion in overseas exports." The report added "with regret" that the August 6 Memorial Day film preview was postponed due to "distribution problems."[7]

These unidentified "distribution problems" continued to impact upon the film's release. By late August the *Asahi* evening newspaper reported that these "problems" arose from all five Japanese national film distributors closing ranks and refusing to release the film.[8] The distributors dictated unanimously that *Hiroshima* would remain unreleased unless the producers "cut the scenes we have demanded."[9]

Several journalists continued to investigate these behind-the-scenes machinations. By 4 September, the *Mainichi* revealed that *Hiroshima* had actually been completed on 6 August and scheduled for release by the Shochiku film distribution on 10 August but the company reneged, explaining that "the content was much too anti–American" and "cruel."[10] A Shochiku spokesman described for the *Mainichi* three scenes that required cutting: the prologue where an American pilot describes the bombing; scenes in which claims were made that the Japanese were "guinea-pigs"; and the end sequence where orphans sell *Hibakusha* skulls to American tourists. The spokesman also justified the company's position by listing other grievances such as Shochiku lending a popular actress under contract to the producers free of charge and also offering their cinemas in Hiroshima, Nagasaki, and Fukuoka for preview screenings.[11]

The Japan Teacher's Union refused to bow to pressure which they identified as coming from "some agents and the government," instead announcing that the organization would "self-distribute the film amongst their large membership."[12] Nearly a half million teachers across Japan had helped finance the film's production.[13] The JTU distribution was trialed first in Hiroshima in late September before expanding to a national audience.[14]

Controversy further dogged the film's release, this time from some *Hibakusha* themselves. According to the *Mainichi* on 13 September, after a public screening in Hiroshima, ten of the famous "Hiroshima Maidens" wrote to the Teachers' Union requesting that a brief newsreel sequence showing the group praying at a church be trimmed, even though they understood the scene was meant to raise sympathy.[15] The JTU replied that the inclusion of the Maidens clip was to protest the lack of support given to bomb victims still eight years on. The Union further noted with regret that the women had joined those forces in vocal opposition to the film. Whether or not the Maidens acted independently or were encouraged to protest at someone else's behest is unclear. But their high public profile on both sides of the Pacific and their medical repatriation by American Christian sympathizers had already made them (perhaps unwittingly) political symbols, if not pawns, paraded both as atomic victims and select beneficiaries of American largess and compassion.[16]

Nevertheless the film certainly had its supporters amongst intellectuals and other elites. For example, writing in the *Mainichi* on 24 September, Professor Kawashima of Hiroshima University publicly supported the film while expressing some mild qualifications concerning the narrative logic and the ending. In a moving passage Kawashima relates how a weeping survivor who watched the film with him had asserted: "It was exactly like that. Please explain for those who did not experience the A-bomb that the depiction was not an exaggeration."[17]

The Professor lauds the realism of Sekigawa's production, noting that Shindō's earlier film had deliberately "dodged the reality of the atomic attack." Reiterating director's Sekigawa's statements on the matter, Kawashima recognizes the limitations of mid–Twentieth Century screen technology to render a true mimetic affect of the experience, while praising the multitude of local *hibakusha* performers whose participation "captured the audience's hearts" more so than the professional actors. For Kawashima *Hiroshima*'s devotion to realism "addresses the A-bomb head on … in a substantive and valid" form.[18] Railing against the historical propensity of the Japanese people to publicly express "inane words like mantras," especially concerning the bomb, the professor concludes his evaluation of *Hiroshima* by describing the production as a refreshing and courageous change of paradigm: "Eight years on from the end of the war, finally a film appears that bluntly confronts the war and provokes strong emotion."[19] Professor Kawashima's article encapsulates the artistic and cultural trend that trauma scholar Adam Lowenstein has identified concerning Hiroshima in Japanese film, arguing that "'realism' trumps 'allegory' as the critical discourse's preferred representational mode."[20]

Despite the growing interest in the film and the producers bypassing traditional distribution networks, *Hiroshima* faced more obstacles, if not a concerted campaign to damage its potentiate audience reach. On 8 November the *Asahi Shinbun* reported that the Ministry of Education, Science, Sports and Culture had intervened to reverse a previous resolution by its own Film Screening Committee, having approved the release of *Hiroshima*. Echoing previous comments by the film distribution cartel, the Ministry stated: "the film is too anti–American to endorse school children's viewing."[21] However, *Asahi Shinbun* drew attention to the reversal of this decision as once again arousing "public concern" about the veracity and independence of the Ministry's film endorsement process. Overturning the decision against the Japan Teacher's Union sponsored film only served to foreground the perceived problem of "maintaining neutrality of education" the newspaper suggested.[22]

In fact, the political interference could not have been any more blatant. As the *Asahi* reported, the Ministry of Education's film endorsement test was unlike pre-war bureaucratic censorship. The applicant film was to be examined solely from an educational perspective to allow viewing by school children. Select committee members from civil society were in charge of assessment screenings. The fully constituted committee concluded *Hiroshima* should be "Endorsed" but the Ministry overturned the decision demanding a re-examination and changed the rating system, thereby reversing the previous resolution to "Not endorsed."[23]

By November *Kinema Junpō* devoted a serious review of the film by Naoki Togawa, one that compared and contrasted it with Shindō's *Children of Hiroshima*. Togawa also touched on the political controversy of the film's production and content.[24] According to the author the JTU was deeply dissatisfied with Shindō's effort produced the year earlier. The Union still wanted to emphasize the graphic and horrendous nature of the atom bombing experience and so commissioned Sekigawa's *Hiroshima*. In comparing the two works Togawa notes that, although the 1952 film by Shindō was "beautiful," it was a "largely symbolic and stylized" treatment that included a "sentimental" happy ending that eschewed the "rawness of the reality" facing contemporary Hiroshima.[25] In stark contrast Togawa describes Sekigagwa's *Hiroshima* as "far from sentimental" in its adoption of a documentary realism that vividly recreates the events and portrays the experiences of *Hibakusha*.

Given the commissioning by the JTU, it was hardly surprising that both Shindō and Sekigawa situated their narratives from the perspective of high school students and teachers during the atom bombing. Further shifting the drama to the then contemporary post-war school setting, according to Togawa, enabled difficult issues to be raised for a contemporary audience. Unlike Shindō's restrained approach: "Sekigawa … seemed intent on overwhelming audiences with a sustained series of shocks rather than densely compressed expressionism." Hence, *Hiroshima's* didactic message "not to repeat the tragedy of war" was amplified by the "shocking scenes of Hiroshima's inferno."[26]

Despite the power of these scenes, Togawa found flaws in the discontinuity of the narrative. Splitting the plot between the horrific effects of the atom bombing and the school students eight years later seemed "unreconciled," like "two independent dramas" within the one narrative. This observation was common among a number of Japanese and Western film critics, including long-time resident of Japan, American film commentator Donald Richie.[27]

Togawa argues that, depending on one's personal perspective, the film "may appear anti–USA," but nevertheless concedes that as a film *Hiroshima* is not particularly effective in agitating anti–American feelings.[28] By describing the A-bomb as an "experiment" and a "human tragedy" does not connote anti–Americanism, according to Togawa, since the filmmakers' "pacifist agenda" was to decry war and the "ongoing re-militarization in Japan and elsewhere."[29]

It is clear there was a significant degree of political sensitivity surrounding the film's perceived ideology and the motivation of the creative team. Editorial comments from an earlier edition of *Kinema Junpō* (70, August 1953) identified *Hiroshima's* principal artists and creative crew (producer, director and photographer) as being "so-called 'progressives,'" noting also that the actors came from "progressive theatrical companies."[30] Donald Richie notes the communist sympathies of several post-war Japanese filmmakers and that director Sekigawa was "an accredited Party member."[31]

For its December 1953 edition *Kinema Junpō* organized a special "Japan Film Round Table" to evaluate *Hiroshima*. Amongst the issues canvassed by the film critics was their surprise at how long the post-holocaust sequence ran, suggesting the duration seemed "cruel" and despite the filmmakers intentions, the production could never truly "express the dreadfulness" of the *Hibakusha* experience.[32] Irrespective of these concerns, and the combined efforts of the Japanese distributors and the Education Ministry to suppress the film, *Hiroshima* won the Best Feature Film award for at the 1955 Berlin Film Festival and ultimately secured an international release.

While the film garnered broad local support during its on-location production—drawing on the resources of tens of thousands of Hiroshima residents, many of them *Hibakusha*—it is not clear what the short or long term effect may have been on this authentic cohort of victims, role playing and re-enacting their horrors. The potential for the production to have re-traumatized those already afflicted by the bomb, whether physically damaged or psychologically impaired, must have been significant. Whatever catharsis may have been afforded individuals by participating in the shoot, hundreds (if not thousands) were featured in many grueling scenes, having to repeatedly limp or stumble across rubble barefoot, wearing torn rags and make-up showing keloids and other scars. Take after take in scene after harrowing scene portraying these citizens wailing, howling, whimpering or screaming maniacally must have taken its toll emotionally.

American Promotion and Reception

It took almost two years for *Hiroshima* to be shown in the USA. The title was acquired by Continental Distributing, Inc., of New York, established in 1954 by Water Reade, Jr., to exhibit foreign films on the east coast and sell to the growing post-war television market.

The company's media campaign was an odd mixture of New York and national film critic hyperbole, along with sensationalist B-movie exploitation and appeals to patriotic civil defense preparedness. It seems Continental was unsure of its audience so rhetorically hedged it bets by appealing to both an art house crowd and those gravitating to film "shockers." The central full-page panel of the press guide reprints a miniature version of the front page of *LOOK* magazine's special feature: "INSIDE HELL: For the first time, a survivor's report on what really happened at Hiroshima when the A-bomb fell…. Read this shattering account by a Japanese doctor and you'll know why there must never be ANOTHER WAR." Under the reprinted *LOOK* cover the promotional guide with a recommendation for theater owners.

PLAN AN ADVANCE CAMPAIGN
All civilian Defense Units have been alerted to cooperate in the
presentation of this film
All Book Stores currently list several outstanding best sellers on HIROSHIMA
Lobby displays should be tied in with Fire Department or Civilian Defense Groups

It is curious that Hiroshima (metonymically represented by Sekigawa's film), as the target of America's first atomic attack, was promoted unproblematically as a tie-in for national civil defense programs. In the lead-up to the tenth anniversary of the bombing of Hiroshima and Nagasaki in mid–1955, fears of a war with the Soviet Union were heightened. The rapid development and deployment of thermonuclear weapons now dwarfed the "primitive" fission bombs used against Japan. Throughout the cold war, across all media and genres, America repeatedly turned to narrative tropes that projected itself as a potential *victim* of atomic attack, rather than as the sole historical perpetrator of such.[33] Amidst the anti-communist discourse of the era, the irony of this revisionism was lost on contemporary reviewers and critics, as their collective cognitive dissonance was sublimated into a culture of victimhood contrasting postwar triumphalism.[34]

The 1955 *Hiroshima* press kit also contains a range of lurid graphics set as large half-tone block advertisements using a line art banner that figuratively shouts off the page: "A BOXOFFICE A-BOMB!" One advertising style features a close-up of a character on fire, seemingly in agony, with the heading:

TERROR AND AGONY BLASTING at *YOU*!
You are caught in the dead center of the first
"A"-BOMB EXPLOSION!
HIROSHIMA
Filmed where it Happened!
A full-length feature—not a documentary!

Two alternative styles were also created for the press campaign. The first draws from the post–*Rashomon* American "discovery" of Japanese cinema that appealed to film aesthetes. This promotional bizarrely concocts the impression that the film is "romantic" by foregrounding a large close-up of two Japanese characters, one gazing at the other, with the tag-line "The [blank] Theatre is proud to present another starling facet of the Japanese cinematic technique. It is a drama rooted in an indelible moment in history. It is a symbol of Japan's remarkable rebirth. HIROSHIMA! The one picture you will never, never forget!"

The second block advertisement draws upon the iconography of the mushroom cloud. An enormous, thrusting stem and billowing cloud-head reveals a splintered city in ruins, over which large lettering proclaims:

It blasts you out of your seat!
The shocking story behind the most ravaged city on earth!
HIROSHIMA
FILMED WHERE IT HAPPENED … WITH A CAST OF 100,000

Two comic-like graphics accompany the display panel, one showing a man engulfed in flames ("A City Is Wiped Out Before Your Eyes!"), the other a ragged soldier and woman on a street ("The Vicious, Shocking Aftermath"). The block advertisement is reminiscent of then contemporary American science fiction film promotion styles, especially of the 1950s wave of mutant-monster films from the U.S. and the imported *kaiju eiga* movies from Japan, a sub-genre expertly critiqued in Susan Sontag's 1966 essay "The Imagination of Disaster."[35]

The *Hiroshima* publicity booklet also drew from extant press reviews. *The New York Times* headlined its review with "Hiroshima After the Bomb: Japanese Film Depicts Catalogue of Horror A Semi-Documentary" where critic Bosley Crowther described the movie as "extraordinary … shocking, nightmarish and agonizing" in its transformation of city in a "sudden blinding flash into a Dantesque place."[36] Jesse Zunser's review in *Cue* magazine echoed the film's sensory impact revealing that *Hiroshima* was "enough to stun any moviegoer," adding the film was "fervent and heartrending" with a directorial style employed "for shock effect—and gets it."[37]

Despite *Time* magazine pronouncing the film as "propaganda-heavy" it nevertheless recommended the film as "well worth seeing … but harrowing" and promoted it weekly among its select "Current Cinema" choices from the film's May release until early July.[38] Writing in *The New York Post* Archer Winsten was similarly conflicted, advising the movie was "a devastating experience [that] cannot be ignored—just as your reaction to it must be a matter of personal conscience, so your seeing it must be."[39] However, *The Herald Tribune*'s critic William Zinsser was almost zealous in his advocacy: "The human tragedy is so enormous that it is hard to comprehend. If everyone in the world could see '*Hiroshima*,' there wouldn't be any more wars."[40]

Arthur Knight in *The Saturday Review* was more measured, praising the film for rendering the subject matter "dispassionately, without protest, without sensationalism, without cheap appeals for pity," noting the effective integration of stock footage with enacted scenes

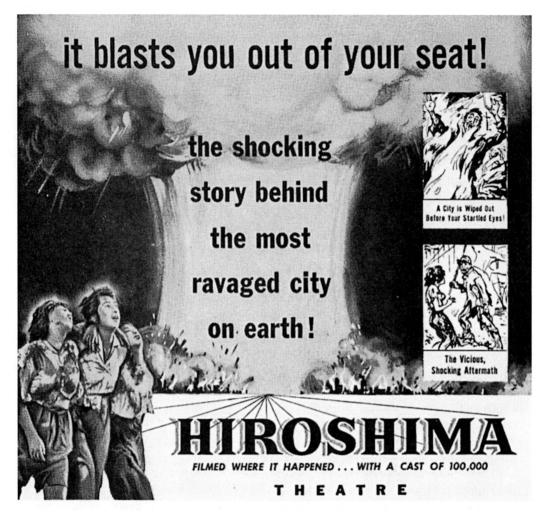

of everyday life. In comparison to other Japanese (mostly period) films, Knight found *Hiroshima* lacked "artistic balance and sureness" but did register "intensity of mood and emotion."[41] Significantly, Knight was one of the few American reviewers to draw attention to the film's "overt criticism ... directed at the Japanese military," specifically the depicted brutal treatment of civilians and the military's refusal to recognize the effects of the A-bomb for fear of alarming the populace. As with *The Herald Tribune*, Knight concluded his review by reiterating the film's "prayer" and coda "that the horror visited on Hiroshima will never occur again anywhere."[42] Knight suggests that the "spirit which animates this shocking film" is something phenomenological and somatic: "For when we have understood the effects of such a bomb not as abstract statistics, but in the agonies of flesh and blood, further recourse to atomic warfare becomes inconceivable."[43] This very public observation and prognostication mirrored what U.S. president Dwight Eisenhower was privately writing in his diary and advising high echelon military advisers in top secret correspondence—that the concept of waging war in the thermonuclear age was "preposterous."[44]

Long denied the suppressed documentary footage of the real human effects of the atomic bombings, American audiences could witness in graphical detail for the first time via the U.S. release of *Hiroshima*, not only the impact of what their military industrial complex had deployed to help end the war, but a potential fate awaiting their own nation. By looking at *Hiroshima* in America, audiences saw the face of the future mirrored in the nuclear victims of the recent past.

Coda

For decades *Hiroshima* was forgotten and little seen in Japan and abroad. From 2011 to 2012 film producer Ippei Kobayashi, the son of the film's assistant director, began a program to restore and subtitle the movie, which was subsequently exhibited in Japan and a range of venues internationally.[45]

Some of the collaborators working on the film's restoration reflected how shocked they were to see similarities between the devastation caused by the 3/11 earthquake, tsunami and reactor meltdowns, and imagery of the post-holocaust devastation in Hiroshima. One subtitler commented, "I was astonished and saddened to find that the footage of the atomic bombing and the region struck by the March 11 disaster overlapped…. We should not allow a recurrence of such a tragedy."[46]

Sekigawa's 1953 film was careful to indict Japanese authorities in sharing responsibility for the after-effects of the bombing, from the military leadership's dismissal of the A-bomb's devastation to their fanaticism in continuing the war. Incompetence, culpability and discrimination within Japanese society against *Hibakusha* remains—evidenced by the recent events at Fukushima and its surrounds. As a polemic cultural intervention *Hiroshima* relates how, eight years from the atomic attack, and after seven years of strict Occupation censorship, Japan had ostensibly "forgotten" the victims of Hiroshima (and Nagasaki). Three years on from the catastrophic explosions and core meltdowns at the Fukushima Daiichi Nuclear Power Plant, a litany of errors and deceit by industry and government has been gradually but continually exposed in the media and online via social networks.[47] For scholars of history, *Hiroshima* stands both as testimony and prophecy—unfortunately—as to how this new generation of *Hibakusha* can expect to be treated in the coming years.

Notes

1. See Mick Broderick, ed., *Hibakusha Cinema: Hiroshima, Nagasaki and the Nuclear Image in Japanese Cinema* (London: Kegan Paul, 1996).

2. See "Atomic Diplomacy: Milestones 1945–52," U.S. Department of State, Office of the His-torian, https://history.state.gov/milestones/1945–1952/atomic (accessed 10 November 2013).

3. Coincidentally, director of *Children of the Atom Bomb*, Kaneto Shindō, made a feature film based on this event. For details on the Bravo test and its impact, see Mark Schreiber, "Lucky Dragon's lethal catch," *The Japan Times*, 18 March 2012, http://www.japantimes.co.jp/life/2012/03/18/general/lucky-dragons-lethal-catch/#.U2rFCdzNZlI (accessed 10 November 2013).

4. On occupation censorship see Kyoko Hirano, *Mr. Smith Goes to Tokyo: Japanese Cinema Under the American Occupation, 1945–1952* (Washington, D.C.: Smithsonian Books, 1994) and Abe Mark Nornes, *Japanese Documentary Film: The Meiji Era Through Hiroshima* (Minneapolis: University of Minnesota Press, 2003).

5. There were some exceptions such as *I'll Not Forget the Song of Nagasaki* (1952), directed by *Hibakusha* Tomotaka Tasaka and dismissed by veteran Japanese film critic Tadao Sato as embarrassing "rubbish."

6. *The Mainichi Shimbun*, 6 August 1953.

7. *Ibid.*

8. *The Asahi Shimbun*, 29 August 1953.

9. *Ibid.*

10. *The Mainichi Shimbun*, 4 September 1953.

11. *Ibid.*

12. *Ibid.*

13. See "Poignant 1953 film on Hiroshima A-bomb returns after 6 decades," *The Asahi Shimbun*, 18 October 2012, http://ajw.asahi.com/article/behind_news/social_affairs/AJ201210180005 (accessed 4 December 2012).

14. *The Mainichi Shimbun*, 4 September 1953.

15. According to Maya Todeschini, "The term 'A-bomb Maiden' (genbaku-otome) was first used for a group of severely disfigured young women who were brought to the United States in the 1950s for plastic surgery in an effort organized by Norman Cousins and Japanese church leaders," see Maya Todeschini, "'Death and the Maiden': Female Hibakusha as Cultural Her-oines, and the Politics of A-Bomb Memory," in Broderick, pp. 222–52.

16. See Robert Jacobs, "Reconstructing the Perpetrator's Soul by Reconstructing the Victim's Body: The Portrayal of the 'Hiroshima Maidens' by the Mainstream Media in the United States," *Intersections: Gender and Sexuality in Asia and the Pacific*, 24, June 2010, http://intersections.anu.edu.au/issue24/jacobs.htm (accessed 10 November 2013).

17. *The Mainichi Shimbun*, 24 September 1953.

18. *Ibid.*

19. *Ibid.*

20. Of course, many scholars have argued that Godzilla and other Japanese mutant monster films are popular precisely because they *allegorize* the Bomb and nuclear holocaust. Adam Lowenstein, *Shocking Representation: Historical Trauma, National Cinema, and the Modern Horror Film* (New York: Columbia University Press, 2005), p. 83.

21. *The Asahi Shinbun*, 8 November 1953.

22. *Ibid.*

23. *Ibid.*

24. Naoki Togawa, *Kinema Junpō*, 77, November 1953, pp. 68–69.

25. *Ibid.*, p. 68.

26. *Ibid.*

27. Donald Richie, "'Mono no aware': Hiroshima in Film," in Broderick, p. 25.

28. Togawa, p. 69.

29. *Ibid.*

30. Editorial, *Kinema Junpō*, 70, August 1953.

31. Richie, p. 25.

32. "Japan Film Round Table Talk," *Kinema Jumpō*, 79 December 1953, pp. 42–43.

33. See Mick Broderick and Robert Jacobs, "Nuke York, New York: Nuclear Holocaust in the American Imagination from Hiroshima to 9/11," *The Asia-Pacific Journal*, 10.11, 6, 12 March 2009, http://www.japanfocus.org/-Mick-Broderick/3726 (accessed 2 February 2014).

34. On this social malaise see Tom Engelhardt, *The End of Victory Culture: Cold War America and the Disillusioning of a Generation* (Boston: University of Massachusetts Press, 2008), and John W. Dower, *Cultures of War: Pearl Harbor, Hiroshima, 9–11, Iraq* (New York: W.W. Norton, 2010).

35. Susan Sontag, "The Imagination of Disaster," *Against Interpretation* (New York: Farrar, Straus & Giroux, 1966).

36. Bosley Crowther, "Hiroshima After the Bomb: Japanese Film Depicts Catalogue of Horror A Semi-Documentary," *The New York Times*, 18 May 1955, p. 35.

37. Jesse Zunser, *Hiroshima* press kit (New York: Continental Distributors, Inc., 1955).

38. "Cinema: *Hiroshima*," *Time Magazine*, 23 May 1955.

39. Archer Winsten, *Hiroshima* press kit.

40. William Zinsser, *Hiroshima* press kit.

41. Arthur Knight, "Hiroshima," *The Saturday Review*, 21 May 1955, p. 45.

42. *Ibid.* However, what both this plea, and Sekigawa's film evades, is the fact another bomb was dropped on Nagasaki three days later on 9 August 1945.

43. *Ibid.*

44. Eisenhower later publically addressed the issue at a late August 1956 Republican nomination ceremony: "We are in the era of the thermonuclear bomb that can obliterate cities and can be delivered across continents. With such weapons, war has become, not just tragic, but prepos-terous." http://presidenteisenhower.net/dwight-d-eisenhower-quotes/501/#sthash.2Ng2I9KJ.dpuf (accessed 31 January 2014).

45. "Poignant 1953 film on Hiroshima A-bomb returns after 6 decades," *The Asahi Shimbun*, 18 October 2012, http://ajw.asahi.com/article/behind_news/social_affairs/AJ201210180005 (accessed 12 March 2104).

46. Asuka Yui quoted in "Poignant 1953 film on Hiroshima A-bomb returns after 6 decades," *The Asahi Shimbun*.

47. See Mick Broderick and Robert Jacobs, "Fukushima and the Shifting Conventions of Docu-mentary: from Cinema and Broadcast to Social Media Netizenship," in Camille Deprez and Judith Perine, eds., *Defining Independent Documentaries? Case Studies in the Post–1990 Context* (Edinburgh: Edinburgh University Press, 2014).

Bibliography

Asahi Shimbun, 29 August 1953.

Broderick, Mick, ed. *Hibakusha Cinema: Hiroshima, Nagasaki and the Nuclear Image in Japanese Cinema.* London: Kegan Paul, 1996.

_____, and Robert Jacobs. "Fukushima and the Shifting Conventions of Documentary: from Cinema and Broadcast to Social Media Netizenship," in Camille Deprez and Judith Perine, eds., *Defining Independent Documentaries? Case Studies in the Post–1990 Context.* Edinburgh: Edinburgh University Press, 2014.

"Cinema: *Hiroshima*," 23 May 1955, *Time Magazine.*

Crowther, Bosley. "Hiroshima After the Bomb: Japanese Film Depicts Catalogue of Horror A Semi-Documentary." *The New York Times*, 18 May 1955, 35.

Dower, John W. *Cultures of War: Pearl Harbor, Hiroshima, 9-11, Iraq.* New York: W.W. Norton, 2010.

Editorial. *Kinema Junpō*, 70, August 1953.

Erdmann, Andrew. "'War No Longer Has Any Logic': Dwight D. Eisenhower and the Thermonuclear Revo-lution," in John Lewis Gaddis et al., eds., *Cold War Statesmen Confront the Bomb: Nuclear Diplomacy Since 1945.* Oxford: Oxford University Press, 1999.

Engelhardt, Tom. *The End of Victory Culture: Cold War America and the Disillusioning of a Generation.* Boston: University of Massachusetts Press, 2008.

Hirano, Kyoko. *Mr. Smith Goes to Tokyo: Japanese Cinema Under the American Occupation, 1945-1952.* Washington, DC: Smithsonian Books, 1994.

Hiroshima press kit. New York: Continental Distributors, Inc., 1955.

Jacobs, Robert. "Reconstructing the Perpetrator's Soul by Reconstructing the Victim's Body: The Portrayal of the 'Hiroshima Maidens' by the Mainstream Media in the United States." *Intersections: Gender and Sexuality in Asia and the Pacific* 24, June 2010.

Knight, Arthur. "Hiroshima," *The Saturday Review,* 21 May 1955, 45.

Lowenstein, Adam. *Shocking Representation: Historical Trauma, National Cinema, and the Modern Horror Film.* New York: Columbia University Press, 2005.

Mainichi Shimbun, 6 August 1953.

Nornes, Abe Mark. *Japanese Documentary Film: The Meiji Era Through Hiroshima.* Minneapolis: University of Minnesota Press, 2003.

Poignant 1953 film on Hiroshima A-bomb returns after 6 decades." *The Asahi Shimbun*, 18 October 2012.

Richie, Donald. "'Mono no aware': Hiroshima in Film," in Mick Broderick, ed., *Hibakusha Cinema: Hiroshima, Nagasaki and the Nuclear Image in Japanese Cinema.* London: Kegan Paul, 1996, 20–37.

Schreiber, Mark. "Lucky Dragon's lethal catch." *The Japan Times*, 18 March 2012.

Sontag, Susan. "The Imagination of Disaster." *Against Interpretation.* New York: Farrar, Straus & Giroux, 1966.

Todeschini, Maya. "'Death and the Maiden': Female Hibakusha as Cultural Heroines, and the Politics of A-Bomb Memory," in Mick Broderick, ed., *Hibakusha Cinema: Hiroshima, Nagasaki and the Nuclear Image in Japanese Cinema.* London: Kegan Paul, 1996, 222–52.

Togawa, Naoki. "Hiroshima." *Kinema Junpō* 77, November 1953, pp. 68–69.

U.S. Department of State, Office of the Historian. "Atomic Diplomacy: Milestones 1945–52." https://history.state.gov/milestones/1945–1952/atomic.

The Shadow of the Bomb
in Hiroshi Teshigahara's
The Face of Another

TONY PRITCHARD

"At the same instant birds ignited in midair. Mosquitoes and flies, squirrels, family pets crackled and were gone. The fireball flashed an enormous photograph of the city at the instant of its immolation fixed on the mineral, vegetable and animal surfaces of the city itself."[1]

Photography rules over the figuring of the first atomic bombs used for military purposes at Hiroshima. From the incinerating flash to the misnamed atomic shadows produced by these blasts, the bombings consistently take on the tropes of photography. In contrast, accounts of the Trinity test do not contain these tropes to describe that initial nuclear blast—even though the test was subsequently analyzed by employing high-speed cameras to capture the event. While the scientists and military personnel at the Trinity site use the word "flash" in their recounting of the test, it is not spoken of as the flash of photography but as the standard flash of an explosive blast. Why does the A-bomb when used in war become euphemistically described as a photographic apparatus? Considering that photography served as a primary means of recording events during much of the twentieth century it logically follows that the images of the aftermath would be key for the world to understand the event—however many of these images were suppressed after the war. Perhaps this was because the atomic shadows were of the bodies of Japanese citizens, who were already constructed in the American mind as stereotypically possessing a passion for photography that such tropes worked. Bringing together the tropes of photography used to describe the event, as well as the suppression of photos of the event, it seems that the means of understanding the framing of the bombing of Hiroshima involves many of the difficulties in the reading images—because Hiroshima and Nagasaki exist for Americans not as events to be responsible for but instead as images produced by a military-industrial camera apparatus. Since Hiroshima and Nagasaki are figured in the American imagination like photography, including both the traditional images of war photography and the walls and other flat surfaces of the two cities that contain atomic shadows, examining this phenomenon necessitates looking at how works of photography and film have subsequently attempted to address the consequences of the bombing. Specifically Hiroshi Teshigahara in his film *The Face of Another* (*Tanin no kao*, 1966) employs a variety of cinematic strategies to delve into the construction of appearances in post-war Japanese society.

From scene to scene, *The Face of Another* purposely works against the standard tendencies of the cinematic apparatus to create a stable narrative. Techniques as varied as still images both in sequences alone, slow pacing, the use of mirrors and planes of glass in the mise en scène, canted frames, stage lighting, and wipes combine to destabilize the viewer throughout the film. Instead of having specific techniques establish the parameters of scenes through a stable diegesis in Teshigahara's film these techniques demonstrate the unsettled nature of the world. In Japan the film met with both critical and commercial success, but unlike Teshigahara's previous films *Pitfall* (*Otoshiana*, 1962) *and Woman in the Dunes* (*Suna no onna*, 1964) which had been acclaimed throughout the world, outside of the country it received little notoriety. While several reasons for the lack of success of this film outside of Japan have been put forward by scholars, one stands out because it has been rarely mentioned. As the film presents the contemporary Japanese psychic landscape after the bomb unflinchingly and the traumas produced by new technologies, *The Face of Another* presents the world with something it not only doesn't want to consider but something it cannot see.

James Quandt in his video essay on the film addresses many of the possible reasons for the film's reception outside of Japan.[2] Among these he notes the formal tension between Teshigahara's use of an older aspect ratio and the variety of contemporary art cinema techniques that he works within the film, the backlash against art cinema in the mid-sixties, and the way that the film complexly works with ideas of East and West. While Quandt gets very close to the curious dilemma surrounding the film, his euphemistic language with respect to the categories of East and West prevents a direct confrontation with the fact that Teshigahara's film does not present another case of existential malaise depicted in the cinema of the sixties but instead approaches the way in which the bombing and the repression of the bombing on a worldwide scale has severe psychic consequences for Japan and the rest of the world. The problems and unsettled historical accounts resist resolution because few dare to consider them in either dialogues or works of art. *The Face of Another* differs in that it boldly presents the concept that the most dangerous masks are the ones that we refuse to see, such as one that covers over the bombings of Nagasaki and Hiroshima by the United States—a fact that the cool reception of the film throughout the world further demonstrates.

In addressing the difficulty of thinking about images produced by technology, theorist Vilém Flusser puts forward the idea that such technical images challenge our abilities to employ critical thought because they employ critical thought in their production.[3] The business of taking a part of the world that consumes the energy of technological apparatuses works like taking a part of the world that consumes the energy of critical thinkers. With the A-bomb the distancing from understanding occurs at two distinct levels. First, the bomb creates an event that needs to be captured with technical images. Second, the bomb presents an event that produces its own technical images—the images burned onto surfaces by the A-bomb.

Addressing either of these two levels, or attempting to frame both of them within a paradigm created by critical thought, compounds the complexity of an already difficult situation to comprehend. Returning to the suppression of the most graphic of the images of the bombs' destruction and the unwillingness of the United States to think about the consequences of their actions results in the observation that beginning to understand Hiroshima and Nagasaki requires a consideration of how we remain unable and unequipped to read images. Seven decades later the U.S. still claims that the loss of military soldiers justifies the use of the A-bomb. Over the same time Japanese literature and film has approached the consequences while the rest of the world remains stunned and fumbling around for direction. But importantly, culturally the work of literature and film has involved a different focus. In American film and literature the bombing are nothing more than a means to victory regardless of the psychic and ecological damage caused.[4] Specifically, *The Face of Another* presents a film that audiences outside of Japan do not want to acknowledge because it presents something that is more complex than a simple binary. Binary thinking shapes American thought on the use of the atom bomb. In *The Face of Another*, Teshigahara places traps for the binary thinking of viewers to spring. In this way the film puts forward a test of its own regarding the ethics and morals of a post-bomb world. Such a test resists binary logic that results in disavowals and instead requires an approach where cinema's very relationship to images and appearances and the construction of illusions occupies the main focus. A result of such a search involves looking at how the power of cinema constructs the grand fiction of identity itself.

The film's strategy of using various techniques to destabilize the audience shapes the introduction to Okuyama (Tatsuya Nakadai), who first appears in a close up, filmed using x-ray film. In the place of the typical facial features, images of the maxilla and the mandible moving in synch with the dialogue fill the shot. The radioactive capturing of the main character eschews the display of a human face and instead provides a focus on the location of fillings in Okuyama's teeth. Within the technological-medical frame Okuyama's voice remains as the trace of his humanity. This voice narrates the particulars of the accident. Okuyama laments that his injuries, since they are the result of industrial accident, prevent him from being placed within pre-existing narratives that would redeem the event; he notes that "nobody remembers me even as a cautionary example."[5] Authority and meaning for events involving industry and technology does not occur at the human level because he is only an operator in a larger industrial system. Since he, like the victims of Hiroshima and Nagasaki, cannot be fixed into a meaningful position in the culture he sees responsibility as being outside of his existence. As a result he places the consequences of his actions with others. When discussing the experiment with the psychiatrist (Mikijirō Hira) Okuyama states, "Remember you will be the one responsible."[6] Additionally, in his encounters with his wife he continually reminds her that it is her fault for reacting to him in the way that she does. Okuyama lives within the logic of the world after the A-bomb, a world where the experimenters hold the final authority for decisions and outcomes; however the power of the experimenters in this world remains in check to the unpredictabilities resulting from the testing situation itself.

Okuyama's desire to participate in the experiment pushes the psychiatrist to overcome his own doubts about the potential far-reaching consequences of the experiment and offer the mask to Okuyama. Where once the limits of the test might have stayed the hand of the experimenter, now the regimes of testing that hold sway in the wake of the bomb push it forward with the slightest force of desire. Avital Ronell in her work on test delineates the consequences of such a shift:

> With the spread of technology, testing lost some of its auratic and exceptional qualities and started hitting everyone with its demands, that is, anyone who wanted to gain admission anywhere, and all institutions started testing to let you in and let you out. If something weird happens, you are taken in for psychiatric testing. Technological warfare belongs to the domain of testing as well, and does much to support the thesis that there is little difference between testing and the real thing. To the extent that testing counts as warfare today, it marks the steady elimination of boundaries between weapons testing and their deployment.[7]

After experimenters pose questions that concern the end of all life on the planet as a possible outcome and such questions fail to slow or delay the test, the types of questions that researchers subsequently ask are destined to raise the stakes of the inquiry and the danger to all. Once the shift between testing and deployment results in a city becoming a test site the logic of testing becomes the dominant course.

Prosthesis frames the film's opening. Early in the film a voiceover speaks to the viewer and poses questions about the images on screen. This voice cements its authority over the viewer by stating, "You have no idea."[8] The psychologist who narrates from an indeterminate location in space and time reminding the audience that they remain in the dark as to what appears on screen. Finally the voice informs that the images present "an inferiority complex in the shape of a finger … that digs holes in psyches and has to be filled in."[9] The doctor's viewpoint presents logic of authority in this film that informs and fills everything with a specific type of meaning. The shots of disembodied parts floating in his tank recall these past atrocities. Haunted by the logic that all prostheses involve a psychic hole the doctor fears that his creation the mask will make us all strangers to each other and radically alter society. Such a fear is a stand in for the bomb, which has already brought forth such a transformation—however only to those willing to see it and think about it. Along these fractures in the doctor's assertions and fears a course is plotted in the film between relief of solitude and the curse of alienation.

Much of the film takes place in the psychiatrist's office that contains panes of glass and mirrors that work as screens that measure and distort the human body within the confines of scientific experimentation. Visual complexity abounds in this environment since the reflective surfaces make it difficult to establish the parameters of the room. From the voice over at the film's outset to the final scene where the doctor's vision of reality is transformed by his creation, the lab and its productions demonstrate how in the factories of illusion the line between real and fantasy does not play a role of normalizing. As a factory for the construction and maintenance of illusions the office works as a means of presenting traps to those who enter into it. As a director Teshigahara exploits these planes as a barrier between two characters or to reveal the way in which they work as a specific framing device.

Full shots of Okuyama's burned face appear only for brief moments throughout the film. At fifteen minutes into the film a first shot of his face occurs. A crane shot shows his head from above and does not allow for the viewer to look directly at his face. During the construction of the mask Okuyama's burned face appears in a brief profile obscured by the flasks in the doctor's lab. This equipment distorts Okuyama's image from the viewer not simply in the traditional logic of horror films where the narrative requires that that audience see the monster at the last possible moment but more specifically so that the burned face does not appear as a surface for the audience to form a human attachment. Literally the technology that creates the mask obscures and distorts Okuyama's face. Such a decision on the part of Teshigahara to present his main character blocks the viewer from identifying with Okuyama's point of view prior to his wearing of the mask. From the film's outset where the doctor's voice claims that his patients' psyches require prostheses to fill the holes within them the power of the narrative resides with the authority of science and technology—that is until Okuyama puts on the mask.

The mask is a device that has taken the power of the technological and fused it with the human sensory apparatus. The result of this experiment radically alters Okuyama's nervous system by isolating him from wind and other sensations touching the nerves of his face. The mask creates a physical barrier that blocks air from Okuyama's face—he cannot feel wind and becomes subject to his skin possibly suffocating underneath the mask if it is worn for more than twelve hours at a time. To capture the initial scenes with the mask Teshigahara borrows from the construction of Chris Marker's *La Jette* (1962) by using still images to emphasize moments and short sequences to mirror the shift in Okuyama's personality. The fragmentation brought about as the mask shifts Okuyama into his new situation works as a rebirth in the film that requires a different cinematic logic from the rest of the film. As he shops for new housewares a sequence of stills presents his choices for furnishing his new life.[10] Since he cannot feel air while wearing the mask, his perceptual world contains a degree of stillness, which further detach his from the outside world. By wearing the mask he enters a world of one.

　　Flusser, in discussing forms, puts forward a consequence of our present world regarding the ability to fashion new worlds:

> Take a form, any form, in fact any algorithm that can be expresses numerically. Feed this form via a computer into a plotter. Stuff the form thus created as complete as possible with particles. And there you have it: worlds ready to serve. Every one of these worlds is just as real as the central nervous system (at least the one we have had so far), providing it manages to stuff the forms just as full as the central nervous system does.[11]

Enabled by the mask, a new life becomes possible for Okuyama. New problems come with the creation of a new world. The world of apparatuses possesses unique motives, ones that do not necessarily match with humanity's motives. Instead the world of apparatuses works according to the motives of critical thought run wild—a world broken down by linear thought. With the advent of the photographic apparatus the problem of understanding a product of critical thought (photography) by using critical thought fails time and again. As Vilem Flusser observes, "photography and other technical images" place "critical thinking … in crisis."[12] Resulting from this crisis the reading and understanding the works of apparatuses requires the exploration and development of new criteria to meet these challenges. Okuyama feels that he can use the old world's criteria of truth as a means of using the mask to test his wife, when instead the test results in a display of his own lack of faith in his wife. The realm of images produced by technology cannot use the previous barometers.

　　Throughout the film as he returns to the psychiatrist's office the mirrors and glass walls display how reflections and screens form the predominant way of interacting with others presently. The fragmented human body with all of its parts spread out throughout the lab on tables presents a series of endless tableaux reminiscent of the carnage of war as to demonstrate that in this world the body can be taken apart and put back together with little concern to the consequences of interpersonal relationships and identity. For Okuyama such malleability becomes a key component of his life with the mask. His plan to be able to work away from the workplace provides a glimpse of a future that many presently live. As he tells his supervisor, "from now on I'll exist via telephone calls, documents, letters." While in the film this seems to be the only way for him to continue working it also provides the freedom to live his double life with the mask. Presently this is the way that many of us exist in our work and social media lives. "Name, work … my bandaged self will take care of that," observes Okuyama in explaining his plan to the psychiatrist. The labor of earning money once outsourced to the former life allows the mask to be set aside for attempting to live a life like that of others. The mask does not result in efficiency but instead acts as a life behind the back of the bandaged life that Okuyama can't live.

"You on the other hand don't have to be anybody," observes the psychiatrist when comparing his own life to that of Okuyama. Such an alibi mirrors the one put forward by the United States for using the atom bomb. The United States didn't have to be responsible, as it existed in a singular position as sole nation possessing the technology—it had no interlocutor to respond to. Like Okuyama with the mask, the U.S. lived alone in a singular world after using the bomb during war—thankfully for the world it remains alone. The key problem as shown above concerns how entering into such a world voids all previous social and ethical contracts. The first one to pass into a new technological realm has no equal to look upon or no other to produce challenges. The psychiatrist remarks in his observations on the "world without friends and family" resulting from widespread use of mask comes closest to linking the fictional world with the actual post-war world: "Suspicion and betrayal would no longer be possible." Okuyama's idea that putting on a mask will open up an opportunity for revenge runs counter to these observations of the psychiatrist about the mask. Okuyama's naive views on identity nature take the form of his determined insistence that his essential identity will never change.

The structure of the shots in the first application of the mask demonstrates that the mask obliterates the former bandaged Okuyama. As the psychiatrist explains about how the mask will change its wearer, Teshigahara employs a series of quick pans and odd tilts to fragment the already complicated space of the office. Specifically there occurs in the sequence a fixed shot that then appears to float counter-clockwise. At this moment in the film the cocktail of a narcotic and a sedative appear to take effect on Okuyama and shift his perception of his self. Much like Teshigahara demonstrates the psychic states of the patients by using the framing of the office lab as a contrasting space for their imagining in the film here the setting and its reflective surfaces contrasts with how Okuyama transitions between his previous identity and his new one with the mask.

The film features numerous repetitions that show Okuyama's dual life. Of these scenes there are two with the superintendent (Minoru Chiaki) of the apartment building where Okuyama rents two apartments, one for his bandaged self and one for his life with the mask, that provide the most direct contrast. Upon arriving at the apartment complex he encounters the superintendent's developmentally disabled daughter (Etsuko Ichihara) who claims to be the superintendent. After this ruse he knocks on the superintendent's door and sets into motion the first of two identically composed scenes. The sole difference between the scenes occurs in the reaction of the superintendent to Okuyama. In the first scene the timid character of the superintendent recoils when he opens the door to the sight of the bandaged man. While the superintendent shows the apartment he stares at the bandages each time Okuyama turns to inspect the place. The second scene while composed of the same shots contains different reactions from the superintendent. With the mask Okuyama does not frighten or shock the superintendent, who goes through what appears to be his standard routine of showing an apartment. After this second scene with the superintendent Okuyama shows how he develops with the mask. Staring into the mirror Okuyama takes the mask for a test drive by making a variety of faces. This scene displays the first time in a great while that he has looked at his face and contemplated it. His rebirth continues as he tests what this mask can do in the privacy of his second apartment. Solitude allows for him to consider the possibilities he can select from to inhabit the mask.

Despite his overwhelming faith in the mask's ability to conceal his identity the superintendent's daughter recognizes him when she comes to the door of his bandaged identity asking for him to give her a yo-yo that his masked self had promised her. The encounter sends him into a panic. Never once does he consider that the encounter could be the result of a simple mistake, since the superintendent's daughter appears to constantly pester the tenants about her yo-yo it is possible that she was going around the whole building asking all the residents for a yo-yo. A shaken Okuyama returns to the doctor with the complaint that the mask does not work. The doctor dismisses Okuyama's claims by observing that since the girl is mentally diminished she potentially uses other senses, like a dog uses the sense of smell, to identify people. The psychiatrist's answer intimates that the processing of faces is a higher-level function in humans. Such a conclusion quells the patient's worries and then the good doctor urges Okuyama to test the mask on someone that he knows. Since the mask itself bears the markings of the technological world at this point in the film it needs the voice of authority to provide the context to justify its further use. Additionally by the voice of scientific reason assigning of the superintendent's daughter to a lower register of human existence, her voice and viewpoint can be disregarded. As a consequence of this move her view of life or events is diminished in its importance. Even though the logic of testing dominates the mask's use in this early phase the fact that Okuyama remains disconnected from his senses similarly places him in a realm of "diminished capacity" never appears after he puts on the mask.

Okuyama's interactions with his wife (Machiko Kyō) demonstrate how the accident places him outside of the domestic relationship and into unfamiliar territory. Teshigahara introduces her with a shot that focuses on the polishing of a gem that contains a close up of only her fingers. In the scene Okuyama assaults her with questions to which she can never provide an answer that satisfies him. His questions demonstrate how the logic of the experiment follows him home. Up to the point in the film where he puts on the mask Okuyama pursues a singular strategy to disarm those who he speaks with in personal interactions. The strategy simply involves Okuyama stating whatever he thinks or he assumes that others are thinking of him. Repeated throughout the first half of the film is the following pattern: Okuyama puts forward his existential dilemma and then his addressee counters with the advice that he should stop tormenting himself with such thoughts—as though this advice were able to be heeded by Okuyama. All who speak to Okuyama do not see anything of value in dwelling upon an accident and subsequently Okuyama retreats further into himself after each encounter. Consequently, these scenes put forward the popular belief that can survive any atrocity as long as decorum and manners remain intact. In contrast to this, the film's efforts to destabilize force the viewer into multiple positions that offer glimpses of the problems that result from a world unable and unwilling to face the psychic aftermath of the bomb.

Much of the first scene with Mrs. Okuyama presents a seated Okuyama facing the camera with his wife behind him. He, in what seems to be part of a nightly denigration of his wife, insists that the face-to-face position remains too uncomfortable for his wife to bear. The selection of this shot for the viewer's location with its attention of the focus on the main character and relegating of his wife to the background results in the conversation quickly mutating into a monologue. "Civilization demands light … a man with no face is free only when darkness rules the world," begins Okuyama's speech.[13] Light, which is necessary for civilization, becomes transformed in the monologue connecting it to the blasts at Nagasaki and Hiroshima—blasts that brought the power of the sun to the surface of the earth. The darkness resulting after the bomb's flash results as a simple fact and provides a world for Okuyama to rule with his mask.

In another scene in the film depicting the couple's nightly conversations Okuyama asks his wife, "I wonder if we see the true face of a gem when it is rough or polished?"[14] She does not want to answer this question because she feels it to be another of her husband's traps. Instead she plies him with a counter question about the reasons behind women's makeup. In this key scene in their relationship he is not able to fathom the ways in which his wife does not operate according to a binary way of thinking.

During the time of the *Tale of Genji* (*Genji monogatari*, written by Murasaki Shikibu) women believed it to be ideal to hide their faces that is why only black hair is mentioned. A woman's face is always hidden. "As long as a woman is a woman her face isn't worth showing without makeup."[15] Okuyama remains blind to the fact that for women masks are always present. Potentially such a fact exists as one that he does not want to face because the consequence would be that he has become feminized.

The constantly under-estimated Mrs. Okuyama provides the location for passing the test of the film—but not the test set up by her husband. Okuyama builds a test informed by binary thinking. In a scene early in the "seduction" she sits at a booth in a restaurant with her husband. Kyō's performance in this scene has her don facial reactions that clearly show that her husband has not fooled her—even though he has certainly fooled himself. Like the previous scenes between the two characters a clear imbalance between the motives of the characters exists. While Mrs. Okuyama reads the seduction as her husband's attempt to behave as her husband again, for Mr. Okuyama revenge never ceases to be the only goal. The act of playing at seduction takes a secondary place for her to her hopes for his future intention. Sadly, his test reveals about his actual opinion of her.

Throughout the remainder of the seduction this discontinuity of viewpoints builds to the tragic conclusion. As the two prepare to enter the apartment building the superintendent's daughter accosts Okuyama about her yo-yo, which he gives to her. Mrs. Okuyama views the giving of the yo-yo as evidence of her husband reforming and re-entering society. For Okuyama the motive of the gift is to simply keep the secret of his multiple identities intact. The dialogue once the two of them are in the apartment continues to keep the two viewpoints separate. She notes that "we must respect appearances" in response to his concerns about the seriousness of the situation. In this scene Mrs. Okuyama makes an observation that marks the ethics of the world after the bomb: "I have so many selves I can't contain them all."[16] The incommensurability of the situation remains lost upon him as well as the capability to empathize, understand or listen to what his wife says to him. Presently many start relationships much similar to how Okuyama sets up his test by stalking the person first on social media and then proceeding to "seduce" them. In our current moment seduction is nothing more than cheating at the game of love to arrive at interpersonal relationships determined by algorithms of compatibility—where all that is left to do is to actually play them out.

After the seduction she reveals her own disappointment in his motives for using the mask and how they do not match what she had hoped: "I thought we must try to keep the masks on."[17] Realizing the reality of the situation shatters him and fully places him outside of everyone. Mrs. Okuyama states before leaving that "pretending that the mask is your real face … that I cannot accept."[18] After his wife flees he sits in the apartment with the mask half-on and half-off. Teshigahara composes these shots to place the deformation of the mask at the center of the frame illustrating Okuyama's in-between status as he shifts from being an avenging husband to a nobody.

Mrs. Okuyama's approach to the mask is to face the mask and to use it to get her husband back. She violates the old code of truth to do this—even though she realizes it is her husband under the mask. Like the task of one facing the photograph involves the development of "new criteria, to critique the myths projected into the world by photographs and the particular magic that results from photography."[19] Mrs. Okuyama attempts to get behind the magic and myths that are features of the mask for her husband.

The soul is what appears to be trapped in Okuyama's view of the world. Similarly, after the war there was no means by which the face of Japan could be seen as anything but a colonized and occupied space. There was no recognition of what happened. The occupation put a waiting period on not only mourning the dead but in recognizing the events that took place. The world changed but the simple fact of that change could not be spoken of or considered as anything else but the right of those who had made the decision. How can anything but a fable or a myth survive here? But it is not constructed specifically in the way that other myths have been.

Teshigahara chooses to introduce the Girl with the Scar (Miki Irie) by transitioning from the main narrative via a soft wipe to a shot of her in profile as she walks down the street. As she moves through the scene catcalls come from off-screen. In this other section of the film Teshigahara adopts a radically different cinematic strategy from that of the main film. Unlike the main story where Okukama's face only appears on screen briefly or obscured by the angle of framing, in this story the girl's face appears in close ups and still frames. Specifically in this first scene when she pauses to respond to her suitors the director shows her face in a still frame close up accompanied by voices of the disgusted men who only seconds before had been admiring her beauty. In this introductory section the injury to her face disrupts the narrative of the film by calling attention to the separation of sound and image. Those who encountered her have to mark her as different and disrupt the newly established narrative thread. The reaction of the men never pauses to consider what has been done to both her and Japan as result of the A-bomb but instead passes straight to disgust and repulsion. Her face in its presentation here operates in a different cinematic language one that works to solidify what other's think of her. Unlike the Duke of Urbino who was able to order that the disfigured side of his face was never to be depicted in art, the Girl with the Scar can only use her hair to temporarily cover over her wounds, which sadly define her. If only she could get free from the pre-existing structures there might be a different outcome. Unlike Okuyama, the option of playing at other identities never opens for her. Where the mask offers a deferral to the authority of science and technology she remains within the structure of family. Her brother remains the point of authority, however his authority only offers reassurances of the closeness of a new war. The structure of the family offers her and her brother few options in this new world. In her stories film's seduction scene she tries her brother's beer and cigarette as a means to find another role. She coughs after smoking and chokes after drinking and fails to find any role but that of little sister. Ultimately she and her brother who Teshigahara frames as being the last survivors of the old world engage in incest. Upon waking the brother finds his sister's suicide note and gazes out the window to see the waves take her. The light of the sun turns his body into an animal carcass recalling the work of Francis Bacon:

> When you go into a butcher's shop and see how beautiful meat can be and then you think about it, you can think of the whole horror of life—of one thing living off another. It's like all those stupid things that are said about bull-fighting. Because people will go in and complain about bull-fighting covered with furs and with birds in their hair.[20]

The result of this narrative thread we see how easily the bodies of humans can be transformed by light and relegated to a non-human state. The narratives are not meant to intertwine they cannot and must not. *The Face of Another* looks at how Japan has been irrevocably changed by the A-bomb. No other nation has experienced what they as a nation have experienced. This is why the film works for the Japanese but not for other countries. Okuyama presents a test case for how to move forward while the Girl with the Scar offers how the views of the past no longer fits in the changed world. If a lack of shared experience were the only factor influencing the reception of the film it might have been different however the presence of an overall unwillingness by the rest of the world to see how the A-bomb augmented the otherness or alterity of Japan results in film's cold reception.

The film exists much like Okuyama's view of the world in that both present something that disarms an audience as a means of challenging what isn't thought or spoken. What the film tries to do it fails at doing—because the world cannot look the Japanese in the face after the A-bomb. Specifically in the work of Emmanuel Levinas the human face works as the fundamental site for the ethics. Levinas's thinking provides insight into the changing scope life brought about with the dropping of the atom bomb.

Consciousness of self outside of self confers a primordial function to the language that links us with the outside. It also leads to the destruction of language. We can no longer speak, not because we do not know our interlocutor, but because we can no longer take his words seriously, for his interiority is purely epiphenomenal. We are not satisfied with his revelations, which we take to be superficial data, a deceitful appearance unaware that it is lying. No one is identical to himself. Beings have no identity. Faces are masks. Behind the faces that speak to us and to whom we speak, we look for the clockwork and microscopic springs of souls.[21]

In Teshigahara's film the play of identity tries to offer a way to live in the shadow of the bomb. However the climate that produces the mask also produces suspicion and doubt—these form the fear of the doctor that he views in the film's final scene. The film presents at least three distinct Okuyama's on screen and perhaps five in total that are presented by the narrative of the film. On screen we encounter an Okuyama as changed by the accident, a masked one who plans to use the mask for revenge, and the one who after the failed revenge becomes a "nobody." Additionally the narrative allows for us to consider both the Okuyama prior to the accident and the character after the murder of the doctor. These five options make it difficult to simply talk about the film in terms of doubles reducible to a binary logic. Teshigahara uses doubling in the film to bait a particular trap for viewers. The viewer either falls into the trap and stays there or like Mrs. Okuyama opens to the reality of possessing a number of identities beyond containment. Ultimately the problem with Okuyama resides in the way that he cannot connect with anyone.

Teshigahara uses then theme of isolation to frame the film by using images of faces at the beginning and masked faces at the ending. These faces demonstrate that after the bomb there is nothing about identity that remains to be important. In the world of apparatuses people are used up. As Flusser notes: "envisoners don't stand over apparatuses that way a writer stands over a typewriter; they stand right in among them, with them, surrounded by them."[22] The problem with the events of Hiroshima and Nagasaki is that it is near impossible to stand within the apparatus and survive.

When J. Robert Oppenheimer put forward his famous quote at the Trinity site he realized his own role in fundamentally changing the world. Events that change everything often resist our ability to share them with others. However the events of testing and using a nuclear bomb are potentially the biggest ones that have taken place and ones that we are still unable to even begin to consider in terms of consequences. At the test site there were a variety of reactions to the test. How does one react to a world-changing event? If one is responsible for the event there is no precedent on how to face the consequences. In an instant everything changed on the planet. Operating as it does a full two decades after the use of the atomic bomb *The Face of Another* presents the difficulty of dealing with both the consequences of the A-bomb and the unwillingness of the world to recognize what happened to Japan. The inability for the film to be received outside of Japan relies not on any technical or aesthetic fault of the film or its director but more specifically on the fact that it presents a face that the world generally, and one that Americans still actively, disavow after seven decades.

Notes

1. R. Rhodes, *The Making of the Atomic Bomb* (New York: Simon & Schuster, 1986), p. 715.
2. J. Quant, *The Face of Another* (New York: Criterion Collection, 2007).
3. V. Flusser, *Writings* (Minneapolis: University of Minnesota Press, 2002), pp. 75–84.
4. Two recent examples of this are the reaction to the news of contamination at the decommissioned Hanford site in early 2013 and the appalling reactions of many Americans to the tsunami and Fukishima meltdown on social media.
5. H. Teshigahara, *The Face of Another* (New York: Criterion Collection, 2007).
6. *Ibid.*
7. A. Ronell, *The ÜberReader* (Urbana: University of Illinois Press, 2008), pp. 298–9.
8. H. Teshigahara, *The Face of Another* (New York: Criterion Collection, 2007).
9. *Ibid.*
10. It becomes clear later in the film that the mask makes these choices and fills the apartment.
11. V. Flusser, *The Shape of Things* (London: Reaktion, 1999), p. 37.
12. V. Flusser, *Writings* (Minneapolis: University of Minnesota Press, 2002), p. 44.
13. H. Teshigahara, *The Face of Another* (New York: Criterion Collection, 2007).
14. *Ibid.*
15. *Ibid.*
16. *Ibid.*
17. *Ibid.*
18. *Ibid.*
19. V. Flusser, *Writings* (Minneapolis: University of Minnesota Press, 2002), p. 44.
20. D. Sylvester, *Interviews with Francis Bacon* (London: Thames and Hudson, 1975), p. 46.
21. E. Levinas, *Entre nous: Thinking-of-the-Other* (New York: University of Columbia Press, 1998), p. 24–5.
22. V. Flusser, *The Shape of Things* (London: Reaktion, 1999), p. 36.

Bibliography

Flusser, Vilém. *The Shape of Things*. London: Reaktion, 1999.
_____. *Writings*. Minneapolis: University of Minnesota Press, 2002.
Levinas, Emmanuel. *Entre nous: Thinking-of-the-Other*. New York: University of Columbia Press, 1998.
Quandt, James. *The Face of Another*. New York: Criterion Collection, 2007.
Rhodes, Richard. *The Making of the Atomic Bomb*. New York: Simon & Schuster, 1986.
Ronell, Avital. *The ÜberReader*. Urbana: University of Illinois Press, 2008.
Sylvester, David. *Interviews with Francis Bacon*. London: Thames and Hudson, 1975.
Teshigahara, Hiroshi. *The Face of Another*. New York: Criterion Collection, 2007.

Nuclear Skin: Hiroshima and the Critique of Embodiment in *Affairs Within Walls*

Julia Alekseyeva

Kōji Wakamatsu's 1965 Pink Film *Affairs Within Walls* (*Kabe no naka no himegoto*) is well known for giving a certain respectability to a genre which had formerly been held in low esteem; the film was submitted to the Berlin Film Festival—predictably, to the great shame of the Japanese government—without the endorsement of Eiren, the Motion Picture Producers Association of Japan. Eiren was dominated by the major studios, and therefore did not recommend independently produced films to international film festivals.[1] Though the film did not by itself revolutionize Pink Film, it did lend the genre a great deal of credibility, showing its aesthetic and political potential to future writers and directors. Although the history of its *succès de scandale* is well known, the film's challenging formal elements, and charged political content, is less discussed—such as the film's most provocative element: a man with a keloid scar from Hiroshima, and therefore an embodiment of the atomic bomb.

In the first few minutes of *Affairs Within Walls* (aka *Secrets Behind the Walls* and *Skeletons in the Closet*), this scarred, lesion-filled body is caressed by a housewife (then still a student activist) in front of an enormous portrait of Stalin. While making love, she states, "You are the symbol of Hiroshima, the symbol of Japan. The symbol of anti-war. I am so happy.... I love you, in order to not forget the war." At first, the use of Hiroshima in the context of Pink Film—a genre of sexploitation films, tailored to a primarily male audience and shown in specialized theaters[2]—might seem surprising; after all, keloid scars are hardly titillating. However, such political symbolism is fairly common in Pink Film, and especially in Wakamatsu's films, in which questions of sexuality, identity, and politics are so often conflated.[3] For the housewife Nobuko who becomes one of the film's protagonists, her keloid-scarred lover Nagai, a boyfriend from her student protest days, becomes an embodiment of Japan's national trauma.[4]

Interestingly, although Wakamatsu could have used this virtual embodiment of Hiroshima as a way of eliciting emotion from the viewer, Wakamatsu frustrates the audience's desire to place the film within a certain standard politico-ethical narrative. In fact, he criticizes this desire for an embodied Hiroshima—for instance, by including the ominous portrait of Stalin behind the two lovers' bodies. This scene is a flashback sequence[5] from the student protest movements in the early '50s, before Stalin's death and the thaw, and before the extent of Stalin's horrifying policies was known to the general public. Therefore, to include a Stalin portrait in a film from 1965 is to place the events unfolding on screen within quotation marks; a critique is always implicit. For *Affairs Within Walls*, what results is a much more ambiguous film which veers away, like Nagisa Ōshima's *Night and Fog in Japan* (1960), from the Stalinist policies of the Old Left: both Wakamatsu and Ōshima's films place the tactics of the old generation into conversation with the new.

In a similarly critical vein, the mise-en-scène of *Affairs Within Walls* contrasts this first lovers' scene with the scenes unfolding afterwards, all of which revolve around the goings-on of *danchi* tenants. As we shall see, Wakamatsu moves away from emotional engagement in his portrayal of two lovers' bodies, and presents us with a *critique* of certain theories of embodiment—theories such as Vivian Sobchack's theory of embodied spectatorship, or Laura Marks's haptic visuality. Instead, Wakamatsu uses distancing techniques and a more static camera. The bulk of the film is decidedly non-fleshly, focusing on voyeuristic gazes and geometric framing. As we shall see, this critique of embodiment has larger implications for the genre of Pink Film as a whole: tailored for the exclusively male gaze, Pink Film sets itself in direct opposition to what can be interpreted as a feminine embodiment. This essay will juxtapose these theories of embodiment with the formal aspects of Wakamatsu's film to discover wherein his critique resides, and will briefly compare the portrayal of Hiroshima in *Affairs Within Walls* with perhaps the most famous filmic representation of Hiroshima—Alain Resnais's *Hiroshima mon amour* (1959), and will conclude with a brief discussion of the possible misogynistic qualities of Pink Film's formal elements, and the theoretical implications that a critique of embodiment entails.

First, it is necessary to trace the types of embodiment that Wakamatsu is trying to refute; although Sobchack and Marks began writing their theories of phenomenology, spectatorship, and the haptic more than a quarter century after *Affairs Within Walls*, their concepts summarize exactly the modes of filming and viewing that it can be claimed that Wakamatsu is trying to avoid, thus making a brief summary of their arguments useful. Although Sobchack's theory focuses more on the sensations of a film's spectator and an embodied experience of filmic viewing, and although Laura Marks's analysis is centered in a film's potential for a "haptic" visuality which calls upon the sense of touch rather than optics, both are modes of viewing which dissolve a separation between self and screen and are based upon *affect*. Here, affect is similar to Brian Massumi's definition, drawn from the writings of Deleuze and Guattari: "a pre-personal intensity corresponding to the passage from one experiential state of the body to another, and implying an augmentation or diminution in that body's capacity to act."[6] In their writings on cinema, both Marks and Sobchack propose a mode of viewership based on this same pre-personal intensity, which is unconscious, unformed, and unstructured.[7] In contrast to emotion, which Massumi claims is the broadcast or display of a feeling into the social world, or feeling, a sensation checked against previous experiences and already labeled, affect has a certain revolutionary potential. In the words of Eric Souse, "affect is what makes feelings feel."[8] However, this visceral, embodied connection to the screen, and, in Wakamatsu's case, the potential for an embodied connection to the A-bomb attack on Hiroshima, is hinted at but inevitably frustrated by the formal devices of *Affairs Within Walls*.

To begin with one potential for embodiment, Vivian Sobchack, for whom embodied spectatorship becomes an ethical aesthetics, posits that "the subjective lived body and the objective world do not oppose each other but, on the contrary, are passionately intertwined."[9] For Sobchack, then, the viewer of a film enters into an interobjective relationship with the screen—"passionately intertwined" with it. What results is, in the vein of Hannah Arendt and drawing from the writings of phenomenologist Maurice Merleau-Ponty, a "passionate devotion to the world" in which the world's "flesh"—its materiality—is enfolded within our own "*senses and with feeling*."[10] Marks writes that this relationship is fundamentally mimetic for Sobchack, in the sense that meaning is not solely communicated through signs but experienced in the body: "The phenomenological model of subjectivity posits a mutual permeability and mutual creation of self and other. Cinema spectatorship is a special example of this enfolding of self and world, an intensified instance of the way our perceptions open us onto the world."[11]

This mode of spectatorship is thus mutually permeable, an "enfolding of self and world" that dissolves the boundary between self and screen. Sharing this desire for a potential passionate involvement with the world through cinema, Marks claims that mimesis—like Henri Bergson's concept of memory—is inherently inscribed in the body,[12] thus making both Marks' and Sobchack's theories a *mimetic* model of film spectatorship that enfolds the events on screen within the viewer's emotions, consciousness, and physical body.

Laura Marks, however, takes this mimetic model a step further by emphasizing the cinematographic elements in films which consciously incite a more embodied mode of spectatorship. While Sobchack's ethics-driven aesthetics is more subjective—Sobchack does not claim that everyone shares her embodied, visceral response to a particular director's (such as Robert Bresson's) films—Marks claims that certain films elicit a "haptic visuality" that leads to a more yielding and porous relationship between self and other, between spectator and screen.[13] Films might evoke this sense of tactility by emphasizing shots of skin or especially hands touching skin (which many erotic, pornographic, and Pink Films in fact do), or by moving the camera in a grazing, loose way which mimics the way our hands move, rather than our eyes. Marks writes: "In haptic *visuality*,[14] the eyes themselves function like organs of touch…. Haptic looking tends to move over the surface of its object rather than to plunge into illusionistic depth, not to distinguish form so much as to discern texture. It is more inclined to move than to focus, more inclined to graze than to gaze."[15] Thus a haptic visuality is inherent in the film's formal elements, in which the camera appears to "touch" the object it is filming, rather than "focusing" in on it. One example is a sequence in Rossellini's *Viaggio in Italia* (1954) in which the camera, taking upon Ingrid Bergman's tourist character's fascination with Roman ruins, slowly "grazes" (to use Marks's term) around the ancient statues in a Naples Museum in a subtly erotic fashion, following the movements of Bergman's eyes. It is no coincidence, then, that haptic visuality is often erotic by nature, evoking the viewer's desire for the image on screen:

> Haptic images are erotic in that they construct an intersubjective relationship between beholder and image. The viewer is called upon to fill in the gaps in the image, to engage with the traces the image leaves. By interacting up close with an image, close enough that figure and ground commingle, the viewer relinquishes her own sense of separateness from the image—not to know it, but to give herself up to her desire for it.[16]

The porous construction of haptic images invites the viewer to "fill in the gaps," to interact with them in a penetrating way that can only be described as erotic. Thus, when the wall between screen and flesh is dropped, and when consciousness and film, the viewer's sense of touch and the objects on screen, commingle, what results is a sexualized mode of film spectatorship. For this reason, generic soft-core pornography in America and Europe is often filmed in lush soft-focus,[17] to emphasize the haptic over the optical.[18] Indeed, "It is hard to look closely at a lover's skin with optical vision," writes Marks, implying that all romantic encounter is viewed haptically rather than optically—an unwritten rule which the fragmented, optical visualities inherent to Pink Film, and Wakamatsu's Pink films in particular, refuse to follow.

To return to Wakamatsu's film, the aforementioned first sequence of *Affairs Within Walls*—a flashback of a housewife caressing her lover's keloid-scarred body in front of a portrait of Stalin—at first appears to follow the mode of haptic visuality. Scenes of hands touching flesh abound, with the scarred flesh from Hiroshima given particular attention. We see Nobuko, the female protagonist, caressing the keloid with both hands and lips, in close-up. Filmed mostly in soft focus, the scene is accompanied by a cello's brooding, low notes, contributing to the eroticism. The viewer is denied a total view of the two bodies, instead focusing on hands traveling around flesh—exactly the haptic visuality described by Marks. This sequence, especially the many shots of elbows, hands, and shoulders, is an explicit reference to French New Wave filmmaker Resnais's *Hiroshima mon amour*, a hugely acclaimed film which Wakamatsu would have inevitably seen.[19] *Hiroshima mon amour* begins with an emphasis on haptic visuality, in which two bodies embrace, filmed from exactly the same angle as *Affairs Within Walls*—a comparison to which we will later return.

Next, Nagai, the Hiroshima victim embraced by Nobuko, states, "The keloid has become a part of me. Radiation will flow through my body forever," thus emphasizing the complete embodiment of the A-bomb within the flesh of this one body—a body that, according to this man, can die at any moment, a kind of nuclear skin, or a bomb capable of exploding at any time. After this, as the couple continue their lovemaking, Nobuko closes her eyes, while the mushroom cloud of Hiroshima is superimposed upon her face as a transparent screen, so that she appears to fantasize about the atomic bomb in the middle of her sexual encounter. The atomic bomb then transitions into documentary footage from the student peace protests of the early '50s in Japan. Sex and politics blur for Nobuko, whose obsession with her lover's keloid scar, and her devotion to "the struggle" reach such heights that they become a sexual fetish; indeed, for her, the scar is itself a fetish object. Here, her conflation of political imagery with the sexual act approach what Sobchack might call an interobjectivity of flesh and screen, certainly a literalization of a "passionate devotion to the world" which has a certain ethical potential.

Clearly, this early sequence from *Affairs Within Walls* is meant to offer a mode of haptic visuality, a Stalinist soft-core porno in which the viewer, following Nobuko's hands, caresses the *Hibakusha*'s flesh and feels herself embracing not only another's flesh, but a political protest movement in its entirety. And alluding to the famous first sequence in *Hiroshima mon amour*, of course, only contributes to this sequence's haptic visuality. However, and most importantly, this scene contrasts greatly with both the tone and framing devices used in the rest of the film. Wakamatsu offers the viewer haptic visuality on a silver platter, seemingly allowing her[20] to, in Marks's words, "give herself up to the desire for it"—but then wrests this hapticity away at the last moment. In fact, what *Affairs Within Walls* offers us is not an embodied, haptic mode of feeling, but a critical distancing and a reliance

Opposite, top: **Nobuko caresses her lover's keloid scarred back in front of a portrait of Stalin. Controversial imagery from Wakamatsu's** *Affair Within Walls.* *Middle:* **In this shot, Wakamatsu denies the viewer a total view of the two bodies, instead focusing on hands traveling around flesh—exactly the haptic visuality described by Marks.** *Bottom:* *Hiroshima mon amour* **begins with an emphasis on haptic visuality, in which two bodies embrace, filmed from exactly the same angle as** *Affairs Within Walls.*

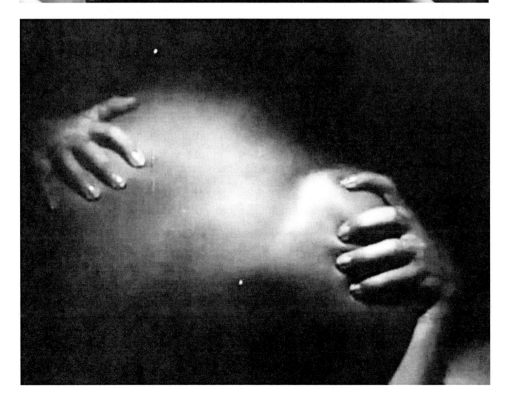

on *optics*. Importantly, the first image of the film is not Nobuko and the *Hibakusha* but an eye—the eye of Makoto, a judging eye. Makoto, a *ronin* or exam failure spending all year studying for the next year's exams, lives in the same *danchi* complex as Nobuko and spends his day peeping into the windows of his neighbors with a telescope and masturbating—hardly a recipe for haptic visuality.

Immediately after the brief shot of Makoto's eye is a sequence of still shots of the *danchi*, emphasizing their unbearably grid-like, restricting qualities, and abstracting the shots so that perfectly geometrical windows, doors, and balconies become Mondrian paintings instead of midcentury Utopian architecture. After this prolonged sequence is a brief scene of Nobuko, now a housewife, injecting medicine into the *Hibakusha*'s flesh. He tells her not to get "hung up" on the keloid, to "just let the past go." Only now does Wakamatsu provide us with the infamous sequence of haptic visuality, in front of a portrait of Stalin. Thus the haptic elements are questioned from the start; clearly the demand that she "let the past go" went unheeded. Nagai, the Hiroshima survivor once deeply involved with the student movement, is now a stock broker profiting from the Vietnam War, an ironic twist of fate. His character, seemingly virile and energetic if not for the scar on his back, seems to forcibly reject the history embodied in his flesh, and nonchalantly listens to the stocks climb on the radio. On the other hand, Nobuko, who decided to sterilize herself during the student protest years to "free herself up for the struggle," is now unhappily married to a complacent union worker and desires a child. She yearns to work for the peace movement but is rebuked by her husband, who, in purely Stalinist fashion, states that "family and communal life" are as important for the struggle as union work. Nobuko's nostalgic desire to reconstruct the past is hopeless, and the realization that she might no longer love her *Hibakusha* lover—no longer the politically engaged youth of the '50s—only deepens her melancholy.

Although Nobuko might at first seem a sympathetic character, Wakamatsu makes it particularly difficult to truly identify with any *danchi* resident. Nobuko, chided by her husband for being too "literary," stays at home and refuses to converse with her neighbors. One extremely lonely resident purposefully drops her lingerie onto Nobuko's balcony while doing laundry in the hopes of befriending her, but Nobuko rebuffs her with cold politeness; later in the film, this woman hangs herself in her apartment. Identification with Nobuko is not easy, thus making haptic visuality according to Marks difficult to apply, since identification with a character's body is usually necessary for the film to evoke what Marks calls a tactile epistemology. Likewise, Sobchack's embodied spectatorship becomes especially difficult for a viewer who, having briefly identified with Nobuko's fetishization of the keloid scar, is forcibly removed from mimetic identification in the scenes that follow.

Sobchack and Marks's passionate, embodied viewing is particularly frustrated by the fact that the camera itself does not follow the gaze (or graze) of Nobuko, but the impotent, frustrated *ronin* Makoto. The image of his eye introduces the film, and, with the exception of the Stalin sequence, the camera-eye and Makoto-eye are merged—a fact exacerbated by Makoto's constant use of the telescope to spy on his neighbors. What results is not haptic visuality but its opposite extreme: an analytical hyper-optics which uses an emphasis on visuality as a distancing effect. This telescope's mechanical, inherently framed elements contribute to its already cinematic quality (it does, of course, mimic the use of an iris in early cinema), and Wakamatsu incorporates many shots of the kino-telescope-eye roving from apartment to apartment.

In fact, the movement of the camera when it mimics the movement of the telescope

After a brief shot of Makoto's judging eye at the beginning of the film is a sequence of still shots of the *danchi*, emphasizing their unbearably grid-like, restricting qualities, and abstracting the shots so that perfectly geometrical windows, doors, and balconies become Mondrian paintings instead of midcentury Utopian architecture.

is one of the only instances of real camera movement. Generally the film includes very little travelling, and the camera remains still. Although there is certainly some amount of montage, the film emphasizes fragmentation and geometrical mise-en-scène. Nobuko's stilted, unpleasant conversations with her misogynist husband are filmed using long or medium long shots, attributing to the sense of emotional distance between them. These scenes usually incorporate a strict symmetrical division of the frame, highlighting the geometrical composition of the *danchi* and contributing to the characters' feeling of suffocation (almost every character, from Makoto to his sister to Nobuko, complains about the restriction of the small spaces between "four walls," and claim to go insane as a result of these framed boundaries). Outside of this sense of alienation caused by architecture, Wakamatsu uses fragments of body parts as another means of critical distancing. For example, early in the film, Wakamatsu films the gossip of housewives by metonymically filming their mouths alone, through Makoto's telescope-lens, and speeding up the dialogue to the point of complete gibberish. Evidently, this immensely experimental use of dialogue is meant to launch the viewer into the mind of Makoto himself, forcing an identification that would otherwise be impossible. After all, in the end of the film, Makoto rapes his sister with phallic vegetables in his refrigerator, attempts to blackmail and rape Nobuko, but stabs her when he proves impotent—hardly a sympathetic character, especially if one is to attempt Marks's mimetic, haptic identification or Sobchack's embodied spectatorship.

This tendency towards fragmentation and the difficulty of identification with any particular character is, however, integral to the Pink Film genre as a whole. Rape and sadomasochism predominate,[21] and Wakamatsu's films in particular are known for their distancing effects, accentuated by deliberately political motifs, fragmented editing, and a flattening-out of emotional affect.[22] In the context of the Pink Film genre then, the use of a Hiroshima victim as a central character seems particularly strange—especially strange when compared to other well-known representations of Hiroshima, such as Resnais's *Hiroshima mon amour*.

Earlier in this essay, I claimed that the lovemaking sequence in front of the Stalin poster in *Affairs Within Walls* alludes to the first few minutes of *Hiroshima mon amour*, but that Wakamatsu's film refuses this potentially haptic visuality later in the film. This would assume that the Resnais film attains the status of a properly "haptic" film, and that it is capable of a kind of embodied, mimetic spectatorship within the viewer. This, however, is not the case: the two lovers embracing in the first few minutes of *Hiroshima mon amour* are symbols, not identifiable people; their bodies are slowly covered with glittering sand, a metaphor for the themes of cultural memory, time, and traumatic experiences caused by World War II that continue to be explored in the course of the film. Importantly, it is not a film about victims of Hiroshima, but memory itself; after all, the film's two protagonists— abstractly named "She" and "He" in the Marguerite Duras script—were not in Hiroshima during the bomb's explosion. I would disagree with Thomas Lamarre when he writes, contrasting the film to *Barefoot Gen*, that in the Resnais film "the experience of the atomic bomb … remains unknowable, unspeakable, unrepresentable."[23] Rather, the film does not really *attempt* mimetic representation of a specific historical event; in the tradition of the *nouveau roman*, the film is about thought, memory, and the impossibility of language to properly signify meaning. Youssef Ishaghpour puts it nicely: "l'image pour lui [Resnais], c'est d'abord «chose mentale»."[24] Wakamatsu's film, then, does not reject the Resnais film because *Hiroshima mon amour* simply follows different paths, and works with different themes. They do, however, share a similar interest in cultural memory, to which Wakamatsu adds a particularly ironic and critical spin in his critical detachment to Nobuko's nostalgic reminisces. Wakamatsu's take on cultural memory, however, is specific to Japan's historical moment, especially in the wake of the 1964 Tokyo Olympics and the demise of the ANPO protests.

Nonetheless, common to both Resnais and Wakamatsu is a critique of standard media representations of the atomic bomb, seemingly echoing Theodor Adorno's famous dictum that to write poetry after Auschwitz is barbaric. Here, it is poetry[25] after Hiroshima which is barbaric, and both filmmakers respond to this crisis of representation with varying uses of experimental cinematographic techniques. However, in Wakamatsu, the representation of the actual event of the Hiroshima disaster is not what is in question.[26] What Wakamatsu interrogates is instead the spectator's temptation for an *embodiment* of the Hiroshima experience—a visual hapticity or embodied spectatorship in which the viewer attempts a passionate engagement with the events unfolding on screen. Although the sexual encounter between Nobuko and the Hiroshima survivor might hint at this sensorial engagement, the film's hyper-optic tropes, fragmentation, and emphasis on geometrical mise-en-scène create a film that refuses what Sobchack might call interobjectivity.

There is, moreover, a

Two lovers embrace in the opening moments of Alan Resnais's *Hiroshima mon amour.*

political purpose to this kind of aesthetic distancing and refusal of cinematic embodiment. Filmmaker Adachi Masao, who collaborated with Wakamatsu on a number of Pink Films in the '60s and '70s, explained this particular political aspect during an interview with Harry Harootunian. Claiming to be influenced by Beckett and Brecht, Adachi stated, "The frame will be there, but, at the same time, the audience should decide. It is fine for the film-maker to put all his feelings into the work, but he should make films where the audience can watch it more freely as well," and that Wakamatsu understood him in that regard.[27] One might see a similar quality to Wakamatsu's films, whose distancing effects, though not entirely Brechtian, might seek to "emancipate the spectator," to use Jacques Rancière's terminology. Wakamatsu's film aims to create an alternative mode of viewership from the standard portrayals of Hiroshima in Japanese mass media—particularly the media circulated by the Stalinist Japanese Communist Party of the 1950s, symbolized by the Stalin portrait in film's flashback sequences.

The politics of *Affairs Within Walls*, then, is one that creates a space of freedom for the spectator, due to the film's formal elements and criticism of embodiment. It is also a politics that criticizes standard media imagery of the Hiroshima tragedy, while asking the taboo question of what comes *after*—not only after Hiroshima, but also the student protest movements in the wake of ANPO. And this, of course, is all accomplished in a film that is, for all intents and purposes, sexploitation, and one of the first historical examples of the Pink Film genre. Thus, to echo Lamarre's argument about *Barefoot Gen*'s potentiality for the comic medium, the invocation of *Affairs Within Walls* might be to *believe in Pink Film*—to believe in its potential for radical formal experimentation, and for engagement with serious political questions. After all, it might have been this invocation that brought writers like Adachi to Wakamatsu Productions in the first place, launching a series of intriguing politically-driven films for the next decade onward.[28]

However, it is important to note that this seemingly utopian, optimistic invocation to believe in Pink Film is directed toward an almost exclusively male audience, especially after the solidification of the Pink Film genre in the late '60s. In its attempt to prevent the viewer from an affect-oriented relation to the events on screen, the hyper-optical framework of Wakamatsu's film is analytical by nature, and can be compared with theoretical paradigms from structuralism to psychoanalysis to semiotics. On the other hand, the haptic frameworks of Sobchack and Marks, by appealing explicitly to this affect-relation to films, fly boldly in the face of these hegemonic theoretical frameworks of the '80s and '90s—and both writers, importantly, are women. Gender, therefore, is a crucial aspect of both frameworks; in Pink Film especially, the gendering of *formal* elements of the genre remain grossly understudied. As Desser states, "It takes no staunch feminist to claim that pink films, which cater to overwhelmingly male audiences, fulfill repressed male desires to rape and torture women."[29] This statement, however, is not followed by any sort of formal analysis, and the misogynistic elements of these films are taken as a given, along with the tropes commonly used within them—an impotent male, a raped schoolgirl, a lonely housewife. I claim, however, that the misogynistic elements of many of these films are evident in their formal construction, in the cinematographic elements which echo the analytical frameworks of the dominant theoretical paradigms of the late 20th century.

In this essay, I have posed Wakamatsu's (inevitably) male-centric film—the kino-eye is Makoto's, after all—against two female theorists, Vivian Sobchack and Laura Marks, whose modes of spectatorship might be interpreted as being feminine by nature—or, more specifically, directly opposed to the hegemonic, heavily male-dominated theoretical frameworks at this time. Both Sobchack and Marks emphasize phenomenology in their writings—not a particularly popular theory at the time of their writing—as well as a turn towards affect, and therefore a clear departure from the dominant discourses of the '80s and '90s.

This, of course, does not mean that Sobchack and Marks are non-theoretical.[30] Indeed, there is much in Sobchack and Marks that has an extremely political and revolutionary potential.[31] Neither Sobchack nor Marks were devoid of politics, and one might say that Sobchack's theory of embodied spectatorship is as political as it is ethical. Likewise, Marks posits an intriguing relation between embodiment and trauma, indicating that "embodiment involves a level of trauma that phenomenology did not initially recognize ... perception is not an infinite return to the buffet table of lived experiences but a walk through the minefield of embodied memory."[32] This theory of embodiment and haptic visuality, in which the perceiving spectator takes a "walk through the minefield of embodied memory," is hardly the hackneyed Stalinist portrayal that Wakamatsu was fighting against. The opposition is not one of politics versus aesthetics, or perception versus sensation. In fact, both modes of spectatorship are enmeshed with the theme of perception, albeit to different ends. Given that one of these approaches derives from an almost entirely male-produced world, and is tailored towards an exclusively male consumer, Sobchack and Marks thus offer an *alternative* gendered mode of viewership and perception—a mode of looking and feeling which is directly opposed to Makoto's distanced male kino-eye.

Notes

1. A. Zahlten: *The Role of Genre in Film From Japan: Transformations 1960s–2000s*, Ph.D. diss., Johannes Gutenberg University Mainz, 2007, pp. 108–109.

2. It is important to note, however, that in 1965, specialized Pink Film theaters were not yet the norm, and films at this time were usually shown in regular theaters. The form of Pink Film was still in flux, and not solidified until the end of the decade. That said, a definition of Pink Film would be extremely useful, and Alexander Zahlten provides a comprehensive one in his doctoral dissertation, which includes the economic, formal, and thematic elements of the genre, as follows: Pink Film is a low-budget alternative to the major studio system which reintroduced independent production and distribution strategies. Each film is shot in a timeframe of merely 3–5 days and with a budget of about 3 million Yen, is around 60 minutes in length, shot on 35mm film on location and without synched sound, and is exclusively shown in specialized Pink Film theaters. Directors are granted a great degree of autonomy, and, as long as a certain number of sex scenes are included at regular intervals (generally about 5–7 per film), the director is free to experiment with form and narrative structure. Genitalia and pubic hair are hidden by either shooting around them or by use of post-production masking techniques. Violence, especially against women, is a mainstay of the genre, and almost every film includes at least one rape sequence. The films often play out themes of nationhood and postwar trauma by making use of the mediated female body. See Zahlten, "The Role of Genre in Film from Japan," 74, 77–78.

3. D. Desser, *Eros Plus Massacre: An Introduction to the Japanese New Wave Cinema* (Bloomington: Indiana University Press, 1988), p. 99.

4. According to Thomas Lamarre, the trauma of Hiroshima and Nagasaki victims were often treated as national trauma. Thus Hiroshima becomes an event that precludes discussion of what came before and after. To take Lamarre's argument a step further, the mass media portrayal of nuclear bomb victims, or *Hibakusha*, becomes a trope that seriously restricts active political discourse on the topic. See T. Lamarre, "Manga Bomb: Between the Lines of Barefoot Gen," *Comics Worlds and the World of Comics: Towards Scholarship on a Global Scale* (Kyoto: International Manga Research Center, 2010), p. 301.

5. Although this famous first scene including the Stalin poster is not often discussed as a flashback (especially in Desser and Standish), the sequence of events shown, and a suggestive use of dissolve, indicates that every scene with the Stalin poster is set during the 1950s.

6. B. Massumi, "Annotated Translation with Critical Introduction of *Mille plateaux* by Gilles Deleuze and Felix Guattari (Volumes I–III)," Ph.D. diss., Yale University, 1987, 84.

7. E. Shouse, "Feeling, Emotion, Affect," *M/C Journal* 8.6 (2005), http://journal.media-culture.org.au/0512/03-shouse.php.

8. *Ibid.*

9. V. Sobchack, *Carnal Thoughts: Embodiment and Moving Image Culture* (Berkeley: University of California Press, 2004), p. 286.

10. *Ibid.*, 290, Sobchack emphasis. Although Sobchack uses the term "feeling" rather than "affect," I believe her writings utilize the sense of both. Interobjectivity has an aspect of the prepersonal as well as the biographical, perhaps even leaning in favor of the former, due to Sobchack's emphasis on phenomenology. Possibly, Sobchack's twin concepts of "sensibility" and "sense-ability" might be linked to Massumi's distinction between feeling and affect.

11. L. Marks: *The Skin of Film: Intercultural Cinema, Embodiment, and the Senses* (Durham: Duke University Press, 2000), p. 149.

12. *Ibid.*, p. 139.

13. "The theory of haptic visuality I advance should allow us to reconsider how the relationship between self and other may be yielding-knowing, more than (but as well as) shattering." *Ibid.*, p. 151.

14. Emphasis Marks.

15. *Ibid.*, p. 162.

16. *Ibid.*, p. 183.

17. D. Desser, *Eros Plus Massacre: An Introduction to the Japanese New Wave Cinema* (Bloomington: Indiana University Press, 1988), p. 101.

18. Indeed, the blurrier the image, the more haptic the mode of visuality becomes. Marks goes so far as to say that anyone with moderately impaired vision can have a haptic viewing experience at the movie theater if they remove their glasses while they watch the film. See Marks, *The Skin of Film*, p. 170.

19. The film was in fact a Franco-Japanese production, and was released in Japan on June 20, 1959, 10 days after its French release. See ヒロシマモナムール (1959), "All Cinema Movie & DVD Database," accessed June 6, 2013, http://www.allcinema.net/prog/show_c.php?num_c=16896.

20. I understand that using the first person feminine pronoun when referring to a viewer of a Pink Film might seem strange, given that the vast majority of Pink Film audiences were male. However, given that this essay's author is female, I have retained it out of a sense of simplicity, and will return to the question of gender later in the essay.

21. D. Desser, *Eros Plus Massacre: An Introduction to the Japanese New Wave Cinema* (Bloomington: Indiana University Press, 1988), p. 101.

22. I disagree with Desser, however, who claims that Wakamatsu's films are known for a "Brechtian air" (100). Instead, I think it is safe to say that Wakamatsu uses distancing effects and experiments with a range of different styles, which might veer towards a kind of Alienation Effect but are far more formally experimental (often incorporating a mix of media and arts with the use of newspaper clippings, cartoons, music collaborations, etc.) and far more politically ambiguous than Brecht would have liked.

23. T. Lamarre, "Manga Bomb: Between the Lines of Barefoot Gen," *Comics Worlds and the World of Comics: Towards Scholarship on a Global Scale* (Kyoto: International Manga Research Center, 2010), p. 301.

24. Youssef Ishaghpour, "For Resnais, the Image Is a 'Mental Thing' First," *D'une image à l'autre* (Paris: Gallimard, 1982), 182.

25. Poetry might be loosely interpreted as prewar aesthetic modes. Here, in the context of film studies, it is akin to something like Noël Burch's concept of the Institutional Mode of Representation (IMR).

26. Instead of other Hiroshima narratives such as *Barefoot Gen* and *Hiroshima mon amour*, *Affairs Within Walls* might be best compared to other *danchi* (or the international equivalent) films with a similar political critique of modern capitalist living, such as Hani Susumu's *She and He* (1963) or Michelangelo Antonioni's *Eclipse* (1962), all produced within the same three year span.

27. H. Harootunian and S. Kohso, "Messages in a Bottle: An Interview with Filmmaker Masao Adachi," *Boundary 2* (Fall 2008), 75–76.

28. The invocation to "believe in Pink Film" might also place Pink Films, shown exclusively in specialized theaters, in opposition to television, which was gaining full swing in popularity in mid–'60s Japan, due especially to the coverage of the Tokyo Olympics. Indeed, Wakamatsu's film is replete with television sets in *danchi* apartments, and with housewives mindlessly watching TV screens—clearly a critical gesture, and meant to signify the rut of daily, habitual existence in the apartment complexes.

29. D. Desser, *Eros Plus Massacre: An Introduction to the Japanese New Wave Cinema* (Bloomington: Indiana University Press, 1988), p. 101.

30. Melinda Barlow, review of *Touch: Sensuous Theory and Multisensory Media*, by Laura U. Marks, *Canadian Journal of Film Studies* 12.2 (Fall 2003), 126–127.

31. Page 4 has an earlier discussion of Massumi's concept of affect, and its potential for ethics and politics.

32. L. Marks: *The Skin of Film: Intercultural Cinema, Embodiment, and the Senses* (Durham: Duke University Press, 2000), p. 152.

Bibliography

Barlow, Melinda. Review of *Touch: Sensuous Theory and Multisensory Media*, by Laura U. Marks. *Canadian Journal of Film Studies* 12.2 (Fall 2003): 126–129.

Desser, David. *Eros Plus Massacre: An Introduction to the Japanese New Wave Cinema*. Bloomington: Indiana University Press, 1988.

Harootunian, Harry, and Sabu Kohso. "Messages in a Bottle: An Interview with Filmmaker Masao Adachi." *Boundary 2* (Fall 2008).

ヒロシマモナムール (1959). "All Cinema Movie & DVD Database." Accessed June 6, 2013. http://www. allcinema.net/prog/show_c.php?num_c=16896.

Ishaghpour, Youssef. *D'une image à l'autre*. Paris: Gallimard, 1982.

Lamarre, Thomas. "Manga Bomb: Between the Lines of Barefoot Gen." *Comics Worlds and the World of Comics: Towards Scholarship on a Global Scale*. Kyoto: International Manga Research Center, 2010.

Marks, Laura. *The Skin of Film: Intercultural Cinema, Embodiment, and the Senses*. Durham: Duke University Press, 2000.

Massumi, Brian. "Annotated Translation with Critical Introduction of *Mille plateaux* by Gilles Deleuze and Felix Guattari (Volumes I–III)." Ph.D. diss., Yale University, 1987.

Shouse, Eric. "Feeling, Emotion, Affect." *M/C Journal* 8.6 (2005). http://journal.media-culture.org.au/0512/03-shouse.php.

Sobchack, Vivian. *Carnal Thoughts: Embodiment and Moving Image Culture*. Berkeley: University of California Press, 2004.

Zahlten, Alexander. "The Role of Genre in Film from Japan: Transformations 1960s–2000s." Ph.D. diss., Johannes Gutenberg University Mainz, 2007.

The Atomic Bomb Experience
and the Japanese Family
in Keiji Nakazawa's Anime
Hadashi no Gen (*Barefoot Gen*)

Kenji Kaneko

Barefoot Gen (*Hadashi no Gen*) is a popular but controversial Japanese manga series that started in *Shūkan Shōnen Jump*, a weekly manga anthology, in 1973, and turned into three live-action films in 1976, 1977 and 1980, and then transformed into two anime films in 1983 and 1986. This successful manga series is now available in English, French, Germany, Portuguese, Korean, Thai and many other languages.[1] *Hadashi no Gen* is a wartime story of Gen Nakaoka (the main character) and his family in Hiroshima City, Hiroshima, Japan, before and after the U.S. atomic bomb known as "Little Boy" was dropped on August 6, 1945. This is the first Japanese manga to portray the effects of the atomic bomb in Hiroshima on that day.

The narrative of Gen Nakaoka is largely based on Keiji Nakazawa, an author who spent his childhood in Hiroshima City before and after the Second World War ended in 1945. This essay refers to the author by his first name, Keiji, instead of his last name, *Nakawaza*, in order to avoid confusion with the main character, Gen *Nakaoka*. Gen and Keiji do not just have similar last names, but Keiji also reveals that Gen is modeled after himself.[2] As discussed later, like Gen, Keiji lost his father, older sister and younger brother on the day of the atomic bombing.[3]

This essay will mainly examine *Barefoot Gen*, the first anime film, released in 1983.[4] The anime film was much more successful than Nakazawa had expected, and it reached a large audience in Japan. Perhaps its anti-nuclear war theme was appropriate in the early 1980s when many Japanese were worried about possible nuclear war between the Soviet Union and the United States. It can be suggested that the success of the anime version of *Barefoot Gen* played an important role in discourse on the early development of Japanese popular culture which in turn became an important part of the process of building an image of a peaceful postwar Japan and its self-confidence in the early 1980s. In addition, this essay will attempt to present a full understanding of *Barefoot Gen* by analyzing two of Nakazawa's books as references: *Hadashi no Gen: Jiden* (1994) (*Barefoot Gen: Autobiography*) and *Hadashi no Gen: Watashi no Isho* (*Barefoot Gen: My Will*) (2012). This essay will focus on how the effects of the atomic bomb are portrayed in the anime film and identify the author's messages.

This essay will start by reviewing three key events which occurred in the film when the atomic bomb was dropped. Gen and his family lived in Hiroshima City, which became ground zero on August 6, 1945. The essay will use Keiji's book *Hadashi no Gen: Jiden* (1994) to explain and elaborate on these events. Next, the essay will analyze the personal views of Keiji on the atomic bomb and how that affected his life until he passed away on December 19, 2012 through analysis of Keiji's last book, *Hadashi no Gen: Watashi no Isho* (2012), alongside *Hadashi no Gen: Jiden* (1994).

Keiji is remembered as an opinion leader who understood what Hiroshima City went through on the fateful day of August 6, 1945, when more than 100,000 Japanese individuals were wounded or killed by thermal radiation and blast winds caused by the atomic bomb. He was not just a popular manga author but also *Hibakusha* ([radiation] explosion-affected person or people) as a socially marginalized group, created after the atomic bomb explosion. His work explains several difficulties and dilemmas *Hibakusha* tend to face and illustrates what they see in Japanese society. As illustrated later, it can be argued that Keiji's work presents the ethnic and social diversity of prewar and postwar Japan.

Barefoot Gen—*Japanese Popular Culture*

Firstly, it is important to review the term "popular culture" as discussed by several scholars before discussing *Barefoot Gen*. It can be strongly argued that the anime version of *Barefoot Gen* has played an important role in constructing particular images and narratives about Japan for many Japanese. In *Barefoot Gen*, the manga series, Japanese civilians are portrayed as victims of the U.S. atomic bombing, and the narrative includes controversial themes such as Japan's colonization of Asia, its former colonial subjects such as the Koreans and the Chinese, discrimination against *Hibakusha* and the wartime responsibility of the prewar Japanese government. But the anime film has a different tone and is less controversial. The anime's primary focus is on how Gen and his family lived in poverty during the wartime, and how their lives changed after the atomic bomb was dropped.

The anime film seeks to explain the way in which the Japanese should understand Hiroshima, the U.S. atomic bomb and the end of the war. Its anti-nuclear theme was (and still is) considered both political and educational; *Barefoot Gen* was far different from other Japanese science fiction and combat-action anime series of that era (1980s) that saw guns, fighting and war as types of entertainment. It can be said that *Barefoot Gen* influenced other war-theme and anti-war theme anime films in the early development of Japanese popular culture.

D. P. Martinez has attempted to define the anthropological meanings of popular culture. He states, "In anthropology as well, the term 'culture' contains a variety of meanings; it can refer to materials produced by a given society (its art, as well as tools, baskets, buildings, etc.); or alternatively to the symbolic or signifying systems of a society … the materials produced by a society are also capable of having symbolic values, and thus the anthropologist's job is to explore the relationships between material culture and symbolic culture. It is the interaction between these apparently separate aspects of society that must constitute the focus of an anthropological study of popular culture."[5] It can be argued, therefore, that the anime version of *Barefoot Gen* has played a symbolic role in building an image of a peaceful postwar Japan. During the postwar period in Japan, anti-militarism became one of the country's main goals, closely related to the pacifist constitution. Through the growing dominance of mass media, especially television and film in the early 1980s, most Japanese individuals shared a mass culture.

The anime film of *Barefoot Gen* portrays the aftermath of the atomic bombing. For many Japanese, Hiroshima has been a symbol of a peaceful nation after the war.[6] Since the release of the anime version of *Barefoot Gen* in 1983, it has been recognized as an appropriate anime movie for young Japanese by both the National Congress of Parents and Teachers Associations of Japan and the Ministry of Education, Science and Culture (the Ministry of Education, Culture, Spots, Science and Technology, MEXT now).[7]

In addition, Koichi Iwabuchi has described Japanese popular culture as *mukokuseki* (lacking any nationality) which means that it has lost its Japanese distinctiveness so it has a universal appeal.[8] Looking at Japanese cutting edge technologies and products such as video games, fashion, films and animation, and personal computers and electric appliances, they are far from the traditional image of Japan. Along with eschewing this traditional image, it can be argued that Japanese popular culture includes elements of post-modernity. Cultural theories of post-modernity emphasize the role of the cultural industries, the definition of lives of individuals as cultural projects, individual choice in identity construction, and "the fragmentation of personal identity which changes over the life-course and between different social settings."[9] By the 1980s, Japanese popular culture no longer meant Japanese language, social customs, and religion, but also various types of commercial products such as karaoke, anime, manga and video games not only in Japan but also abroad.

Keiji believes that "Hiroshima" should not be forgotten as long as there are *Hibakusha* and nuclear weapons in the world.[10] Since its release, the film has also been available outside Japan in different languages. In the global context, the film does not just seek to explain how the Japanese understand Hiroshima, the U.S. atomic bomb and the end of the war, but also to educate an audience why nuclear weapons should not be used. Keiji sees that war acts as karma: what you give, you get.[11] Now, this essay will present a full understanding of *Barefoot Gen*, a popular semi-autobiography.

Barefoot Gen—*The Animated Amine Story of the Atomic Bombing of Hiroshima City, Hiroshima*

Here, the essay will review the anime version of *Barefoot Gen* (1983). This section is divided into four parts: (1) Hiroshima city, Hiroshima, (2) *pika-don* (the explosion of the atomic bomb), (3) the aftermath of the atomic bomb, and (4) Keiji's atomic bomb experience on August 6, 1945. After the manga version of *Barefoot Gen* was released in 1973, Keiji began to show a strong interest in making an anime version of *Barefoot Gen* in the early 1980s. According to his book, Keiji was shocked to see that his daughter was very excited to watch bombings and explosions in Japanese combat-action anime series in spite of reading the *Barefoot Gen* comic books.[12] Keiji heard his daughter say, "Yatta!" (Yeah!) as she watched the atomic bomb being dropped on the city in the combat-action anime series. He expected that she would have been more sensitive to war and war-related subjects. Seeing how the anime series was able to attract and reach its young viewers, Keiji felt that he should make an anime version of *Barefoot Gen*. The anime version of *Barefoot Gen* could tell the audience what was exactly going on behind war-scenes in which people would often get killed or injured by bomb explosions.

Barefoot Gen is about what Hiroshima City, Hiroshima, went through on the day the

U.S. atomic bomb was dropped. The anime film can be divided into two main parts: the first describing what life was like in Hiroshima City, Hiroshima, Japan, before the *Enola Gay*, an American B-29 bomber, dropped the atomic bomb at 8:15 on August 6, 1945, the second part describing the chaotic situation with shocking and horrifying images in which buildings, roads and streetcars were melted down and blown away. This part vividly portrays suffering atomic bomb victims desperately looking for help. The film changes its entire tone after the "fateful" event.

The main character, Gen Nakaoka, copes with the worst situation and creates something good out of it. This can be interrupted as the main theme of this anime film: resilience and not giving in (*ganbaru*). In the film, Gen's father, Daikichi, tells Gen to grow up strong and tough like wheat: it is resilient, and it is able to survive a cold winter. The act of *ganbaru* against adversity is seen in the entire film. The value of *ganbaru* is embedded in Japanese culture and society. The Japanese phrase also includes the meaning of determination. It has a positive connotation as one may go through a harsh experience but come out of it stronger.

HIROSHIMA CITY, HIROSHIMA

Gen and his family lived in Hiroshima City, Hiroshima, Japan. Gen was a six-year-old boy who just started elementary school as a first grader. His father was an artisan who painted on wood sandals (*geta*), and his pregnant mother, Kimie, helped the family business. He had an older sister, Eiko, and a younger brother, Shinji. They were a struggling family and were always hungry.

The beginning of the film sets up what Hiroshima City was like before August 6, 1945. It was regarded as a "spared" city since it had not been a target of air raids by the U.S. bombers unlike other major cities such as Tokyo, Yokohama, Nagoya, Osaka and Okinawa. Gen and his family often spent time in the air-raid shelter, but nothing usually happened except for a few incidents. They wondered why Hiroshima City had not been targeted yet.

PIKA-DON (THE EXPLOSION OF THE ATOMIC BOMB)

The Japanese phrase *pika-don* was often used to express and explain the explosion of the atomic bomb on Hiroshima by many Japanese who had no idea what the explosion was at that time. *Pika-don* is a Japanese onomatopoeia: when the atomic bomb was dropped on Hiroshima, they saw or recalled a bright light, "*pika*," followed by an explosive sound, "*don*."

The morning of August 6, 1945, began with an early warning siren at 7:15 as Gen's family evacuated to the shelter. Gen's father said, "The enemy showed up earlier than usual today." Although the U.S. aircraft flew over Hiroshima City, they were quite relaxed. Gen said, "That was just another spy plane" when he and his family came out of the shelter. They quickly went back to the house. Gen was prepared to leave to go to school, and his mother hung out the laundry on the roof balcony. But the B-29 that had earlier appeared in Hiroshima City that morning was sent to check weather conditions. The second aircraft, the *Enola Gay*, approaching Hiroshima City was informed that the weather condition was "favorable for bombing." According to the film, no early warning was given to the people in Hiroshima City as there was no real chance of escape. The atomic bomb was dropped while Gen was on his way to go to the school at 8:15. Gen stopped to talk to his friend near the entrance of the elementary school when the atomic bomb exploded in the sky.

The film shares with its audience the horrific atomic bombing experience in Hiroshima city. There was a large mushroom-shaped cloud: the explosion consisted of thermal radiation as a bright light that instantaneously burned children and adults to ashes, and then blast winds that blew away homes, buildings and streets. There was a tremendous sound. Human bodies melted away like wax figures, and broken glass from windows flew into the air.

When the bomb exploded in the sky above the city, Gen was picking up the rock he had dropped to the ground. Suddenly, Gen was blown away and fell onto the ground, and so was everything else in the area. Broken pieces of concrete walls, houses and buildings covered him. The destruction was immediate with dust particles floating in the air, and everything became dark. But he was unharmed and was able to stand up. He looked around and tried to collect himself, but he did not understand what had happened. He found his friend on the ground and noticed that she was already dead. He was scared but tried to look for help. He then realized that something terrible had just happened to the city. He started to worry about his family and decided to go back home.

The Aftermath of the Atomic Bomb

Gen ran past burning houses and saw not only many dead bodies lying on the ground but also injured people walking slowly on the street: he described them as *obake*, Japanese ghosts. There were shocking images of the effects of the atomic bomb explosion on atomic bomb victims: a mother and her young son were severely burned. They were both badly wounded. Their clothes were gone. Shards of glass were stuck in their bodies. Their skin was ripped off by the heat of the blast wave. There was a man following them, his eyeballs popping out of their sockets. There was another man whose guts spilled out. Many faces were burned by the heat of the blast. Gen also realized that nobody was screaming.

Gen reached home and met his mother, Kimie. Then he saw his father, older sister and younger brother caught underneath the rubble of their house which had collapsed. They were stuck between two large pillars and about to get burned alive. Gen and his mother desperately tried to move the pillars, but they were just too heavy. At this point, Kimie realized it was a hopeless situation. Their Korean neighbor, *Paku san* (Mr. Pak), showed up and helped Gen and his mother leave the collapsed house. It was just too dangerous to stay.

That evening Gen and his mother tried to sleep on the ground. They heard wounded people crying in pain. They did not really understand the agony they were suffering, but they tried to help them by giving them cups of water. Gen and his mother soon realized that there were just too many wounded people, and they could not do anything much for them. *Kuroi ame* (Black Rain) began to fall. It mainly fell on the west side of Hiroshima City and contained radioactive materials which seeped into the ground. Nobody knew how harmful the black rain was at the time. Many survivors were exposed to radiation from the black rain.

There are three key events before and after the atomic bomb was dropped. The first is that Hiroshima City was regarded as a spared city since the city had not become a target of air raids by the U.S. bombers unlike big cities. Like the Nakaoka family, many people in the Hiroshima City were quite relaxed despite the frequent early warning sirens. The first B-29 showed up in the sky at 7:15 to check the weather conditions, and the *Enola Gay* dropped the atomic bomb at 8:15.

The second event was the atomic bomb explosion, *pika-don*. According to the film, no early warning siren was given to the people of Hiroshima City when the atomic bomb was dropped at 8:15 on August 6, 1945. There was a loud explosion and a large mushroom-shaped cloud that consisted of thermal radiation as a bright light which instantaneously turned people to ashes and then blast winds that blew away homes and buildings. Just at the time of the blast, Gen was behind the concrete walls that shielded him from the explosion. His mother was also saved, although she had been blown away from the roof by the blast.

The last event was that there were many dead and injured people after the explosion. Gen saw not only many bodies lying on the ground but also injured people slowly walking on the street. The destruction was felt everywhere. As discussed, the manga author intended to show the audience what was going on behind the scenes—to accurately depict that many people would be killed and injured by the bomb explosion. The scenes presented the aftermath of the effects of the atomic bomb on Hiroshima City with horrific images.

KEIJI'S ATOMIC BOMB EXPERIENCE IN HIROSHIMA CITY ON AUGUST 6, 1945

It is important to review Keiji's book *Hadashi no Gen: Jiden* (*Barefoot Gen: Autobiography*) (1994) to compare and explain these events in the film. Like the film, there was a rumor that the United States would spare Hiroshima City and turn it into a vital military base when the war was over.[13] Keiji remembered that many people in Hiroshima City believed and actually felt relieved by this rumor, although they still evacuated when early warning sirens for air-raids were activated. They might see airplanes in the sky, but they tended to assume that they were just spy planes. Later, Keiji thought about the situation and believed that it was just a set-up before the Americans dropped the atomic bomb.

Keiji argues that if the bomb had dropped at that time, many would have stayed in the shelter and survived the effects of the atomic bomb.[14] There was supposed to be an early warning siren at 8:15 by NHK Hiroshima, but the atomic bomb exploded before the siren. The atomic bomb was dropped while Keiji was on his way to go to elementary school. According to him, he found himself lying on the ground and covered by pieces of the concrete walls like Gen. Keiji stood up and tried to understand what happened.[15] But unlike the film, he was talking to his friend's mother when the *Enola Gay* dropped the bomb. He found her lying on the ground severely burned and dead but still looking at him. Like the film, Keiji started to worry about his family in the house and ran as fast as possible.[16] Then, he saw the hordes of injured people walking with scattered glass fragments stuck on their bodies. Many were severely burned and wounded.

In the film, after the atomic bomb explosion, Gen witnessed many injured people walking slowly on the street, *obake* (Japanese ghosts). In his book, Keiji describes the walking injured people as *yūrei* instead of *obake*.[17] Both *yūrei* and *obake* are Japanese words for [Japanese] ghosts. He did not mistake them as ghosts, but the way they were walking, he thought, looked like Japanese ghosts. As Keiji recalled, they were severely burned but continued walking. They did not just look awful but also walked in a peculiar manner. The skin on their arms was ripped off from their shoulders to their fingers. The skin was barely hanging by the nails. They put their arms high when they walked so that they did not have to drag their skin on the ground. The skin on their back was also ripped off to their waistlines. The skin on their legs was ripped off from their thighs to their ankles. Although each part of all their skin was dangling they continued walking with their arms up. They could only walk in this *yūrei* style.

Keiji recalled his Japanese neighbor fortunately saw him and told him that his mother also escaped from the blast of the explosion, while Keiji was crying on the street afterward.[18] When Keiji met her, he was so relieved, then realized that she was holding a newborn baby. She had already given birth to a baby girl, Tomoko, on the street.[19]

The black rain began to fall, but it stopped as the clouds shifted to the northeast of Hiroshima City.[20] Nobody knew what the black rain was, and Keiji and his mother did not even think that they were exposed to radioactive materials. He later thought that if they had escaped to the northeast where the clouds shifted, they would have developed acute leukemia and died with the high radiation exposure. Unlike Gen, Keiji could not go back to his house when his father, older sister and younger brother died there. His mother was the sole survivor. She often told him that she could never forget their voices shouting and screaming before she managed to escape from the fire.[21]

It is clear that the anime film effectively portrays the aftermath of the effects of the atomic bomb on Hiroshima City, with not just horrific but realistic images. One gets the feeling that the film reminds the audience that the atomic bombing of Hiroshima is part of the history of Japan, and many Japanese civilians were killed on the day. It happened just a few decades ago, and survivors are still alive and living in Japan. At the same time, the film helps the audience think and acknowledge what it means to live in a peaceful country like Japan that has chosen not to participate in war and war-related activities, supported by the Pacific constitution. In this sense, the film has played a symbolic role in building an image of a peaceful postwar Japan.

In addition, reviewing the three events in the film and Keiji's book, it is possible to understand what Gen and his family went through on that day in comparison to what Keiji and his family did: Gen and Keiji experienced the same three events, but had different outcomes. Both Gen and Keiji witnessed the atomic bomb explosion that killed and wounded more than 100,000 people as a six-year-old boy, and thus the narrative of Gen is a semi-autobiography of Keiji himself. One also gets the strong impression that Keiji could never overcome this horrific experience as an adult, which clearly fed his work as an artist and the adaption from manga to anime. Through watching the anime film and reading his book, one becomes compelled to know who Keiji Nakazawa is and why he has decided to share his atomic bomb experience with others. Keiji believes that the atomic bombing of Hiroshima is a life-changing event not just for the people of Hiroshima but also Japan or anywhere in the world and what Hiroshima City experienced on that day should never be forgotten.

Who Is Keiji Nakazawa?

This essay will now examine who Keiji Nakazawa is and his personal views on the effects of the atomic bomb through close examination of Keiji's latest books, *Hadashi no Gen: Watashi no Isho* (2012) and *Hadashi no Gen: Jiden* (1994). The two books overlap each other, and the main emphasis is on the former book as opposed to the latter. The later book will be used to discuss his later years before he passed away. First, it is important to start off by discussing two of the most influential figures in Keiji's life, his parents, Harumi and Kimiyo, before exploring how he became a manga writer and what he thought of the nuclear incident in Fukushima on March 11, 2011, when Japan suffered the devastating Tōhoku earthquake. The March 11 disaster reminded him of his own experience in the past.

Keiji had never thought about writing about the U.S. atomic bomb until 1966 when his mother passed away in Hiroshima.[22] They may have survived the atomic bomb, but they were often stressed over social problems and unemployment. For a long time, they worried about the possibility of developing many atomic bomb–related illnesses such as acute leukemia and different types of cancers.[23]

KEIJI'S FATHER, HARUMI

Like Gen's father, Keiji's father, Harumi, was an artisan who drew pictures on wood sandals, and he passed away on August 6, 1945. Keiji described Harumi as an artist who hated money-hungry business people.[24] Thus, Harumi never tried to be good at his business, and as Keiji remembered, his family was always poor. When Harumi was younger, he was interested in becoming a stage actor and eventually joined a left-wing theater group.[25] The theater group played the works of Japanese liberal thinkers and writers such as Tōson Shimazaki, author of *Yoakemae* (*Before the Dawn*), that were labeled as inappropriate by the Japanese authoritarian government. One day, Harumi was arrested as an anti–Japanese activist and taken to a detention center for a year and a half. When he came back from the detention center in October 1941, he became weak and lost weight.

Keiji was told by his uncle, a former Imperial Japanese navy officer, that Harumi was a great man. Before the end of the war when many Japanese blindly believed in the Japanese government, backed by the emperor system, Harumi told his younger brother, "The emperor system should be abolished. This war is wrong. Absolutely, Japan is going to be defeated. You should not waste your life [for the war or the emperor]."[26] At that time Harumi's brother was just about to leave Japan to join the mission to attack Pearl Harbor. He had remembered Harumi's words and tried to protect himself from being killed. He returned to Japan when the war ended.

Harumi often criticized Japanese fascism.[27] Because of Harumi, his family was picked on and became the target of bullying by the members of the same community. There was a Korean man, Mr. Pak or *Paku san*, who lived near Keiji's house in Hiroshima City in real life, just like *Paku san* in *Hadashi no Gen*.[28] In the film, Mr. Pak had a particular and even peculiar role as he gave the Nakaoka family food and helped Gen and his mother escape from the fire. In real life, Keiji often played with his daughter. One day, Keiji innocently made fun of Koreans by singing a racial song, and his father scolded him. Harumi explained to him that Japan colonized Korea and took all of its natural resources. Many Koreans including *Paku san* were forced to come to Japan and live as cheap laborers.[29] Keiji was only a six-year-old boy, but Harumi treated him like an adult in this matter. Keiji did not even know what discrimination was, but he understood that he should not have made fun of them.

NAKAZAWA'S MOTHER, KIMIYO

Keiji's mother, Kimiyo, spent three years before her death in 1966 in a hospital in Hiroshima. Keiji had seen how weak she had become over the years due to the late effects of radiation. He was told by his older brother that the Atomic Bomb Casualty Commission (ABCC), *Genbaku Shōgai Chōsa Iinkai*, supported by the American government, came to their house immediately after she died and were very interested in taking her body to the United States for autopsy to examine causes of her health problems.[30] His brother was upset that there was no way that he would let the ABCC dissect her body. Keiji himself had received many letters from the ABCC asking him to be a voluntary patient among the atomic bomb survivors for medical research. He thought that he would never let the ABCC study him like a guinea pig. He had torn up those letters and hated that the United States and their atomic bomb destroyed their lives in Hiroshima.

At the crematory, Keiji looked at his mother's body being cremated and turned into ashes on the bed. In following the Japanese Buddhist funeral rituals, he tried to collect a throat bone and other main bones, but all of her bones were so fragile that there were hardly any remains left.[31] Because of the late effects of radiation exposure, her body had become very weak, and the entire bones turned to ash. He was upset about the atomic bomb again and felt that it was so painful to see that his mother had become like that.

HIBAKUSHA AND THE CREATION OF BAREFOOT GEN

Keiji may have survived the bombing, but he continued to live as *Hibakusha*, a marginalized group in Japanese society, until he passed away. Every summer, Keiji had to hear the same debate over the atomic bombing in Hiroshima. Keiji felt depressed about himself as *Hibakusha* and hated to hear the phrase *genbaku* (the atomic bomb). This also reminded him of his poor childhood. Many Japanese were trying to collect signatures to support antinuclear weapons, and he felt guilt and remorse, as if he had done something terrible before.[32]

Keiji was discriminated against as *Hibakusha* when he moved to Tokyo to become a manga writer in the 1960s. When Keiji talked about his atomic bomb experience, his colleagues suddenly looked at him differently and behaved differently when he was around. He did not understand at the time. Later, he found out that there was a rumor about *Hibakusha* in Tokyo: you might be exposed to radiation through *Hibakusha* so you should not let them close to you or you should not share a cup with *Hibakusha*.[33] Keiji was upset with their attitude. People in Tokyo had no idea about radiation at all. He was also amazed by their double standards. They claimed that "Japan is the only country that has suffered from the atomic bomb," but they lacked sensitivity and discriminated atomic bomb survivors.[34] They were just ignorant.

Barefoot Gen started in *Shōnen Jump* in June 1973.[35] Keiji was surprised to receive positive reviews from fans. Keiji wanted to tell a younger audience how horrible war was through the manga series. Keiji intentionally drew ugly images of atomic bomb *genbaku* victims. He felt that there was no way to sugarcoat what Hiroshima City went through on that day. The drawings of the atomic bomb victims should be real enough to tell them that *genbaku* was awful.[36] Keiji intended for his audience to feel repulsed by reading *Barefoot Gen*. He believed that these ugly images of the atomic bomb victims would make young children despise war.

HIROSHIMA AND FUKUSHIMA

Many people acknowledge Hiroshima City's *Genbaku Dōmu* (Hiroshima Peace Memorial) as a symbol for peace, but Keiji remembered that there was a debate over *Genbaku Dōmu* in early postwar Japan. The debate was whether the building should be demolished as it could spoil the beauty of a new Hiroshima City.[37] Back then, many people in Hiroshima City were not comfortable seeing anything that reminded them of either the war or the atomic bomb. Keiji thought differently and believed that the building should be kept as a reminder that Japan was involved in the war and the atomic bomb was dropped on Hiroshima City. The nuclear weapons dropped on Hiroshima and Nagasaki were small.[38] But nuclear weapon technology has advanced considerably over the past years. If nuclear weapons are used now, they would be the end of humanity. The real danger may lie ahead for all nations as long as there are nuclear weapons in the world. Nuclear weapons do not just kill instantaneously but they cause long-term health problems for survivors.

Keiji attended the Hiroshima Peace Memorial Ceremony on August 6, 2011, for the first time. He did not usually like this type of ceremony because it seemed inadequate or insufficient: a bell rang, doves flew away, a chorus sang, and prayers for peace were said.[39] Keiji felt that neither war nor nuclear weapons will ever go away by doing any of these things in any ceremony. Keiji imagined that he would love to attend a peace memorial ceremony in which Japanese individuals could throw rocks at the figures of Japanese war criminals. Keiji saw an image of the execution of Benito Mussolini. Keiji was amazed to see that people were dragging his dead body to the street, and everyone, children to the elderly threw rocks at it. Looking at the image, Keiji thought that Japanese people should be angry when they need to be. Otherwise, they may not remember what happened in Hiroshima.

In addition, according to his book, Keiji was still apprehensive about the emperor system.[40] If the Shōwa emperor had said, "No" to the attack on Pearl Harbor, the attack could have been prevented. Many lives could have been saved. The Shōwa emperor did not do anything but let it happen. After the end of the war, the Shōwa emperor was as if he had not done anything wrong.

When Japan experienced the devastating earthquake that hit the Tōhoku region of Japan, Keiji saw shocking images of a tsunami striking the coastlines including Fukushima where the two nuclear energy power stations were located. Keiji always opposed building nuclear energy plants in an earthquake-prone country like Japan.[41] The Japanese government often claimed that there were differences between nuclear weapon and nuclear energy technologies as if making nuclear energy plants was much safer than nuclear weapons. The government had built as many nuclear energy power stations as it could, and many Japanese people had not said anything to oppose them. These irresponsible attitudes of the Japanese made him resentful. Keiji did not expect it to happen like that, but he did suspect that this type of nuclear-related incident might happen sooner or later. In addition, soon after the Fukushima nuclear incident, some people began to spread a rumor that the effects of radiation exposure may be "contagious" through the survivors from Fukushima.[42] This reminded Keiji of what he went through in the 1960s when people did not know about the effects of the atomic bomb and radiation exposure. Keiji realized that many Japanese people still did not understand them at all. His antiwar and anti-nuclear weapon messages were spread through the manga/anime series of *Barefoot Gen* so that future generations would know the true horrors of atomic warfare and the devastation and destruction the use of such bombs can cause.

Discussion

The anime version of *Barefoot Gen* aims to connect with young Japanese who do not know what war is like. In the film, Gen coped with the terrible situation and was determined to overcome the adversity he faced during and after the atomic bombing. The anime movie can be interpreted as a means to educate about what happened in Hiroshima with Japanese cultural values such as *ganbaru*. Thus, the anime film has played a symbolic role in building an image of a peaceful postwar Japan, supported by its popular culture.

Having presented a full understanding of *Barefoot Gen*, the film/manga can be considered a type of anti-*nihonjinron* literature, although it is a manga series. During the mid–1970s through the early 1980s, many Japanese scholars, magazine writers and newspaper columnists were interested in writing about the supposed ethnic homogeneity of Japanese society, and the vast collection of publications about the uniqueness of Japan and its culture led to the development of a new genre, *Nihonjinron* (theories of Japaneseness).[43] The long-lasting popularity of *nihonjinron* literature has constructed particular images and narratives of Japan, providing a way of thinking which recognized the strong ties between Japanese individuals and their society.

Nihonjinron literature often emphasizes stereotypical images of Japan and its people: Japan is presented and understood as a unique homogeneous society with the essence of "Japaneseness" which tends to undermine its ethnic, cultural and social diversity.[44] *Nihonjinron* literature also tends to omit historical facts that may become a disadvantage to postwar Japan, i.e., the notions of inner/outer (*uchi/soto*), front/back (*ura/omote*), and on-stage /off-stage (*tatemae/honne*).[45] But Keiji's work, particularly the manga series and essays, portray the diversity of Japanese society before and after 1945. He has claimed a type of social oppression his family experienced in prewar Japan, based on what they believed, and they were labeled as anti–Japanese (*hi-kokumin*). He has described his wartime experience as Japanese fascism. His work also acknowledges that Japan was an empire, and its government was an aggressor before and during the Second World War. He talks about a form of social discrimination he and his mother experienced as *Hibakusha*, a marginalized group.

Keiji's work is remarkable in the sense that he gave his critical opinion about the atomic bombing of Hiroshima and the prewar Japanese authoritarian government by writing *Hadashi no Gen* in the early 1970s when many *nihonjinron* writers were pleased to see their nation's rapid economic growth and discussed its cultural uniqueness. Keiji's work stands at a unique position in the field of Japanese studies, although he may not be a scholar or researcher.

Conclusion

This essay has examined how the effects of the atomic bomb are portrayed in the anime version of *Barefoot Gen* and also attempted to identify the manga author's messages in the film. Keiji's work portrays the aftermath of the effects of the atomic bomb on Hiroshima City, Hiroshima, with horrific but realistic images, and he also shares his experience through the manga and anime series. Keiji started to write about the U.S. atomic bomb explosion in Hiroshima such as *Kuroi ameni utarete* (*Struck by Black Rain*) in 1968 that eventually led to the creation of *Barefoot Gen* in 1973. Despite his success, Keiji had not been so keen to write any manga series about the atomic bomb until his mother passed away in 1966. When *Hadashi no Gen* was released, Keiji was surprised to receive positive reviews from its readers. That helped him continue to write the manga series and tell his young audience about the horrors of war and the plight of *genbaku* victims of Hiroshima.

This essay has found that Keiji's work is a type of anti-*nihonjinron* literature. His work discussed ethnic and social conflicts before and after the end of the Second World War in the early 1970s when many Japanese described Japan as a unique homogeneous society. Keiji became critical of Japan and its people: the Japanese government did not do much to help *Hibakusha* victims, and he strongly felt that the Japanese should not forget what the people of Hiroshima City went through on that day. Although he passed away on December 19, 2012, his central message through his work remains: "Hiroshima" should not be forgotten as long as there are *Hibakusha* and nuclear weapons in the world.

Notes

1. K. Nakazawa, *Hadashi no Gen: Watashi no isho* (Tokyo: Asahi gakusei shinbunsha, 2012), p. 193.
2. K. Nakazawa, *Hadashi no Gen: Jiden* (Tokyo: Kyōikushiryō shuppansha, 1994), pp. 3–5.
3. *Ibid.*
4. *Hasashi no Gen* (*Barefoot Gen*) 1983, motion picture, Gen Production, Tokyo. Nakazawa *Hadashi no Gen*, p. 219.
5. D.P. Martinez, "Gender, Shifting Boundaries and Global Cultures," in D. P. Martinez, ed., *The Worlds of Japanese Popular Culture: Gender, Shifting Boundaries and Global Cultures* (Cambridge: Cambridge University Press, 1998), pp. 1–18.
6. See, for example, J. Orr: *The Victims as Heroes: Ideologies of Peace and National Identity in Postwar Japan* (Honolulu: University of Hawaii Press, 2001); R. Lifton, *Death in Life: Survivors of Hiroshima* (Chapel Hill: North Carolina University Press, 1991).
7. K. Nakazawa, *Hadashi no Gen: Jiden* (Tokyo: Kyōikushiryō shuppansha, 1994), p. 225.
8. K. Iwabuchi, *Recentering Globalization: Popular Culture and Japanese Transnationalism* (Durham: Duke University Press, 2002), pp. 28–33.
9. N. Abercrombie, S. Hill and B. Turner, *Dictionary of Sociology*, 3d ed. (London: Penguin, 1994), pp. 326–327.
10. K. Nakazawa, *Hadashi no Gen, Jiden*, pp. 228–229.
11. K. Nakazawa, *Hadashi no Gen: Watashi*, p. 202.
12. *Ibid.*, pp. 191–192.
13. K. Nakazawa: *Hadashi no Gen: Jiden*, p. 45.
14. *Ibid.*, p. 49.
15. *Ibid.*, pp. 52–54.
16. *Ibid.*, pp. 55–59.
17. *Ibid.*, pp. 61.
18. *Ibid.*, pp. 60. In the film, Gen's *Korean* neighbor showed up and helped him and his mother.
19. *Ibid.*, p. 62.
20. *Ibid.*, p. 64.
21. *Ibid.*, p. 171.
22. *Ibid.*, pp. 189–194.
23. *Ibid.*, pp. 108, 112–113, 118–119, 137–138, 150–151, 156–157 and 168–169.
24. *Ibid.*, pp. 13–14.
25. *Ibid.*, pp. 17–18 and 20–22.
26. *Ibid.*, p. 25.
27. *Ibid.*, pp. 24–25 and 27–30.
28. *Ibid.*, p. 43.
29. *Ibid.*, p. 44.
30. *Ibid.*, pp. 190–191.
31. *Ibid.*, p. 192.
32. *Ibid.*, p. 185.
33. *Ibid.*, p. 186.
34. *Ibid.*, p. 186.
35. *Ibid.*
36. *Ibid.*, pp. 211–212.
37. *Ibid.*, p. 202.
38. K. Nakazawa: *Hadashi no Gen: Watashi*, pp. 202–203.
39. *Ibid.*, p. 204.
40. *Ibid.*, p. 205.
41. *Ibid.*, p. 206.

42. *Ibid.*, pp. 208–209.

43. P. N. Dale, *The myth of Japanese Uniqueness* (London: Routledge, 1986), p. 15. Popular Japanese scholars such as Chie Nakane and Takeo Doi supported the argument of the cultural uniqueness of Japanese society. C. Nakane Chie, *Tate shakai no ningen kankei* (*Human Relations in a Vertical Society*) (Tokyo, Kōdansha, 1967); T. Doi, Takeo: *Amae no Kōzō* (*The Anatomy of Dependence*) (Tokyo: Kōbundō, 1971).

Shoichi Watanabe, a scholar and Japanese cultural critic and Shintaro Ishihara, a novelist and politician have also contributed to the argument of the uniqueness of Japanese society by discussing an assumed Japanese total loyalty to the emperor and its emperor system and stereotypically comparing Japan with Western countries, especially the United States (e.g., one race, cultural homogeneity, and groupism in a small island nation in Northeast Asia vs. mixed races, cultural heterogeneity, and individualism in a large nation across the North American continent). S. Watanabe, *Kokumin no Kyōiku* (*The Education of Japanese People*) (Tokyo: Sankei Shinbunsha, 2000), S. Ishihara and A. Morita, *"No" to ieru Nippon* (*Japan That Can Say "No"*) (Tokyo: Kobunsha, 1989).

44. See, for example, Yoshio Sugimoto, *An Introduction to Japanese Society*, 3d ed. Cambridge: Cambridge University Press, 2012, pp. 2–4, pp. 13–14, and P.N. Dale, *The Myth of Japanese Uniqueness*. The period between the late 1970s and the early 1980s was considered as the peak of the popularity of the distinctiveness of Japanese culture for the majority of the Japanese. But in the mid–1980s, many Western and Western-educated Japanese anthropologists and sociologists began examining the diversity of Japanese society or the "Other" Japanese such as women, part-time workers, minority groups and foreign migrants.

45. Compare with the work of N. Rosenberger, ed., *Japanese Sense of Self* (Cambridge: Cambridge University Press, 1992), p. 62.

Yuichi and Jizō in *Black Rain*: Imamura's Phenomenological Attempt to Render a Hiroshima Wormhole Experience Among His Audience

Keiko Takioto Miller

First an unprecedented crisis brings the world to a sudden halt. Then journalists rush to the location of the incident, collect facts and report the event objectively. Reactions differ, from primal expression of shock to indifference. Some are swift enough to transfer responses into actions of service. Give us days, weeks, months or years, however, always in the multiples of three; the universe makes its survivors and witnesses reflect through a matrix of time and space. In turn, we rely on other genres to craft reflections that challenge the test of time and our ever-shifting lens. No matter. Eventually, even our testimonials carry an unsuspecting voice of grandeur, if not humanity. The stuff of our culture, too, has been made this way.

Words alone may be powerful in helping us cognitively order the otherwise chaotic sensory data in our memory. Yet no sooner do they enter into our cranial furrows than our bodies become numbed to them; they dangle in the void, if not forgotten completely. Since the advent of the first reels, film as a literary medium has been more than a simplistic visual transliteration of its textual prototype. Its potential ability to invite its audience into the field of re-enactment by opening up all five senses synesthesically through a narrow audio-visual gate is left at the mercy of its creator. The latter must transcend technical temptations of idealizing characters and their surroundings as a means to an end. Thus, whether the creator can leave a lasting imprint on his/her audience's sensory bed depends on his/her detachment of ego. This critical step allows them to phenomenologically process their cinematographic experience into the realm of symbolic clarus. For it is here, in this aesthetically charged field of human senses and mind that a director may have chanced to awaken the authenticity in both his/her characters and audience.

By investing his craftsmanship in subtle elements, the director of *Black Rain* (*Kuroi ame*, 1989), Shōhei Imamura, phenomenologically awakens human perceptions among his audience, who, in turn, is invited to co-participate in the symbol making. To this end, he infuses a sub-character, not present in Masuji Ibuse's story, based on which he crafted his film. His name is Yuichi, the Jizō stonecutter. This essay will focus on the essence of this Buddhist stone deity not only as a vehicle imbued with Imamura's intentions behind its uncanny presence, but also how it is effective as a symbolical restorer of archetypal Japanese aesthetic-based ethics in the face of the catastrophic events of the Hiroshima and Nagasaki bombings. To this end, both the language and method of the Western phenomenology will be used to analyze the awakening of authenticity in the characters of the film whose lives become intertwined with the hidden operative in the enigmatic Jizō.

The Co-Arising Autochthonous Origin of Symbols

In his book *The Face of Jizō: Images and Cult in Medieval Japanese Buddhism*, Hank Glassman writes, "Images speak to the human mind and heart in a direct way that text cannot. [I]nterpretation of the numinous power of icons was from the beginning ambivalent."[1] If so, Glassman seems to imply that there is something inherently sacred which, in the advent of textuality, humans have since failed to comport themselves in balance with "it." In its stead, we have come to honor conformity, relying more on competitive displays of our highest quality in technicality only devoid of the essence. However, given our opportunity to travel back to where we had concealed "it" in the first place, we may be able to recall the auspice intrinsic in the dynamic union of two opposites. It is during our very posturing with both-footedness that the numinous presences itself multi-dimensionally within our reach. The Greek origin of the word icon, eikon, means "akin to."[2] Accordingly, then, an icon, per se, is not absolute; its totality must be understood necessarily by unraveling that to which it is akin.

As a practitioner of Japanese calligraphy, *shodō*, I am constantly made aware of such numinosity at the co-arising origin. With a certain primordial significance, the brush and I move as one when scripting each ideograph (Ch: hanzu, Jp: kanji). Allow me to describe the process: My entry into a ritual realm begins by first tapping fresh water into a small porcelain vessel. No matter, I clutter the surface on which to practice my *shodō* by arranging each tool in its proper place, respectively: an ink stone, ink stick, water vessel, and a brush on my right, a sheet of felt, and a paper weight. The writing space now aligns with my torso directly opposite it. There is nothing but the edge of the table that separates these dormant tools and myself. I meditate in the moment's given stillness until I feel a mutual omphalus connection with the earth. It signals me to pour the water into the stone inkwell. Like a seasonal monsoon rain, it takes its own course flowing from a high plateau to a depression. Grabbing the ink stick firmly with all my fingertips, I begin to grind it against the hard surface of the "plateau," dipping it now and then into and out of the "waterhole." No sooner do I notice the glistening of the oil from the eroding ink stick, now an aquified black fluid, I feel myself enveloped by a subtle aroma of its earthy essence wood, fire, metal, and soil. The forces of river current have pulverized the hardened earth to smooth silt. The aqueous motility within me tries to attune with the aqueous movement of my grinding the ink. We are about to enter into our mutually aqueous threshold. The table's edge becomes blurred. The ink is ready. I pause to rest my ink stick against the upper rim of the ink stone. Methodically, I place a sheet of rice paper onto the surface of the felt piece. This act itself is punctuated by my strategically placing the paperweight at the top and a gentle stroke of my hand vertically across the paper, for me, to retrieve its arborous origin. I mimic the erect posture of an ancient tree whose invisible root system upholds its visible dignity. In this way my spine aligns with the verticality of my bamboo brush handle now held firmly in my right hand with the middle thumb acknowledging their mutual centeredness. I dip my brush in the ink, draining any excess on the grinding stone's "plateau." I pause for a moment and breathe deeply. I feel myself entering into a primordial threshold where a certain human first crafted a glyph. The undifferentiated brush point, now imbued with the living ink, is about to meet the sacred nexus between the embodied essence of the experienced reality lived by the ancestral creator of a given script, and the "emerging field of understanding" of the Logos, the rationality, or the language, of what human senses have embodied as Eros.[3] In this curious way, I am able to temporarily return to an ambivalent liminal realm, and recall and dialogue in a "pre-ontological"[4] and holistically unconscious way, that which has been concealed behind/beneath the symbol I am about to brush on a blank sheet of rice paper. In his book *The Body's Recollection of Being: Phenomenological Psychology and the Deconstruction of Nihilism*, David Michael Levin makes an attempt to "educe, by appropriately hermeneutical strategies, the hidden presence of Eros [in "a symbolic manifestation of the primordial Logos"] in an emerging body of understanding [in search of] an auspicious beginning."[5] This "auspicious beginning," or "emerging body of understanding," corresponds to no other than the "autochthonously"[6] realized origin mentioned by Glassman.

At one time, any given indigenous group was left in relative isolation to be able to pre-ontologically geo-embody the dynamically operative male-female essence of their locality during the process of their culture-in-the-making. Owing to its most eastern geographical location from the original departure point of the first human migration out of Africa, the first Eurasian stock,[7] of which one happened to arrive on the Japanese archipelago to dwell there, were able to enjoy a relatively long period of uninterrupted geo-embodiment process until their first prehistoric contact from the Asian Continent as late as 300 BC. These were the Jōmon people. Thus, for them, in an ever-diversifying world since then, that "auspicious beginning" had to be given its own organic time, hence autochthonous," not by the human clock, through each phase—foundation, construction, deconstruction, recollection, re-enactment, redemption, retrieval, and regeneration—in order to redefine themselves as a cultural group. The roots of the more recent infamous reputation that Japanese turn what they have learned from others into uniquely their own may literally lie deeply in this Jōmon sediment, owing to its relatively long spatio-temporal isolation from the rest of the world. When such time to retrieve their bodily imprint was denied to them, their access to the Eros became blocked at the expense of having to obey an artificially choreographed ideology of a given dominant other.

Suppression of the "Auspicious Beginning" During the Japanese Acculturation of the West

In the case of the Japanese, as a cultural group, their abrupt exposure to and blindingly expedient emulation of the technologically advanced West during the Meiji Restoration and beyond put them on the fear-based ideological path of the then imperialist West. The inauthentic behavior on the part of the Japanese government is evident in their ironical violation of the "auspicious beginning" inherent in the prehistoric Jōmon and Yayoi archaeological evidences. No sooner than reacting with primal fear imprinted first by the sight in 1852 of the ominous Black Ships under the commandership of Commodore Matthew Perry, the Japanese found themselves ushered into the military mode of the West. Presently, the self-appointed oligarchy conveniently summoned the 16-year-old emperor out of his lineage's centuries-long political refuge in Kyoto to make his emblematic presence as "the genuine hereditary evidence" of Japan's existence, both physically and spiritually. This was crucial in justifying their action for reclaiming the "native" Shintoism as the basis for their nationalism. In this bi-polar mode, Japan was able to fuel 100 percent of its national energy into technologically masculinized manifestation, Logos, at the expense of suppressing its feminine essence, Eros. The rest is history, as we say, but this essay will not settle for a cliché; it is moved to question our own nihilistic behaviors ignorant of what is dynamically in store beneath this so-called "auspicious beginning."

As his aesthetic response to the humanity, which had met its nihilistic end, Imamura unravels this "auspicious beginning" in his film *Black Rain*. It is particularly present in his peculiar attempt to ground his audience phenomenologically. The idea is to question with Imamura the motive behind his insertion of the iconography of Jizō, and the sub-character Yuichi who crafts them. Neither is present in Ibuse's textual work upon which Imamura based his cinematographic oeuvre. A brief discussion concerning the role of Yuichi's mother, as Imamura's another sub-character, will be added to elucidate the operative behind the so-called Levinian "auspicious beginning" which corresponds to Glassman's "autochthonous."[8]

Taking advantage of an inherently visual field, literally and figuratively, of the film, Imamura plants, into its furrow, a secret seed. This seed offers ontologically powerful visuality, but it does not presence itself until the end—and only to those who cared enough to open up to its hidden potential. Deliberately concealing the uncanny in his sub-characters, rather than in the protagonists, he leaves at the discretion of his audience to undergo their own, "labor," if not struggle, of cultivating the soil to see the subtle in order for them to be able to truly able to savor its fruit. As part of their philosophical practice, neither Levin nor Glassman categorically proclaims one school of exigent metaphysical principle over another. Their mediatory, inclusive, and pragmatic approaches themselves resonate not only with each other but also with Imamura's use of Jizō both as a symbol and method. For example, while critiquing the theoretical formality found in Heideggerian phenomenology, Levin takes it into account as an earlier but crucial phase of the whole phenomenological movement which took its turn towards a more "corporeal schema" with Merleau-Ponty.[9] Similarly, Glassman, who realizes Jizō's "embodied interventions on behalf of believers"[10] in Japan, adapts the art historian Aby Warburg's methodology, which challenged the convention of his time by insisting that "while image and word certainly form an opposition in his thought, he also saw them as an inevitably linked synergistic pair."[11] For Imamura, too, simplistically sensationalizing cinematographically the catastrophic event of Hiroshima/Nagasaki atomic bombs would only prolong the already meaninglessly divided animosities between Japan and the West. He does not only realize his internally felt need to transcend the divide; he also uses this newly retrieved internal compass to guide him through the dark passage back into the prehistoric Jōmon, Yayoi and Kofun realms in which to see himself lay bare with the primordial materiality of the terracotta *dogu* or *haniwa*, a possible Japanese archetype of Jizō—its "autochthonously realized origin." That is, first, as it is evidenced by both utilitarian and ritually symbolical (in that order), figurines and terracotta vessels, the original human migrants who had settled on the Japanese archipelago were, were able to attain, on their own, their sense of who they were on this very geo-climatically dynamic aqua-terra earth formation by the end of the Jōmon period. But, second, it wasn't until the advent of the arrival and assimilation of the "other" from the Continental Asia during the Yayoi period that the Japanese had been given their first opportunity to post-autochthonously realize their origin. The Japanese affirmation of what their underlying aesthetic essence from origin is best conveyed by Paul Varley in his *Japanese Culture*:

The serene and elegant appearance of Yayoi pottery suggests that the civilizing influences that brought new technology to Japan in this age also advanced the mentality of its people. The untamed spirit reflected in the shape and ornamentation of some Jōmon pottery and in the dogu figurines was either lost or suppressed by the craftsmen of Yayoi. But perhaps the most striking difference between the two kinds of pottery is that in Jōmon the stress is on decoration and in Yayoi it is on form.… In aesthetic terms, the cherishing of primitive pottery rests on the value of naturalness, or the preference of things in their original, unaltered states. For the artist or craftsman, naturalness means staying close to his materials, [without] seek[ing] to disguise the clay he uses.[12]

In a similar vein, it is interesting to note that all three, Levin, Glassman and Imamura, as products of more recent schools of thought, embrace ambivalence as their only viable soil in which to nurture their seed of truth in its primal intimacy within into a dynamic tree of knowledge. In this sense their philosophy automatically precludes a methodology, which demands of us to participate in life fully as a whole being, not as an over-active rational mind disconnected from its sensuous partner in flesh in the latter's interest of winning a metaphysical argument as a means to an end. For all three, the only end they would settle for is a kind, which is able to renew itself as part of the eternally evolving and dynamic cosmic cycle. As method-practicing philosophers, they all demand our undergoing its process deliberately at its own organic pace to be able to feel its hidden universal aesthetics in the oscillation of its elements. Evolutionarily speaking, this is esotericism at its best.

Samurai Paradox in Imamura's Art

So how does Imamura help his audience find themselves "in" their own both-footing suited for their homage towards the hidden aesthetics, if not ethics, behind the "autochthonously realized origin" in his cinematographic use of Jizō in his *Black Rain*? As to why he based his film on Ibuse's novel in the first place is a speculation on my part. Clearly the story's credibility lies in the novel's author Ibuse's inclusion of the *Hibakusha*'s words based on their lived experience. He also sprinkles with intermittent haiku-like lyrical passages, which surrounds the main plot dealing with the challenge of the A-bomb radiated young maiden Yasuko, whose uncle, Mr. Shizuma, tries to dutifully seek an opportunity to find a good suitor for before his own death as a promise to his deceased sister. They seem to idyllically hint either the Japanese resignation ethics of "*Shikata ga nai!*" ("There's nothing you can do!") and "*hara hachi-bu*" (Literally, "eight-tenth of the belly," hence "moderation") and/or aesthetics of "*mono no aware*" ("the pathos of nature" and "transiency of life") making his Western readers close the book with such wonderment as "Why aren't Japanese angry at us?" Imamura's art is like a samurai paradox based on the 17th century deeply Zen sword master Ichiun Odagiri 小田切一雲 (1630–1706). As a disciple of his master Hariya Sekiun's school "The Sword of the No-abiding Mind" 無住心間, Ichiun reached enlightenment amidst his practicing his master's sword technique called ai-uchi 相打ち("mutual-strike"). It is used to mark one's reaching a pinnacle of swordsmanship through a rigorous Zen discipline.[13] Daisetsu Suzuki records in his book *Zen and Japanese Culture*, an account written by Ichiun on how the spirit and conduct of a swordsman is no different than an ordinary man's deep understanding of the earth's elements at work in an ordinary person within and without:

> When Heavenly Reason [t'ien-li 天理] is present in us it knows how to behave on every occasion: when a man sees fire, his Reason knows at once how to use it; when he finds water, it

tells him at once what it is good for; when he meets a friend, it makes him greet him; when he sees a person in a dangerous situation, it makes him go right out to his rescue. As long as we are one with it, we never err in our proper behavior however variable the situation may be.[14]

Essentially, for Ichiun, when one's feet are firmly rooted in the ground, he or she is able to meet any unexpected situation with a situationally appropriate comportment because his or her reasoning is derived from the immovable origin, hence the expression *fudō-shin* 不動心.

Realizing a human possibility to spiritually transcend this technically limited optimal edge, Ichiun, then at thirty-something, comes up with a higher alternative: ai-nuké, or "mutual passing-by."[15] While they are basically the same thing, Ichiun makes it ontologically more powerful by indicating that in order to liberate oneself truly from the worldly bondage (technique-based competitiveness), one must first bodily undergo diligent mind-body practices. As such, at the zenith of one's technical skills, if realized mutually with that of the opponent's, two enemies can then occupy the same seat, or "auspicious beginning" together in another dimension of primordial ecstasy. There they are able to dance in an eternal Merleau-Pontian chiasm.[16] According to Abe, the Chinese and Japanese ideograph for Zen Emptiness wu (Ch)/mu(Jp) 無 is derived from its ancient root wu (Ch)/bu(Jp) 舞, meaning "dance."[17] Note the difference between the lower radicals in their otherwise mutually similar upper one. In the former, the four dots signify fire, hence deconstruction. In the latter, two sub-radicals signifying two opposing elements facing back to back, hence a turning point within a cycle. In a further examination based on L. Wieger, S.J.'s *Chinese Characters: Their Origin, Etymology, History, Classification and Signification*, we learn that with the upper portion carrying the shared radical meaning "a multitude … of 大 men, acting upon a 林 forest, felling the trees, clearing of wood a tract of land.… Hence chuan-chu the general abstract notion of vanishing, defect, want, negation,"[18] it is easy to see that both ideographs convey the essence of ambivalence of the death and regeneration simultaneously in chiasmic motion, to use the Merleau-Ponty's term. Imamura is moved deeply to continue his shared mission with Ibuse to dance their ai-nuké through his re-enactment of the Hiroshima and Nagasaki bombings, and rise from their ashes anew. For by modeling thusly, according to guild of Japanese craftsman of old, perhaps others, too, may join their primordial dance, defying all boundaries. Such an act of compassion was not too far removed from the way the medieval dramaturge Zeami Motokiyo (1363–1443) designed his architectural space of noh as a liminal space of re-enactment and redemption as evident in his play Atsumori which, like Imamura's film, transcends its 12th century epic predecessor "The Death of Atsumori" in *The Tales of Heike*. In all three parallels, the time plays a critical role in allowing the latter's spiritual awakening and transformation beyond the former's well-lauded technical prowess. The study of phenomenology and Zen helps to elucidate this point in the discussion of the Ibuse-Imamura pair.

Imamura's Adaptation of Ibuse, in Essence

Like Ichiun who transformed his master Sekiun's method, Zeami who existentially transcended his father Kan'ami's technical edge both in theater and the latter's physical death, Imamura takes his predecessor Ibuse's textual attempt to convey the reality of the Hiroshima/Nagaski bombings by ontologically crafting the visual medium to help his audience summon the hidden Eros as a necessary step to move them to "dance." Particularly powerful are the elements found in the following two passages in Ibuse's novel that are also present in Imamura's film.

> In the direction of the city, smoke was rising high up into the sky. [I]t was no ordinary smoke. My knees as I squatted there shook so uncontrollably that I pressed against a rock, heedless of a small white flower clinging to it.[19]
>
> August 7. Fine
> I tried to sit up in bed, but an excruciating pain shot through my shoulders and down my lower back and legs.... To turn on my side was agony, but I had a bright idea. With my right hand, I tugged at the seat of my pants so as to turn my body on its side. Then I hunched up my body and got my buttocks in the air, then got onto my knees and so succeeded, little by little, in raising the upper part of my body. Sufferers from lumbago get up in the same way ... as when someone doing a classical Japanese dance gets up off the floor. I found myself wondering: perhaps the originator of the Japanese dance had suffered from lumbago?[20]

In both passages by Ibuse, the hope of regeneration is poignantly rendered. But the same determination with which the lumbago patient in the second passage struggles to get up from the ground zero is metaphorically the same as the white flower which clung on the rock on the day of the bombing. Applying the convoluted motion apparent in the second, Imamura turns the passivity in the first into effective moving images through his character Yuichi. Effective, because, through Yuichi, he succeeds in making his audience undergo their corporeal diligence, and subsequently embody the method with which to carry their actions holistically and meaningfully once return to the world after their cinematographic hiatus.

Besides the inherent given in the film—the motion, at first Imamura's choice of adding the stone statue Jizō alone doesn't seem compelling enough as a metaphor. Like the prehistoric Yayoi potters, he realizes that the ontological significance of a metaphor is not in its external décor, but in its subtle operative of origin hidden in its native clay. Thus, through his creation of the sub-character Yuichi, the Jizō stone cutter, he is able to animate the stone statues and in turn his audience. Not only that. There is something more to Imamura's presenting Yuichi as a war victim of a PTD (post-traumatic depression). By our worldly standard, he is a broken human being living at a margin of the society, no different than, we would also come to learn, the film's protagonist Yasuko, who is faced with the challenge of meeting a good suitor as a damaged product. Looming over any temptation to sensationalize war victims, Imamura instead employs Yuichi's PTD symptoms openly in the film, like a lumbago sufferer, as a viable catalyst to involve not only his other characters, including the protagonist Yasuko, but in the process, his audience. Every time Yuichi hears an engine sound roaring outside his stone-cutter's hut, be it a bus, jeep or motor bike, he goes into a fit and madly dashes out into the street with a pillow and a hoe, yelling something unintelligible. When he finds himself able to stop the vehicle's wheels, he screams triumphantly, "Seiko! Seiko!" ("Good, I got them"). Let us dwell briefly on this creation of Imamura by simultaneously wearing both Levin's corporeally rooted phenomenological and Glassman's non-dualistic conciliatory lenses.

First of all, it is clear that neither Levin nor Glassman takes image or word as a means to an end.

> [I]f we cling to the dominant tradition ... which the prevailing "world picture" continues to conceal and suppress and exclude,... we are lost; but if we break away,... a retrieval of the "origins" of that tradition ... can be emancipatory, a source of strength.[21]
> Icons are not art per se; to read them is to mistake them for something else. The powerfully

affecting properties of paintings and statues depicting Jizō, while they are certainly also grounded in an aesthetic response, are really at core about the sacred power or efficacy of the object.[22]

Imamura realizes the "efficacy of the object" in Jizō as a dynamic way to "retrieve ... the 'origin'" of the Japanese archetypal cultural psyche. By having his audience befriend its unadorned primordial lithic materiality, self-contained womb-phallus dualities in one, and locally and globally appropriated familiar expressions hide untold stories within—he offers a visual amulet for them to carry around with corporeal vigilance throughout their life once out of the theatrical realm. In this sense, Imamura follows the two-step method suggested by the Levenian phenomenology: (1) Erinnerung: He makes diagnoses of the war afflictions clearly to his audience by making them "go deeply into our experienced body of perception; (2) Wiederhoung: He evokes in his audience "the sense that we feel a need to retrieve, from the very depth of our pain, our affliction, our ontical dissatisfactions, an experience of Being its more hospitable, more who wholesome dimensionality.[23] Essentially, to do so, he convenes three critical points in our body: eyes, navel, and feet. Calling the affliction "essentially a characteristic tendency of the optical ('egological' dimensionality of our visionary being," he offers "[t]he anamnesis by which we go down into the preontological (or proto-ontological) body of felt sense, deepening our contact with its panoramic attunement and holistic awareness, lifts up this dark understanding into the clearer light of thought (Thinking begins, fundamentally, in the feet. It roots are there. But the level, or phase, or pre-understanding we mostly tend to contact and work with first is always significantly connected with the experiencing taking place in the region of the navel)."[24] By establishing this optical-biped triad with the navel posited at its center, Levin urges us to awaken our "guardian awareness" of the Being, and get rid of our "historically deepseated guilt and shame, flaming into a terrible hatred of the body" as a separate entity."[25] Jizō, like an ancient omphalous stone, serves to awaken this dimension within us.[26] In his book *Menhirs, Dolmen and Circles of Stone: The Folklore and Mythology of Sacred Stone*, he quotes Devreux who states, "The omphalos is the mythic point where the figuratively vertical axis of mind intersects the figuratively horizontal plane of the physical world, contained within the round of mundane time."[27] Accordingly, when Japan became trapped in the path toward a technological state of military art as a praiseworthy means to an end, it became separate from its ecologically sustainable mode characteristic of the Edo period, according to Kiyoyuki Higuchi 樋口清之, the author of 「梅干と日本刀」 *Umeboshi and the Japanese Sword*.[28] Adapting the new slogan *fukoku-kyōhei* 富国強兵, "Enrich the country, and strengthen its arms"[29] as its metaphysical ideology, it began to suppress its agrarian tradition since the pre-historic Yayoi. The latter understood the secret of sustaining the hidden primordial force in the twining of the chords as had been done by their Jōmon ancestors. As a Buddhist icon, Jizō summons its sentient beings to balance the masculine and feminine principles into one at their axial omphalos. How does Imamura help us phenomenologically delve into this triad's very center in question?

The year is 1950, five years after the end of the World War II. In Hiroshima, those who survived the physical and emotional debris of the bombing have moved onto the next cycle of three years. Finding themselves technically adjusted back to their quotidian lives, they can now focus on other things that matter in life. During this earliest transitional scene of the film, we reacquaint our middle-aged protagonists Mr. Shizuma and his niece Yasuko return. We find them on a bus from Hiroshima to his rural homeland. Yasuko is a young *Hibakusha* who was affected by the atomic radiation upon coming into contact with a rainfall blackened by the soot of the Hiroshima atomic bombing on August 6, 1945. Her uncle Mr. Shizuma is on the mission to keep his promise made to his sister on her death bed that Yasuko be handed over to a good suitor for marriage. We witness a scene of havoc as the bus is about to approach the edge of the village. Suddenly both the characters in the film and audience are interrupted unexpectedly by a peculiar human voice of battle enactment by a sub-character named Yuichi. At first he appears a creature to be pitied, if not avoided. Now that the war is over, his animal-like symptom of PTD is in stark contrast not only to the scenery of the peaceful countryside, but also to the urbanized civility of the two members of the Shizuma family, who carry themselves properly according to the social codes of the time. Needless to say, our thoughts are farthest from even our temptation of wildly guessing him as Yasuko's ideal suitor. Suddenly caught off-guard by the act of this seemingly insane character, the audience, too, find themselves unknowingly caught up in the moment with such a tension. What, another war episode? All we hope, at this point, is to be able to move on to a more peaceful scene. In so doing, we see, out of the corner of our eyes, an uncanny glimpse of his mother desperately helping to rescue her son.

By clarifying the role of phenomenologists Martin Heidegger and Merleau-Ponty and psychologist Carl Jung, respectively, Levin importantly offers a "rigorous method"[30] in order for us to reclaim the Hideggerian "primordial essence of Being," or the "authentic Self," or the "eternal child" which is hidden in the typical adult.[31] According to him, Merleau-Ponty's phenomenology is one "which is capable of working with the body of understanding that is implicitly operative in our sensibility—our feelings, our perceptions, our gestural components."[32] What is at work in Imamura's film is his sense-evoking choreography to grip his audience with his bare "turnip picking"[33] hand, as if it were, and shove them into the dusty scene, so that they can go through the post-war human sufferance in flesh. To achieve this end, he repeats the scene several times with different sets of characters. Then the audience is made to anticipate with fear every time they hear the sound of an engine. On the second occasion, Yuichi reacts to a sound of the jeep driven by a bunch of former military officers. In order to minimize the havoc, his mother inadvertently instructs them to get down on the ground. In desperation, these veterans follow her and the feat ends with Yuichi yelling again, "Seiko! Seiko!" While Imamura may have put Yuichi as a metaphor of human suffering due to war, it is really his mother who, driven by both maternal instinct and compassion, matter-of-factly instructs others to join her son, who now pretends to be "the Captain," in the moment of his insanity. We are all forced to practice our Dōgen's "shinshin datsuraku" (心身脱落), or "casting off of the mind-body."[34] At first, Imamura appears to create a slapstick humor at the expense of his reversing the conventional social hierarchy—the socially inferior woman and her mentally disabled son are now leading the males officers, including Mr. Shizuma. Yet, underneath all this visually burlesque quid pro quo, he inadvertently grabs everyone physically (sensorially) to the ground zero. And there he stirs bitter-sweetly, like the lumbago dancer, something more serious deep inside us: a message that in the face of human sufferance, wars cannot be used as an excuse to put any sentient beings above or below any man-rationalized hierarchy. This is an utter irony to what the Meiji advocate of modernity Fukuzawa Yukichi (1835–1901) said in his Gakumon no Susume 「学問の進め」 or Encouragement of Education (1872–1876): "Heaven does not create one man above or below another man."[35] His avid promotion of independence as a signature of a civilized man got the best of the Japanese who, as a group, blindly emulated the West as the object of their new moral consciousness, devoid of kenshō 顕正, or realizing their true nature.[36]

Like a seven-year itch, no matter what attempts Shizuma makes, the world according to the newly installed modernity's formula, is wearing thin. For example, in order to convince Yasuko's potential suitors, he relies heavily on textuality to legitimize Yasuko's immunity from the "black rain." He takes great pain transcribing his niece's journals in order to use it to obtain an official medical document of proof. But finally it's his words against "theirs." The audience perceives that the world which is too caught up in its technicality is yet to become awakened to the source. Even the Buddhist abbot, from whom Shizuma receives his advice on performing his amateur funeral rites, appears lethargically half-dead, moving only his lips as a service. The six figures which appears on the Japanese byobu screen painting behind him suggests *rokudo noge jizō bosatsu* 六道能化地蔵菩薩 or six manifestations of Jizō signifying his "tireless travels through all regions of this samsaric Saha (J. Shaba)[娑婆]world."[37] The last figure in the painting is mounted on a tortoise. We take a notice of it as the abbot finishes his business and sinks into the same posture as the sixth figure. It corresponds to the sixth of the Daoist and Buddhist "Ox Herding" showing one's "riding the ox back home."[38] Mr. Shizuma has physically reached his home, but has not quite figured out how to be on the right path to his liberation; he is still on his mission to do the right thing by the worldly standard. At this point, he has three choices: one, he can push it in the same direction to its nihilistic end; two, he can switch to a new skill and try perfecting it; or three, he can go beyond his technical correctness by facing his own truth. For the moment, the only thing that seems to be coming circumstantially in his way is the second choice—to try his new skill at reciting Buddhist sutras to meet the increasing rise in demands to perform amateur funerary rites for his dying fellow villagers one after another, including eventually his wife Shigeko's. Through his practice, his "six organs are purified" even amidst vexations.[39] Yet, because this elusiveness alone does not resonate with his whole being, the chaos surmounts exponentially at this junction of the movie. One can hear, at an alarmingly annoying rate, the female shaman's crazed chanting of "Nan'myo horen gekkyo!"; Shigeko hired her as her last hope to better her medical condition. Instead, it, too, only seems to veer the entire family off the illusionary path that mankind has created. We feel the urgency: This has got to stop now!

The modernity's aimless trod on such a wrong path is accentuated in the third PTD scene involving Yuichi. We see a motorcycling punk momentarily paralyzed by Yuichi's anticipated erratic behavior and exclamation, "Seiko!" What does he succeed this time around? Could it be that Imamura sees that our rush to modernity at the expense of the speed of technology creates imbalance in adults because our child within us is forced to meet the standard of Logos at the expense of suppressing our Eros? Imamura further illustrates this by depicting the punk's connection to the village's disfunctional family whose members—the mother and daughter—seek sensuality as their aesthetic response to the humanity's problems. Their disengaged female whole being has been over-compensated by acts of fulfilling their insatiable sexual desire. By removing themselves too far from the cosmic center, they continue to circumnavigate as wander lusts on the periphery of their world.

Yasuko Has Walked Jizō on Her Own Feet!

By this time, Yasuko herself becomes instrumental in stopping Yuichi in the absence of his mother. The cinematic timing is right: Yasuko, too, has not been making much progress with the prospect of her marriage and her health is failing. She is not convinced with her suitor Mr. Aono; she is turned off by his aggressiveness fueled only by his superficial display of his physical attraction to Yasuko as an object of his desire. Curiously, here, the audience is forewarned of this awkward nuptial arrangement when they hear a voice from Yasuko's paternal Grandmother. Under the spell of her dementia, she, too, dwells in a marginal space, but more like a ghost who is closer to the realm of the dead than a worldly being. Now and then she appears from the darkness, dropping a line or two which makes one stop and think. Her messages are at once unintelligible and profound. They carry a half-truth. For example, by mistaking Yasuko for her dead mother Kyoko, she warns Yasuko, "'Kyoko,' if you marry, you will be killed!" While chuckling at the cliché directed to the old woman's senility, the audience could not, at the same time, dismiss Yasuko's "internally felt" awakening emerging on her facial expression. The truth behind Grandmother's message is further reinforced by her abrupt interruption of the Shizumas' discussion to sell the family's mountain. She adamantly, though with such a disinterested voice, insists her opposition to it based on the family's shame (Jp. haji) put on their ancestors, if and when they choose to sell it. Having had her say, she turns around, like a spectral noh shité character, and begins to pray to Buddha. Geo-climatically resituating his audience in their embodied memory of a "mountain," the ancient source of life on whose summit the life-giving rainwater descended from the sky, the urgency for us to reconnect ourselves with this "auspicious beginning" becomes ever more evident in this work of Imamura.

Symbolically powerful is the way Yasuko makes "her official" refusal of her marriage with Aono. It could also be interpreted as Imamura's subtle move against modernity. Four times during the film, Yasuko gets up on the chair to recalibrate manually the clock in the Sizuma's family room with the sound of "pip, pip, pi … ip!" The clock symbolized the modern West and the Japanese relied on the start of the NHK's evening news at seven o'clock to set it every day until the advent of an electric clock. The first time, she obeys her uncle's order as part of her daily chores in a new place. However, on the third occasion when we see her do this in the film, she takes this man-made time telling machine and uses it to adamantly refuse her marriage to Aono. She realizes it as another meaningless way to be praised as a dutiful daughter, and expresses her wish to stay with her Uncle and Aunt. In this way, Yasuko ironically shatters the man-made illusion, by "announcing her own news" precisely at 7 p.m.! Otherwise, why should she keep continuing to blindly weave a shiny ribbon of convenient rules only to end up sleepwalking ignorantly on it until they meet another catastrophic end? Imamura is arousing his audience's omphalos-containing optical-biped triad to help themselves discover the hidden dharma whose timing only obeys the rhythm of the cosmological cycle. By having Yasuko play an instrumental role in this, Imamura first deconstructs the missteps made by the society that failed to truly liberate women as part of democratization in order to realign the essence of women Eros with the primordially "auspicious beginning." Incidentally, the Chinese/Japanese ideograph "beginning" 始 is comprised of the radical "woman" 女, and "foundation"台, which can be further broken down into radicals 厶 denoting, "nose" or "breath" and 口, or "mouth" or "language."[40] Without the essence of woman as an inalienable partner with that of man, no action takes roots.

This is the film's turning point, strategically. After Yasuko sends her suitor Aono off on the bus, her gaze meets that of Yuichi on the other side of the stone fence. Is this Imamura's humorous idea of real "omiai" (a formalized "pre-nuptial engagement" arranged by elders according to the society's rules)? The attention consumed earlier by the hype involving Yuichi's PTD now shifts towards his quotidian task—the carving of Jizō, the Buddhist stone statues. Here, the audience find themselves in a new space with Yuichi. He is not quite what we have been led to believe. Who is he? What's in it for us? Why this Buddhist icon, the Jizō, and why now?

According to Levin, "a Jungian interpretation of cultural symbols, myths and ritual of self-transformation can significantly clarify Heidegger's [not only] discourse concerning our returning to this realm of our deepest self-understanding and our existential possibilities-for-becoming, [but also] formulation of the three dimensions of human existence—the pre-ontological attunement, the ontical reduction in characteristic everydayness, and Self."[41] Yuichi's well-wishing gift of Jizō to Yasuko and the motorcycle episode trigger the rekindling of their childhood friendship—their mutual "pre-ontological" fertile soil, which is the same as the essence of the Jōmon or Yayoi clay. The face of this Jizō bears a peaceful expression. Yet, Imamura is not about to craft a happy ending story at the expense of Yasuko and Yuichi tying their knot; he is more concerned with impacting his audience with this message: "Face the truth, if you want to be free!" At this point Imamura bombards his audience with several why questions uttered from the mouths of Shokichi, one of the villagers: No longer wanting to suffer, Shizuma's buddy wonders why the United States bombed Japan, why Hiroshima and Nagasaki, and not Tokyo, why so much suffering, etc. Presently we learn that Yasuko and Yuichi themselves have been asking the same questions and searching for their answers together in his stone cutting shed. In the film, Imamura creates a theater within a theater, in a noh-like disinterested inter-space. When Yasuko asks about his condition, Yuichi begins animated, and so do Jizō statues, in turn. The director uses a spotlight as his camera follows Yuichi's move from one Jizō image to another, each bearing a human expression of angst, fear, horror, joy, peace, and so on. As if we were transported to the graveyard at Kōya-san, or Mount Kōya in Kyoto, the audience are made to begin their journey into the underworld "traveling about the dharmadhatu" the whole of the phenomenal world in order to save "beings from suffering."[42] As Glassman points out, in each of the stories told, "the [Jizō] statues fly, they walk, they speak. They are images in motion. Jizō is a dynamic figure, described as bustling here and there.... [T]here is a conflation, or ... unity ... between the deity and particular statue.... Yet images of Jizō are not strictly bound by place.... Jizō statues are ambulatory. In this way we see Yuichi making round like a 'mawari Jizō.'"[43] By paving the way to this open road, Yuichi becomes one with the primordial essence of Jizō, as goes the old Japanese saying: 「道路を造る人は地蔵の一子成ること」 or "A person who builds road is a child of Jizō."[44] In this way, Imamura defies the lack of visual outflow into the abundance of outflow of the invisible energy, thus affirming the symbol's power to access the phenomenologically operative "motility" within.[45] Yuichi's chiseling away a stone piece into an animated Jizō is a therapeutic method and metaphor for eradicating his own mental illness, but also Yasuko's own illusion, and, in turn, that of the world. Finally in this cleared field where the emerging body of deepest understanding is imminent, the two are reborn together as did Buddha on the lotus flower. No doubt, here, Imamura finds himself having done his justice to Ibuse's white flower on the stone. This brings them to one of the most critical element Levin points out—the Heidegger's notion of "reversal," or Kehre.[46]

"Kehre," meaning "hairpin bend,"[47] precisely aligns, interpreting from my internalized calligraphic practices, with the U-turn in the second stroke of the Chinese and Japanese ideograph *kokoro*. Preceded by its left stroke, representing the first phase, be it one's childhood, or primary familial environment, the second stroke U-turn consists of our being-in-the-world. It's a relatively long journey during which an individual acquires technical skills, customs, systems, etc., necessary to survive in the world. However, our eventual questioning of this world's ways is imminent. The hairpin bend corresponds to a period of dilemma, or angst. One may receive numerous hints from the wise, but may miss it or be made aware of it depending upon the degree of his or her worldly concern. A sudden urge to turn upward is often viscerally felt, as the simultaneous gravitational pull downward disperses all fibers whose knots we thought of having importantly made. It is at this very Heideggerian pivotal turn, the "reversal Kehre," where we may be able to finally focus on the "ontological affirmation" of a "new[ly realized] origin" from that omphalos threshold.[48] As Levin writes, "[T]he turn involves a revolutionary awareness, and an explicitly herme- neutical acknowledgment, that it is in relativity, in a relatedness Heidegger calls openness- to-Being."[49] Furthermore, "what gives feeling its truth-disclosive nature, then, is that it is inherently directed toward an experience which is global and holistic."[50] Levin calls this feeling "feeling attunement" or "guardian awareness."[51] It is here that he claims that one is in "'Rapture' (Rausch) … the 'aesthetic' experience of this ek-static inherence in Being."[52] The Japanese aesthetic consciousness of "profundity in simplicity" and *mono no aware* ("pathos of nature") could have been realized pre-texually as early as during the later Yayoi period as its pottery subtly whispers to our child within the same essence of which both the earth and we are made and thus attune each other just so. This coincides with what is known in Japanese, according to Glassman, as *muen no jihi* (無縁の慈悲). "This is the deepest and most sincere sort of universal love within the Buddhist taxonomy of compas- sion."[53]

Both Yasuko and Yuichi are united by their internally and ceaselessly generated selfless force of *muen no jihi*, the very nexus of that "auspicious beginning." In the study of the ideograph *kokoro*, especially when rendered calligraphically in a swift cursive, the last two strokes form a figure eight, or infinity, which carries the operative essence of the Being. Coming to one's sense with this universal omphalos changes one's perspective on love also. After all, in their loving, neither Yuichi nor Yoko seeks any worldly gain: Yuichi is a recov- ering mental patient and Yasuko is a victim of radiation suffering from her disabling keroid, now darkly hidden in her buttocks. As if what is happening between them is not enough to cure the world, much less please his audience with this bittersweet ending, Imamura once again activates the character of Yuichi's mother to stir the world. This time, she makes a deliberate visit to ask, on behalf of her son, Shizuma's permission to marry Yasuko to her son. Shizuma's hesitation is expected. But it makes him think twice. And the audience is moved humorously and refreshingly by the honesty displayed by Yuichi's mother, as if to declare, "Folks, never mind the indecisiveness on the part of Mr. Shizuma!" Her uncon- cerned plain honesty, "Ah, now that I said my piece, I feel such relief!" couldn't be more powerfully cathartic for cleaning anyone's "hara" or belly, much less with a good humor. Like *Ame no Uzume*, the Japanese parallel of the Western Baubo,[54] the laughing hag deity, she seems to have triumphantly opened up the emerging field of understanding paving others the way toward it. In the Japanese creation myth, she is instrumental in coaxing the sun goddess Amaterasu out of the darkness into the light. This act of opening is equivalent to her exposure of sexuality "seen as the best way to drive away dark or evil influences and invite good fortunes and blessings."[55] In retrospect, the audience is reminded of the geo- graphical importance of the stonecutter's dwelling. It is "the place at the fork in the road," representing "sexual organs," according to Glassman, who affirms the pagan-rational bridg- ing via Jizō.[56] Known as varyingly from region to region as *chimata no kami* (岐又の神), *sae no kami* (斎の神) or *dosojin* (道祖神), they are found, in the likeness of Jizō, at "crossroads and liminal spaces."[57] In brief, sexual intercourse and ecstasy can be considered as metaphors for a dynamic union, or differently put, one's return to the undifferentiated whole, or sacred source. Thusly understood, the Jizō maker Yuichi's PTD can be interpreted symbolically as a shamanistic dance in trans, or inter-space, whereby to gyrate the two opposing forces of the dead and living into an ecstatic chiasm, to use Merleau-Ponty's term. Accordingly, Yukichi's Jizō-crafting hut serves not only a geographical "check point" where the bus stops, but also its Zen tea-hut-like doorway creates an entry into a liminal space. As Glassman puts it, "Jizō has always been a bridging figure in Japan; … Jizō's liminal nature made him essential element in the creation and implementation of the logic of honji suijaku (literally, 'original ground and trace manifestation') whereby Buddhist deities were identified with local gods."[58] In such a synchrony of the visual and the textual, Imamura achieves not only as an effective cinematographer but as a phenomenological philosopher à la Levinianne by bringing Ibuse's textual work onto the field of embodiment of the wholeness. Like the female deity *Ame no Uzume*, her laughing dance is contagious. Sooner or later, even Mr. Shizuma is made to pause, reflect and question his own traditionally correct actions, which have none-the-less short-circuited his genuine honesty.

Mesmerized by the giant carp thrusting itself out of the pond and then twisting and twirling in the air, Yasuko suddenly utters an untamed ecstatic cry none has ever heard before. Yasuko returns home weak yet free. Somewhat normalized by the morning routines at the house, Shizuma tunes the clock radio to the 7 a.m. announcements. The news of another nuclear threat by the U.S. against the communism in Korea frustrates him. Suddenly there is a shift in the mood; Yasuko now turns for the worse. Like an "ambulatory" Jizō, Yuichi makes his self-forgetting moves to put his feeble friend into the vehicle and accompanies her to the hospital. Her uncle, now left behind, stands alone in front of his country house. Imamura's lens moves farther and farther away from him, exposing the greater Mother Nature whence we all come and return.

We remember, though, that somewhere in their back yard, the aloe plants tended by the Shizumas is now at the peak of their growth. Their succulent rigor now reminds us to sustain our own aqueous motility within to help heal those of us who may be treading on a less honest path, including ourselves.

Notes

1. H. Glassman, *The Face of Jizō: Images and Cult in Medieval Japanese Buddhism* (Honolulu: University of Hawai'i Press, 2012), p. 2.

2. P. Bobcok-Gove, ed. in chief, *Webster's Third New International Dictionary of the English Language: Unabridged* (Springfield, MA: Merriam-Webster, 1993) p. 1211.

3. D.M. Levin, *The Body's Recollection of Being: Phenomenological Psychology and the Deconstruction of Nihilism* (London: Routledge and Kegan Paul, 1985) p. 2.

4. *Ibid.*, p. 101.

5. *Ibid.*, p. 3.

6. H. Glassman, "Dare we call them indigenous, even autochthonous?," *The Face of Jizō* (Honolulu: University of Hawai'i Press, 2012), p. 6.

7. S. Wells, *The Journey of Man: A Genetic Odyssey* (Princeton: Princeton University Press, 2002), pp. 182–183.

8. H. Glassman, *The Face of Jizō: Images and Cult in Medieval Japanese Buddhism* (Honolulu: University of Hawai'i Press, 2012), p. 6.

9. D.M. Levin, *The Body's Recollection of Being: Phenomenological Psychology and the Deconstruction of Nihilism* (London: Routledge and Kegan Paul, 1985), p. 67.

10. H. Glassman, *The Face of Jizō: Images and Cult in Medieval Japanese Buddhism* (Honolulu: University of Hawai'i Press, 2012), p. 5.

11. *Ibid.*, p. 4.

12. P.H. Varley, *Japanese Culture*, 3d ed. (Honolulu: University of Hawai'i Press, 1984), pp. 5–6.

13. D.T. Suzuki, *Zen and Japanese Culture* (New York: MJF Books, 1959), pp. 173–174.

14. *Ibid.*, p. 174.

15. *Ibid.*, p. 172.

16. M. Merleau-Ponty, *The Visible and Invisible* (Evanston: Northwestern University Press, 1968), pp. 130–155.

17. Y. Abe 阿部吉雄, *Kanwa Jiten*「漢和辞典」(*Dictionary of Chinese-Japanese Ideographs* [my translation]) (Tokyo東京: Obunsha旺文社, 1964), pp. 641 and 825, respectively.

18. S.J.L Wieger, *Chinese Characters: Their Origin, Etymology, History, Classification and Signification: A Thorough Study from Chinese Documents* (New York: Paragon, 1965), p. 36.

19. M. Ibuse, *Black Rain*, John Bester, tr. (New York: Kodansha International, 1969), p. 22.

20. *Ibid.*, p. 128.

21. D.M. Levin, *The Body's Recollection of Being: Phenomenological Psychology and the Deconstruction of Nihilism* (London: Routledge and Kegan Paul, 1985), p. 3.

22. H. Glassman, *The Face of Jizo: Images and Cult in Medieval Japanese Buddhism* (Honolulu: University of Hawai'i Press, 2012), p. 6.

23. D.M. Levin, *The Body's Recollection of Being: Phenomenological Psychology and the Deconstruction of Nihilism* (London: Routledge and Kegan Paul, 1985), pp. 52–53.

24. *Ibid.*, p. 54.

25. *Ibid.*, p. 56.

26. G. Varner, *Menhirs, Dolmen and Circles of Stone: The Folklore and Mythology of Sacred Stone* (Baltimore: Angora, 2004), p. 44.

27. P. Devereux, *Symbolic Landscapes: Dreamtime Earth and Avebury's Open Secret* (Glastonbury: Gothic Image Publications, 1992), p. 92.

28. K. Higuchi 樋口清之, *Umeboshi and the Japanese Sword*「梅干と日本刀」(Tokyo: Shodensha, 1990).

29. P.H. Varley, *Japanese Culture*, 3d ed. (Honolulu: University of Hawai'i Press, 1984), p. 222.

30. D.M. Levin, *The Body's Recollection of Being: Phenomenological Psychology and the Deconstruction of Nihilism* (London: Routledge and Kegan Paul, 1985), p. 13.

31. *Ibid.*, p. 6.

32. *Ibid.*, p. 16.

33. Referring to Kobayashi Issa's *haiku* poem:
The turnip farmer rose
And with a fresh-pulled turnip
Pointed to my road

34. Dōgen, *Shōbōgenzō: Zen Essays by Dogen*, trans. Thomas Cleary (Honolulu: University of Hawai'i Press, 1968).

35. P.H. Varley, *Japanese Culture*, 3d ed. (Honolulu: University of Hawai'i Press, 1984), p. 210.

36. Y. Sheng, *Ox-herding at Morgan's Bay* (New York: Dharma Drum, 1988).

37. H. Glassman, *The Face of Jizō: Images and Cult in Medieval Japanese Buddhism* (Honolulu: University of Hawai'i Press, 2012), p. 26.

38. Y. Sheng, *Ox-herding at Morgan's Bay* (New York: Dharma Drum, 1988), pp. 27–28.

39. *Ibid.*, p. 28.

40. The analysis of the *kanji* radicals and their constructs are my own.

41. D.M. Levin, *The Body's Recollection of Being: Phenomenological Psychology and the Deconstruction of Nihilism* (London: Routledge and Kegan Paul, 1985), p. 18.

42. H. Glassman, *The Face of Jizō: Images and Cult in Medieval Japanese Buddhism* (Honolulu: University of Hawai'i Press, 2012), p. 15.

43. *Ibid.*, p. 24–25.

44. *Ibid.*, p. 125.

45. D.M. Levin, *The Body's Recollection of Being: Phenomenological Psychology and the Deconstruction of Nihilism* (London: Routledge and Kegan Paul, 1985), pp. 93–94.

46. *Ibid.*, p. 26.

47. Collins Dictionary, http://www.collinsdictionary.com/dictionary/german-english/kehre.

48. D.M. Levin, *The Body's Recollection of Being: Phenomenological Psychology and the Deconstruction of Nihilism* (London: Routledge and Kegan Paul, 1985) p. 26.

49. *Ibid.*, p. 27.

50. *Ibid.*, p. 49.

51. *Ibid.*, p. 50.

52. *Ibid.*

53. H. Glassman, *The Face of Jizō: Images and Cult in Medieval Japanese Buddhism* (Honolulu: University of Hawai'i Press, 2012), p. 39.
54. W.M. Lubell, *The Metamorphosis of Baubo: Myths of Women's Sexual Energy* (Nashville: Vanderbilt University Press, 1994), p. 180.
55. H. Glassman, *The Face of Jizō: Images and Cult in Medieval Japanese Buddhism* (Honolulu: University of Hawai'i Press, 2012), p. 168.
56. *Ibid.*, p. 169.
57. *Ibid.*
58. *Ibid.*, p. 6.

Bibliography

Abe, Yoshio 阿部吉雄. *Kanwa Jiten* 「漢和辞典 *Dictionary of Chinese-Japanese Ideographs*. Tokyo東京: Obun-sha 旺文社, 1964.

Bobcok-Gove, Philippe, ed. in chief. *Webster's Third New International Dictionary of the English Language: Unabridged* (Springfield, MA: Merriam-Webster, 1993).

Colins Dictionary. http://www.collinsdictionary.com/dictionary/german-english/kehre.

Devereux, Paul. *Symbolic Landscapes: Dreamtime Earth and Avebury's Open Secret*. Glastonbury: Gothic Image Publications, 1992.

Dogen. *Shōbōgenzō: Zen Essays by Dōgen*. Trans. Thomas Cleary. Honolulu: University of Hawai'i Press, 1986.

Glassman, Hank, *The Face of Jizō: Images and Cult in Medieval Japanese Buddhism*. Honolulu: University of Hawai'i Press, 2012.

Higuchi, Kiyoyuki 樋口清之. *Umeboshi and the Japanese Sword* 「梅干と日本刀」. Tokyo東京: Shodensha 祥伝社, 1990.

Ibuse, Masuji. *Black Rain*. Tr. John Bester. New York: Kōdansha International, 1979.

Imamura, Shohei. *Kuroi Ame (Black Rain)*. 1989. DVD.

Levin, David Michael. *The Body's Recollection of Being: Phenomenological Psychology and the Deconstruction of Nihilism*. London: Routledge and Kegal Paul, 1985.

Low, Albert. *Hakuin on Kensho: The Four Ways of Knowing*. Boston: Shambala, 2006.

Lubell, Winifred Milius. *The Metamorphosis of Baubo: Myths of Women's Sexual Energy*. Nashville: Vanderbilt University Press, 1994.

Merleau-Ponty, Maurice. *The Visible and Invisible*. Evanston: Northwestern University Press, 1968.

Sheng-Yen. *Ox Herding at Morgan Bay*. New York: Dharma Drum Publications, 1988.

Suzuki, Daisetsu T. *Zen and Japanese Culture*. New York: MJF Books, 1959.

Varey, H. Paul. *Japanese Culture*, 3d ed. (Honolulu: University of Hawai'i Press, 1984).

Varner, Gary. *Menhirs, Dolmen and Circles of Stone: The Folklore and Mythology of Sacred Stone*. New York: Algora, 2004.

Wells, Spencer. *The Journey of Man: A Genetic Odyssey*. Princeton: Princeton University Press, 2002.

Wieger, L. S. J., *Chinese Characters: Their Origin, Etymology, History, Classification and Signification. A Thorough Study from Chinese Documents*. New York: Paragon, 1965.

Trauma and Witness
in Hideo Nakata's *Ring*

TIENFONG HO

While the world still waits to know the long-term effects of the nuclear accident at Fukushima Daiichi Power Station, the psychological effects were felt immediately. Operating like the structure of psychic trauma, the more recent disaster on March 11, 2011, a three-part storm of earthquake, tsunami, and nuclear disaster, revivified the events of August 6 and 9, 1945, when the U.S. dropped atomic bombs on the cities of Hiroshima and Nagasaki.

In 1937 Sigmund Freud described a theory for psychic trauma in *Moses and Monotheism* that also accounted for the history of a culture. Of key importance in this study would be his concept of "latency," how the memory of a tragedy is lost over time but then retrieved in the context of second event reminiscent of the earlier one.[1] In this way personal history like cultural or national history, plays out as a sequence of traumatic events for which subsequent traumas invoke previous catastrophes. Thus the experience, memory, and consequence of a particular disaster are not unique or discrete but mediated through the lens of the past.

It seems presently in the United States there continues to be a need to visit the topic of trauma given the repetitions of violent catastrophes depicted in popular culture. In the summer of 2013 we had both *World War Z*, Marc Forster's filmic interpretation of Max Brooks' apocalyptic horror novel about a zombie pandemic, and Guillermo del Toro's *Pacific Rim*, a film about enormous human-piloted robots saving the earth by battling gigantic monsters. Borrowing heavily from Japanese monster movie director Ishirō Honda of *Gojira* fame, *Pacific Rim* with its relatively satisfying and redemptive conclusion reprises in 2013 the compulsive repetition of repressed trauma presented in nuclear bomb cinema of the 1950s and '60s. As Susan Sontag explained in her 1965 essay "The Imagination of Disaster," "Science fiction films are not about science. They are about disaster, which is one of the oldest subjects about art."[2] Suggesting nuclear disaster as the traumatic impetus behind these films, Sontag writes, "One gets the feeling, particularly in the Japanese films, but not only there, that mass trauma exists over the use of nuclear weapons and the possibility of future nuclear wars. Most of science fiction films bear witness to this trauma, and in way, attempt to exorcise it."[3] Sontag's use of the term "exorcise" evokes the idea of ghosts and hauntings. In *Moses and Monotheism,* Freud himself had written about the delayed completion of his book, and the trauma of leaving Vienna in terms of a haunting as well. He writes, "I had decided to put [the book] away, but it haunted me like an un-laid ghost...."[4] Thus if we recognize that repetitions of repressed trauma, such as discourses like atomic bomb cinema, are attempts to exorcise the ghosts that haunt us, then the ghost story may be a particularly apropos trope for expressing trauma. While Japanese films dubbed atomic bomb cinema or *Hibakusha* cinema (*Hibakusha* meaning "explosion-affected persons"[5]) tend to be the science fiction type, Noël Carroll places science fiction cinema in the category of horror: "I think that, historically, movie science fiction has evolved as a sub-class of the horror film."[6] In the chapter on Japanese atomic bomb cinema, film historian Jerome Shapiro describes Tokihisa Morikawa's *Summer Girl* (*Natsushōjo*) as a film that exploits the shared experiences of *Hibakusha*. Released in Hiroshima in 1995, the fiftieth anniversary of the bombing of Hiroshima, this indie film is a ghost story channeling the emotions of guilt and regret over lost chances through the narrative of a family dealing with the trauma of the atomic bomb.[7] Thus an area of overlap occurs between the categories of ghost story and atomic bomb cinema.

English professor Jay McRoy identifies two dominant genres in Japanese horror films: the *kaidan* (ghost story) about the martyred woman as *onryō* (vengeful spirit), and the *daikaijū eiga* (giant monster film), the genre that had inspired del Toro's *Pacific Rim*. According to McRoy, while *daikaijū eiga* like Honda's *Gojira* (1954), *Rodan* (*Radan*, 1956), and *Mothra* (*Mosura*, 1961) tend to follow narratives about disasters and the fear of nuclear attack, onryou narratives like Takashi Shimizu's *Ju-On: The Grudge* (2002) and Hideo Nakata's *Ring* (1998) are films about family issues arising from the conflict between Japan's traditional past, and evolving influences following the American occupation.[8] In other words, these films, which are on the outset about confronting monsters and ghosts, are allegorical representations of societal crises such as trauma and loss incurred from nuclear disaster and the conflicts arising within post-war Japanese identity. Film scholar Collette Balmain notes the topics shared by both monster and ghost films made in post-war Japan, stating, "*Godzilla* clearly elucidates societal, economic and political concerns in Japan at the time of production that are mirrored in the ghost story, which emerges almost simultaneously."[9]

This essay attempts to analyze Nakata's *Ring* in terms of nuclear disaster and trauma. While *Ring* may be the prime example of Japanese cinema's commercial success due to the fact that its 2002 Hollywood remake, *The Ring*, by Gore Verbinski, was one of the highest grossing horror films in history, it has also proven to be a rich source for academic discussion. By delving into the structure of psychic trauma the essay brings focus to the film's centerpiece, the cursed video itself. An avant-garde film in its own right, the poetic stream of shadowy black and white images signifies a lack conscious control, reminding us of the nature of the "unassimilable experience." The unassimilable experience according to Cathy Caruth, that returns as a flashback is not a product of disavowal, repression, or amnesia, "but an event that is itself constituted, in part, by its lack of integration into consciousness."[10]

Quite unlike many American horror films about a psychotic murderer that cannot be killed, e.g., *Halloween*, *Friday the 13th*, and *Nightmare on Elm Street*, *Ring* presents horror as a consequence of obligatory witness. Reiko, the film's main protagonist, learns to defer the spell of a cursed video by copying and sharing the video with others. Horror is characterized as the endless transfer or sharing of witness necessitating the expansion of suffering beyond the individual. Furthermore, unearthing the repressed event proves insufficient since, in perhaps the film's single most unexpected and spectacular scene, death continues the day after the murdered girl's corpse is pulled out of the well. Thus *Ring* teaches that (as Caruth has described) history, like trauma, is not one's own, but a condition of being involved in each other's experiences and memories.[11] Moreover, through the film's narrative, which unfolds like a detective thriller, viewers learn that while it is possible to make sense of historic data by weaving a unified story with a logical redemptive meaning, the effects of trauma cannot be fully contained within the bounds of corroborated facts and scientific knowledge. To accept a list of statistics and facts, e.g., six million Jews or August 6, 1945, as an adequate expression of trauma would be effectively to misunderstand or misrecognize the event.

References to the nuclear bombing of Japan in *Ring* are perhaps less explicit than those made in *daikaijū eiga*. The date is Sunday, September 5, when Sadako's first victim dies in *Ring* is close to VJ Day, the date of Japan's surrender aboard the USS *Missouri* in Tokyo Bay on September 2, 1945. Both are the first Sunday of the month. Sadako's name inevitably evokes Sadako Sasaki, a real Japanese girl born during the Second World War.[12] Sadako Sasaki was two years old and living in Hiroshima when the atomic bomb destroyed the city. As a result of radiation exposure the young girl would contract leukemia and die from the disease at age ten. While in the hospital, Sadako folded hundreds of paper cranes to no avail believing that she would recover if she folded a thousand. The story today continues to be a call for peace and a morality tale about the consequences of war. The *Children's Peace Monument* in Hiroshima Peace Memorial Park commemorates Sadako and other children who died as a result of the atomic bomb.

Film historian Linnie Blake makes a connection between the Japanese *onryō* tradition and the circumstances in Japan following the American occupation. Blake contends that the Japanese vengeful ghost narrative gained recognition during the American occupation of Japan between 1945 and 1952. This period in Japan was marked by drastic cultural changes imposed by the American occupiers. The Americans instated the Shōwa Constitution which required the renunciation of war, and promoted universal adult suffrage, gender equality, and work and trade union membership.[13] The idea was to impart the American model of civil liberties and human rights as a move to drive out Japanese wartime militarism. American control over Japanese life and culture was so thorough that even traditionally Japanese cultural products, such as sword-fight dramas, kabuki plays, and poetry were censored or banned entirely. Shintoism was abolished and according to Blake, "even Mount Fuji, the object of Shintoist nature worship, became a forbidden subject for visual representation."[14] In response, the Japanese became ideologically fragmented with many believing the military had victimized the Japanese people by instigating the dropping of nuclear bombs on Hiroshima and Nagasaki. The ambivalent status of Japan as both victim and perpetrator figure into the inconsistencies of Sadako herself who is both an evil aggressor and an innocent victim. In the American remake, Verbinski eliminates all doubt that good could exist in the onryou and she is revealed in the end to be fully evil. While more legible to American viewers, Verbinski's version is perhaps less Japanese and less interesting in this aspect.

Some of the post-occupation *onryō* films are essentially morality tales that further anti-militaristic and leftist ideals, such as Kaneto Shindō's *Onibaba* (1964). Set in medieval Japan, *Onibaba* advances a wrathful critique against the *bushido* code (the militaristic samurai code of honor), instructing how male-dominated militarism is the cause of social depravity and perversion of women.[15] Balmain notes how Kenji Mizoguchi's *Tales of Ugetsu* (1953) is often identified as the prototypical *onryō* film. *Tales of Ugetsu* takes a rather different stance from *Onibaba* and locates the source of societal corruption in the destruction of traditional Japanese paternalism, a consequence of Japan's defeat in the Second World War. To Balmain, *Tales of Ugetsu* "seems to suggest that a return to traditional values is necessary for a post-military masculinity."[16] Similarly, in 1967 literary critic Jun Etō would publish *Maturation and Loss: The Destruction of the Mother*. According to historian Yumiko Iida, Etō interpreted Japan's modernization in terms of the destruction of the sensual bond between mother and son. To Etō the American postwar incursion effected "the symbolic castration of the Japanese father," and was therefore the root of all social ills in Japan.[17] Believing that a man's bond to his wife (the core of stable family relations) was an extension of the earlier bond that men have as boys with their mothers, Etō called for a restoration of the traditional Japanese image of the selfless mother.[18] Attitudes towards the gender identity crisis in post-war Japan are thus highly nuanced and while the militaristic warrior male of the past was not acceptable having caused the nation's catastrophic defeat, neither was the enfeebled, Americanized father of post-occupation Japan.

In *Ring* one can distinguish a narrative about identifying and punishing divorced parents, and Ryūji's spectacular death scene does feel like retribution against the father. The camera cuts to a close-up of Sadako's face covered by a disgusting curtain of unkempt hair but revealing her one dreadful eye. An eyeline match follows showing Ryūji's look and the two finally meet eye-to-eye, or even more so perhaps, an *eye for an eye*. Like all of Sadako's victims Ryūji's features contort in a paroxysm of terror. In retribution for the past wrong of father killing daughter, this time daughter kills father. Tracing a filmic lineage back to Teinosuke Kinugasa's *A Page of Madness* (*Kurutta ippēji*, 1926) film historian Ruth Goldberg argues that *Ring* is a contemporary version of the "Uncanny Mother" film and as such it asserts an "implicit critique of the alienated Japanese social landscape and the loss of traditional family values."[19] To Goldberg, the fiendish Sadako is thus only a reflection of the real monstrosity in the story, Reiko the single mother whose professional lifestyle goes against traditional Japanese family values. Goldberg believes that Ryūji dies in the end because he failed to reclaim his responsibility as a father and husband.[20]

However, it can be argued that Ryūji's death also makes a statement about the contrast between mathematical logic, and emotional experiences that can be illogical or incoherent. Seconds prior to Sadako's shocking and horrific arrival into Ryūji's apartment through the television screen, Ryūji, a professor of mathematics at the university, is shown working on his paper which he had put off completing in order to attend to his ex-wife's emergency with the videotape. The camera reveals that his work, written in English, is a mathematical proof. We can make out words and phrases like "suppose that," "then there are two elements," and "the following two conditions." At this time, Ryūji also notices an incorrect minus sign in the equations he was working out on the chalkboard. Earlier in the film we had seen his lively young female assistant rub out and change something on the chalkboard as a prank against her professor. Ryūji's ability to catch the mistake and restore the plus sign shows us the character's keen aptitude for mathematical accuracy and detail. This small event preceding the spectacular death scene speaks to the film director's interest in conveying this aspect of Ryūji's character which proves ineffectual in preventing his own death.

Perhaps once again, this attitude towards mathematical logic says something about the contrast between old Japan which is aligned to nature and intuition, and contemporary Japan which has become associated with science, technology, and the industrial West. However, it should be noted that historically in Japan even this stance is unstable and has been interpreted in conflicting ways. For example, while the atomic bomb may be linked to the discipline of science in the West, science itself is not necessarily seen to be completely at odds with peace. Director of *Children of Hiroshima* (1952) Kaneto Shindō writes, "we might say the atomic bomb had been given to [the] Japanese as a revelation of science who preferred savageness, fanaticism and intolerant Japanese spirit to freedom, culture and science. The atomic bomb was an alarm to civilization and the awakening towards peace for [the] Japanese."[21] In the film Ryūji's character, although logical and scientific, is also a psychic with abilities to speak to the dead. His son Yōichi has inherited this ability and the psychic father and son pair balances the mother-daughter pairing of Shizuko and Sadako who are also both psychics. In his discussion of Honda's *daikaijū eiga*, Shapiro argues how through gender designation, characters and creatures in these films signify the restoration of balance and harmony: "In these films, men have become too strong, that is, their weapons or political powers are too strong, and society is out of balance with nature; so nature, which is highly anthropomorphized in Japanese tradition, retaliates (usually against modernity). Thus the feminine element must assert itself and transform the masculine element in order to restore balance and harmony."[22] Through Shapiro's explanation we can easily find in Japanese monster films, the same anti-military, post-occupation attitudes towards the male, which are simultaneously present in the *kaidan* films. One also discovers layers of this kind of balance, or perhaps harmonizing ambivalence, occurring throughout the characters of *Ring*. We may take for example the flashback scene in which Shizuko gives a public demonstration of her clairvoyance. The scene is striking in that Shizuko is visible as the only woman in a room filled with men wearing Western-style business suits. Sitting on the stage in a kimono, Shizuko's exceptional gender stands out more than her psychic abilities. Unconvinced by the demonstration a skeptical reporter accuses Shizuko for being a fake. The rest of the audience stands up and joins in the angry accusations. Shizuko is clearly distraught, but Sadako comes to her mother's rescue, and kills the angry skeptic using her supernatural powers. The scene illustrates all at once the balance between the rational and irrational, East and West, and male and female.

As already suggested the Japanese post-war identity as both aggressive instigator and innocent victim corresponds to Sadako's ambivalent character. But this same complexity is also echoed in Japanese attitudes toward the forces of nature. For example while winds and typhoons blowing inland from the sea have proven repeatedly to be catastrophically destructive, historically these same winds have also served to protect the Japanese. Shapiro reminds us that Kublai Khan's two assaults on Japan in 1274 and 1281 were both neutralized by typhoons.[23] With their fleets destroyed, the Mongols were forced to retreat. Thus the belief in a god wind or *kamikaze* that blows from the sea and protects Japan's island people very likely arose from this and other similar historical events.[24] It is also implied in *Ring* that Sadako was conceived when Shizuko was impregnated by a supernatural entity of the sea. Thus Sadako, both human and demon, also exemplifies the ambivalence of nature and its forces.

Equally important, however, is the structure of the film narrative overall. *Ring* is a story that is driven forward like a detective thriller. The plot advances as the protagonists chase down clues one after the other. Although the film pays homage to the American teen slasher flick by beginning with two teenaged girls discussing an overnight stay with boys in a cabin and a scary urban legend, the film very much sticks to the storyline of detective thrillers, or perhaps closer yet, of *Scooby-Doo* episodes in which protagonists put clues together to solve a crime. After Reiko tracks down the video and enlists Ryūji's help, the pair analyzes the video images as a set of clues. For every image there is an explanation or identification. When gathered together the images and explanations tell a complete story which the characters assume will provide a method for ending the curse. Let us take a closer look at the video which Reiko views for the first time in the cabin in Izu.

The noisy sound of random static suddenly cuts out and we see the first image, a perfectly circular section of clouded sky floating in the middle of an otherwise blackened frame, as if we were looking through a round window at night. Between one and two o'clock, facing us with head pointing towards the circle's center, a person is visible from the shoulders up. While the figure remains still, the clouds behind are moving quickly upwards at an angle from right to left, as in a time-lapse recording. Next, we see an oval mirror hanging on a wall positioned off-center to the left of the frame. In it we see the reflection of a woman from the chest up combing her hair. She faces front as if looking out at us from behind the television screen, her gaze directed towards her own reflection. Looking at this image Reiko remarks to Ryūji that the camera should be visible in the reflection, a fact further corroborating the possibility of a supernatural video "not of this world." The two protagonists later learn that the mysterious woman in the mirror is Yamamura Shizuko, a woman with psychic abilities who had killed herself by jumping into a volcano forty years ago.

The shot pairing is a formal match of two figures framed by circular rings, suggesting that the first image of the circle of sky might be a reflection like what one sees looking down into a pool of still water. We learn later that the first image was the view seen by Sadako looking up from the bottom of a well, i.e., the view of Professor Ikuma peering into the well where he had just pushed Sadako, backed against the circle of sky delineated by the well's rim.

By applying the circle as the main visual motif in these frames, Nakata is also making a direct reference to Zen Buddhism. In classical Zen literature circles and round mirrors signify enlightenment and the indiscriminate reflection of truth.[25] Portraits of Zen masters and patriarchs have historically been painted within circular formats, serving as images of their true natures and signifying their attachment to heavenly realms remote from quotidian life.[26] The circular format of the images in the video allude to this old Japanese artistic convention of depicting the sacred and thus signify as well the otherworldly nature of the individuals and images shown.

The next image is a very brief shot of the mirror now positioned towards the right side of the screen. In the mirror's shadowy reflection a full-length figure of a person (who we later identify as Sadako) appears wearing a white gown. Cutting back to the previous shot we see that Shizuko has since stopped grooming, and has now turned to face the frame's right edge. It is as if she, too, had glimpsed the figure in white and the direction of her look reaffirms our experience. The sequence works like an eyeline match in reverse; the object of the look is followed by the shot of the person looking. Reiko and Ryūji eventually discover that Shizuko had a daughter with supernatural abilities.

The next image is of a field of shifting Japanese characters. The solid black forms turn and float against a white background, and some of the characters are tilted or even lying on their sides. In constant movement they overlap and tumble into each other. Due to the erratic positioning the text is illegible, but by using hi-tech video equipment to pause the tape Ryūji eventually makes out the term "eruption." Reiko and Ryūji discover later that the image comes from two actual newspaper articles entitled "Mount Miharayama Eruption Alert to Local Residents" and "Did Local Woman Predict Eruption?" about a volcano eruption on Ōshima Island.

Next, the video shows some very grainy footage of people crawling on their hands and knees, and then cuts to a standing figure wearing a shirt and slacks. The figure's right arm is lifted straight out away from the body to just below shoulder height with the index finger pointing towards something off-screen to the left. A white cloth is draped over the figure's head, hiding the person's face and identity. Behind the pointing figure is a backdrop of waves as if the person were standing on the shore of a large body of water. But by omitting the horizon line the composition pulls the backdrop of waves up close against the figure, and erases the normal sense of depth and space. This is a prophetic vision and not a memory as the identity of the pointing figure turns out to be Ryūji's ghost. After he is murdered Ryūji appears to Reiko in the glare seen reflected on the television screen and guides her to the copy of the video by pointing to it. This is how Reiko figures out that she survived the curse by copying the video and showing it to Ryūji.

An extreme close-up of an eye follows this scene. The shot is very dark or underexposed and we are unable to distinguish pupil from iris since the eyeball is almost entirely black. What may appear at first to be a white reflection on the eye, on second glance is actually the Japanese character *sada*, meaning chaste and a reference to Sadako. Also, as already mentioned references to reflections, circles, and mirrors occur frequently in classical Zen literature. After the final shot, which is a long shot of the well out of which they eventually find Sadako's corpse, the video ends with the jarring return of loud static.

This string of images is meant to be disturbing, but it is also meant to pique our curiosities. Darkness, unusual perspectives, graininess, shrouding and other devices ensure that the images remain only partially legible. Even though the protagonists diligently follow the trail of images, in the end we all learn that their strategy had been a red herring. By creating a rather classic detective narrative in which the protagonists are thrown off-course and led to a false conclusion, Nakata also pits Western mathematical logic against Japanese traditions of nature, intuition, and superstition.

The film also performs the structure of psychic trauma. In "Unclaimed Experience," Cathy Caruth discusses Freud's concept of latency from *Moses and Monotheism*. Adding further clarification to Freud's example of an accident (such as a train collision) as the source of traumatic neurosis, Caruth explains that the experience of a traumatic event is irretrievable in its entirety, not because the victim forgets the facts and details, but because the event as it was occurring was too shocking to be fully comprehended:

> What in fact constitutes the central enigma revealed by Freud's example, is not so much the period of forgetting that occurs after the accident, but rather the fact that the victim of the crash was never fully conscious during the accident itself: the person gets away, Freud says, "apparently unharmed." The experience of latency, would thus seem to consist, not in the forgetting of a reality that can never be fully known; but in an inherent latency within the experience itself.[27]

The disjointed, illegible stream of images in the video thus also stands for the moment of traumatic encounter and the absence of conscious control. The failed detective strategy tells as that an abundance of newspaper articles, video footage, identified persons and geographical locations, testimonies, and names (i.e., the where, what, who, and when) in the end tell nothing about the truth or reality of Sadako's suffering. Her unique experience of pain and terror, and the injustice of being forgotten are not fully knowable through facts and evidence. Thus the curse could not be ended by constructing a cohesive narrative in accordance to data and facts, achieved through detective work, logical reasoning, and expensive video technology. The ghost takes vengeance not merely to settle the facts of Sadako's death, but to teach the impact of a different kind of truth, the trauma that *disrupts* the narrative because it was never fully known in the first place. As professor of Jewish studies Michael Bernard-Donals explains, "The horror (what was seen but is not contained by language or knowledge) remains disruptive and leaves a mark."[28] The cursed videotape in *Ring* is therefore also very much a metaphor for the *testimony*, as described by comparative literature professor Shoshana Felman. Felman argues that while testimony has become a crucial mode by which we relate to contemporary traumas, as such it does not provide full closure. Hence, "what the testimony does not offer is, however, a completed statement, a totalizable account of those events. In the testimony, language is in process and in trial, it does not possess itself as a conclusion, as the constatation of a verdict or the self-transparency of knowledge."[29]

The curse is never lifted but endlessly deferred. In the final scene Reiko drives away in her car vowing that beginning first with her son and then with her father (yet another father) the video will be copied ad infinitum in order to stave off the effects of the curse. The video's curse of obligatory witness points to the impossibility of bearing witness at all. As Bernard-Donals explains, "Witness is a moment of forgetting, a moment of seeing without knowing that indelibly marks the source of history as an abyss," or as in the case here, a well.[30] By implying that the world will be forced to bear witness, *Ring* brings us back to Sontag's comment about the *mass trauma* that exists over the use nuclear weapons. Sontag makes no distinction in terms of the immediacy of the event. While the definition of *Hibakusha* only refers to immediate survivors of the atomic bomb, *Ring* suggests that the trauma of nuclear disaster is not limited to just *Hibakusha* but shared by anyone who knows about nuclear weapons. Anticipating a future when even perpetrators, become *Hibakusha*, the message expresses more generally that until everyone accepts a share of the agonizing burden of war's consequences, wars and deaths will continue. By embedding the structure of trauma in a horror story, *Ring* points to the unavoidable consequences of listening and of bearing witness which Caruth describes as "the danger, as some have put it, of the trauma's 'contagion,' of the traumatization of those who listen. But it is also its only possibility for transmission."[31] More than anything else, *Ring* may evoke the Fortunoff Video Archive for Holocaust Testimonies at Yale University. A collection of over 4,400 videotaped interviews with witnesses and survivors of the Holocaust this archive is a premier example of how the burden of trauma can be shared. For Caruth the sharing of such stories "is also a means of passing out of the isolation imposed by the event: that the history of a trauma, in its inherent belatedness, can only take place through the listening of another. The meaning of the trauma's address beyond itself concerns, indeed, not only individual isolation but a wider historical isolation that, in our time, is communicated on the level of our cultures."[32]

Notes

1. S. Freud, *Moses and Monotheism*, trans. Katherine Jones (New York: Vintage, 1939), 84.

2. S. Sontag, "The Imagination of Disaster," *Commentary* 44 (Oct. 1965): 44.

3. *Ibid.*, 46.

4. S. Freud, *Moses and Monotheism*, trans. Katherine Jones (New York: Vintage, 1939), pp. 131–132.

5. J. Shapiro, "1945–2001: Japan's Atomic Bomb Cinema," in *Atomic Bomb Cinema: The Apocalyptic Imagination on Film* (New York: Routledge, 2002), p. 252.

6. N. Carroll, "Nightmare and the Horror Film: The Symbolic Biology of Fantastic Beings," *Film Quarterly* 34, no. 3 (Spring 1981): 17.

7. J. Shapiro, "1945–2001: Japan's Atomic Bomb Cinema," in *Atomic Bomb Cinema: The Apocalyptic Imagination on Film* (New York: Routledge, 2002), pp. 258–262.

8. J. McRoy, *Nightmare Japan: Contemporary Japanese Cinema* (New York: Rodopi, 2008), p. 6. With long unkempt hair hiding her face and dressed in white like a corpse, Sadako the avenging spirit in *Ringu* appears as the typical Japanese *onryō*.

9. C. Balmain, "Horror After Hiroshima," in *Introduction to Japanese Horror Film* (Edinburgh: Edinburgh University Press, 2008), p. 32.

10. C. Caruth, "Introduction to Recapturing the Past," in *Trauma: Explorations in Memory*, ed. and intro. C. Caruth (Baltimore: Johns Hopkins University Press, 1995), p. 152.

11. C. Caruth, *Unclaimed Experience: Trauma, Narrative, and History* (Baltimore: Johns Hopkins University Press, 1996), p. 24.

12. E. Coerr, *Sadako and the Thousand Paper Cranes*, illus. Ronald Himler (New York: Putnam, 1977).

13. L. Blake, "Nihonjinron, Women, Horror: Post-War National Identity and the Spirit of Subaltern Vengeance in *Ringu* and the *Ring*," in *The Wounds of Nations: Horror Cinema, Historical Trauma and National Identity* (Manchester: Manchester University Press, 2008), p. 45.

14. *Ibid.*, p. 46.

15. *Ibid.*, pp. 47–48.

16. C. Balmain, "Horror After Hiroshima," in *Introduction to Japanese Horror Film* (Edinburgh: Edinburgh University Press, 2008), p. 47.

17. Y. Iida, *Rethinking Identity in Modern Japan: Nationalism as Aesthetics* (New York: Routledge, 2002), p. 137.

18. *Ibid.*, pp. 134–37.

19. R. Goldberg, "Demons in the Family: Tracking the Japanese 'Uncanny Mother Film' from a *Page of Madness* to *Ringu*," in *Planks of Reason: Essays on the Horror Film*, ed. Barry Keith Grant and Christopher Sharrett, rev. ed. (Lanham, MD: Scarecrow Press, 2004), p. 380.

20. *Ibid.*, pp. 380–381.

21. K. Hirano, *Mr. Smith Goes to Tokyo: Japanese Cinema Under the American Occupation 1945–1952* (Washington, D.C.: Smithsonian Institution Press, 1992), p. 64.

22. J. Shapiro, "1945–2001: Japan's Atomic Bomb Cinema," in *Atomic Bomb Cinema: The Apocalyptic Imagination on Film* (New York: Routledge, 2002), pp. 279–280.

23. *Ibid.*, p. 269.

24. *Ibid.*

25. D. Riggs, "Meditation for Laymen and Laywomen: The Buddha Samādhi (Jijuyū Zanmai) of Menzan Zuihō," in *Zen Classics: Formative Texts in the History of Zen Buddhism*, ed. Steven Heine and Dale S. Wright (Oxford: Oxford University Press, 2006), pp. 247–274. The section on seeing is useful for understanding the significance of mirrors in Shigenori Nagatomo, "Japanese Zen Buddhist Philosophy," in *The Stanford Encyclopedia of Philosophy*, ed. Edward N. Zalta, http://plato.stanford.edu/archives/win2010/entries/japanese-zen/ (accessed May 20, 2013).

26. D. Keene, "The Portrait of Ikkyū," *Archives of Asian Art* 20 (1966/67): 54–65.

27. C. Caruth, "Unclaimed Experience: Trauma and the Possibility of History," *Yale French Studies* 79, Literature and the Ethical Question (1991): pp. 186–187.

28. M. Bernard-Donals, "Beyond the Question of Authenticity: Witness and Testimony in the Fragments Controversy," *PMLA: Publications of the Modern Language Association of America* 116, no. 5 (Oct. 2001): 1313.

29. S. Felman, "Education and Crisis, or the Vicissitudes of Teaching," in *Trauma: Explorations in Memory*, ed. and intro. C. Caruth (Baltimore: Johns Hopkins University Press, 1995), pp. 16–17.

30. Bernard-Donals, "Beyond the Question of Authenticity," 1313.

31. C. Caruth, "Introduction to Trauma and Experience," in *Trauma: Explorations in Memory*, ed. and intro. C. Caruth (Baltimore: Johns Hopkins University Press, 1995), p. 10.

32. *Ibid.*, 11.

Bibliography

Balmain, Colette. "Horror After Hiroshima." *Introduction to Japanese Horror Film*. Edinburgh: Edinburgh University Press, 2008.

Bernard-Donals, Michael. "Beyond the Question of Authenticity: Witness and Testimony in the Fragments Controversy." *PMLA: Publications of the Modern Language Association of America* 116, no. 5 (Oct. 2001).

Blake, Linnie. "Nihonjinron, Women, Horror: Post-War National Identity and the Spirit of Subaltern Vengeance in Ringu and the Ring," in *The Wounds of Nations: Horror Cinema, Historical Trauma and National Identity*. Manchester: Manchester University Press, 2008.

Carroll, Noël. "Nightmare and the Horror Film: The Symbolic Biology of Fantastic Beings." *Film Quarterly* 34, no. 3 (Spring 1981).

Caruth, Cathy. *Unclaimed Experience: Trauma, Narrative, and History*. Baltimore: Johns Hopkins University Press, 1996.

_____. "Unclaimed Experience: Trauma and the Possibility of History." *Yale French Studies* 79, Literature and the Ethical Question (1991).

_____, ed. *Trauma: Explorations in Memory*. Baltimore: Johns Hopkins University Press, 1995.

Coerr, Eleanor. *Sadako and the Thousand Paper Cranes*. Illus. Ronald Himler. New York: Putnam, 1977.

Felman, Shoshana. "Education and Crisis, or the Vicissitudes of Teaching," in *Trauma: Explorations in Memory*, ed. and intro. Cathy Caruth. Baltimore: Johns Hopkins University Press, 1995.

Freud, Sigmund. *Moses and Monotheism*. Trans. Katherine Jones. New York: Vintage, 1939.

Goldberg, Ruth. "Demons in the Family: Tracking the Japanese 'Uncanny Mother Film' from a *Page of Madness* to *Ringu*," in *Planks of Reason: Essays on the Horror Film*, ed. Barry Keith Grant and Christopher Sharrett, rev. ed. Lanham, MD: Scarecrow Press, 2004.

Hirano, Kyoko. *Mr. Smith Goes to Tokyo: Japanese Cinema Under the American Occupation 1945–1952*. Washington, D.C.: Smithsonian Institution Press, 1992.

Iida, Yumiko. *Rethinking Identity in Modern Japan: Nationalism as Aesthetics*. New York: Routledge, 2002.

Keene, Donald. "The Portrait of Ikkyū." *Archives of Asian Art* 20 (1966/67): 54–65.

McRoy, Jay. *Nightmare Japan: Contemporary Japanese Cinema*. New York: Rodopi, 2008.

Nagatomo, Shigenori. "Japanese Zen Buddhist Philosophy," in *The Stanford Encyclopedia of Philosophy*, ed. Edward N. Zalta. http://plato.stanford.edu/archives/win2010/entries/japanese-zen/ (accessed May 20, 2013).

Riggs, David E. "Meditation for Laymen and Laywomen: The Buddha Samādhi (Jijuyū Zanmai) of Menzan Zuihō," in *Zen Classics: Formative Texts in the History of Zen Buddhism*, ed. Steven Heine and Dale S. Wright. Oxford: Oxford University Press, 2006.

Shapiro, Jerome F. "1945–2001: Japan's Atomic Bomb Cinema," in *Atomic Bomb Cinema: The Apocalyptic Imagination on Film*. New York: Routledge, 2002.

Sontag, Susan. "The Imagination of Disaster." *Commentary* 44 (Oct. 1965).

The Fragile Roots of Memory

ROBERT MCPARLAND

Japanese filmmakers have long sought to express how the profound human tragedy of Hiroshima is remembered. Memory and commemoration of the repercussions of the atomic bombs at Hiroshima and Nagasaki upon Japanese society and the psychology of individuals have been at the center of some of their work. This essay seeks to explore *Children of Hiroshima* (*Genbaku no ko*, 1952), *Women in the Mirror* (*Kagami no onnatachi*, 2002) and *The Face of Jizō* (*Chichi to kurasebe*, 2004) and how these films recollect the human factor in the aftermath of the bombings. Memories of Hiroshima and Nagasaki are deep and they have been cast by these films as vivid markers of modern history. These films present stories of struggle, relationships, and longing. We see in them our own humanity; we see the faces and hear the voices of characters who attempt to make sense of cultural memory. In contrast with remembrance, the films suggest how the pain of these events has been submitted by some to a form of amnesia. In striking images and scenes, they represent what the aftermath of these events mean for the Japanese people and for our world.

Each year, on August 6, the world remembers what a *New York Times* (Sunday, August 6, 1995) headline called "an act that haunts Japan and America." In an article on the fiftieth anniversary of the bombing, Nicholas D. Kristoff began his article by mentioning "one of the unlucky survivors." Like the writers of the screenplays of films that recall those fateful events, he wrote of "those ghosts" who persist and "the survivors who are unable to rest in peace." This is the human face of what Kristoff called "one of the great moral and historical tangles of modern history."[1] It is that profound tangle, on a quite human level, that Japanese filmmakers have often sought to address.

Children of Hiroshima (1952), directed by Kaneto Shindō, reveals the potentially unseen impact of this incident. The psychological and social consequences of the bombing are explored by this director, who was born in Hiroshima in 1912. The United States occupation ended in 1952 and Kaneto Shindō was able to return to film in the city of Hiroshima. He did so near the sites of destruction and his images are arresting. He casts his partner, Nobuko Otowa, as Takeko, an attractive, youthful school teacher who returns to her city years after the bombing. The film begins with Takeko working with her students, who are standing in lines for a school exercise. She then bids farewell to her co-workers and we soon see her aboard a ferry that sails across the water toward Hiroshima. This gives us our first view of the city and we reach the shore with her. She is our viewpoint character for what we begin to observe. The condition of human struggle after the bomb is soon brought to our attention as Takeko meets her former neighbor, who is now a blind beggar. The man appears forlorn, embarrassed by his handicap, and Takeko desires to help him. This scene was filmed near the Aioi bridge, the center where the bomb fell. We are soon given a chilling montage of memories of that consequential day.

We follow Takeko into the world she is now exploring. A child runs to see his mother who is with workers constructing the Peace Memorial Museum. Takeko stands in the ruins of the Prefectural Industrial Promotion Hall where tourists snap photographs and have their pictures taken, as if unmindful of what occurred there.

Whereas Yashito Matshusige is the only known photographer of the original blast, hundreds of photos have been taken by tourists since that fateful day. The visual record of photography and film raises questions about how historical memory operates. Studies like those of Robert Jay Lifton and Greg Mitchell specifically probe the aftermath, while reflections on cultural memory, such as those of Pierre Nora, and Dominick La Capra's work on trauma and memory, may provide us with a context in which to view the film and think about the personal and social devastation wrought by the bombs on Hiroshima and Nagasaki. In his introduction to *Realms of Memory*, Pierre Nora tells us that "history is needed when people no longer live in memory but recall the past through the assistance of documents that help to recall it." While Nora's reflections concern French history, they are more broadly applicable. He speaks of a society's sense of "belonging, collective consciousness ... memory and identity" and suggests for our period the term "the age of commemoration." As Nora puts it, "the most continuous or permanent feature of the modern world is no longer continuity or permanence but change."[2]

Change affects how the Japanese and the American public today each remember Hiroshima and Nagasaki. Film now acts as a repository of cultural memory. Films like *Children of Hiroshima*, *Women in the Mirror*, and *The Face of Jizō* inscribe a stirring sense of the unforgettable human tragedy. They help to overcome what Kristoff, in his *New York Times* article, referred to as a "glossing over war's atrocities" in both Japanese and American accounts of the Second World War.[3]

Children of Hiroshima was a breakthrough film. In the late 1940s, there were few open protests about the American use of the bomb. The pain of the survivors was not openly acknowledged in the media. Yet, the impact upon Japanese social life portrayed by later filmmakers was unmistakable. In 1954, at the Peace Memorial Ceremony, members of the Imperial family attended activities in national recognition of the victims of the bombings.

For many years there was a reluctance to speak about the disaster. This only began to wane in the 1970s and 1980s. Films like *Black Rain* (1988) and *Rhapsody in August* (1991) forcefully brought out the human consequences of the bombing of Hiroshima and Nagasaki. *Black Rain*, based on a novel by Masuji Ibuse, was directed by Shōhei Imamura. It moves from the journal entries of Shigematsu Shizuma (Kazuo Kitamura) in 1945 to those of 1950, when he and his wife, Shigeko Shizuma (Etsuko Ichihara) have become guardians for Yasuko (Yoshiko Tanaka), their niece, and have to find her a husband. The film unfolds the human cost and legacy of the bomb in Yasuko. She was in the "black rain" fallout, some say. So no one wants her. Shizuma sees more people (*Hibakusha*) getting radiation sickness and Yasuko meets with a man who is experiencing post-traumatic stress disorder, who now thinks that cars are tanks. In *Rhapsody in August* (1991), directed by Akira Kurosawa, the lives of the *Hibakusha* are brought into focus. This film shows three generations affected by the bomb at Nagasaki. Sachiko Murase is Kane, who is the mother of this family. In the Summer, Kane's children fly to Hawaii to visit a man who claims to be Kane's lost brother.

Japanese film had something to offer that was more direct and disturbing than the textbooks provided in Japan's schools. As Nicholas Kristoff pointed out in his 1995 *New*

York Times article, school textbooks in Japan avoided direct confrontation with the issue of the bombings, as well as Japan's invasion of China and its attack upon Pearl Harbor. Instead, these texts were "describing them in a way that makes them sound like natural disasters unrelated to human behavior."[4]

It can be argued that the films tend to portray Japan as victim (*higai-sha ishika*) rather than as a militant aggressor in the war. Little context is provided concerning the fighting that led to America's decision to drop the bomb. However, what is most universally captured by the films is the human cost of war. Japan's cultural amnesia is shaken. For American audiences, the once dehumanized Japanese are brought into awareness with lifelike human features, as people who have suffered. By the time of Yoshida's film, *Women in the Mirror* (2002), Japan was distant enough from the Second World War to face its memories. Yoshida's film dealt with the human factor of loss and trauma.

Japan, long before the twentieth century, had become a proud nation, one of the nation states Max Weber once called a "community of memories."[5] Yet, collective memory, in Japan and elsewhere, depends upon commemoration. Contemporary Japan's history includes the Second World War and this cannot be easily forgotten. The community of memories that defines social identity needs to have memories with what Hilgartner and Bosk have called "carrying capacities" across generations, according to changing historical circumstances.[6] In the immediate postwar period, Japan, under the supervision of United States, was evidently stunned by its experience. Some critics have suggested that Japanese "memory" of Hiroshima and Nagasaki was suppressed and only "official" versions' were permissible. Yet, survivors were left with what Jeffrey Alexander has called "a horrendous event that leaves indelible marks upon their group consciousness, marking their memories forever and changing their future identity in fundamental and irrevocable ways."[7]

Films about the interpersonal consequences of the atomic bomb that destroyed Hiroshima and Nagasaki have been a means of coming to terms with this history and healing the society. In 1957, Japan began providing for survivors (*Hibakusha*), changing the Japanese from spectators to "wounded actors," observes Hiro Saito. The traumatic event, Saito asserts, "violently disrupts processes of memory construction and shakes existentially the sense of who we are."[8] From the time of *Children of Hiroshima*, Japanese filmmakers attempted to face this.

In *Present Pasts* (2003), Andreas Huyssen speaks of a conflation of memory and history at the end of the twentieth century. Huyssen observes that "technological change, mass media and new patterns of consumption, work and global mobility" prompts one to seek to slow down "to heal wounds of past mistakes and create a livable future. Kaneto Shindō and other Japanese filmmakers became involved in this process.[9] His work reflects what Pierre Nora, in his reflections upon French cultural memory, has called a sense of "belonging, collective consciousness … memory and identity." Nora suggests for our period the term "the age of commemoration" and this is clearly an aspect of the filmmaker Kaneto Shindō's project. As Nora puts it, "the most continuous or permanent feature of the modern world is no longer continuity or permanence but change."[10] Shindō has seen change in modern Japanese society and, to use Pierre Nora's terms, communes with the past "through vestiges" that "hold the key to our identity, to who we are." As Nora explains, "The idea that collectivities have a memory implies a far-reaching transformation of the status of individuals within society and of their relationship to the community at large." The work of Shindō and the directors and writers of these other films also echoes Dominick LaCapra's observation that survivors work through memories of traumatic times. This working through is an act of memory, and may be seen as a variation on what La Capra views as a "working through" of trauma.

However, some works show the difficulty of working through of trauma which has reverberated across generations. *Women in the Mirror* (2002) is an example of this. The film was directed by Yoshishige "Kijyu" Yoshida, a significant director of the Japanese New Wave in the late 1960s and 1970s. His wife Mariko Okada was cast in this film as Ai Kawase, a woman who is ever haunted by the destruction of Hiroshima.

"Kijyu" Yoshida came to work on this film after several other inquiries into social issues. He had studied French existentialist philosophy at Tokyo University. This informed his work in film and his writing on film and the arts. The Shochiku studio recruitment drive in the late 1950s brought Yoshida to work in film. It was not until 1965 that Yoshida produced his first feature film, *A Story Written on Water*, independent of Shochiku. Early in Yoshida's career, he was involved in the use of youth film cycles (*taiyozoko*) that young directors were assigned to. He directed *Good for Nothing* (*Rokudenashi*) and *Blood Is Dry* (*Chi wa kawaiteru*) in 1960. Then, in 1962, came a momentous turn in his life. He received an offer to write on post-war disillusionment in *The Affair at Akitsu* (*Akitsu onsen*) and he met actress-producer Mariko Okado. He married her and they would do thirteen films together. Kijyu Yoshida would become one of the most highly-esteemed directors in Japan. In a key work of the Japanese New Wave, he directed *Eros Plus Massacre* (*Erosu purasu gyakusatsu*, 1969), exploring radicalism and the intellectual roots of Japanese politics. *Coup d'etat* (*Kai genrai*) (1973) investigated Japan's military history. *The Human Promise* (*Ningen no yakusoku*, 1986) explored euthanasia. He directed *Wuthering Heights* (*Arashi ga oka*, 1988), an adaptation of the Emily Bronte classic. Yet, it was with *The Women in the Mirror* (*Kagami no onnatachi*) (2002) that Yoshida turned to melodrama to present three generations of a family dealing with a shared memory of Hiroshima. The interconnected puzzle of women's lives in this film interacted with the national imagination.

This was Yoshida's first feature film in fourteen years. It is a humanist film that shows how multiple-generations of people were affected by the bombing. Yoshida uses broken mirrors and troubled dreams to depict the fractured reality. Hiroshima reverberates within the lives of each generation.

Ai Kawase (Mariko Okuda) is an elderly woman. Her daughter Miwa ran away twenty-four years ago. Ai searches for Miwa, who is now known as Masako. Ai calls her other daughter, Natsuki, who lives in the United States, and asks her to return home. Ai Kawase's husband was a doctor who treated soldiers who were victims of radiation sickness. Her daughter returns home after many years. When Ai meets Musako she wonders at the change she sees in her daughter.

At this point, a television producer (Mirai Yamamuto) visits Ai Kawase. He wants her to assist with a program about a U.S. soldier who was saved at Hiroshima by her husband, a doctor who treated victims of the bombing. Ai refuses, saying that she does not know of this. Or, perhaps she does not want to recall the trauma of war. The documentary filmmaker wants to ask her about her husband's experiences at Hiroshima. She will not respond.

When Ai meets her daughter Musako, her daughter's appearance is that of a shocked girl with a blank face. Natsuki, meanwhile, has felt abandoned by her mother. She feels unable to trust others. Her daughter is experiencing amnesia: a memory of forgetfulness. Only an image of the bombed devastation of the city remains in her mind. The film uses broken mirrors to show this fractured mind and this fractured country. The breaks in this family suggest the shock waves that echo across generations. What Yoshida presents implies the severity of the many hidden, psychological and social consequences of Hiroshima. Life issues are strained, generation after generation, because painful memories linger.

Critics have asked whether a younger generation can relate to this film. Is this, they ask, only for an older audience? They have expressed the concern that younger generations will lose memory. However, the work of Yoshida on this film provides each generation with a marker of memory. Indeed, it is a reminder that this incident still echoes across time. Yoshida recalls the spiritual costs of the war and its broader social dynamics.

Another film that addresses social and personal memory is *The Face of Jizō* (2004), which emerged from a 1994 stage production about the lasting suffering of the survivors of the bombings of Hiroshima and Nagasaki. *The Face of Jizō* (2004) directed by Kazuo Kuroki was a play by Hisashi Inoue. This was the thirty-fourth play performed by Komatsuza, between September 3 and 18, 1994. It has since been performed worldwide. *The Face of Jizō* reminds us that the destruction of Hiroshima and Nagasaki resulted in thousands of personal human tragedies. The play originated when the playwright Hisashi Inoue was sent to Hiroshima to work for a summer on an anti-nuclear program. There he met victims of the bomb and found it "too awful" to write about. Yet, at this time, novelist Kenzebaurō Ōe was beginning to write about the atomic bombing of Hiroshima. Hisaki Inoue decided to deal with the human consequences of that event.

In Inoue's play a father and his daughter engage in fiery dialogue. The setting is Hiroshima in the summer of 1948. A father and daughter appear in the gradually rebuilt city. Mitsue (Rie Miyazawa) is lectured by her father Takezo (Yoshio Harada) on how she ought to live her life. We learn that Mitsue lives alone: her father is a ghost and he died in the bombing. Mitsue is stuck, feeling guilt as a survivor she cannot move forward with her life. Mitsue and Takezo are in a room—perhaps it is the kitchen. Mitsue sits with her knees to her chest. Takezo, her father, wears a long white apron. Their conversation is lively indeed but Takezo is a ghost. Mitsue is stuck, frozen in time, emotionally paralyzed by what has occurred. She experiences anguish as a survivor: wondering why she should be allowed to live when others have died. This psychological immobilization affects her entire life. She is a young librarian, a curator of the repository of the race. Her work is that of a holder or retainer of culture. Yet, she is stunted and feels burdened. "People were killed in my place," Mitsue says. "I do not have the right to find happiness."[11] She meets Kinoshita, a handsome man, in the library. But she cannot allow herself to have feelings for him. He has come to the library to research on the bombing. Mitsue is also a victim of the bombing because her life is psychologically and emotionally arrested.

A ghost is a sign of memories. He is a sign of ancestors: Mitsue's father may be identified with Jizō, who is a guardian of the children. The father, Takezo, is identified with Jizō, the guardian of children. Mitsue, representing the generation of the children, forever struggles with herself, trying to forget. "I am the daughter whose father fell into a sea of flames worse than hell and I ran away from it," she says.[12] Amid all this self-recrimination, she is someone forever affected by the war. She feels guilt about being a survivor.

Kazuo Kuroki directed the film, which brought Rie Miyazawa to the screen with Yoshio Harada. The drama is clearly about the anguish of a survivor, a young librarian who may represent a holder and preserver of culture, as well as the youth and future of Japan. The prizes the film has won—the Hochi Prize, the Asaki Best Film award, and the Blue Ribbon Award for Rie Miyazawa as best actress—are not nearly as important as the message of how Mitsue's conscience has been affected as a survivor and the question about whether she can ever move forward with her life.

Like *Hiroshima mon amour* (1959), directed by Alain Resnais, these Japanese films are Proustian studies of time and memory. They delve deeply into Japanese culture in their examination of the human cost of the destruction and its after-effects. The way that other filmmakers have treated the use of the atomic bomb in 1945 has been generally different from the approach of Renais, or those of Japanese filmmakers Shindō and Yoshida. *Hiroshima* (1995), a three hour Japanese and Canadian film made for television by Koreyoshi Kurahara and Roger Spottiswoode, examined the decision making process that led to the bomb. The film includes interviews, documentary footage, and dramatic recreations of events. Documentary was the also the vehicle for a film on Hiroshima and Nagasaki that Oliver Stone and Peter Kuznick assembled in 2012–2013 for a Showtime cable television series on American history. They brought this segment with them to address several hundred academics and graduate students in Spring 2013. The setting was the American Popular Culture Association Conference in Washington, D.C., at the end of March 2013, and their documentary was highly critical of the American decision to drop the bombs. As in the great Japanese treatments of this tragic story, a central concern was memory. Stone and Kuznick suggested that events would have evolved differently if Henry Wallace had become the American president, rather than Harry Truman. Their selective use of footage made a striking case against the use of the bomb and their images graphically depicted its horror.

Even so, the direct dramatic encounter with human lives in films by a director like Shindō, a playwright like Inoue, or the psychologically probing drama of Yoshida, may evoke more feeling and reflection in viewers than even the most passionately critical of documentaries. Notably, *The Face of Jizō* was screened at the Washington, D.C., embassy on August 17, 2011, less than a year after the playwright Inoue's death. As such films become better known, they may have an effect upon how future generations look back and remember. The future of cultural memory and how history is remembered today depends, in part, upon film. In speaking of history to new generations, these films—*Children of Hiroshima, Women in the Mirror, The Face of Jizō*—make present the small, personal, and hidden moments; the struggles of lives hidden behind the official versions of these events. They offer a timeless human face, a poignant memory, which belongs to the historical record and sustains the fragile roots of cultural memory.

Notes

1. N. Kristoff, "Hiroshima: An Act That Haunts Japan and America," *The New York Times*, August 6, 1995: 1, 11–13.

2. P. Nora, *Realms of Memory* (New York: Columbia University Press, 1996), pp. 4–5.

3. N. Kristoff, "Hiroshima: An Act That Haunts Japan and America," *The New York Times*, August 6, 1995: p. 11.

4. *Ibid.*

5. M. Weber, *Economy and Society*, ed. G. Roth and C. Wittick (Berkeley: University of California Press, 1978), p. 903.

6. Stephen Hilgartner and Charles L. Bosk, "The Rise and Fall of Social Problems: A Public Arenas Model." *American Journal of Sociology* 94.1 (1988): 53–54.

7. J. Alexander, "Toward a Theory of Cultural Traces," *Cultural Trauma and Collective Identity*, ed. Jeffrey Alexander, R. Eyerman, et al. (Berkeley: University of California Press, 1982), p. 30.

8. H. Saito, "Reiterated Commemoration: Hiroshima as a National Trauma. *Sociological Theory* 24.4 (December 2006): 354.

9. A. Huyssen, *Present Pasts: Urban Palimpsests and the Politics of Memory* (Stanford: Stanford University Press, 2003).

10. P. Nora, *Realms of Memory* (New York: Columbia University Press, 1996) p. 4.

11. H. Inoue, *The Face of Jizō*, 1994.
12. *Ibid.*

Bibliography

Alexander, Jeffery. "Toward a Theory of Cultural Traces," in *Cultural Trauma and Collective Identity*, ed. J.C. Alexander, R. Eyerman, et al. (Berkeley: University of California Press, 1982)

Hagen, Michael J, *Hiroshima in History and Memory*. Cambridge: Cambridge University Press, 1996.

Halbwachs, Maurice. *Social Frames of Memory (Sociaux de la Memorie)*. Chicago: University of Chicago Press, 1992. First published 1925 by University of Paris Press.

Hilgartner, Stephen, and Charles L. Bosk. "The Rise and Fall of Social Problems: A Public Arenas Model." *American Journal of Sociology* 94.1 (1988): 53–78.

Huyssen, Andreas. *Present Pasts: Urban Palimpsests and the Politics of Memory*. Stanford: Stanford University Press, 2003.

Inoue, Hisashi. *The Face of Jizō*. 1994.

Kristoff, Nicholas D. "Hiroshima: An Act That Haunts Japan and America." *New York Times*, August 6, 1995: 1, 11–12.

LaCapra, Dominick. *History and Meaning After Auschwitz*. Ithaca: Cornell University Press, 1998.

_____. *Rethinking Intellectual History*. Ithaca: Cornell University Press, 1983.

_____. *Writing History, Writing Trauma*. Baltimore: Johns Hopkins University Press, 2001.

Nora, Pierre, *Realms of Memory*, 3 vols. New York: Columbia University Press, 1996–98.

Renais, Alain. dir. *Hiroshima mon amour*.

Saito, Hiro. "Reiterated Commemoration: Hiroshima as a National Trauma." *Sociological Theory* 24.4 (December 2006): 353–54.

Shindō, Kaneto, dir. *Children of Hiroshima*. 1952.

Stone, Oliver, and Peter Kuznick, dirs. *Oliver Stone's Untold History of the United States*. Showtime. 2013.

Weber, Max. *Economy and Society*. Ed. G. Roth and C. Wittick. Berkeley: University of California Press, 1978.

Yoshida, Yoshisige. *Woman in a Mirror*. 2002.

Inconceivable Anxiety: Representation, Disease and Discrimination in Atomic-Bomb Films

Yuki Miyamoto

For better or worse, one's experience of surfing the Hub [Human Rights media] is shaped by the do-I-or-don't-I-want-to-watch-this question, as in: Do I or don't I want to watch a Tibetan pilgrim being shot dead by the Chinese police at Nangpa La Pass? How about cell phone footage of a man being hung upside down and sodomized with a rod in an Egyptian prison? Or the testimony of women in Bangladesh whose faces have been disfigured by acid? Well intentioned and effective as the operation may be, scrolling through such choices makes me feel as though I've arrived at the hub of a problem rather than its solution.—Maggie Nelson, The Art of Cruelty[1]

In March 2012, I came across an article by Abigail Haworth in the *Guardian*, entitled "After Fukushima: Families on the edge of meltdown." The article describes people's lives in Fukushima two years after the meltdown of the nuclear power plant following the earthquake and tsunami of March 11, 2011.[2] Focusing on how radiation leakage from the crippled reactors at the Fukushima Dai'ichi Nuclear Power Plant strained people, especially couples with children, emotionally, mentally, and physically, Haworth's article sheds light on a matter not often taken up in public contexts: anxiety and discrimination surrounding victims of radiation-related disasters.

As Haworth writes, "Couples are being torn apart over such issues as whether to stay in the area or leave, what to believe about the dangers of radiation, whether it is safe to get pregnant and the best methods to protect children."[3] As clinical psychologist Noriko Kubota claims in Haworth's account, "People [in the Fukushima region] are living with constant low-level anxiety."[4] Uncertainty surrounding the dangers of radiation has the side-effects of generating prejudices and discrimination, further straining those living in Fukushima. Yet, as Haworth observes, such discrimination goes largely without mention. "Most unmentionable of all, cases of discrimination against people from Fukushima are arising within Japanese society. Social stigma attached to victims of radiation goes back to the aftermath of the wartime atomic bombings of Hiroshima and Nagasaki, when men could not find work and women were unable to marry due to fears they were 'tainted.'"[5]

Discrimination against victims of radiation is expressed, regrettably, in quite tangible ways: some people from Fukushima were turned down when offering blood donations, their car windows were smashed, and they were asked to disclose their cesium levels on job applications.[6] Haworth reports that "prejudice against women is the most pervasive"; they are considered "damaged goods." At about the time Haworth's article was published, the Hiroshima City council announced it was removing the three effigies at the Hiroshima Peace Memorial Museum, citing the objective to replace these imagined bodies with more fact-based materials.[7] The three figures, representing a woman, a schoolgirl, and a boy—all non-masculine figures—represent bodies injured as a result of the atomic bombing. Although one motivation for removing these figures from the grounds might be to help mitigate against the prejudices against women as "damaged goods," I will suggest in the following pages that removing such images from the public eye—making them unmentionable, invisible—will not alleviate discrimination and may in fact render both discrimination and the anxiety around injured bodies all the more trenchant.

Thus we are confronted with the question of how to represent and respond to the "abnormal" body, and in what the socially sanctioned "normal" body consists. I want to respond to this question by examining representations of bodies injured or made ill by radiation, considering the ethical problems and possibilities of representing such bodies. In doing so, I will examine popular representations and social constructions of "normal" and "abnormal" bodies, with the aim of better understanding not only why certain representations of injured bodies are repressed while others are romanticized for public display, but also why discrimination against injured bodies so often occurs.

Toward this end, I investigate several atomic-bomb films that, in their representations of afflicted bodies, romanticize or repress those injured bodies. I pay special attention to the depiction of the bodies of women, as they are so often the object of discriminatory treatment, suggesting that the representation of bodies made "abnormal" through injury or illness tends to be widely accepted only if those bodies are romanticized, that is, euphemized, aestheticized, and idealized through the neutralization of pain and the more gruesome aspects of suffering.[8] Such romanticization,[9] I submit, effectively erases the genuine physicality of the injured or ill bodies, thereby rendering them less threatening to the orders and norms of a given society, in this case, Japanese. The romanticized bodies represented in the mass media—movies in particular—tend also to be the bodies of women, stripped of their full physicality and individuality through their romantic aestheticization and idealization.

As I hope to show, this romanticization of injured and ill bodies in atomic-bomb movies corresponds to social norms complicit with nationalist ideologies. The sentiments of nationalism enforce stereotypes of male and female "normal" bodies while suppressing those injured and ill bodies that do not conform to this imposed standard. My hope is that raising to critical visibility the problematic relationship between the representation of ab/normal bodies and the perpetuation of discrimination is a modest step toward resisting those structures through which such discrimination persists. Alleviating suffering from prejudice and discrimination against those with exceptional bodies may ultimately require values at odds with those that currently prevail within and beyond Japanese society.

Norms and the Body

For the purposes of these reflections, I want to follow Judith Butler's conception of a norm as comprising "various standards" based upon "restrictive ideas about what the human is,"[10] in such a way that determines who is accepted and who is excluded within a given society—for no society always accepts anybody. I will emphasize that the body is a contested element, a site of vulnerability and particularity that remains a threat to the structures of control, discipline, and predictability upon which modern societies are predicated. Sunaura Taylor, a painter and disability activist who was born with anthrogryposis, remarks on the threats presented by the particularities of human bodies: "I think what's ultimately threatening about it … the way in which someone moves or the way in which someone uses their bodies or the way in which someone speaks differently, is that it's a threat to our most basic categories that we've built our systems of power on."[11] Bodies, always to some extent uncontrollable and unpredictable, and inevitably exhibiting a uniqueness or difference that threatens stability, is one key element that norms seek to govern.

One such method of neutralizing the rather intractable aspects of the body, especially ill or injured bodies, is romanticization. Through romanticization, the body that resists the norm is tamed and is made "acceptable." But romanticization not only mitigates the differences of the unique body; it also legitimates inequitable treatments of "abnormal" or unacceptable bodies, which in turn promotes discriminatory attitudes toward those bodies that do not conform to prevailing norms. As we will see, nationalism is one source of governing normativity, defining the normal body as the specifically masculine and militarized body, able to stand up and fight for the nation. Other bodies are repressed, romanticized, or otherwise discriminated against.

Why are "abnormal" bodies, particularly ill and injured bodies, so persistently objects of discriminatory treatment and "social violence"? In what does their "threat" consist? As Butler points out, such bodies display human vulnerability, a vulnerability that threatens to undermine the stability of social structures. "I think," writes Butler, "there are a lot of different reasons for social violence toward people who are perceived to be on the margins of gender, the margins of able-bodiedness, the margins of racial normativity, and a lot of it has to do with fear of contact and contagion, that maybe somebody else's vulnerability will become one's own."[12] The fear of encountering another's vulnerability and in turn of recognizing one's own vulnerability, generates discrimination, because such fear, as Taylor puts it, "hits people at … an emotionally uncontrollable level."[13] As this essay will contend, removal or romanticization of the injured or ill body from the public eye will not resolve or alleviate discrimination. Rather, cultivating a willingness to face our own vulnerability and a sensibility toward uncontrollable and unpredictable nature will help us to recognize and appreciate differences.

Broaching the issue of prejudice and discrimination against those with injured, diseased, or otherwise "abnormal" bodies, medical doctor and anatomist Takeshi Yōrō asks why dead bodies inspire fear. Yōrō observes that the corpse is "stripped of all social meaning," that is, deprived of the markers of identity—professional, familial, etc.—that secured a place for the now-deceased person within the social structure. And although death is a natural (and final) stage for all human beings, in today's (post)industrial societies, dead bodies are largely felt to be alien, other, and therefore must be removed from public visibility. And yet, even the dead body vividly exhibits its physical particularity. In light of this observation, Yōrō claims that exposing the human body—dead or alive—in its nakedness is a taboo, to certain extent, in any society.[14] This is precisely because the body belongs to nature; it is, in other words, something "unpredictable and uncontrollable," and therefore in tension with human civilization, which is founded and organized on the basis of predictability and human control.

For Yōrō, it is not only the human body that is taboo. The natural world more broadly elicits an ambivalent uncanniness (*bukimi*), an anxious but fascinated response to that which is beyond predictability and human control. That which provokes this uncanny response—attraction and repulsion—is expelled from the social structure. Therefore those who engage most directly with nature—hunters and fishers, for example—are often assigned places outside the social order in the course of European as well as Japanese history.[15] Some are consecrated, taken as holy, while others are scorned or shunned.[16] But in the modern world, what is unpredictable and uncontrollable, Yōrō argues, tends not to be elevated, but rather scorned, held in suspicion, and discriminated against.

Literary critic Noboru Okaniwa supports this point, claiming that discrimination against "abnormal" bodies stems not precisely from the deformity of the bodies, but rather from the sheer physicality that such deformities—whether in the form of excess or lack—exhibits. In other words, what is considered an "abnormal" body is, as Yōrō suggests, the body that reminds and confronts us with an unpredictable and uncontrollable nature, one opposed to stable social norms organized around predictability and control. Abnormal bodies, Okaniwa goes on to claim, deviate from the norm, and therefore seem to undercut predictability and resist control. Escaping the social norms and physical normality, which are predicated on sameness, abnormal bodies exhibit unique individuality.

I would suggest that it is precisely because abnormal bodies are idiosyncratic and distinctive, unique in their physical particularity, that they are often suppressed from public view and the popular media, which functions in complicity with prevailing norms. Synthesizing the insights of Okaniwa and Yōrō, it is clear that any social order, any set of norms, predicated upon predictability and controllability will fail to countenance diversity—or even worse, it will tend to avoid recognizing distinctive differences.

Diseased Bodies of Women in Film

This failure to attend to difference may seem to contradict the ever-intensifying affirmative rhetoric of diversity in the academy and segments of the mass media. French philosopher Alain Badiou sees such embrace of diversity as symptomatic of a banalization of the concept of "difference"—and a suppression of real difference: "Respect for differences, of course!" Badiou writes. "But on condition that the different be parliamentary-democratic, pro free-market economics, in favour of freedom of opinion, feminism, the environment.... That is to say: I respect differences, but only, of course, in so far as that which differs also respects, just as I do, the said differences."[17] In the terms of the present essay, abnormal bodies are acceptable as long as their differences do not threaten prevailing social norms—as long, that is, as they do not pose a challenge to norms through their affiliation with "nature"—unpredictable and uncontrollable. Injured and diseased bodies are a reminder of powerlessness, vulnerability, and mortality—things that must be covered over or eliminated in upholding the stability of social norms.[18]

As noted, one way to tame and transform such abnormal bodies into "acceptably" different bodies for public display is through romanticization. According to Susan Sontag in her well-known discussion of "illness as metaphor," tuberculosis, once identified with death[19] and defined as "a disease thought to be intractable and capricious—that is, a disease not understood—in an era in which medicine's central premise is that all diseases can be cured,"[20] has been romanticized. Tuberculosis "had already acquired the associations of being romantic by the mid-eighteenth century,"[21] and in turn, images of "romantic agony" in literature derive from "tuberculosis and its transformation through metaphor."[22] This romanticization conceals actual suffering. "Agony," writes Sontag, "became romantic in a stylized account of the disease's preliminary symptoms (for example, debility is transformed into languor) and the actual agony was simply suppressed."[23] The suffering body is aestheticized and depictions of suffering transformed into portraits of alluring lassitude.

Similarly, the visual rhetoric of romanticization in a-bomb movies tends to suppress the actual suffering undergone by *Hibakushas*, neutralizing and banalizing their distinctive pains, scars, and traces of violence, such that their differences become acceptable, "normal." As a result, besides the critical problem that romanticized representations fail to address the *Hibakushas'* plight and the very real anxieties for their health, such visual rhetoric distracts the audience's attention from those norms that suppresses the real differences, and thereby legitimates and perpetuates discrimination. In order to discern the filmic romanticization that banalizes the plight of *Hibakushas*, let us turn to two movies that came out in the 1980s: *Yumechiyo nikki* (*The Diary of Yumechiyo*, hereafter *Yumechiyo*) and *Kuroi ame* (hereafter *Black Rain*), both of which depict the ill bodies of women living in rural villages of Japan.

Yumechiyo debuted as a television program in 1981 on NHK, the Japanese public broadcasting station. Thanks to its popularity, two more seasons followed in 1982 and 1984. A movie, the subject of the following discussion, was made in 1985. The eponymous protagonist, exposed to radiation while still in her mother's womb in Hiroshima, is taking over her late mother's occupation, running a geisha house at a rural onsen (hot spring) town in Japan. She falls in love with Munakata Masaru, who visits Yumechiyo's village as part of his performance group. It turns out that he is being pursued by police, wrongly accused of the murder of his own father. Yumechiyo flees with him into exile, though she has been diagnosed with leukemia.

Feminist writer Maya Morioka Todeschini attributes the success of the *Yumechiyo* series to its melodramatic plot: "[*Yumechiyo*] contains all the ingredients for commercial success: a long-suffering, beautiful heroine who dies fashionably in the end; romantic love and sex; traditional dance, song and popular theater; intrigue, female suicide and murder—all set in a romantic, rustic hot-spring resort far from the tensions of urban life."[24] The many romanticized aspects of the story obscure through aestheticization brutal facts of suffering that victims of leukemia, functionally suppress the real agony of radiation-related illnesses. Fatal illness cast in a romantic light and love relations cut short due to premature death are widespread melodramatic tropes in a-bomb films depicting *Hibakushas*. In *Yumechiyo*, the protagonist's illness is highly aestheticized: she was prenatally exposed to radiation and as an adult is diagnosed with leukemia and given a life expectancy of three months. The prenatal exposure to radiation does not affect Yumechiyo's external beauty, nor her intellectual abilities. In other words, the effects of the disease have no visible, outward manifestations, but rather imbue the Yumechiyo character with an alluring sense of romantic melancholy.

But of course, real-life illness from radiation is never so attractive, a point made painfully clear when comparing the fictional melodrama with illnesses portrayed in documentary films. For instance, Steven Okazaki's 2005 documentary *The Mushroom Club* features three women who, like the fictional Yumechiyo, were exposed to radiation prenatally. Narumi and Toshiko were conceived three months prior to the bombing. As a result of their prenatal radiation exposure, they were born with small brains, a condition called microcephaly; they each have a mental capacity roughly that of an eight-year-old. The third victim, Yuriko Hatanaka, 59 years old at the time of the filming, has a mental capacity of a two-year-old. Yuriko's father, more than 80 years of age, has been taking care of her, and is concerned about Yuriko's future after he passes away. The women featured in this documentary have appearances that do not conform to the norms of "ideal" feminine beauty. And though they have the intellectual capacities of children, their relatively long lives, not romantically cut short by their illness, are lived out alongside parents and other caregivers whose compassion is matched by agonized concern for their loved ones' wellbeing.

Yumechiyo, meanwhile, is portrayed as outwardly lovely and intellectually capable, free of the microcephaly and attendant conditions suffered by some who have been exposed prenatally to radiation. Even her leukemia is romanticized. Sontag again sheds light on this matter. "One non-tumor form of cancer now turns up in commercial fiction in the role once monopolized by TB, as the romantic disease which cuts off a young life," namely leukemia.[25] In a-bomb movies like *Yumechiyo*, the female protagonists' deaths are aestheticized through leukemia, the "romantic disease" that can end life while it is still in the full blossom of youth and "ideal" beauty.

Leukemia brings a premature death to the lovely Yumechiyo, thereby also cutting short her love relationship with Munakata. The melodramatic narrative is one of too-brief love that further glorifies the self-sacrificial Yumechiyo in her devotion to Munakata. But these melodramatic tropes of romantic love serve to cover over the anxieties—among both victims and others—provoked by possible genetic disorders associated with radiation and the discrimination that stems from these anxieties. In the context of the movie, the discriminatory sentiments so often directed at radiation victims seem to be internalized by the protagonist. In her youth, Yumechiyo was eager to have a baby, yet after conceiving, she terminates the pregnancy out of fear that the child might suffer some form of radiation sickness. This decision is a complicated matter. On the one hand, terminating the pregnancy might seem to be an act of compassion, a decision undertaken in the hope of preventing another living being from suffering. And yet, it is still uncertain that a child born from an a-bomb victim will suffer any illness. In light of this fact, the character of Yumechiyo represents a kind of internalization of discriminatory attitudes toward victims of radiation. In aborting the pregnancy, she is reproducing the attitudes that suggest that a life with radiation sickness is not worth living. This in turn reflects the character's attitude concerning her own life as a victim of radiation illness.

Yumechiyo's anxiety around reproduction—so severe as to compel her to terminate her pregnancy—is, of course, a melodramatic trope designed to hook an audience—but, unfortunately, it is not entirely groundless. What I have referred to as the internalization of the discriminatory sentiment has its basis in a sad reality. Journalist Kazuo Chūjō reports that in the 1970s, three decades after the nuclear bombing, Nobuyoshi Kondō, a doctor and member of the Tokyo Metropolitan Assembly, proposed that *Hibakusha* be sterilized. He believed that *Hibakushas'* children tended to be genetically damaged.[26] *Hibakusha* groups protested Kondō's proposal, prompting an apology from Kondō. The protest and apology did not, however, substantially change the situation. Despite Kondō's discriminatory statement, he was elected ōhe assembly for another four consecutive terms.[27] Such discriminatory attitudes toward *Hibakusha* and other radiation victims remain very much alive. As Haworth reveals in her article on Fukushima, "Last year, prominent anti-nuclear activist Ikeya Hobun, the head of the Ecosystem Conservation Society of Japan, said at a public meeting: 'People from Fukushima should not marry because the deformity rate of their babies will skyrocket.'"[28]

The real-life examples above convey a clear and troubling message: certain bodies are not deemed worthy of life and integration into the social sphere. Within the fictional context of the movie, Yumechiyo's decision to terminate her pregnancy signifies not only a personal decision but also an internalization of discriminatory social norms that refuse certain bodies. This discrimination, as we will now see, often devolves along gender lines.

The 1980s also saw the release of the popular a-bomb film *Black Rain*, based upon renowned writer Masuji Ibuse's semi-fictional 1963 novel,[29] which was shot in black and white by Imamura Shōhei in 1989.[30] The story's protagonist, Shizuma Shigematsu, is about a mile away from the hypocenter when the atomic bomb explodes over Hiroshima. His niece, Yasuko, is to the west of the city, witnessing from afar the rising mushroom cloud over Hiroshima. Yasuko leaves for the city to find her uncle Shizuma and his wife Shigeko. On her way to the city, she is caught in nuclear fallout, or "black rain," but is able to reunite with her uncle and aunt. Together, they flee the city. Seven years later, we find the Shigematsu family leading a quiet life in a rural village eighty kilometers east of Hiroshima.

But one concern for Shigematsu is the prospect of marriage for Yasuko. Her suitors break off relations with her once they learn that she was in Hiroshima on August 6. Again, the real-life correlates to this story are troubling. Having been in Hiroshima on August 6 became a stigma for young women hoping to be married. They were often considered less desirable as wives and mothers, because *Hibakusha* were believed to be prone to falling sick or dying prematurely, and to being barren or producing deformed or ill offspring. In the story *Black Rain*, Shigematsu decides to rewrite Yasuko's diary in the hope of "proving" that she was not in the city at the time of the bombing. But before he has finished this task, Yasuko begins to show symptoms of radiation sickness.

The film version of *Black Rain* includes a young male character named Yuichi Okazakiya, who does not appear in the original book. Yuichi suffers from shell shock, and is unable to bear loud noises. Suffering from this mental condition, Yuichi withdraws to live with his aged mother. In his spare time, he carves logs into bodhisattva statues. Eventually Yasuko, relating to Yuichi's loneliness and emotional suffering, befriends him. Yet, predictably, the incipient love between these two characters, both deeply traumatized by the war, ends in melodramatic fashion; Yasuko falls ill and Yuichi's mental disorder continues to incapacitate him from taking care of himself.

Though themes of illness and trauma pervade *Black Rain*, their melodramatic treatment in fact distracts viewers' attention from the horror of long-lasting radiation effects from the bombings—the ostensible focus of the story. In this connection, consider the discriminatory gender implications of Shizuma's concern for Yasuko's marriage prospects, and his failed attempts to find her a spouse. This aspect of the story shifts the focus from the violence of the atomic bombing to the sadness of a woman with a social stigma who cannot find her romantic partner—while downplaying the fact that it was Shizuma who was directly impacted by the bomb's explosion. In other words, though the male character is more quintessentially a *Hibakusha*, he does not suffer from the same social stigma as Yasuko. Moreover, Shizuma appears destined to live into old age, whereas Yasuko exhibits signs of radiation sickness; everything indicates that her life will reach an early end while she is still outwardly beautiful.[31]

The apparent critique of the atomic bombing forwarded by the movie falls along gender lines; the bombing is condemned not because of its long-lasting effects—effects that in fact do not discriminate between male and female (or any other such divisions)—but rather because of the social stigma customarily attached to women—a stigma perpetuated, rather than undermined, by the movie's romantic tropes. In this sense, the movie is complicit with the norm surrounding marriage in Japanese society in the 1950s, whereby the female body is treated as a commodity, the object of barter or sale, deprived of autonomy. Her anxieties and struggles are expressed through a male character, her uncle. As Todeschini points out, "victims' subjective experiences are de-emphasized, and illness becomes romanticized."[32] This point is brought home by the real-life notion cited by Haworth—that women suffering from radiation are "damaged goods." Discrimination is not problematized or critiqued in *Black Rain*, but "explained" by recourse to social stigma and tacitly affirmed through the privileging of the male character and the portrayal of the woman as an object lacking genuine subjectivity.

Leukemia in *Yumechiyo* and radiation sickness in *Black Rain* are "romantic" diseases, such as described by Sontag—diseases that do not mar the outward aspect of the victim, but rather lend them an aestheticized aspect of "sensitivity" and allure. According to Sontag, the association of women with these diseases arise in literature of the late eighteenth and early nineteenth centuries, in correspondence to social norms for women as weak, submissive, and deprived of subjectivity. The normative image of men, meanwhile, is one of increasing size and strength: "Gradually, the tubercular look, which symbolized an appealing vulnerability, a superior sensitivity, became more and more the ideal look for women—while great men of the mid-and late nineteenth century grew fat, founded industrial empires, wrote hundreds of novels, made wars, and plundered continents."[33] Fatal diseases are thereby romanticized—trivialized through aestheticization, made a facet of feminine beauty.

Like literary depictions of tuberculosis in European fiction, leukemia in Japanese fiction and film is consistently associated with women. In her own researches, Todeschini has been able to find only one film, *Ai to shi no kiroku* (*Record of Life and Death*, Koreyoshi Kurahara, 1966), in which a male protagonist who experienced the atomic bombing at the age of four dies from leukemia.[34] As journalist Kazuo Chūjō has observed, "women suffering from 'A-bomb disease' or leukemia make popular tragic heroines.... Men, somehow, don't seem to go along very well with leukemia, and are therefore hardly ever depicted as victims of this disease."[35] Of course, the absence of representations of men afflicted with leukemia is not insignificant, and is at odds with empirical facts. As Todeschini observes, "statistics reveal that the rate of leukemia in women was consistently lower than in men, for any age group."[36] The woman's body is romantically weakened, affording her a "sensitivity" and "sadness" that obscures the agony of disease, while the male body as depicted in popular film is an image of strength and health, and not the object of pity.

"Sadness," Sontag contends, is a feminized trait, and to be sad is to be "powerless."[37] The male body, on the other hand, should not evoke sadness and powerlessness. The normative image of the male body, in Japan as in Europe, has one source in nationalism. In his book *Nationalism and Sexuality*, historian George L. Mosse unveils the close relationship between the emergence of nationalism and the transformation of body image in eighteenth- and nineteenth-century Western Europe—at around the same time tuberculosis became a romantic, feminine disease. "The wars of the French Revolution and Napoleon and the rise of a new national consciousness," writes Mosse, "served to transform soldiering into an attainable and much admired profession. Soldiers were now citizen-soldiers whose status was quite different from that of their predecessors, even if most of them came from the so-called lower classes."[38] Mosse's observation suggests that the outward accouterments and dispositions of the body—attire, accessories, mannerisms, and the like—once fragmented along geographic, occupational, and social lines, became unified and homogenized through military service. The male body was, in this manner, nationalized, made an emblem of the state in its full might.

In this connection, becoming a citizen within a modern nation-state does not entail merely an inner disposition in which one subscribes to a national ideology. Rather, allegiance and loyalty to the nation must be demonstrated outwardly, through the body and its gestures—in singing the national anthem,[39] or reciting the pledge of allegiance in a specific posture. The body becomes an essential vehicle for communicating national ideologies, literally embodying its norms—the norms by which the nation-state is upheld. As the unified body image was solidified, bodies that did not fit that image were denigrated. "The Enlightenment and the science of medicine" writes Mosse, "sharpened the distinction between vice and virtue, insider and outsider, which the religious revival had also encouraged. During the early nineteenth century, the normal and abnormal were irrevocably fixed—each encompassing a set of morals, manners, looks, and intellectual qualities."[40] The normal body is the body that can stand up and fight for the nation. The body unable to fight is "abnormal."

As the demarcation between normal and abnormal bodies, dispositions, and morals were established in the war in Europe and brought forth with the emergence of the modern-nation state, similar changes were occurring in Japan, which was undergoing its own modernization and construction of the "normal" body. Historian Hajime Imanishi examines the correlation between nationalism and the process of homogenizing the body image in nineteenth- and twentieth-century Japan, particularly with the regime change from the feudal Tokugawa Shogunate in 1868—the Meiji Restoration. The newly instituted Meiji government, aiming at establishing a modern-nation state on the Japanese archipelago, issued edicts and ordinances regarding the bodies of the general public. Whereas bodies under the shogunate were regulated according to social status and occupation, the birth of the modern Japanese nation-state under the Meiji government coincided with new regulations of people's bodies. The Meiji government sought to homogenize bodies of the citizenry more broadly, compelling greater conformity to a national standard embodied in the emperor himself.[41]

According to art critic Kōji Taki, prior to the Restoration, the Meiji emperor-to-be, Prince Mutsuhito, wore traditional attire and sported idiosyncratically outmoded make-up, plucking off his eyebrows and whitening his face in a manner after the aristocrats. But when ascending to the throne, his appearance changed. In the portrait distributed to local governments for display in public halls in the 1870s and intended to provide a visualization of the head of the nation for the purpose of unifying national identity, the Meiji emperor appeared in a military uniform, with short hair, no make-up, thick eyebrows, and mustache.[42] This transformation of the emperor's image epitomizes the new norm of the body of the nation, with its elevation of manliness and military aptitude.

As the Meiji emperor's portrayal exemplifies, the normal body exhibits "ideals of manliness." But as Mosse reveals, those masculine ideals served to situate not only "insiders who accepted the norms," but also "the place of women" and "outsiders, those considered abnormal or diseased."[43] That is to say, the emergence of the normal body generated by service to the modern nation-state inevitably defines women's bodies as "other" than the norm. The construction of the masculine body as normal, and the concomitant situation of the female body as abnormal or other, illuminates why the atomic bomb films overwhelmingly and repeatedly depicts ill bodies as women's bodies. The female body, in its very difference from the male body, is a socially ill or injured body, and also therefore a body deemed incapable of combat—abnormal, helpless, and pitiable. Male bodies, which must uphold the social norms of masculinity, strength, and military ability, must be depicted as relatively invulnerable.

For this reason, in contrast to the bodies of female protagonists, the bodies of male protagonists in a-bomb movies are by and large healthy bodies. But I want to investigate the vulnerable male body in filmic treatments of the atomic bombings. As we have seen, depictions of injured or diseased bodies of male characters in atomic bomb films are quite rare. One notable instance of this rarity is the movie adaptation of Keiji Nakazawa's auto-biographical graphic novel *Hadashi no Gen*, or *Barefoot Gen*, the first installment of which appeared in 1972. Nakazawa draws upon his own experiences as a six-year-old in Hiroshima at the time of the bombing, portraying himself in the protagonist Gen.[44] The story opens in pre–1945 Japan before moving into depictions of the horrific damage to human bodies from the atomic bombing, and on to post-war sufferings from radiation sickness, discrimination against *Hibakusha*, and poverty.[45]

Although Nakazawa's graphic novel was translated into more than ten languages, and though the animated film version of 1983 continues to captivate audiences within and beyond Japan, the trilogy of action films made in 1976, 1977, and 1980 remain relatively unknown. Among them, the 1977 installment of the Gen trilogy, *Hadashi no Gen: Namida no bakuhatsu*, or *Barefoot Gen: The Explosion of Tears*, is one of a very few movies to deal in depictions of an injured male body of a main character. The episode in question concerns the friendship between Gen and Seiji Yoshida, a once-aspiring painter who was badly burnt in the atomic bombing. Frightened by his appearance, even Seiji's family avoids him. Gen is hired to take care of Seiji. Although Gen had seen many dead bodies—charred, blackened, unidentifiable—while roaming through the burnt ruins of Hiroshima on August 6, it is not easy for him to attend to Seiji's wounded body, which is melted, deformed, and exudes an awful smell. Such afflictions were common among *Hibakusha*; their injuries often remained unhealed for years, due to a lack of white blood cells resulting from radiation exposure.

Seiji is ashamed of his body, embittered toward the world, and hides himself in his house. Gen, also a *Hibakusha*, has suffered from discrimination, with people shunning him out of fear of contracting disease. As a victim of such discrimination, Gen identifies with Seiji, and tries to help him regain the confidence needed to go out in public. Gen devises the plan to wheel Seiji on a cart through the city, publically displaying his grotesquely injured body. Despite Gen's good intentions, the exposure of Seiji's body stirs up fear and disgust among people in the neighborhood.

Such feelings stem in part from the fact that Seiji's exposed body breaks many taboos. Indeed, the responses to his body crystallize the attitudes of discrimination that attend injured or ill male bodies. First, as Yōrō and others argue, display of the exposed body itself is taboo in modern industrialized societies founded on controllability and predictability; Seiji's nakedness is a reminder of nature's unpredictability and of human mortality. Second, the intact and nationalized male body, able to engage in combat, is the normative body. Injured and diseased male bodies like that of Seiji, in failing to conform to this norm, go largely unrepresented in atomic bomb films. The absence of such representation reflects discriminatory attitudes toward male bodies that are not combat-able. Finally, those bodies which are deemed fit for display are controlled bodies, that is, bodies whose individuality and particularity are neutralized or erased either through romanticization, or through the enforced conformity to the normative construction emblematized in the image of the Meiji emperor. But the representation of Seiji's body is neither romanticized nor does it follow the normative image. Rather, it challenges norms and taboos surrounding the body. One may surmise, then, that the relative lack of popularity of this version of the otherwise celebrated Gen story derives at least in part from the fact that it challenges the general public's sensibilities; the audience would seem to react to this filmic representation in much the same way as the neighbors in the film react to encountering Seiji's body.

Conclusion: Accepting Vulnerability

What kind of attitude toward bare, injured, ill bodies should be cultivated? How might discrimination against such bodies be overcome? A-bomb survivor Sumiteru Taniguchi provides insight into this matter. Taniguchi appears in Steven Okazaki's documentary *White Light/Black Rain: The Destruction of Hiroshima and Nagasaki*, which appeared in 2007, two years after *The Mushroom Club*. As a 16-year-old boy, Taniguchi was crushed to the ground by the force of the atomic blast in Nagasaki, and severely burnt by its heat. Sixty years later, he removes his shirt before Okazai's camera, revealing a dislocated rib cage. The skin of Taniguchi's entire back consists of scar tissue; his wife applies oil to prevent cracking and breaking. He must be cautiously gentle when coughing, so as to avoid breaking a rib. The sight of his body, mutilated by the atomic blast, is shocking, and all the more so because adult males' damaged, vulnerable bodies so rarely appear in a-bomb films, whether fictional or documentary. Even the footage collected by the *Atomic Bomb Casualty Commission* (ABCC), often used in atomic-bomb documentaries, trains its focus primarily upon the bodies of women and children.

When Taniguchi turns to speak into the camera, he says that he reveals his scars in the hope that such suffering not be repeated. "I've shown you my wounds because I want you to know this can't happen again."[46] It is with this gesture that I want to conclude, for Taniguchi's statement offers ethical insight into the question of how to represent and respond to injured bodies. We must face injured bodies neither with scorn nor romanticization. Rather than attempting to refute, eradicate, or repress such traces of violence, we must promote an attitude of acceptance that extends to the acknowledgment of the vulnerability of our own bodies, rather than anxious attempts to cover over vulnerability—one's own or that of others.

Unless we cultivate a sensitivity toward human vulnerability and allow for real differences—the sometimes troubling particularities, the reminders of contingency, uncontrollability, and mortality—that everybody in fact exhibits, we will fail to alleviate discrimination. The tendency to romanticize bodies erases difference in the name of "acceptability," at once obscuring and upholding the norms that legitimate and perpetuate discrimination. Bringing such norms to visibility, as I have tried to do here, reveals that the normal body is dictated by conformity to an image of a masculine, nationalized body image. If we take seriously the injunction to respect diversity, we must seek for pluralistic, multiple, de-homogenized value systems. Doing so is difficult, and likely to face resistance, because it forces us to confront our own vulnerability to contingency within social structures aiming at control and stability. But incorporating the perspectives of the injured and diseased, voices speaking from positions of vulnerability, stands to enrich our lives, which otherwise may be stifled within a system of norms and values dedicated to erasing particularity.

Notes

1. M. Nelson, *The Art of Cruelty: A Reckoning* (New York: W.W. Norton, 2011), p. 38.

2. A. Haworth, "After Fukushima: Families on the edge of meltdown," *The Guardian*, 23 February 2013, http://www.guardian.co.uk/environment/2013/feb/24/divorce-after-fukushima-nuclear-disaster.

3. *Ibid.*

4. *Ibid.*

5. *Ibid.*

6. Cesium levels indicate degrees of internal radiation exposure.

7. Chūgoku Shimbun, 19 March 2013.

8. Caroline Brothers discusses the euphemization of suffering in war photography in her book *War and Photography: A Cultural History.* See Chapter 8 for a discussion of the euphemization of soldiers' injured bodies in war photography in newspapers.

9. As I discuss further below, I am drawing upon Maya Morioka Todeschini, who argues that atomic-bomb films tend to romanticize injured bodies. Todeschini does not define "romanticization" in her essay; I am thus adapting the term for my own purposes here, even while building on some of her insights. "'Death and the Maiden': Female Hibakusha as Cultural Heroines, and the Politics of A-bomb Memory," in *Hibakusha Cinema: Hiroshima, Nagasaki and the Nuclear Image in Japanese Film* (London: Kegan Paul International, 1993).

10. J. Butler and S. Taylor, "Interdependence," in *Examined Life: Excursions with Contemporary Thinkers*, ed. Astra Taylor (New York: The New Press, 2009), 206.

11. *Ibid.*

12. *Ibid.*, p. 207.

13. *Ibid.*, p. 206.

14. T. Yōrō, *Kami to hito tono kaibougaku* (*Anatomy of Gods and Men*) (Tokyo: Chikuma shobō, 2002), p. 263.

15. Yourou cites *Chūsei senmin no uchū* (*The Cosmos of Medieval European Outcastes*) by Abe Kinya, medieval European historian.

16. In this connection, many Japanese folk tales portray the conversion of the lowly elements into the holy figures. See my "Sacred Pariahs: Hagioraphies of Alterity, Sexuality, and Salvation in Atomic Bomb Literature," *Japan Studies Review* 13 (2009).

17. Yōrō, Kami to hito to no kaibougaku, p. 24.

18. Judith Butler also notes, "The body implies mortality, vulnerability, agency: the skin and the flesh expose us to the gaze of others, but also to touch, and to violence, and bodies put us at risk of becoming the agency and instrument of all these as well. Although we struggle for rights over our own bodies, the very bodies for which we struggle are not quite ever only our own. The body has its invariably pubic dimension." J. Butler, *Precarious Life: The Powers of Mourning and Violence* (London: Verso, 2004), p. 26.

19. S. Sontag, *Illness as Metaphor* (New York: Farrar, Straus and Giroux, 1978), p. 18.

20. *Ibid.*, p. 5.

21. *Ibid.*, p. 26.

22. *Ibid.*, p. 29.

23. *Ibid.*

24. M.M. Todeschini, "'Death and the Maiden': Female Hibakusha as Cultural Heroines, and the Politics of A-bomb Memory," in *Hibakusha Cinema: Hiroshima, Nagasaki and the Nuclear Image in Japanese Film* (London: Kegan Paul International, 1993), p. 225.

25. S. Sontag, *Illness as Metaphor* (New York: Farrar, Straus and Giroux, 1978), p. 18. Emphasis mine.

26. *Ibid.*, p. 21.

27. *Ibid.*, p. 22.

28. Haworth, "After Fukushima; families on the edges of meltdown."

29. The story is based upon an actual atomic bomb victim's memoir. Ibuse published the first few episodes, entitled *Mei no Kekkon*, or *My Niece's Marriage*, in a monthly journal in 1963 before changing the title to *Black Rain*.

30. Imamura's 1989 film, *The Eel*, won him the Palm d'Or at Cannes Film Festival.

31. Although one scene in the movie depicts Yasuko losing her hair due to radiation sickness, no later scenes in the movie betray any baldness, underscoring the movie's tendency to aestheticize or suppress the symptoms of illness.

32. M.M. Todeschini, "'Death and the Maiden': Female Hibakusha as Cultural Heroines, and the Politics of A-bomb Memory," in *Hibakusha Cinema: Hiroshima, Nagasaki and the Nuclear Image in Japanese Film* (London: Kegan Paul International, 1993), p. 231.

33. S. Sontag, *Illness as Metaphor*, p. 30. In Japan, tuberculosis was romanticized, according to Sakai Shizu, medical historian, who also points out that though many male writers contracted tuberculosis, they wrote stories about women afflicted with the disease. Sakai also claims that Tokutomi Roka's Hototogisu began

the trend of portraying tuberculosis as a romantic disease. Sakai Shizu, *Yamai ga kataru Nihonshi* (*Japanese History Through Diseases*) (Tokyo: Kōdansha, 2008), p. 262 and pp. 269–270.

34. M.M. Todeschini, "'Death and the Maiden': Female Hibakusha as Cultural Heroines, and the Politics of A-bomb Memory," in *Hibakusha Cinema: Hiroshima, Nagasaki and the Nuclear Image in Japanese Film* (London: Kegan Paul International, 1993) p. 229.

35. K. Chūjō, "The World of Fiction," *Asahi Evening News*, 5 August 1985.

36. M.M. Todeschini, "'Death and the Maiden': Female Hibakusha as Cultural Heroines, and the Politics of A-bomb Memory," in *Hibakusha Cinema: Hiroshima, Nagasaki and the Nuclear Image in Japanese Film* (London: Kegan Paul International, 1993), p. 249.

37. S. Sontag, *Illness as Metaphor* (New York: Farrar, Straus and Giroux, 1978), p. 31.

38. George L. Mosse, *Fallen Soldiers: Reshaping the Memory of the World Wars* (New York: Oxford University Press, 1990), p. 19.

39. Enforcing playing and singing the national anthem in public schools in Japan is still a controversial issue, and teachers who do not sing the national anthem or remain seated during the anthem at commencement ceremonies are often punished. See the documentary *Watashi o ikiru* (*Live My Own Life*), directed by Doi Toshikuni, 2010.

40. G. L. Mosse, *Nationalism and Sexuality: Middle-Class Morality and Sexual Norms in Modern Europe* (Madison: University of Wisconsin Press, 1985), p. 13.

41. I. Hajime, *Bunmei kaika to sabetsu* (*Civilization, Enlightenment, and Discrimination*) (Tokyo: Yoshikawa Kōbunkan, 2001), p. 150. In attempting to regulate the body, the Meiji government public nudity and forbade the distinctive hairstyle (*mage*) of the Tokugawa period. Imanishi points out that the traditional way of walking and running in Japan, called Namba, in which one moves the right arm and leg forward at the same time, was westernized as well. *Ibid.*, pp. 149–150.

42. K. Taki, *Tenno no shōzō* (*Emperor's Portrait*) (Tokyo: Iwanami shoten, 1998).

43. G. L. Mosse, *Nationalism and Sexuality: Middle-Class Morality and Sexual Norms in Modern Europe* (Madison: University of Wisconsin Press, 1985), p. 1.

44. Gen is two years older than Nakazawa was at the time of the events depicted in the graphic novel.

45. Though beyond the scope of the present paper, Nakazawa's portrayal of pre–1945 Japan captures the lack of commodities, the prevalence, censorship of and violence against those expressing sentiments critical of Japanese national policies, and discrimination against Korean residents that afflicted Japan. These matters deserve further scholarly treatment.

46. Steven Okazaki, *White Light, Black Rain: The Destruction of Hiroshima and Nagasaki*, 2007.

Bibliography

BOOKS

Abe, Kinya. *Chūsei senmin no uchū: Yōroppa genten e no tabi* (*The Cosmos of Medieval European Outcastes: Travel to the Origin of Europe*). Tokyo: Chikuma shobō, 1987.

Broderick, Mick, ed. *Hibakusha Cinema: Hiroshima, Nagasaki and the Nuclear Image in Japanese Film*. London: Kegan Paul International, 1993.

Brothers, Caroline. *War and Photography: A Cultural History*. New York: Routledge, 1997.

Nelson, Maggie. *The Art of Cruelty: A Reckoning*. New York: W.W. Norton, 2011.

Butler, Judith. *Precarious Life: The Powers of Mourning and Violence*. London: Verso, 2004.

Imanishi, Hajime. *Bunmei kaika to sabetsu* (*Civilization, Enlightenment, and Discrimination*). Tokyo: Yoshikawa Kōbunkan, 2001.

Mosse, George L. *Fallen Soldiers: Reshaping the Memory of the World Wars*. New York: Oxford University Press, 1990.

_____. *Nationalism and Sexuality: Middle-Class Morality and Sexual Norms in Modern Europe*. Madison: The University of Wisconsin Press, 1985.

Sakai, Shizu. *Yamai ga kataru Nihonshi* (*Japanese History Through Diseases*). Tokyo: Kōdansha, 2008.

Taki, Kōji. *Tenno no shōzō* (*Emperor's Portrait*). Tokyo: Iwanami shoten, 1998.

Taylor, Astra, ed. *Examined Life: Excursions with Contemporary Thinkers*. New York: The New Press, 2009.

Yōrō, Takeshi. *Kami to hito to no kaibougaku* (*Anatomy of Gods and Men*). Tokyo: Chikuma shobō, 2002.

ARTICLES

Chūjō, Kazuo. "The World of Fiction." *Asahi Evening News,* 5 August 1985.

Haworth, Abigail. "After Fukushima: Families on the edge of meltdown." *The Guardian*, 23 February 2013.

Miyamoto, Yuki. "Sacred Pariahs: Hagiographies of Alterity, Sexuality, and Salvation in Atomic Bomb Literature." *Japan Studies Review* 13 (2009).

FILMS

Doi, Toshikuni. *Watashi o ikiru* (*Live My Own Life*). 2010.
Imamura, Shōhei. *Kuroi amei* (*Black Rain*). 1989.
Kumai, Kei. *Chi no mure* (*Apart from Life*). 1970.
Kurahara, Koreyoshi. *Ai to shi no kiroku* (*Record of Life and Death*). 1966.
Kuroki, Kazuo. *Chichi to kuraseba* (*The Face of Jizō*). 2004.
Ōba, Hideo. *Nagasaki no kane* (*The Bells of Nagasaki*). 1950.
Okazaki, Steven. *The Mushroom Club*. 2005.
_____. *White Light, Black Rain: The Destruction of Hiroshima and Nagasaki*. 2007.
Resnais, Alain. *Hiroshima mon amour*. 1959.
Sasabe, Kiyoshi. *Yūnagi no machi Skura no kuni* (*Town of Evening Calm, Country of Cherry Blossom*). 2007.
Shindō, Kaneto. *Genbaku no ko* (*Children of Hiroshima*). 1952.
Silvia, M.T. *Atomic Mom*. 2010.
Urayama, Kirio. *Yumechiyo nikki* (*Diary of Yumechiyo*). 1985.
Yamada, Shōgo. *Hadashi no Gen: Namida no bakuhatsu* (*Barefoot Gen: Explosion of Tears*). 1977.

Kazuo Kuroki and Hisashi Inoue's *Chichi to kuraseba*: Remember, Protest and Return to Ordinary Life

Yoshiko Fukushima

Since the dead are not returning,
What are the survivors to understand?
Since for the dead there is no way to lament,
About whom and what should the survivors lament?
Since those who died cannot but keep silent,
Should the survivors do the same?
                    —Jean Tardieu, "Glory of a Poet," 1943[1]

In a 2003 special issue of *Kokubungaku* (*Japanese Literature*) featuring Hisashi Inoue (1934–2010), the author of the play *Chichi to kuraseba* (*The Face of Jizō*; literally, "Living with Father," 2004),[2] Japanese critic Komori Yōichi wrote: "The ordinary people's voice conforming to human rights would not allow us to use a single nuclear weapon since Hiroshima and Nagasaki. What stop nuclear weapons are not nuclear weapons, but the voices from ordinary people."[3] The war is a dramatic event that transforms ordinary people into heroes and heroines. It gives ordinary people a chance to be awarded a medal of honor to commemorate their achievement at war. At home, however, another group of ordinary people live a normal life supporting soldiers fighting at the war front. The atomic bombs were suddenly dropped on top of such ordinary people living in Hiroshima and Nagasaki and instantly took away ordinary life. The opening quote from Jean Tardieu's poem, from the Introduction to *Kike wadatsumi no koe* (*Listen to the Voices from the Sea*), is resonant with how the director Kazuo Kuroki (1930–2006) looked at atomic bombs in his film adaptation of Inoue's *Chichi to kuraseba*.[4] Three years after World War II, what haunts Mitsue, the heroine of *Chichi to kuraseba* from returning to an ordinary life, is survivor guilt. In order to save Mitsue's soul, her father, killed in the blast of the atomic bomb in Hiroshima, appears as a ghost and starts living with her. Her father helps Mitsue learn the importance of returning to an ordinary life and asks her to "tell people sad things an' happy things" for her children.[5] This essay discusses how Kuroki came across and adopted Inoue's anti-war and anti-nuclear message in his play and developed it further using a variety of cinematic techniques—such as close-up, flashback, props and settings—to narrate and remember traumatic war experiences.

171

Kazuo Kuroki and Survivor Guilt

Kuroki, born into a militarist family in Miyazaki Prefecture, southern Kyūshū, moved to Shinkyō (current Changchum), the capital of Manchuria in 1935 to join his father working for the Manchurian Railroad. In 1942 he returned alone to Miyazaki to attend a Japanese junior high school. In April 1945 Kuroki was assigned to work in the factory of the Kawasaki Aircraft Industries Company in Miyakonojō under the Student Mobilization Act. One month after, the U.S. Grumman Hellcats sent from Okinawa attacked his factory and killed eleven classmates in the middle of evacuation to a bomb shelter. Later, Kuroki's survivor guilt caused by the fact of not saving his friends in his escape appeared as recurring anti-war and anti-establishment motifs in his entire film career. From the mild leftist perspective, Kuroki began his criticism against the major political powers in his earlier independent films such as *Kyūba no koibito* (*Lovers in Cuba*, 1969), *Nihon no akuryō* (*Evil Spirits of Japan*, 1970), and *Ryōma ansatsu* (*Assassination of Ryōma*, 1974).

Kuroki's filmography includes four anti-nuclear films treating atomic bombs, three fiction films—*Tobenai chinmoku* (*Silence Has No Wings*, 1965), *TOMORROW/ashita* (1988), *Chichi to kuraseba* (2004)—and one non-fiction TV documentary, *Kayoko Sakura no saku hi* (*Kayoko, on the Day of Cherry Flowers Blooming*, 1985). Kuroki articulates why he makes anti-nuclear film:

> The Japanese film and TV worlds tend not to produce a work dealing with atomic bombs.... The reality is that the majority of the people in the world do not know much about atomic bombs. They know the atomic bombs were dropped [in Japan] but not been taught what have happened after that.... It is sad to see many people thinking the dropping of atomic bombs was a good means as it ended the war. Japan is the only country that has been atom-bombed. That's why Japanese people must tell how dreadful nuclear weapons are. Japanese people, who were responsible for the war, protest against nuclear weapons not because they are the victims of the atomic bombs but because they are against unforgivable violence against human beings.[6]

Kuroki has felt a desperate call, witnessing years have passed since the atomic bombs were dropped, and the number of people who remember the incidents and can speak about them is becoming smaller and smaller. Interviewed by Roger Pulvers for his film review for *Chichi to kuraseba*, Kuroki also explains the background to create the film:

> [T]he war was not over inside me. In fact, it has never been brought to a conclusion in this country because responsibility for its heinous actions has never been taken, neither by the emperor, the government not by the people. Japan today is like a wolf in lamb's clothing. The country is preparing itself, in the name of self-defense, for warlike action. Oh, I vividly remember the day we found out Pearl Harbor was bombed. Of course I was a kid, in occupied China, but you should have seen it. Everybody jumped for joy. And the same thing happening all over Japan. Japanese people became convinced, on that day, that they were fighting to liberate Asia from the white man [*The Japan Times*, August 4, 2004].[7]

Kuroki's filmmaking approach is not just to remember wartime experiences, but to use them as a catalyst to urge Japanese people to be aware of Japan's responsibility for atrocities against neighboring Asian countries. And, more productively, to encourage them to learn the Japanese government's interest in being a military ally of the United States and to understand the capability and potential intent of denying disarmament spelled out in Article 9 of the postwar Japanese constitution. In the prologue of *Chichi to kuraseba*, Inoue also articulates his similar standpoint for how to remember atomic bombs in Hiroshima and Nagasaki. Inoue contends it is not "wrong to keep acting as if the Japanese were the victims"[8] when Japan talks about bombs. Inoue asserts: "Those two atomic bombs were dropped not only on the Japanese but on all humankind.... Feigning ignorance of the human catastrophe that occurred in those cities would constitute ... the immoral choice."[9]

It is not a coincidence that Kuroki decided to make an anti-nuclear film using the script written by Inoue. Inoue is one of the founders of the Article 9 Association (2004–), which "strives to shine the light of Article 9 upon this turbulent world, in order to join hands with the peace-seeking citizens of the world."[10] Kuroki and other filmmakers also form the Article 9 Association for Film People (2004–). Both Kuroki and Inoue share the same pacifist political view and strong interest for nuclear disarmament. Naturally, Kuroki and Inoue's approach for how to remember Hiroshima traces another founding member of the Article 9 Association and anti-nuclear activist Kenzaburō Ōe's approach. Ōe (1935–) writes in his *Hiroshima Notes*, "If survivors would overcome their fear of death, they too must see some way of giving meaning to their own death. Thus, the dead can survive as part of the lives of those who still live."[11] Ōe's remark echoes with Homi Bhabha's call for how to remember the past in the postcolonial society that has been a necessary process to live the present after World War II: "Remembering is never a quiet act of introspection or retrospection. It is a painful re-membering, a putting together of the dismembered past to make sense of the trauma of the present."[12]

The 1960 political movement against the renewal of the United States–Japan Security Treaty sparks pacifist sentiment among young leftist intellectuals. It helps them shift their eyes from the oppressed Asia colonized by Japan to another oppressed inside Japan, a political minority group regarded by others as disturbing Japan's ideal of homogeneity. Their attitude to deal with atomic bombs is not hiding Japanese atrocious actions against other Asian countries, but learning a methodology, for example, from how to look at horrifying genocides during the Holocaust. The Holocaust, as Jewish Studies scholar Zygmunt Bauman points out, cannot be sociologically treated as the work of "morally deficient individuals" or a prejudice or ideology-oriented "deviant phenomena" by those who are "sane and morally normal" or "as if the Holocaust did not happen."[13] Inoue is against such socially enforced moral systems when interpreting atomic bombs. Obversely, Bauman asserts, "Moral behaviour is conceivable only in the context of coexistence, of 'being with others,' that is, a social context."[14] Immoral behavior, as Bauman defines, is "a conduct which forsakes or abdicates responsibility for the other."[15] Thus, remembering atomic bombs urges mankind to take moral responsibility for the misery. It never diminishes Japan's responsibility as colonizer during World War II, but that is how Kuroki has read his role as an artist when dealing with nuclear issues in his filmmaking process.

Tobenai chinmoku, distributed by Japanese independent film production company ATG (Art Theatre Guild) in 1966,[16] is Kuroki's first fiction film made after he quit the Iwanami Film Production Company.[17] The film is about an elementary school boy's despair against the adults who do not believe his story of having caught a Nagasaki swallowtail in Hokkaido. As the film traces the Nagasaki swallowtail's long journey from Nagasaki to Hokkaido, Kuroki criticizes war advancement planned by the United States and Japan incorporating anti-war and anti-nuclear shots. In the beginning scene of a-bombed Nagasaki, the camera captures the destruction of Nagasaki and the military truck of the U.S.'s Atomic Bomb Casualty Commission (ABCC, 1946–1975) that was investigating the effects of radiation among the atomic-bomb survivors without providing treatment for the patients. *Tobenai chinmoku* has a strong influence of French New Wave released by ATG in the 1960s in the use of flashbacks and the nonlinear style of storytelling. Kuroki specifically named the influence of two French New Wave films, Jean-Luc Godard's *À bout de souffle* (*Breathless*, 1960) and Alain Resnais's anti-nuclear film *Hiroshima mon amour*.[18] *Tobenai chinmoku* reflects Kuroki's reaction against the Self Defense Forces' secret planning of the Three Arrows Study in 1963 and the arrival of the first nuclear submarine Seadragon to a Japanese port at Sasebo in 1964. The Three Arrows Study, simulating a crisis on the Korean Peninsula, allows U.S. to have its bases to receive supplies of ammunition, fuel and food. Seadragon's arrival was a part of operations for the Vietnam War.[19]

The second anti-nuclear fiction film, *Genshiryoku sensō* (*Nuclear War*), also distributed by ATG, is a film adaptation of the book written by former Iwanami Film Production's colleague and TV director Sōicihrō Tahara.[20] The film deals with concealment of the nuclear power plant accident in 1978. Location shooting was done near Tokyo Electric Power Company's Fukushima I and II Nuclear Power Plants, which suffered partial nuclear meltdowns after the earthquake and subsequent tsunami that hit Japan on March 11, 2011.

The TV documentary *Kayoko sakura no saku hi* provides him with the prototype for the following two anti-nuclear films, *TOMORROW/ashita* about Nagasaki and *Chichi to kuraseba* about Hiroshima. The documentary is a coproduction by TV Nishi-Nippon, TV Nagasaki, and the National Documentary Film Studio (WFD) in Poland. The subject, proposed by Kuroki, is Nagasaki's atomic bomb. The motif is the Kayoko Zakura, a row of cherry trees planted in memory of Tsue Hayashi's daughter and atomic bomb victim Kayoko. Kuroki has created a fictional story of a Polish female university student Joanna Socha, visiting Nagasaki in order to research about Father Maximilian Maria Kolbe. Father Kolbe is a Catholic missionary who stayed in Nagasaki between 1930 and 1936 to found a monastery. After he returns home, he volunteers to die in place of a Jewish prisoner in Auschwitz in 1941.[21]

With the fortunate encounter with the Shōchiku producer Toshio Nabeshima, Kuroki completed his third anti-nuclear film, *TOMORROW/ashita*, a film adaptation of Mitsuharu Inoue's William Faulkner–style novel about the atomic bomb in Nagasaki.[22] The fourth, *Chichi to kuraseba*, was one of Kuroki's last three films about war, with *Utsukushii Kirishima* (*Beautiful Kirishima*, 2002) and *Kamiya Etsuko no seishun* (Kamiya Etsuko's *Young Days*, 2006). These films were made as Kuroki observed with uneasiness that the Japan Self-Defense Forces sent the Iraq Reconstruction and Support Group to southern Iraq to help the Iraqi people. It was the first foreign deployment of Japanese troops since the end of World War II, following the Junichirō Koizumi administration's swift legalization of the Humanitarian Relief and Iraqi Reconstruction Special Measures Law.

Kuroki's war films depict no scene of severe ground battle or aerial bombardment, nothing spectacular, no war heroes, no guns, no tanks, no warships and no war airplanes. Probably it comes from how Kuroki remembered his war from a 15-year-old boy's perspective. When Kuroki visualizes his war experience, he does not go to the front outside Japan, unlike the earlier generation films such as Masaki Kobayashi's *Ningen no jōken* (*The Human Condition*, 1959–1961) and Kon Ichikawa's *Nobi* (*Fire on the Plain*, 1959). Kuroki looks at how ordinary people lived in Japanese towns during wartime. The struggles with death arrive unexpectedly to the family and friends waiting for the soldier's return at home. Also, Inoue, belonging to the same generation, has indirectly portrayed in his plays social issues in relation to the war through historical figures—such as General Maresuke Nogi, Fumiko Hayashi—and ordinary people.

The news of the atomic bomb dropped on August 6, 1945, in Hiroshima did not reach the people living an ordinary life immediately. On the day, Kuroki was at home under medical treatment for post-traumatic stress disorder—his own survivor guilt—caused by the U.S.'s attack on his factory and his classmates' death. It was the beautiful summer day when children were playing, with the cicadas' chorus all around the countryside. The atomic bomb interrupts the heroine of *Chichi to kuraseba*, Mitsue's ordinary summer day. Mitsue leaves her father in "a sea of flames worse than hell."[23] Mitsue tells her father: "Your face was so badly burnt then, daddy, melted away just like the face of Jizō. I just did nothing, left you there and ran away."[24] Mitsue's survivor guilt is similar to Kuroki's in the interview with film historian Yoshio Yasui:

> One of the boys ... had been knocked over by the blast, and when he finally got up, thinking he had survived, his face began to split right down the center in front of my eyes.... And there he stood extending his arm up towards the sky.... I was overcome with terror and shock, and I ran away just leaving him there [*Nihon Cine Art* 16, 2001].[25]

Without doubt Mitsue is Kuroki's double.

Collaboration with Hisashi Inoue—From Theater to Film

Chichi to kuraseba is one of the Hiroshima Trilogy written by Inoue, together with *Kamiyachō sakura hoteru* (*Kamiyachō Sakura Hotel*, 1997), a play about the Sakuratai, the only theater group based on Hiroshima when the atomic bomb dropped in Hiroshima and *Shōnen Kōdentai 1945* (*Little Boy, Big Typhoon*; literally "Boy Messenger," 2008), Inoue's only dramatic recitation about Hiroshima's atomic bomb and attack of the Makurazaki typhoon in 1945. Kuroki, who had been "an admirer of Inoue's drama for many years," saw Inoue's theater group Komatsuza's first production of *Chichi to kuraseba* at Kinokuniya Hall in Tokyo in 1994 (*New York Times*, August 4, 2004).[26]

Chichi to kuraseba does not have Inoue's well-known comedic features such as loquacity, puns, and jokes. Instead, the play focuses on the aftermath of the atomic bomb dropped in Hiroshima. It represents how the atomic bomb took a normal life away from ordinary people living in the town. Similar to Ōe, Inoue attempts "to comprehend a situation directly accessibly only to its immediate victims" through interviewing them.[27] Inoue, according to Kuroki, has spent two years to read memoirs written by over 10,000 atomic bomb victims.[28] During the interview process, Inoue recognizes that many atomic bomb survivors have felt sorry to stay alive. The words of the atomic survivors are directly and indirectly quoted as Mitsue's words in Inoue's play.[29]

Soon after Kuroki saw Inoue's theater production of *Chichi to kuraseba*, he contacted Komatsuza's producers Shinichi Takabayashi and Miyako Inoue to ask for permission to make a film version of the play. Inoue immediately agreed with Kuroki's proposal. Inoue didn't give any specific restrictions for how to use his script in the film. Inoue, who had seen his successful foreign productions in France in 1997 and in Russia in 2001, was especially interested in Kuroki's offer as he thought the film would be an easy medium to allow audiences living abroad to see his play.[30] Due to the difficulty of funding a film treating an atomic bomb, however, Kuroki had to wait a few more years to produce *Chichi to kuraseba*. In 2002, Seigō Fukada, Shōchiku-affiliated Eisei Theatre's film producer for Kuroki's film *Suri* (*The Pickpocket*, 2000), introduced him to film producer Wataru Suzuki. Suzuki, known as a pacifist, was a producer of many experimental horror and cult films. Suzuki produced Kuroki's final two films, *Chichi to kuraseba* and *Kamiya Etsuko no seishun*.[31]

Most of the dialogues in Inoue's original play are imported in Kuroki's film. No changes are added in the plot. As a result, this collaboration produces a remarkably beautiful unison, consolidating their position against nuclear disarmament. In *TOMORROW/ashita,* using the heavy Nagasaki dialect, Kuroki successfully documents 24 hours of the people's ordinary life living near the Urakami Cathedral until the blast of the atomic bomb in Nagasaki. Similarly, Mitsue and her father Takezō speak to each other in the heavy Hiroshima dialect in Inoue's play. The play focuses on four days three years after the blast of the atomic bomb in Hiroshima. The cruelty of the war is delivered mainly through the words of Mitsue and Takezō. With the help of Inoue's skillful playwriting, the audience can "see" it well using their ears. Kuroki's focus is to add his own film language to Inoue's well-written original. It requires Kuroki to develop Inoue's theatrical realism into his cinematographic realism through images of actors, settings and objects.

Different from the script of *TOMORROW/ashita,* Inoue's play *Chichi to kuraseba* has a very eccentric motif—the supernatural being, "ghost" or "living dead." The use of the "living dead" is a familiar motif in Hollywood since the 1968 horror film *Night of the Living Dead* directed by George A. Romero. Mitsue's father appears in Japan's ghost season, the summer. Yet *Chichi to kuraseba* is not a horror film but a comedy film. Inoue's living dead can appear both night and day. It is not the same as a Hollywood comedy film *Ghost Dad* (1990) directed by Sidney Poitier, either. Bill Cosby's ghost dad Elliot loves his children as much as Mitsue's father and continues working at his company for his family's survival during the day. He also tells his daughter not to waste her life when she, seriously injured, arrives in his afterlife world. In the end, however, the audience learns Elliot, in fact, is not yet dead. The film stays as a twisted home drama, in which the father and the children reconfirm their love of each other and learn about family values. In a more spiritual, fantasy romance film, *Ghost* (1990), the ghost Sam helps his girlfriend Molly quite actively, even saves her life. But the film's focus is Molly's grief recovery after she lost her love, murdered by his friend to cover his money-laundering scheme. The ghost Sam is simply completing a long good-bye to this world.

Inoue's use of the ghost does not follow the style of Japanese traditional theater, *Noh.* Parodying the structure of *Noh* plays, the deceased appears to tell something to the living and exits the scene slowly and quietly from a black entrance without a door and a curtain, like that used on the stage. Yet the deceased—the father Takezō—appears not once, but four times, four days in a row. More precisely, Takezō does not appear just to tell his story from the past unilaterally to his daughter. Situation comedy-style, comical and ingenuous dialogues between the father and the daughter develop. He makes positive advice for happiness and the future of his daughter and his family. As Takezō finds that the daughter is in love with Kinoshita, the father tries to take over a matchmaker's role, even making his favorite dish, small fry *miso* for Kinoshita as a gift. What makes Inoue's play strong is that all words by the characters, both the dead and the living, are the testimonies of their experience with the atomic bomb. Inoue's political and social statement is voiced through dialogues between the father and the daughter.

As mentioned in the afterword of the play, Takezō may not be a ghost in Inoue's plan. Takezō is "a visual" in Mitsue's mind[32] Inoue explains: "I divided Mitsue into the woman who forbids herself happiness and the woman who wishes it to come…. I gave the latter one to her father, who symbolizes all of the people who died in Hiroshima."[33] In other words, the father in the play is performing Mitsue's alter ego. In Kuroki's film, the audience sees the difference of bodies, the daughter who wants to join the dead and the father who wishes her to live. Mitsue, performed by Rie Miyazawa, is extremely skinny, fragile-looking. The camera shows her skin extremely white, almost like a ghost. She is alive, but her scars stay deep in her mind. She seems to have suffered from minor radiation sickness, too. As the film progresses, the camera begins to show her regaining energy using different make-up and lighting every time she feels happy. In contrast, the father Takezō performed by Yoshio Harada (1940–2011) is big, tall, and massive, nicely tanned, and wears brownish make-up. He is extremely active and does not look like the dead. In reality his healthy body is already lost because of the blast of the atomic bomb. Harada's acting convinces that Takezō's energy and wisdom need to be remembered and rediscovered using Mitsue's body as the medium.

As well as the actors, Kuroki's long time collaborators, Tatsuo Suzuki (1935–) for camera, Teizō Matsumura (1929–2007) for film score, and Takeo Kimura (1918–2010) for set design contribute to generating Kuroki's interpretation of Inoue's dialogues. Suzuki, a former colleague at Iwanami Film Production, successfully integrates Kuroki's point-of-view shots made in studio and location shootings with computer generated images and sounds. Suzuki and his younger staff have handled the post production phase of the film—such as actual documentary footage of the destruction of Hiroshima, sounds of bombs, cicadas, crickets, birds, thunders, winds and rain. Words, images and sounds together, Kuroki brings Hiroshima closer to the audience. Kuroki's images directly catch the audience's eyes, not just imagining from the words spoken by the actors. His Hiroshima becomes more real.

Kuroki's Chichi to kuraseba

The film begins with the image of the Atomic Bomb Dome in Hiroshima with the peaceful and gentle leitmotif—repetition of a set of two different keys, played by the piano and the pipe organ.[34] Behind the dome, a white flash of lightening appears in the screen with the sounds of thunder. The camera first shows a close-up of Mitsue's feet in clogs, running through the ruins of Hiroshima, and then catches her from the back entering into her house. Mitsue's house, designed by Kimura, is not Inoue's Japanese style shack, but the half-burned and wrecked Fukuyoshiya Inn, built in an eclectic style of architecture, Japanese and Western. The house has a Japanese style closet, *oshiire* and the central pillar, the two symbols of the Japanese traditional house. Takezō, already in the *oshiire*, invites Mitsue inside. The atomic bomb is called *"pika"* by Hiroshima people, using the same word as a flash of thunder. Mitsue is afraid of thunder because the thunder reminds her of the bomb. Takezō's friend Nobu at the Tomita Photo Shop is afraid of the flash of magnesium bulbs. When Takezō tells her the story about how Nobu gave up photography, the instant flash, hinting the blast of the atomic bomb, is spread screen-wide.

Different from Inoue's script, Professor Kinoshita, performed by Tadanobu Asano, appears as the third character on the screen and speaks his own lines, conversing with Mitsue. Thus, Kinoshita becomes more autonomous, given a body and words. Kinoshita appears in flashbacks when Mitsue tells a story about him. The first flashback goes back to a few days earlier when Mitsue met him at the library for the first time. Inside the library, a coworker is sitting next to Mitsue, but her face not shown. Then, the camera shows Kinoshita asking for materials related to the atomic bomb, killing his emotion to give a neutral expression. And the shot of Mitsue at the reception desk follows, Mitsue answering Kinoshita's question. The next shot is the black and white documentary footages showing the ruins of Hiroshima near the Atomic Dome. Supporting Mitsue's criticism against the occupation forces, the shot of the U.S. Military Base in Hiroshima in 1948 appears. The sign on the metal fence reads: "UNAUTHORIZED ENTRY BY JAPANESE PROHIBITED." The camera returns to Mitsue's library and zooms in on atomic bomb related documents piled up on the table behind the bookshelves, the sign "PROHIBITED By OCCUPATION FORCES" posted. Returning to the original shot of Mitsue and Kinoshita, Mitsue lies that the library does not collect such materials. The white lilies, the flower for the dead are in a vase on top of the wooden catalog drawers. The dull and weak series of the computer-generated sound of the bombs recall the memory of bombing during World War II. She adds: "I have burnt absolutely everything that would remind me of my father."[35] Takezō appears in the next shot sitting on the burned stairs of Mitsue's house, listening to her words. As Takezō explains he has started to appear in front of Mitsue to make her fall in love with Kinoshita, the same scene of Kinoshita's first visit to the library is repeated. This time the scene begins with the shot of the Western style library building from the outside. In the next shot, the camera catches Mitsue and her coworker sitting at the library's reception from the front. Then, the scene of the first dialogue between Mitsue and Kinoshita is filmed in exactly the same way to intensify their destined encounter.[36]

On the following day, Kinoshita appears on the screen again when Takezō criticizes Mitsue who had a fight with Kinoshita in the pine forest of the suburbs of Hiroshima, Hijiyama. The next location shot shows Mitsue and Kinoshita walking through the forest, talking to each other happily. The sound is off so that their conversation is not audible. Kinoshita has asked her something. Suddenly, Mitsue, darkening her face, her words—"I absolutely cannot do"—are heard from the screen. Kinoshita hands a box wrapped with the Japanese wrapping cloth, *furoshiki*. Yet the audience does not know what is inside.

Words in Inoue's play verbally document traumatic experiences of the atomic bomb survivors in Hiroshima. In contrast, images of Kuroki's film capture and archive objects melted from the heat of the blast of the atomic bombs. The objects, made by the Art group led by Kimura's student, Norifumi Ataka, are not original, but look real on the screen. In a way, the film plays the role of a war memorial museum collecting copies of the original, which are visual records of the history in Hiroshima. The box Kinoshita wanted Mitsue to keep is now at her house. Takezō opens the box and jumps away from it with fear. The camera moves to the objects inside the box and shoots them in close-up. Among them are tiles covered with thorns, a medicine bottle twisted out of shape, and pieces of glasses, all instantly created by the heat and the shock of the atomic bomb blast. Images accompany a tensional, high pitch sound of the piano. Following a series of dissonances, accompanied by the dull sounds of the blast, comes another close-up of Mitsue's hands. She holds a piece of glass that was removed from the body of an atomic victim. After returning to the dialogue between Mitsue and Takezō, a moment of flashback of the same forest scene in Hijiyama is incorporated twice when Kinoshita tells Mitsue two requests—"I know I am asking you too much, but could you keep my stuff from the bomb in the library?" and "Isn't it a good idea to use my atom bomb objects in trying to tell the children about what happened to me in the bomb an' everything?"

Kuroki, using the *cinéma vérité* style, records the two storytelling performances performed by two actors, Eri Miyazawa and Yoshio Harada—Mitsue and Miyazawa's storytelling collected as an activity of her high school storytelling research club and Takezō and Harada's storytelling modified as suggested by Kinoshita. Mitsue's scene is a rehearsal for Children's Summer Storytelling Club in her room. Mitsue tells a comical story of a stingy old man and his wife in a *rakugo* style, sitting on a Japanese cushion called *zabuton* and playing the roles of an old man and an old woman imitating their voices.[37] The subject of rejuvenation in the folk tale also makes Mitsue rejuvenate and return to Mitsue before August 6, 1945. Mitsue regains her normal form, cheerful and energetic. Because Mitsue is opposed to Kinoshita's idea to tamper with the original when telling children a story of the atomic bomb, Takezō takes over the role and tells the Hiroshima version of *Issun bōshi* (Little Inch-High Warrior) to the camera imagining children sitting in front of him. Takezō, spotlighted, performs the role of Little Inch-High in a *taishū engeki* (traditional popular theater)'s exaggerated style of speech and acting, accompanied by the dissonances of the piano. Hiroshima's Little Inch-High goes inside the body of the demon and attacks it from the stomach using a tile having thorns created by the heat of the atomic bomb. At the climax, when Takezō mentions the moment of the blast in the story, the camera shows a parachute from a B-29 in the blue sky, the destruction of Hiroshima and the mushroom cloud of the atomic bomb. Mitsue feels terrified and yells out, "Stop it!" Takezō apologizes and exits.

On Day Three, Mitsue begins to reveal one of the causes of her survivor guilt. For the scene, Kuroki, using a flashback, brings the audience back to Hiroshima on August 6, 1945. This first flashback scene, shot in black and white, begins with Mitsue leaving for work, Takezō cleaning his garden. The moment the heat of the blast gets to a black and white world, a circle with a "weird kind of yellow and red outline" spreads on the screen for a second. Then the entire screen turns into white.[38] The camera returns to Mitsue in close-up three years after, telling her story. In the next shot the camera catches Mitsue and Takezō standing in front of the opened window from the outside. There is no trademark of Ozu, the "round sitting dinner table," but Ozu's "lamp" hanging in the living room. There is a central pillar in the middle, hinting how Mitsue is protected by the mainstay of the house— Takezō. Mitsue's survivor guilt is expressed in her lines: "There are countless people who, by all rights, should have been able to lead a happy life."[39] But this does not mean she is trying to forget about the atomic bomb. The camera repeatedly catches the images of Mitsue's collections to keep the dead alive—her friend Akiko's pencil, the Japanese wedding doll whose part of face is burnt with the heat of the blast of the atomic bomb, the stone lantern that has saved her, and the head of Jizō.

The head of the Jizō, the guardian deity of children is a significant prop to guide the audience to the origin of Mitsue's survivor guilt in Inoue's play. In the film Kuroki uses the close-up shot of the head of the Jizō multiple times starting on Day Three and portrays how Mitsue gradually remembers the horrific moment in Hiroshima. On Mitsue's first return to her house after the blast of the bomb, shot in flashback in black and white, she walks through the ruins of Hiroshima. Once she arrives in her house, the camera shoots the head of the Jizō on the ground as it catches Mitsue's eyes. The right side of the Jizō's face is melted away by the heat of the blast of the atomic bomb, burned like keloids, which does not remind her of Takezō's face yet.

On Day Four, the scene starts with a shot of Mitsue's house, which is full of Kinoshita's collected objects burned and melted by the heat of the atomic bomb blast. In contrast with the eeriness created by the objects, Mitsue's face in close-up is beaming with joy, having seen Kinoshita. As soon as Mitsue sees the head of Jizō, she turns Jizō's face and makes the damaged side of the face more visible. Here Mitsue in Kuroki's film does not voice out "an unintended shriek."[40] to show her immediate understanding of the real cause of her survivor guilt—her father's death as in Inoue's play. Kuroki delays her decision to let Kinoshita go, in order not to disturb Mitsue and Takezō's cheerful dialogues about how Mitsue entertains Kinoshita with food, drinks and a hot bath as a guest of the house. Thus Kuroki's Mitsue does not have to pretend to make her father happy. After Takezō leaves the kitchen to check the fire of the bath, Mitsue alone is given a moment to make up her mind. Kuroki's camera catches Mitsue, softly saying "Daddy" with a sad face. Then, Jizō's face in close-up appears in the entire screen.

The third flashback is used in order to show the moment of the atomic bomb blast as Mitsue recalls. Different from the first and second flashbacks in black and white, the third is colored. The camera catches a hellish scene—injured Takezō's white face, his body trapped under a large beam, and orange fire burning in the town of Hiroshima. The camera shifts to a painting titled *Inferno*, drawing the agonizing look of the men, women, mothers and babies. It visualizes what Mitsue talks about, what she saw on that day. The voices of pains hear from the screen. To Mitsue, who is still stubbornly saying, "I should have died beside you, daddy,"[41] Takezō angrily responds: "You're really the stupid pigheaded daughter you say you are and there's no way I can ever depend on you. Just as soon have some other child instead.... A grandchild ... a great grandchild!"[42]

As soon as Takezō's words end, Yōko Tajima's soprano requiem, composed by Teizō Matsuyama, is heard. In the next shot, Kinoshita, on the back of the truck, is heading toward Mitsue's house. The truck is running through the city of Hiroshima on a sunny day, ruined but showing signs of recovery, cars and a streetcar running and people walking. The camera returns to the kitchen of Mitsue's house and shoots her lower stomach, anticipating the future birth of the child. Getting the sun on her face, Mitsue gains color and looks healthy, cutting carrots to prepare a dinner for Kinoshita.

The film ends as a comedy as Mitsue changes her mind, overcomes her survivor guilt and decides to live with Kinoshita, listening to her father's wish. Yet Kuroki does not end the film with a song of praise. Instead, the piano still plays a series of discords as used repeatedly throughout the film. Kuroki, using Brecht's *verfremdungseffect* (estrangement effect), asks the audience "to look critically even at what [the spectator] has so far taken for granted" Mitsue's happy ending.[43] Kuroki knows that it is not that simple and easy as it did not happen to many survivors of the war including Kuroki himself.

At the very end of the film, the camera moves upwards and shows the empty ceiling of the Atomic Bomb Dome in the ceiling. Mitsue's house is inside the Atomic Bomb Dome, the ruins of the Hiroshima Prefectural Industrial Promotion Hall. According to Kuroki, the scene is inspired by the endings of Andrei Tarkovsky's *Nostalgia* (1983) and Kenji Mizoguchi's *Ugetsu monogatari* (*Tales of Moonlight and Rain*, 1953). In *Nostalgia* the camera first shows a shot of the main character Andrei Gorchakov, a dog and their house. After the camera is pulled back, the audience sees everything is inside the ruins of an enormous Italian church. In the last shot of Mizoguchi's *Ugetsu Monogatari*, following the shot of a child playing in the ancestor's graveyard, the camera is pulled out to show the mountains surrounding the graveyard.[44] The ending of the film tells the audiences that we humans must live where you are from with the weight of this tragic incident in the history.

Conclusion

We all know the atomic bomb film masterpiece, Shōhei Imamura's *Kuroi ame* (*Black Rain*, 1989), inspired from Masuji Ibuse's novel. Both Ibuse and Imamura are from the war generation having been more directly involved in World War II than Inoue and Kuroki. Ibuse was in Singapore during World War II, publishing a Japanese language newspaper as a Japanese army officer. He entered Kiryū Technical High School not to be drafted and lost his elder brother during the battle in the Philippines. Both *Kuroi ame* and *Chichi to kuraseba* attempt to document similar subjects, the atomic bomb in Hiroshima and the uncle's and father's wish for his niece and daughter's marriage. Both extend their subjects to the aftermath of the bomb and touch on the survivor guilt. *Kuroi ame* portrays "the normal lives of normal people in abnormal times."[45] On the other hand, *Chichi to kuraseba* portrays the wishes for a normal life by portraying an "already lost" normal life between a daughter and a father. A normal father in an abnormal shape—a ghost—helps his daughter to return to a normal life. *Chichi to kuraseba* could go a step beyond from *Kuroi ame*'s "a politics of understatement," which avoids Dorsey and Matsuoka's criticism of *Kuroi ame*, regarded by them "a tacit acceptance of the unacceptable."[46] Takezō's statement is different from the uncle Shigematsu's passive perspective: "Rather than a just war, an unjust peace is not so bad."[47] Takezō explicitly delivers the voice of the dead, who absolutely deny the atomic bomb. Inoue and Kuroki's generation, who lived the 1960s tumult, have seen enough of an "unjust peace" under U.S. hegemony, continuing with the threat of Japan's rearmament in alliance with the U.S.

"*Otottan, arigato gozaimashita*" ("Thank you, Daddy"). Mitsue's word of gratitude for her father helps the audiences to think about how to live an ordinary life after knowing what happened to Hiroshima, remembering and protesting against it. We should not dilute Inoue and Kuroki's message with the homogeneous look of veneration of the dead, unique to Japanese culture. The father Takezō on the screen is too real and too alive to stay dead. After death, Takezō appears to Mitsue and repeats his dying words: 'Live. Live my life for me too!' So, you see, you will go on living because of me."[48] Yet remember that Takezō is Mitsue's alter ego. Mitsue the living is the one who makes him stay alive in her mind. It is not a coincidence that who is dead in *Chichi to kuraseba* is a father. Kuroki's camera captures the father, wearing an apron to cook and kneeling down and bowing to apologize and appreciate the daughter. How many fathers were like that from Inoue's and Kuroki's generation? Takezō represents Inoue and Kuroki's political statement against the prewar constitution that recognized Emperor Hirohito as the state, and venerated as the nation's father figure during the war. Inoue and Kuroki, in common, seem to tell us that women are the ones who take the lead in an ordinary life and decide the future of the nation.

Notes

1. The poem was originally quoted by Kazuo Watanabe in the Introduction of the 1949 version to *Kike Wadatsumi no koe*. The English translation of the poem was made by M. Yamanouchi and J. L. Quinn in *Kike Wadatsumi no koe* (Scranton: University of Scranton Press, 2000), p. 3.

2. *The Face of Jizō* was the title created by the translator of the English version of the play, Roger Pulvers.

3. Y. Komori, "*Kokka towa nani ka, Kokkyō towa nani ka* (What is the nation? What is the border?" *Kokubungaku* 48, no. 2 (February 2003): p. 37.

4. Kuroki noted he was inspired by Tardieu's perspective when creating *TOMORROW/ashita*. See K. Kuroki: *Watashi no sensō* (Tokyo: Iwanami Shoten, 2004), p. 158.

5. H. Inoue, *The Face of Jizō/Chichi to kuraseba*, trans. Roger Pulvers (Tokyo: Komatsuza, 2004), p. 168.

6. K. Kuroki, *Watashi no sensō* (*My War*) (Tokyo: Iwanami Shoten, 2004), p. 156.

7. Translated by the author.

8. H. Inoue, *The Face of Jizō/Chichi to kuraseba*, trans. Roger Pulvers (Tokyo: Komatsuza, 2004), p. 168.

9. *Ibid.*

10. See the English version of the Article 9 Association website, http://www.9-jo.jp/en/index_en.html (accessed May 29, 2013).

11. K. Ōe, *Hiroshima Notes*, trans. David L. Swain and Toshi Yonezawa (New York: Grove Press, 1981), p. 111.

12. See H.K. Bhabah, *The Location of Culture* (New York: Routledge, 1994), p. 40, and also Y. Igarashi, *Bodies of Memory: Narratives of War in Postwar Japanese Culture, 1945–1970* (Princeton: Princeton University Press, 2000), p. 6.

13. Z. Bauman, *Modernity and the Holocaust* (Ithaca: Cornell University Press, 1989), p. 176.

14. *Ibid.*, p. 179.

15. *Ibid.*, p. 183.

16. According to Kuroki, *Tobenai chinmoku* was originally scheduled to release in 1965 by the Toho Film Country nationwide, but it was cancelled after the film was shown to the Toho's executives. See K. Kuroki, *Watashi no sensō* (Tokyo: Iwanami Shoten, 2004), p. 88.

17. In 1954 Kuroki joined the Iwanami Film Production Company, which was founded by the physicist Nakaya Ukichirō with the help of the publisher Iwanami Shoten's Kobayashi Isao. The company first mainly produced documentary film on science and education. But it eventually shifted its share to producing PR movies for Japanese corporation. In 1962, Kuroki quit the company and became independent. See T. Satō, *Kuroki Kazuo to sono jidai* (Tokyo: Gendai Shokan, 2006), pp. 14–24.

18. K. Kuroki: *Watashi no sensō (My War)* (Tokyo: Iwanami Shoten, 2004), pp. 79–80.

19. *Ibid.*, pp. 83–89.

20. Tahara was an assistant cameraman in the Iwanami Film Production Company before he joined TV Tokyo Corporation in 1964.

21. K. Kuroki, *Watashi no sensō (My War)* (Tokyo: Iwanami Shoten, 2004), p. 90.

22. Since 1983, Kuroki has been thinking of making the film adaptation of *Ashita*. See Y. Abe and T. Himukai, *Eiga sakka Kuroki Kazuo no zenbō* (Tokyo: Firumu Ātosha, 1997), p. 90 and p. 165.

23. H. Inoue, *The Face of Jizō/Chichi to kuraseba*, trans. Roger Pulvers (Tokyo: Komatsuza, 2004), p. 160.

24. *Ibid.*, p. 158.

25. See http//eigageiutsu.blogspot/2009/06/interview-with-kuroki-kazuo … (accessed May 19, 2013).

26. *Chichi to kuraseba* was Inoue's first play about the atomic bombs in Hiroshima and Nagasaki. Since the first production that Kuroki attended, the play was continuously staged: in August 1995 at Benisan Pitt, Tokyo; in October to December 1995 at Kinokuniya Hall, Tokyo, followed by the 3-month-long national tour; in February 1997 at PARIS21, Paris, France; in August in 1997 at Ōta Kumin Plaza, Tokyo; in June to July 1998 at Kinokuniya Southern Theatre, Tokyo; in May to June in 1999 at Kinokuniya Southern Theatre, Tokyo; in June 2001 at Etcetera Theatre, Moscow, Russia; in July to August 2004, Kinokuniya Southern Theatre, Tokyo; in December 2004 in Hong Kong; in June 2008 at Kinokuniya Southern Theatre; and in August 2011 Kinokuniya Southern Theatre, followed by the national tour.

27. J.W. Treat, *Writing Ground Zero: Japanese Literature and the Atomic Bomb* (Chicago: University of Chicago Press, 1995), p. 230.

28. K. Kuroki, *Watashi no sensō (My War)* (Tokyo: Iwanami Shoten, 2004), p. 173.

29. Inoue tells Kuroki that he "has not written a single line of the play by himself" (*Kokkōrō* [Japan Federation of National Service Employees] *Newspaper* 1226, January 10, 2006). See http://kokkororen.com/old/shinbun/s1226.htm#5 (accessed May 29, 2013).

30. K. Kuroki, *Watashi no sensō (My War)* (Tokyo: Iwanami Shoten, 2004), p. 174.

31. Kuroki also mentioned that he wanted to make a film about an atomic bomb in Hiroshima for his junior high school friend, Ōmuta Minoru, a journalist at Chugoku Newspaper Company. Ōmuta, who witnessed a mushroom cloud of the atomic bomb from Yamaguchi in 1945, published many reports about atomic bomb victims. Ōmuta was also one of the three secretariats in the Kinoko-kai (The Mushroom Club) established for atomic bomb victims diagnosed as Microcephalic, also known as small-head syndrome and the family. Ōmuta passed away in 2002 before Kuroki found the producer for *Chichi to kuraseba*.

32. H. Inoue, *The Face of Jizō/Chichi to kuraseba*, trans. Roger Pulvers (Tokyo: Komatsuza, 2004), p. 180.

33. *Ibid.*, p. 178.

34. Most likely, both sounds were created by an electric key board. Kuroki does not use a timpani drum as in Inoue's stage directions. A timpani drum is often used to create the sound of thunder.

35. H. Inoue, *The Face of Jizō/Chichi to kuraseba*, trans. Roger Pulvers (Tokyo: Komatsuza, 2004), p. 38.

36. Kuroki chose the former building of the Japanese and British joint investment Explosive Production Company built in 1906. The building was later purchased by the Japanese navy and used as the officers' club. The character of Inoue's play, Kinoshita was a lieutenant of the navy during World War II.

37. K. Kuroki, *Watashi no sensō (My War)* (Tokyo: Iwanami Shoten, 2004), pp. 195–96.

38. H. Inoue, *The Face of Jizō/Chichi to kuraseba*, trans. Roger Pulvers (Tokyo: Komatsuza, 2004), p. 118.

39. *Ibid.*, p. 108.

40. *Ibid.*, p. 136.

41. *Ibid.*, p. 166.
42. *Ibid.*
43. J. Willett, *The Theatre of Bertolt Brecht* (New York: New Directions, 1960), p. 179.
44. K. Kuroki, *Watashi no sensō* (*My War*) (Tokyo: Iwanami Shoten, 2004), p. 187 and p. 204.
45. J.T Dorsey and N. Matsuoka, "Narrative Strategies of Understatement in *Black Rain* as a Novel and a Film," in Mick Broderick, ed., *Hibakusha Cinema: Hiroshima, Nagasaki and the Nuclear Image in Japanese Film* (London: Kegan Paul International, 1996), p. 219.
46. *Ibid.*, p. 220.
47. *Ibid.*, p. 219.
48. H. Inoue, *The Face of Jizō/Chichi to kuraseba*, trans. Roger Pulvers (Tokyo: Komatsuza, 2004), p. 166.

Bibliography

Abe, Yoshiaki, and Himukai Teratarō, eds. *Eiga sakka Kuroki Kazuo no zenbō* (*Film Creator: All Aspects of Kuroki Kazuo*). Tokyo: Firumu Atosha, 1997.

Bauman, Zyfmunt. *Modernity and the Holocaust*. Ithaca: Cornell University Press, 1989.

Bhabah, Homi K. *The Location of Culture*. New York: Routledge, 1994.

Broderick, Mick, ed. *Hibakusha Cinema: Hiroshima, Nagasaki and the Nuclear Image in Japanese Film*. London: Kegan Paul International, 1996.

Kike wadatsumi no koe. Listen to the Voices from the Sea: Writings of the Fallen Japanese Students. Nihon Senbotsu Gakuseu Kinen-Kai. Ed. Midori Yamanouchi. Trans. Midori Yamanouchi and Joseph L. Quinn. Scranton: University of Scranton Press, 2000.

Komori, Yōichi. "Kokka towa nani ka, Kokkyō towa nani ka" ("What is the nation? What is the border?"). *Kokubungaku* 48, no. 2 (February 2003): 32–37.

Kuroki, Kazuo. *Watashi no sensō* (*My War*). Tokyo: Iwanami Shoten, 2004.

Ōe, Kenzaburō. *Hiroshima Notes*. Trans. David L. Swain and Toshi Yonezawa. New York: Grove Press, 1981.

Igarashi, Yoshikuni. *Bodies of Memory: Narratives of War in Postwar Japanese Culture, 1945–1970*. Princeton: Princeton University Press, 2000.

Inoue, Hisashi. *The Face of Jizō/Chichi to kuraseba*. Trans. Roger Pulvers. Tokyo: Komatsuza, 2004.

Sato, Tadao. *Kuroki Kazuo to sono jidai* (*Kuroki Kazuo and His Age*). Tokyo: Gendai Shokan, 2006.

Treat, John Whittier. *Writing Ground Zero: Japanese Literature and the Atomic Bomb*. Chicago: University of Chicago Press, 1995).

Yamanouchi, Midori, and Joseph L. Quinn, eds. and trans. *Listen to the Voices from the Sea* (*Kike wadatsumi no koe*). Scranton: University of Scranton, 2000.

Willett, John. *The Theatre of Bertolt Brecht*. New York: New Directions, 1960.

Breaking the Silence of the Atomic Bomb Survivors in the Japanese Graphic Novel *Town of Evening Calm, Country of Cherry Blossoms* and the Film Adaptation

Senjo Nakai

The atomic bombings of Hiroshima and Nagasaki have been highly sensitive issues for Japan–U.S. relations. The long-standing silence of the atomic bomb survivors was first imposed by the Allied Powers during the 1945–52 occupation, and then followed by self-censorship of the Japanese people. At first, the strict censorship was imposed by the Allied Powers to ban on any reports on the atomic bombings that might evoke anti–U.S. sentiment among Japanese people. In addition, both the rightist and the leftist camps have been reluctant to allow the survivors to express the subjective views of the event. The post-war regime, which was led by the dominant group in the ruling Liberal Democratic Party, prioritized the economic and security partnership with the United States. Therefore, the issue of "Hiroshima" could be addressed only if it would not damage the bilateral relationship. On the other hand, the leftist camp supported the atomic bomb survivors to form the anti-nuclear weapon organization *The Japan Council Against Atomic and Hydrogen Bombs* in 1955. In the following year, the first atomic bomb survivors' own organization *Japan Confederation of A- and H-Bomb Sufferers Organizations* was formed during the Second World Meeting against Atomic and Hydrogen Bombs. However, the survivors' movement was mired by the bitter infightings between the communist and socialist factions over nuclear testing and possessions of nuclear weapons by Soviet and China during the 1960s.[1] It was both Japanese and the U.S. governments' interest to downplay the role of the United States in the atomic bombings of Hiroshima and Nagasaki because their alliance was regarded as a crucial part of regional security in Asia Pacific during the Cold War period.

The survivors have been facing difficulties in talking about their own experiences of the atrocities. Even if the survivors break the silence, they are often countered by the United States, Korea and China, which argue that Japan was an aggressor in the war, and therefore the deploying of atomic bombs was justifiable. As a result, the survivors grew hesitant to talk about their own experiences of the bombing because their views were likely to be dismissed as illegitimate within the political context of the Cold War both within and outside the Japanese society. In particular, pronouncing the United States' role in "Hiroshima" and

"Nagasaki" has been carefully avoided. Thus, the hegemony of silence effectively left a majority of casualties voiceless for more than 60 years.

Orthodox Marxists are generally skeptical about the power of popular culture in resisting dominant ideology. They rather view popular culture, e.g., films, novels and popular music, as inferior copies of genuine arts, or cheap forms of entertainment. For them, popular culture is considered as an apparatus of the ruling groups to preserve the current social condition by impeding the imagination of the subordinate classes, and turning them into a passive mass. In contrast, Antonio Gramsci viewed that domination is neither entirely dictated by the economic structure of the society, nor imposed upon the subordinated classes by a few elite. The dominant group's ideology is formed and disseminated in not only state institutions but also civil society in order to operate "without 'sanctions' or compulsory 'obligations,' but nevertheless exerts a collective pressure and obtains objective results in the form of an evolution of customs, ways of thinking and acting, morality, etc."[2] Domination in civil societies can be accomplished when people at every social stratum consider the current order of society as natural, and voluntarily accept the status quo.[3] In Gramsci's theory of hegemony, culture is regarded as a key to both domination and resistance. In order to resist hegemony, Gramscian theorists propose that the subordinated groups must challenge "common sense" by creatively utilizing their own cultural resources, which reflect their own understanding of the society.[4] Gramsci describes that their struggle is waged "first in the ethical field and then in that of politics proper, in order to arrive at the working out at a higher level of one's own conception of reality."[5]

Fumiyo Kōno's graphic novel of the atomic bombing of Hiroshima *Town of Evening Calm, Country of Cherry Blossoms* was published in a popular comic magazine in 2003, and was adapted to a film in 2007. In fact, there is a long history of cultural expressions by atomic bomb survivors, but no other stories have been cherished by Japanese audiences in recent years. *Town of Evening Calm, Country of Cherry Blossoms* can be viewed as a form of cultural representation by the subordinated groups against the hegemony over the representations of the atomic bombings in the post–Cold War period.

This study is aimed at examining both the graphic novel and the live action film of *Town of Evening Calm, Country of Cherry Blossoms* through Gramscian view of counter-hegemonic actions in order to discuss (1) difficulties in expressing the survivors' subjective views of "Hiroshima," and (2) the role of popular media in negotiating the representations of the atomic bombing. Given the post–Cold War reconfiguration of Japan–U.S. relations, it is timely to examine a popular representation of the atomic bombing of Hiroshima. The positive reception of this tale may signal a shift in the long standing hegemony over the representations of the atomic bombings and possibly the Japan–U.S. relations.

Fumiyo Kōno

Fumiyo Kōno was born in 1968 in the city of Hiroshima. As a child, she read a variety of comics and developed her interest in drawing her own comics. Her passion for comics led her to drop out of university in order to pursue her career as a professional cartoonist in Tokyo. Her first professional work was published in 1995. As she continued to publish her works, she developed a distinctive drawing style, which is characterized with comical deformation. Kōno's works often narrate everyday life of ordinary people in a relaxed and subdued manner, which can also be observed in *Town of Evening Calm, Country of Cherry*

Blossoms. The success of this graphic novel was surprising in many ways; Kōno was far from a mainstream graphic novelist. In addition, she created *Town of Evening Calm, Country of Cherry Blossoms* by her imagination and research of the event because she is not a *Hibakusha* or an atomic bomb survivor. She recalls her reaction to the publisher's offer to create a story of "Hiroshima" as follows:

> Although I was born and raised in Hiroshima, I am neither a *Hibakusha* survivor of the atomic bomb, nor am I a second generation *Hibakusha*. I don't have any relatives who can talk about their experience. For me, the atomic bomb is a tragedy that occurred in the distant past. At the same time, it was a circumstance that existed in the background of "other people's households." I always thought all I needed to know about the bomb was that it was a terrifying thing that happened once upon a time, and a subject best avoided.[6]

Even for Hiroshima native Kōno, the atomic bombing of Hiroshima is a challenging task to address. Take Japanese chemist turned peace activist Hideto Sotobayashi for example. As a high school student, Sotobayashi survived the blast, but lost his mother and school friends. It was only a few years before his death in 2011 that Sotobayashi finally broke silence and started talking about the fateful event. In an interview with a journalist, he explained why he had chosen not to tell his experience of the atomic bombing for 61 years:

> For example, my brother has a son and a daughter, and once said to me, "Please don't talk openly [you are an atomic bomb survivor] because it would hurt my children's prospects of marriage." Due to the spread of various rumors, the survivors are ostracized, as is the case with AIDS. Apart from that, I wished to register my late mother to the official list of atomic bomb victims in Hiroshima. But people around me stopped me; they are unwilling to let others know their relatives are atomic bomb survivors. Ostracization of the survivors remains both in and outside Hiroshima until now.[7]

As Sotobayashi's testimony attests, Kōno sensed the complexity surrounding the silence of the survivors, and the risk of addressing "Hiroshima." However, she started creating a story of "Hiroshima," which later turned into *Town of Evening Calm, Country of Cherry Blossoms* after being encouraged by a magazine editor a few years before the 60th anniversary of the atomic bombing. Interestingly, she chose the issues of the survivors' lives after the blast and their silence as the central theme rather than the atomic bombing itself. She described her decision to tell the tale of the atomic bombing as follows: "Post-war comics have always been dealing with most pressing issues of the times. War-related comics are one of such traditions in this industry. Although it is a difficult task, I have to do it; I thought that it was my duty."[8] In order to compensate for her lack of direct experience of the event, Kōno conducted research on a number of works on "Hiroshima," some of which left a profound influence on the creative process of her work. She noted as inspirations for *Town of Evening Calm, Country of Cherry Blossoms* a 1953 memoir of a female survivor *Seven Years Diary* (*Nananen no ki*) in the anthology *Living an Atomic Bombing* (*Genbaku ni ikite*). This memoir led her to create a story of losses of family members in the first episode whereas Masuji Ibuse's *Black Rain* (*Kuroi ame*) and Kenzaburō Ōe's *Hiroshima Note* (*Hiroshima nōto*) were referred to as useful in recreating the atmosphere of the 1955 Hiroshima in which the first episode is set.[9]

Town of Evening Calm, Country of Cherry Blossoms

Town of Evening Calm, Country of Cherry Blossoms was first published in 2004 by a *Futabasha*'s graphic novel magazine. Founded by successful grain trader Ryōichi Yazaki in

1948, *Futabasha* has always been trying to satisfy the tastes of young adult and working class male. The company has run a number of entertainment magazines, such as gossip-filled *Weekly Taishū* in 1958 and weekly magazine *Weekly Manga Action* in 1967.[10] *Futabasha* also boasts a wide range of popular comic series, such as Monkey Punch's *Lupin III*. Etsumi Haruki's *Jarinko Chie* and Yoshito Usui's *Kureyon Shinchan*. In recent years, *Futabasha* has diversified its venture to video game manuals, gambling books and popular novels. After more than 60 years of its corporate existence, the company remains one of the leading publishing houses in Japan.

As is always the case with *Futabasha*'s other publications, *Town of Evening Calm, Country of Cherry Blossoms* was created, sold and consumed primarily as a commodity. The first two episodes of *Town of Evening Calm, Country of Cherry Blossoms* were respectively published in *Weekly Manga Action* in September 2003 and *Manga Action* in August 2004. Later in 2004, Kōno added the final episode of the series called *Country of Cherry Blossoms 2* to combine all three episodes as a *tankōbon* monograph. Although Kōno was then relatively unknown to the general public, *Asahi Shimbun* published a positive review of her work in its weekly book review on November 28, 2004.[11] Book review magazine *Da Vinci* also chose it as a book of the month in the January 2005 issue.[12] Kōno's graphic novel eventually won two prestigious prizes; one from Japan Media Arts Festival Grand Prize from Japan's Agency for Cultural Affairs in 2004, and a "creative award (*Shinsēshō*)" from the ninth Tezuka Osamu Cultural Prize in 2005. *Town of Evening Calm, Country of Cherry Blossoms* also drew attention from overseas; it has been translated into a number of major languages, including the English translation from *Last Gasp* in 2007. Although the popularity of *Town of Evening Calm, Country of Cherry Blossoms* may, to some extent, be attributed to the fact that Year 2005 fell on the 60th anniversary of the atomic bombing of Hiroshima, it appealed to an exceptionally wide audience in Japan. According to one survey, this graphic novel was acquired by 12 out of 44 U.S. academic libraries of educational institutions with leading Japanese studies programs. It was listed as top Japanese graphic novels published in 2007.[13] The graphic novel was then adapted to a radio drama in 2006 by NHK-FM, a novel in 2007, public readings, and finally a live action film by veteran film director Kiyoshi Sasabe in 2007.

Prior to *Town of Evening Calm, Country of Cherry Blossoms*, there are a sizable number of graphic novels about the atomic bombing of Hiroshima. Perhaps, the best known is late graphic novelist Keiji Nakazawa's *Barefoot Gen* (*Hadashi no Gen*). The losses of his father, elder sister, and younger brother in the atomic bombing left him too traumatized to talk about "Hiroshima." However, his mother's death led him to address his experiences in graphic novels. After a number of short stories on the atomic bombing of Hiroshima, such as *Kuroi ame ni utarete* (1968) and *Ore wa mita* (1972), appeared in comic magazines, *Barefoot Gen* was serialized in popular magazines between 1973 and 1974, and later reprinted in monograph format.[14] *Barefoot Gen*, dubbed as a "trauma manga," appeals to graphic realism of the atomic bombing that Nakazawa experienced as a child, as well as blunt political statements, including condemnation of the Japanese emperor.[15] Despite mounting controversies, *Barefoot Gen* is the best known *genbaku* manga (comics on the atomic bombings) to date.

In addition to *Barefoot Gen* and Nakazawa's other *genbaku* mangas, there are more graphic novels on the atomic bombings, most of which are short stories: Kazuhiko Tanigawa's *Hoshi wa miteiru* (1957), Sanpei Shirato's *Kieyuku shōjo* (1959), Kōji Asaoka and Tatsuo Kusaka's *Aruwakusei no higeki* (1969), Kōji Sugito's *Heiwa no toride o mezashite* (1974), Ryōko Yamagishi's *Natsu no gūwa* (1976), Riyoko Ikeda's *Mariko* in comics anthology

Ikiteteyokatta! (1976), Kenichirō Suzuhara's *Mata auhi made* (1983), Tetsuo Aoki's *Akaikutsu haita* (1991), Kenji Iwasaki's *Kaze no yōni honō no yōni Tōge Sankichi* (1993), Yoshihiro Sae-gusa's *Kataritsugareru sensō no kioku* (2002), Kazu Gotō's *Ikirunda—Hiroshima kara ima inochi no messēji* (2006, 2010), Shiyori Matuo's *Kimi ga kureta taiyo* (2008), Yuka Nishioka's *Natsu no zanzō* (2008), *Hachigatsu kokonoka no santakurōsu Nagasaki genbaku to Hibakusha* (2010) and Susumu Nishiyama's *Anohi no koto boku no kienai kioku·1945.8.9* (2005). How-ever, in comparison with *genbaku bungaku* (literature on the atomic bombings), *genbaku mangas* are relatively neglected as a serious research topic.

The original graphic novel of *Town of Evening Calm, Country of Cherry Blossoms* com-prises three interrelated episodes, which revolve around three generations of atomic bomb survivors. It depicts the silence over the atomic bombing of Hiroshima and the struggle to overcome it, which spans about 60 years.

The first episode, set in 1955, depicts the brief life of female survivor Minami. She lives in a shanty town called *genbaku suramu* (atomic slum), which was located along the Ōta River in Hiroshima. Minami survives the atomic bombing despite her losses of the father and a younger sister, and later an elder sister possibly from a radiation sickness. This episode is set three years after the end of the Allied Powers' occupation, and also a year before the Japanese government declared that "it is no longer 'post-war.'"[16] Despite economic hardship, Minami's life takes a positive turn when she starts working at an architect studio, where she meets new friends, including her lover Uchikoshi.

However, underneath the surface of restored peace in the city, the people are still struggling with memories of the bombing. For example, mere a sight of the scarred bodies of women in a public bath house reminds Minami of the images of badly wounded casualties in the aftermath of the blast. Later, it is revealed in Minami's recollection of the blast that she feels guilty for surviving the blast by abandoning victims, and even stealing shoes from a deceased woman.[17] In response, she tries to forget the atomic bombing, saying to herself, "If only I could forget that all this had happened."[18] Minami also expresses the dilemma of the survivors not being able to talk about the atomic bombing: "There's something not quite right in this town. Nobody talks about it. I don't really understand what happened, even to this day. All I know is that somebody wanted us dead. They wanted us to die, but we survived. And the most horrifying thing is that I've become the sort of person one ought to wish dead since that day. That's what I've come to realize."[19]

Indeed, the post-war peace was achieved through the survivors' silence over the atroc-ity. It is well documented that the survivors of the atomic bombings are unable to talk about their experiences.[20] The survivors' silence is also the central theme of late Hisashi Inoue's 1994 stage play *Chichi to kuraseba* and the film adaptation in 2004. However, Minami eventually breaks the silence by telling Uchikoshi the aftermath of the atomic bombing: "Please.... Please tell me that it's okay for me to be here in this world. Let me talk about what happened ten years ago. Maybe then, I can make sense of why I was spared. Maybe then, I won't think about my sisters and the others and feel guilty about having met you."[21]

After breaking silence, Minami's health deteriorates. Minami starts showing a number of symptoms that resemble those of her late sister: lack of appetite, fever, vomiting blood, blindness, and loss of hair. This episode ends with Minami's death, but Kōno carefully avoids adding too much sentiment to the portrayals of her death. Minami's monologue is narrated in blank panels, which represent her blindness and eventual demise. At her deathbed, Minami contemplates those who dropped the atomic bomb: "Happy now? It's been ten years. I wonder if the people who dropped the bomb are pleased with themselves—'Yes! Got another one!'"[22] It is shocking to hear such an aggressive remark from a dying heroine. Rather than turning Minami into a helpless, innocent victim, Kōno defies a stereotypical image of atomic bomb victims by articulating those who dropped the bomb and killed the people in Hiroshima.

The second episode is set in 1987 in a fictional town in Tokyo called *Cherry Blossom Country*. This episode revolves around the carefree life of fifth grader Nanami, who is a niece of Minami. She is depicted as a lively and mannish girl while her friend Tōko is quiet and feminine. Minami's younger brother Asahi, who appears only briefly at the end of the first episode, becomes the retired father of Nanami and frail son Nagio, who is hospitalized for asthma. He takes shelter in Ibaragi Prefecture at the time of the bombing, and does not return until he enters a university in Hiroshima. Minami's mother Fujimi in this episode lives with Asahi and her grandchildren in the town. Her concern, although not being explicitly expressed, is about her grandchildren's health. Even Nanami's nosebleed makes her alarmed probably because she mistakes it with a sign of radiation sickness.[23] Fujimi's reaction indicates that the second and third generation survivors cannot escape from fear of radiation exposure-related illnesses. Overall, the second episode is the most light-hearted among all three. This episode is centered on Nanami's relationships with her family and friends mainly through the depictions of various episodes at school, home, and hospital. Curiously enough, no explanation is available to the absence of Nanami's mother and their relationships with "Hiroshima."

The final episode is about Nanami's reconciliation with her own memories of "Hiroshima." Nanami grows up to become an office clerk whereas her brother Nagio recovers his health and becomes a doctor. This episode starts with their father Asahi's bizarre behaviors; secret phone calls and outings at night. Growing suspicious about her father's behaviors, Nanami decides to follow him only to find out he is going to Hiroshima. In her pursuit, Nanami accidentally meets Tōko, who is an old friend from Cherry Blossom Country. Nanami later discovers that she is Nagio's lover. This episode reveals that all characters are haunted by memories of the atomic bombing although they have no direct experience of the blast. Nanami's seemingly joyful reunion with Tōko in fact reminds her of her grandmother Fujimi at deathbed, who hallucinates as if she were meeting her deceased daughter's friend after the blast.[24] She also recalls her mother lying in a pool of blood on the floor before she dies at the age of 38.[25] Nanami confesses that she does not wish to meet Tōko again[26] and tries to forget "everything that happened to me back in our old neighborhood."[27]

For Asahi, his visit to Hiroshima is for the 50th anniversary of her sister Minami's passing. While sitting on the bank of the river, where his home used to be located, he recalls how he met his future wife Kyōka. At that time, she is rumored to be mentally retarded due to radiation exposure as a child. Unfazed Asahi confides to his mother his plan to marry Kyōka. However, his mother first reaction is fear—the fear of losing family from radiation sickness: "Why do you think we sent you away to be raised by others? And how would I explain this to your foster parents Ishikawa? Oh, why can't I die? I don't want to see any more people I know die from the bomb."[28]

As for Nagio, who is born and grows up in Tokyo, "Hiroshima" is a distant event. However, as Nanami describes, "people stubbornly believe that both Nagio and I [Nanami] could die at any time because of the bomb."[29] The atomic bomb continues to cast a long shadow over Nagio's life, particularly his relationship with his lover Tōko. Because they grow up together in Cherry Blossom Country, Tōko and her parents are aware of his poor health and the untimely death of his mother. As a result, Tōko's parents pressure Nagio to leave her, and he complies with their request by writing a goodbye letter to Tōko. The first half of the final episode depicts the context of the survivors' silence by revealing every character is traumatized by "Hiroshima." A number of factors, such as fear of radiation exposure-related illness, losses of families, survivor guilt, and ostracism against the survivors, continue to haunt the second and third generations of atomic bomb survivors.

Nanami and Tōko's visit to Hiroshima proves to be a shocking revelation about the atomic bombing. Yet, it helps them face "Hiroshima"; Tōko decides to return to Nagio while Nanami returns to Cherry Blossom to rediscover her own childhood. During her stroll in the town, Nanami stops over the bridge, and tears Nagio's letter into pieces. As letting them go in the wind, she experiences a moment of realization about her relationship with the mother. Nanami asks, "Mom, you are watching, aren't you?"[30] This scene, followed by a series of her parents' life events from Hiroshima to Cherry Blossom Country: her mother watching falling petals of cherry blossoms, and then her parents deciding to marry and moving to this town, symbolizes Nanami's reconciliation with her mother, "Hiroshima" and Cherry Blossom Country, all of which she once tried to forget.

The Film Adaptation

Despite the success of the graphic novel version of *Town of Evening Calm, Country of Cherry Blossoms*, the film adaptation proved to be a difficult task. Veteran director Sasabe was so impressed by the graphic novel that he contacted major Japanese film distributors for the film adaptation, but his proposal was all but rejected as "unattractive and hard to sell."[31] After facing rejections by Japanese distributors, the director turned to an American distributor instead. Yet again his proposal was rejected; this time it was due to Minami's line at her deathbed. Nonetheless, the producers and the director's persistence eventually paid off when they managed to assemble 12 production companies and 2 distributors for the film adaptation. Although the film adaptation is not listed even within top 29 box office hits among Japanese films released in 2007,[32] it was recommended by a number of organizations, such as the Agency for Cultural Affairs, the Advisory Council on Children's Film Viewing of Film Classification and Rating Committee, the Japanese Film Pen Club, and The Parent Teacher Association in Japan.

Overall, the film adaptation of *Town of Evening Calm, Country of Cherry Blossoms* is true to the original graphic novel. Despite the melodramatic ending, it succeeds in cinematically recreating the silence surrounding "Hiroshima," and Nanami's reconciliation with Minami and by extension "Hiroshima" to show how the silence is broken. However, the director had to overcome the challenge of visualizing the survivors' silence within the conventional length of feature films. In an interview, the director explained how he had recreated the graphic novel in relation to the graphic novel's title:

> [A]t the time of *Town of Evening Calm*, which was 13 years after the atomic bombing, the issue of "radiation exposure" was a grave reality only inside "the Atomic Slum," which was a small town in Hiroshima. However, I suppose, after 60 years of the postwar period have passed, the issue may have spread from a small town in Hiroshima to nationwide, that is, *"Country of Cherry Blossoms"* [in which the second and third episodes are set].[33]

In order to represent an event which occurred in Hiroshima more than 60 years ago to the present-day Japan, Sasabe focuses the film on the process of reconciliation between

Minami and Nanami. He reduced the narrative structure to the two interconnected episodes about the two persons. In order to symbolically bridge the temporal and spatial gaps between them, the scene of Minami's death is inserted at both ends of the first and second episodes. New scenes are also added to the end of the second episode; dying Minami asks young Akira and her lover to live long to remember "us."[34] This scene is followed by the final scene of the second episode, which is set in present-day Tokyo. In this scene, the picture of Minami is shown to Nanami as Akira talks about her for the first time. In addition, Sasabe expanded the role of Minami's hairpin, which appears only briefly in the graphic novel. It is originally given to Minami by her father before the bombing, and then to her mother by dying Minami. The film details how this item has been passed on from one generation to another. At the end of the second episode, Nanami witnesses young Akira presenting the hair pin to her mother while making a marriage proposal to her.[35] Thus the director uses the hairpin as a token of Nanami's reconciliation with her mother through a shared memory of "Hiroshima."

Among a number of other differences between the film and the graphic novel, the most striking is a dialogue between Asahi and Minami in the first episode of the film:

ASAHI: Why was it Hiroshima? Why did the atomic bomb fall on Hiroshima?
MINAMI: That's wrong. It did not fall, but it was dropped.[36]

This dialogue indicates the role of the United States in the atomic bombing of Hiroshima, but it also reveals that the pervasiveness of the hegemony over the representations of "Hiroshima" in today's Japanese society. Even to this day, the survivors' emotions have to be carefully controlled in Japanese society.

The Missing Subject: The Silence over the Atomic Bombings in the Cold War Era

On August 6, 1945, the U.S. army deployed a nuclear weapon against the city of Hiroshima. B-29 bomber *Enola Gay* detonated a uranium-based nuclear bomb called "Little Boy" over the central business district of the city. According to a survey by Hiroshima City, a total of 118,661 civilians (38 percent of the registered civilian population) were presumed dead, 79,220 were injured, and 3,655 were missing as of August 10, 1946.[37] However, many did survive the bombing, but with both physical and psychological scars. The survivors also have to endure *hibaku* or radiation exposure related health problems, such as leukemia and other types of cancer, as well as social stigma.

Despite a great deal of suffering, the survivors have difficulties in expressing their own experiences of the bombing. One of the earliest obstacles was the officially sanctioned ban on telling "Hiroshima." It is well documented that after the atomic bombing of Hiroshima, the Supreme Commander of the Allied Occupation (SCAP) imposed the Press Code to ban any publication of reports and studies on damages caused by the atomic bombings of Hiroshima and Nagasaki. The SCAP set up Atomic Bomb Casualty Commission (ABCC) in 1946 with a directive order of President Harry Truman to conduct long term studies of atomic bomb casualties, in collaboration with Japanese authorities, such as doctors, scientists and government officials.[38] Until the end of the occupation, the damages were kept secret and remained largely unknown to the general public.

Until the end of the occupation in 1952, literary works became one of a few platforms where survivors could tell their experiences and feelings about the bombing. For example, amateur poet and atomic bomb survivor Shinoe Shōda illegally printed 100 to 150 copies of *tanka* poem anthology titled *Sange* (*Repentance*) in March 1946, and handed it to other survivors.[39] After Shōda, a number of survivors tried to represent their experiences of the atomic bombing through poems, novels, picture books, essays, and reports. Although their expressions had to be compromised, if not banned, under the official censorship, it was the birth of the literary genre popularly called *genbaku bungaku* (the atomic bomb related literature).

The SCAP, which was practically directed by the United States government, initiated the wide-ranging post-war policies for Japan. Initially, these policies were designed to prevent Japan from becoming any forms of threat to the United States. It was only after the growing sympathy for socialism and communism among Japanese people, and the breakout of the Korean War in 1950 that the United States realized the necessity to rehabilitate Japan as a pro–American partner. In 1952, San Francisco Peace Treaty and the bilateral security treaty with the United States were enacted. From then on, Japan has been collaborating with the United States in Cold War conflicts. It was the Cold War tension that dictated the bilateral relationship between the two countries despite the bitter enmity during the war. In spite of occasional conflicts, Japan's post-war administrations under the prolonged rule of Liberal Democratic Party considered the bilateral partnership as the pillar for security and economic prosperity of the country. The Japanese government has been downplaying the U.S.'s role in the atrocities in Hiroshima and Nagasaki.

Quoting Donald Richie's analysis of Japanese films on the atomic bombings, Chizuko Tezuka points out that the Japanese generally accept the events as if they were natural disasters, and do not express anger toward the United States.[40] Although his view is not entirely correct, it is shared by other observers like Gunther Anders, who pointed out with surprise at the unexpected reactions of Japanese people to the atrocities.[41]

However, the hegemony of silence was not created without controversy. In fact, it had to be won through heated debates at the local level. In 1952, Hiroshima City installed the cenotaph for the atomic bomb victims in Hiroshima Peace Memorial Park. The inscription reads "Let all the souls here rest in peace; For we shall not repeat the evil." The epitaph was written by English Professor Tadayoshi Saika upon the request of then Hiroshima Mayor Shinzō Hamai. In Japanese, the sentence was left ambiguous about who made the evil due to the missing subject in the second sentence. Since then, the epitaph has been an object of controversy over the identity of the "we" in the English translation. When Indian jurist Radhabinod Pal criticized the epitaph for the absence of reference to the U.S.'s role in the bombing, Saika retorted to Pal's criticism by stating the "we" in the epitaph meant to be all of humanity.[42] In 1983, the Hiroshima City administration installed an explanatory panel in order to clarify that the missing subject is meant to be "all human beings, not any particular country or individuals."[43] Thus, the cenotaph in the Peace Memorial Park is a site of contestation over the representations of "Hiroshima" in the Cold War.

In fact, the cenotaph has been vandalized at least six times: February 1965, August 1976, March 5, 2002, July 26, 2005, January 4, 2012, and September 21, 2012. In August, 1976, the original cenotaph was covered by a stone tablet, which reads "President Truman."[44] In the 2005 attack, local nationalist Takeo Shimazu damaged a part of the epitaph, and subsequently sent a statement to the mass media, the mayor of Hiroshima City and the governor of Hiroshima Prefecture to claim that his act was a protest against the content of the epitaph. In response, the Japanese media almost unanimously condemned the attacker. For example, a local newspaper, which regularly covers issues of the atomic bombings, condemned Shimazu as follows:

> The 2005 attack was carried out by a member of a right wing group. He damaged the cenotaph in the part of the phrase "the evil." He confessed to the police that he is not satisfied with the word because the wrongdoer was the United States. This crime was intended to provoke another round of debate. But using the cenotaph as a ploy to instigate anti–U.S. sentiment, he will not be able to attract sympathy from anyone, not to mention atomic bomb survivors.[45]

Shimazu was subsequently arrested and sentenced to imprisonment for two years and eight months for damaging public property. Although the controversy over the cenotaph continues, the Japanese media, the local administrations, and leaders of atomic bomb survivors' organizations have asserted the official line of how the epitaph should be interpreted without referring to the U.S.'s role in the bombing. As the public responses to the protests against the cenotaph indicate, the hegemony over the representations of the atomic bombing is defended by the local government, the legal system, and mass media. The hegemony was created by the U.S. censorship, but it is defended and maintained by the Japanese, even those in Hiroshima.

In Japan, the hegemony over the representations of "Hiroshima" has also been asserted by Japanese leaders. Shōwa emperor, prompted by Toshihiko Akinobu, who was a journalist from a Hiroshima-based broadcaster, in his first ever press conference on October 31, 1975, expressed his view about the atomic bombing of Hiroshima: "It was very regrettable that the atomic bomb was dropped, and I feel sorry for the people of Hiroshima. However I think that it could not be helped because it was an incident during the war."[46] In 2007, Defense Minister Fumio Kyūma stated in a lecture that the atomic bombings "cannot be helped." Kyūma, who is known for his outspokenness, and being critical about some of the U.S.'s foreign policies, expressed his view of the atomic bombings as a strategic means to end the war before the Soviet would enter the war with Japan.[47] Meeting mounting criticism from the leaders of Hiroshima and Nagasaki and representatives of the atomic bomb survivors' organizations, Kyūma eventually resigned from the Cabinet. In a sense, Japan has been contradicting itself on the issue of nuclear weapons. It has been pursuing the total abolition of nuclear weapons while it has been living under the doctrine of nuclear deterrence against the communist bloc, which was provided by the United States. Such a Japanese attitude has cast a long shadow over how the atomic bombings can be represented.

In contrast, the U.S. government's stance has been consistent in its justification of the use of atomic bombs. In a reply to a journalist who supported his order to bomb Hiroshima, Harry Truman retrospectively stated his justification of the atomic bombings in 1963: "I knew what I was doing when I stopped the war that would have killed a half million youngsters on both sides if those bombs had not been dropped. I have no regrets and, under the same circumstances, I would do it again."[48]

His view still resonates in today's American society. In 1994, the Smithsonian Museum's National Air and Space Museum revealed its plan of an exhibition on the atomic bombings of Hiroshima and Nagasaki "The Last Act: The Atomic Bomb and the End of World War II" in order to commemorate the 50th anniversary of the end of World War II. The exhibition was initially planned to display the effects of the atomic bombings, and to critically examine the atomic bombings from various perspectives. As soon as the details of the plan were made public, the U.S. veterans' organizations and policy makers started condemning the Smithsonian's plan:

As early drafts of the exhibit text became known, the 180,000 member Air Force Association, the 3-million-member American Legion a small group calling itself the Committee for the Restoration and Proud Display of the *Enola Gay*, and conservative members of Congress, some genuinely offended, some sensing the issue's demagogic potential, denounced the exhibit as "anti–American," insensitive to veterans, and overly sympathetic to the bomb victims.[49]

Despite negotiations initiated by the museum and some historians, many of display items, such as pictures and belongings of atomic bomb victims, were removed from the display. This event, which intended to facilitate mutual understanding about the atomic bombings, ironically highlighted how deep the gap runs between the two countries:

American refusals to issue an official apology give conservatives and nationalists in Japan a trump card: "why should we apologize when others do not?" Many people, such as nationalist manga artist Kobayashi Yoshinori, ask simply: "Why was Nanking a crime but not Hiroshima?" Progressives have also compared Hiroshima and Nanking, or even Auschwitz and Hiroshima, but face the problem of convincing Japanese people to accept a perceived double standard: Japan must apologize for its war crimes even though the Allies refuse to apologize for what, in Japanese eyes, is their major war crime.[50]

In November 1994, the U.S. Postal Service announced a commemorative stamp of the atomic bombings of Hiroshima and Nagasaki as a part of World War II stamp series. The design shows a mushroom cloud with a caption reading "Atomic bombs hasten war's end, August 1945." This time, the Japanese survivors protested against the U.S.'s proposal, and the Japanese government lobbied U.S. representatives in Japan and policy makers in Washington, D.C. Eventually, the proposal was cancelled despite protest from U.S. veterans. However, this incident reveals an undertone of ambiguity over the atomic bombings within American society:

In one way or another, across America, journalists, pundits, and ordinary citizens found themselves unexpectedly wrestling with the historical meaning of Hiroshima and Nagasaki in the angry months leading up to the fiftieth anniversary of the bombings. In a Gallup poll jointly commissioned by U.S.A Today and the Cable News Network, 59 percent of Americans expressed approval of Truman's decision, with 35 percent disapproving. Fifty years after the event, Americans remained uncertain and deeply divided about its meaning.[51]

Resisting the Silence of the Atomic Bomb Survivors

During the Cold War era, individual atomic bomb survivors were allowed to express their views of the event only if their views were in line with the goals of political camps, i.e., the pro–American conservatives who tried to defend the Japan–U.S. partnership and the leftists who followed party lines of the communist party and the socialist party. In addition, the survivors feared social stigma as well as the long term effects of radiation exposure; through repeated encounters with such obstructions, the survivors gradually learned to refrain from expressing their own views of the atomic bombing, or stopped talking about the atomic bombings at all. They accepted the status quo surrounding "Hiroshima," and their inaction in turn contributed to maintaining the Japan–U.S. relations in the Cold War era.

However, it is not saying that discontent toward the hegemony does not exist among the atomic bomb survivors. Japan Confederation of A- and H-Bomb Sufferers Organizations conducted a survey of 1,622 survivors, "'My appeal' 60 years after radiation exposure."[52]

Fifty-seven point seven percent of the valid respondents were survivors of Hiroshima. To a question about who holds the responsibility for the atomic bombings of Hiroshima and Nagasaki, 20.7 percent considered the United States government, 9.7 percent the Japanese government, and 56.9 percent both governments, with 5.7 percent considering that "it cannot have been helped because it was [an incident in] a war." Selected comments from the correspondents indicate that there is a shared understanding that "Japan started the war and the United States dropped the bombs."[53] The survey results indicate that the atomic bomb survivors do have their opinions, but the majority of them keep their views of the bombings private.

It is worth noting that Hiroshima and Nagasaki, which both suffered destruction and human losses from the atomic bombings, are in contrast in reaction to the bombing. Three days after the bombing of Hiroshima, another atomic bomb "Fat Man" was detonated over Christian dominant Uragami district of Nagasaki City. Since then, Nagasaki has come to terms with the U.S. bombing in a way that is best exemplified in local doctor Takashi Nagai's *The Bells of Nagasaki*, who called the event as "God's providence."[54] The Nagasaki city administration even chose to demolish the damaged Uragami Cathedral despite the locals' wish to preserve it in memory of the catastrophic event. As expressed in the well-known phrase "Hiroshima's anger, Nagasaki's prayer," the atomic bombing survivors in Nagasaki are said to be more inclined to reconcile to their own fate than their counterparts in Hiroshima.

Nonetheless, memories of the atomic bombings still trigger strong sentiments among Japanese people, particularly those in Hiroshima. In fact, at the early stage of the postwar period, anger was expressed toward the United States by the survivors. For example, atomic bomb survivor Yōko Ōta expressed discontent with both the United States and the Japanese authorities. In her novel *Yunagi no machi to hito to: 1995-nen no jittai* (*The Town and People of the Evening Calm: The Real Condition of 1953*), she captured the emerging hegemony of silence over "Hiroshima." through the critical eyes of the protagonist, who investigates as a writer the transformation of "H City" into a "peace city."[55] The story ends with the protagonist interviewing with a lawyer who plans to take legal action against President Truman for the atomic bombing.

Nobel laureate Kenzaburō Ōe also explained that it was the survivor's anger that made him a novelist. However, Ōe conceded that he is not certain if he can create a story that reflects experiences of the survivors without downplaying the Japan's role as an aggressor in the war.[56] Ōe's confession is a testimony of the Japanese society, which has been haunted by traumatic memories of Hiroshima and Nagasaki, and Japan's own responsibility in the war. A British scholar describes the Japanese's dilemma as follows: "More than 60 years have been passed, yet the Japanese are still struggling to find a word for the sufferings of Hiroshima. Their silence is not only personal. It arises out of a complex interaction of personal, social, cultural, historical and political forces—the relationship between the personal narrative and social discourse."[57]

While Ōe struggled with the difficulty in representing "Hiroshima," aforementioned novelist Ōta became increasingly frustrated with indifference to "Hiroshima" in the Japanese society, and eventually stopped writing about "Hiroshima." Nonetheless, their struggles did give rise to *genbaku bungaku*, and other forms of cultural representations of the atomic bombings, including *Town of Evening Calm, Country of Cherry Blossoms*. Although *Town of Evening Calm, Country of Cherry Blossoms* was produced and consumed primarily as a cultural commodity, it challenges the long standing cultural hegemony over the representations of the atomic bombing of Hiroshima. Despite the popularity among the general public, Japanese academics' responses are not always positive. In fact, this tale has become a site of contestation over cultural representations of "Hiroshima."

For example, literary critic Takayuki Kawaguchi argues that the feminization of the atomic bomb survivors in Kōno's graphic novel serves to obscure Japan's role as an aggressor or a colonizer, and in turn reinforces the hegemony of Japanese nationalism.[58,59] His critique is reductionistic; It is true that Kōno does follow the generic representation of atomic bomb survivors in atomic bomb-related literature as either women or children, but Minami—the protagonist in the first episode—is portrayed as a more complex figure than a mere victim as her bold remarks attest. Tomoko Ichitani, resonating with Kawaguchi's view, criticizes Kōno's work from the point of view of the colonized as follows: "However, this new narrative is not free from the ethnocentric remembering of Hiroshima and generates the image of post-war Japan as a peaceful, harmless and innocent nation by forgetting the city's military history and the nation's acts of colonial aggression against the people of Asia and the Pacific."[60]

Both Kawaguchi and Ichitani further criticize this tale for the absence of Koreans from the portrayals of the post-war Hiroshima. During the post-war era, many ethnic Koreans were living in the slum, which is home to the protagonists in the first episode. Although their criticism presents an alternative reading of the tale, their analysis slips into a question of ethnicity and an attack on colonialism. Although their criticism makes us realize ethnic Japanese survivors were the dominators in relation to ethnic Korean survivors, it, unwittingly or not, serves to maintain the hegemonic silence of the survivors.

Due to the collapse of the Soviet Union, the relative importance of Japan as a regional partner of the United States diminished. In addition, after Deng Xiaoping's economic reforms came into full effect in the early 1990s, China presence in the global market grew as the factory of the world. In fact, China has become the U.S.'s second largest trading partner. The U.S.–China relations have come to the point where the U.S. State Department under Bill Clinton's presidency called for the development of a constructive strategic partnership. Thus, the end of the Cold War had a considerable impact to the U.S. policies in East Asia.

The end of the Cold War also changed Japan's stance toward East Asia. The Japanese Democratic Party (JDP) led government tried to take more initiative in East Asian politics under the premiership of Yukio Hatoyama in 2009. The shift in the Japanese government's policy was symbolized in its demand for the relocation of the Futenma U.S. Marine Corps airbase in Okinawa in 2009. During the Cold War era, Okinawa was one of the most important military bases in the Asia-Pacific region. The pro–U.S. policy makers in the Liberal Democratic Party criticized the JDP government's move as destabilizing the regional security in the Asia Pacific while the JDP government claimed that this move will improve Japan's relationships with other East Asian countries. Hatoyama's plan was short-lived, but his move signaled a shift in the Japan–U.S. relationship.

According to Japanese Ministry of Health, Labour and Welfare, 192,719 were recognized as living survivors of the atomic bombings, as of the end of March, 2014.[61] In Hiroshima, 61,666 were registered as *Hibakusha* or atomic bomb causalities. Considering their average age was as old as 79.44, accessing firsthand accounts of the atomic bombings will become increasingly difficult in the near future. If nuclear weapons are not deployed against human beings again, personal accounts of the atomic bombings will be accessible only in a mediated fashion. Therefore, it is expected to witness more efforts to represent "Hiroshima" and "Nagasaki" in the future. As the case of *Town of Evening Calm, Country of Cherry Blossoms* attests, cultural products, such as films and graphic novels, will be sites of contestation over how to represent the atomic bombings. Cultural products will become important media through which the consumers are introduced to distant pasts, which they cannot experience directly.

Notes

1. James Arthur Ainscow Stockwin, *Collected Writings of J. A. A. Stockwin: Part 1: The Politics and Political Environment of Japan* (London: Routledge, 2004), pp. 117.

2. Antonio Gramsci, *Selections from the Prison Notebooks of Antonio Gramsci*, ed. and trans. Q. Hoare and G.N. Smith (New York: International, 1971), p. 242.

3. *Ibid.*, p. 244.

4. *Ibid.*, p. 197.

5. *Ibid.*, p. 333.

6. Fumiyo Kōno, *Town of Evening Calm, Country of Cherry Blossoms*, trans. Andy Amemiya and Naoko Amemiya (San Francisco: Last Gasp, 2007), p. 103.

7. Hideto Sotobayashi, "Dokunichijin Interview # 836," 1 October 2010, *Doitsu News Digest*, intvw. and ed. M. Nakamura, http://www.newsdigest.de/newsde/person/deutschland-japan/3019-hideto-sotobayashi.html (accessed 29 May 2014) (the author's translation).

8. Fumiyo Kōno, "Genbaku ya sensō manga de hyōgen Hijiyamadaitankidaigakubukyakuinkyoju Fumiyo Kōno-san," *Chūgoku Shimbun Online*, 5 September 2012, intvw. by K. Watanabe, http://www.hiroshimapeacemedia.jp/mediacenter/article.php?story=20120905103128261_ja (accessed 22 September 2012) (the author's translation).

9. Interview with Kōno Fumiyo, "Genbaku no saika o tōi kako no higeki dewanaku ima no kotoba de tsutaetai," *Gensuikyō Tsūshin on the Web 0.1*, 6 February 2005, http://www.antiatom.org/blog/2005/02/post_136.html (accessed 22 September 2012) (the author's translation).

10. *Futabasha*, "Kaisha gaiyō," http://www.futabasha.co.jp/company/ (accessed 12 January 2012).

11. Minami Nobunaga, "Minami Nobunaga no komikku kyōyōkōza," *Asahi Shimbun*, 28 November 2004, morning edition, p. 16.

12. Editorial Department, "Yūnagi no machi sakura no kuni," Fumiyo Kōno, *Da Vinci* (January 2005), pp. 8–9.

13. Glenn Masuchika and Gail Boldt, "Japanese Manga in Translation and American Graphic Novels: A Preliminary Examination of the Collections in 44 Academic Libraries," *The Journal of Academic Librarianship* 36.6 (2010): p. 514, http://www.sciencedirect.com/science/article/pii/S0099133310002156 (accessed 10 June 2014).

14. Keiji Nakazawa, *Kuroi ame ni utarete* (Tokyo: Dino Box, 2005), pp. 285–86.

15. Kenji Kajiya, "How Emotions Work: The Politics of Vision in Nakazawa Keiji's Barefoot Gen," in *Comics Worlds and the World of Comics: Towards Scholarship on a Global Scale* (Global Manga Studies, vol. 1), ed. Jaqueline Berndt (Kyoto: International Manga Research Center, Kyoto Seika University, 2010), p. 221, http://imrc.jp/images/upload/lecture/data/20101227Comicspercent20Worldspercent20andpercent20thepercent20World percent20ofpercent20Comics.pdf (accessed 20 September 2012), pp. 245–61.

16. Japanese Government Economic Planning Agency, "*Showa sanjūichinendo Nenjikeizaihōkoku*," http://www5.cao.go.jp/keizai3/keizaiwp/wp-je56/wp-je56-010501.html (accessed 4 August 2010).

17. Fumiyo Kōno, pp. 23–24.

18. *Ibid.*, p. 26.

19. *Ibid.*, pp. 15–16.

20. Chizuko Tezuka, "An Analysis of the Japan–U.S. Perception Gap Regarding the Atomic Bombing from the Perspective of Silence and Silencing," *Intercultural Communication Studies* 14 (2002), pp. 79–97.

21. *Ibid.*, p. 28.

22. *Ibid.*, p. 33.

23. *Ibid.*, p. 49.

24. *Ibid.*, p. 63.

25. *Ibid.*, p. 80.

26. *Ibid.*, p. 62.

27. *Ibid.*, p. 87.

28. *Ibid.*, p. 84.

29. *Ibid.*, p. 86.

30. *Ibid.*, p. 91.

31. Kiyoshi Sasabe, *Director Sasabe Kiyoshi-san Interview Vol. 2*, "Sakura no kuni ni himerareta imi to

kantoku no omoi" (Tokyo: Pia eigaseikatsu, 2007), http://blog.eigaseikatu.com/yunagi-sakura/2007/05/post_2.html (accessed 5 May 2012).

32. Motion Picture Producers Association of Japan, *"Nisennana nen (Showa jūkyu nen) kōshū jūoku en ijō bangumi"* http://www.eiren.org/toukei/img/eiren_kosyu/data_2007.pdf n.d. (accessed 3 May 2012).

33. Kiyoshi Sasabe, *"Pia eigaseikatsu Director Sasabe Kiyoshi-san Interview Vol. 2 'Sakura no kuni' ni himerareta imi to kantoku no omoi,"* http://blog.eigaseikatu.com/yunagi-sakura/2007/05/post_2.html 25 May 2007 (accessed 5 May 2012).

34. Kiyoshi Sasabe, dir., *Yunagi no kuni sakura no machi* [DVD], (Tokyo: Art Port, 2012) 01:49:25, the author's translation.

35. *Ibid.*, 01:44:42.

36. *Ibid.*, 00:45:59.

37. Hiroshima City, *"Hiroshima genbaku sensaishi: Dai ni-kan dai ni-hen kakusetsu dai ichi-shō shinai kaku chiku hibaku jōkyō"* (Hiroshima: Hiroshima City, 1946), pp. 5–6, http://a-bombdb.pcf.city.hiroshima.jp/pdbj/bookdownload/sensai2.pdf (accessed 20 May 2014).

38. Atsuko Shigesawa, *Genbaku to ken-etsu amerikajinkishatachi ga mita Hiroshima·Nagasaki* (Tokyo: Chūkōshinsho, 2010).

39. Kuwajirō Mizuta, *Genbakubunken o yomu genbakukankeisho 2176-satsu* (Tokyo: Chūkōbunko, 1997), pp. 18–9.

40. Tezuka, p. 83.

41. Claude Eatherly and Günther Anders, *Burning Conscience: The Case of the Hiroshima Pilot, Claude Eatherly, Told in His Letters to Günther Anders* (New York: Monthly Review Press, 1962), p. 5.

42. Yoshiteru Kosakai, *Hiroshima Peace Reader*, trans. Akira Tashiro, et al. (Hiroshima: Hiroshima Peace Culture Foundation, 1978), p. 50.

43. *Ibid.*, p. 47.

44. Chūgoku Shimbun Online, "Genbaku irēhi ni toryō Hiroshima mimē 50-dai otoko? Tōsō," Hiroshima Peace Media Center, 5 January 2012, http://www.hiroshimapeacemedia.jp/?p=5498 (accessed 13 August 2013).

45. Chūgoku Shimbun Online, "(Shasetsu) genbakuirēhi hason hibun o yomikomu kikai ni," Hiroshima Peace Media Center, 29 July 2005, www.chugoku-np.co.jp/abom/05abom/edit/Ae05072901.html (accessed 22 September 2012).

46. Japan National Press Club (Nihon kisha kurabu), *Nihon kisha kurabu kishakaiken amerika hōmon o oete Shōwa tennō·Kōjunkōgō ryōhēka,* 31 October 1975, p. 4, http://www.jnpc.or.jp/files/opdf/120.pdf (accessed 22 September 2012) (author's translation).

47. Rui Abiru, *"Kyūma bōēshō no genbaku 'shōganai' hatsugenbun,"* 30 June 2007 (corrected 1 July 2007), http://abirur.iza.ne.jp/blog/entry/211450/ (accessed 22 September 2012).

48. Harry S Truman, "Correspondence between Irv Kupcinet and Harry S. Truman, including draft copies of Truman's letter, July 30 and August 5, 1963, Papers of Harry S. Truman: Post-Presidential Files," The Harry S. Truman Library. http://www.trumanlibrary.org/flip_books/index.php?pagenumber=1&titleid=236&tldate=1963-07-30&collectionid=ihow&PageID=-1&groupid=3707 (accessed 12 June 2014).

49. Paul S. Boyer, *Fallout: A Historian Reflects on America's Half-Century Encounter with Nuclear Weapons* (Athens: Ohio State University Press, 1998), pp. 247–248.

50. Philip A. Seaton, *Japan's Contested War Memories: The "Memory Rifts" in Historical Consciousness of World War II* (Oxford: Routledge, 2007), p. 64.

51. Boyer, p. 250.

52. Japan Confederation of A- and H-Bomb Sufferers Organizations (Nihon gensuibaku higaisha dantai kyōgikai), "Hibaku 60-nen 'Watashi no uttae' Chūkan hōkoku," 2005, p. 2. http://www.ne.jp/asahi/hidankyo/nihon/about/img/057myappealjapanese.pdf (accessed 22 September 2012).

53. *Ibid.*, p. 12.

54. Tsuyoshi Takase, *Nagasaki kieta mōhitotsu no "Genbaku dōmu"* (Tokyo: Heibon, 2009), pp. 89–90.

55. Yōko Ōta, "Yunagi no machi to hito to [The town and people of the evening calm]," in *Yōko Ōta Shū 3* (Tokyo: Nihon Tosho Sentā, 1955), pp. 5–294.

56. Kenzaburō Ōe, "Hiroshima and the Art of Outrage," *New York Times Online,* 5 August 2010, http://www.nytimes.com/2010/08/06/opinion/06oe.html?pagewanted=all (accessed 20 September 2012).

57. Nigel C. Hunt, *Memory, War and Trauma* (Cambridge: Cambridge University Press, 2010), p. 114.

58. Takayuki Kawaguchi, "Fukuma Yoshiaki-cho: 'Hansen' no media-shi sengonihon niokeru seron to yoron no kikkō, Yoshimura Kazumasa·Fukuma Yoshiaki-cho 'Hadashi no Gen' ga ita fūkei Manga·sensō·kioku," *Journal of Genbaku Literature* 5 (2006), p. 52.

59. "Media toshiteno manga, yomigaeru genbaku no kioku: Kono Fumiyo 'Yunagi no machi Sakura no kuni' shiron," *Genbaku Literature* 4 (2005), p. 91.

60. Tomoko Ichitani, "Town of Evening Calm, Country of Cherry Blossoms: The Representation of Hiroshima Memories," *Journal of Narrative Theory* 40.3 (2010), pp. 387–388.

61. Ministry of Health, Labour and Welfare, Hibakusha-sū (Hibakusha kenkō techō shojishasū) (The

Number of Atomic Bomb Survivors, 2014, http://www.mhlw.go.jp/stf/seisakunitsuite/bunya/0000049130.html (accessed 10 July 2014).

Bibliography

Adorno, Theodor W. *The Cultural Industry: Selected Essays on Mass Culture.* Ed. J. M. Bernstein. London: Routledge, 2001.

Jones, Steve. *Antonio Gramsci.* Oxford: Routledge, 2006.

Kawaguchi, Takayuki. *Genbaku toiu mondairyōiki* (*The Area of Inquiry Called Atomic Bombs*). Fukuoka: Sōgensha, 2011.

Kuroko, Kazuo. *Genbaku bungakuron, Kakujidai to sōzōryoku* (*On Atomic Bomb-Related Literature: The Atomic Age and Imagination*). Tokyo: Sairyūsha, 1993.

_____. *Genbaku wa bungaku ni dō egakaretekitaka* (*How Have Atomic Bombs Been Portrayed in Literature?*). Tokyo: Hassakusha, 2005.

Nakazawa, Keij. *Barefoot Gen Volume 01: A Cartoon Story of Hiroshima.* Trans. Project Gen. San Francisco: Last Gasp, 2008.

NHK. *NHK Special Fūinsareta genbakuhōkokusho* (*NHK Special Sealed Reports Atomic Bomb Investigation*). Documentary, 49 minutes. 2010.

NHK Hiroshima. *Furusato-hatsu "Genbaku no hi" mamoritsuzuketaotoko* (*From Home Town: The Man Who Preserved "the Flame of the Atomic Bomb"*). Documentary, 28 minutes. 2007.

The Sound of the Bomb: Gō Shibata's *NN-891102*

Johannes Schönherr

Reiichi is a five-year-old boy living in Nagasaki in 1945. His father works in air defense and he has been entrusted with one of those rare open-reel tape recorders that had recently been developed in Germany and of which a few found their way to war ally Japan. He keeps the tape machine in an air raid shelter in his own garden on the periphery of Nagasaki. Proudly, he shows his son how to operate the mysterious new gadget and on occasion lets him play with it.

On August 9, 1945, the father leaves the house as usual for his job in the city. It's a sweltering hot summer day and young Reiichi, ever fascinated with the new machine, prefers to enter the shelter. The family cat had already sought refuge from the heat in there. Reiichi turns on the tape recorder, hoping to catch the voice of the cat.

Right then, at 11:02 a.m., the earth shakes and a huge air pressure wave sweeps over the hills, flattening everything in its path. With it came the mightiest sound wave ever to have been recorded up to that moment ... the moment of the nuclear destruction of Nagasaki.

Reiichi's father perished in the city but Reiichi and his mother survive unscarred. Well, not quite. Though physically unharmed, Reiichi will never forget the sound of the bomb again. In fact, he will spend the rest of his life trying to recreate that sound just one more time.

NN-891102, Gō Shibata's film, is named after the moment the bomb hit Nagasaki: August 9, 11:02 a.m. It's the moment which profoundly shapes the fictional main character Reiichi and which leads to all the resulting developments.

The film leaves it open as to whether Reiichi was actually able to capture the sound of the blast on tape or if an electrical blackout stopped the machine first. It doesn't seem to matter to Reiichi. What he wants is to achieve the recreation of the full impact of the sound ... something a 1940s tape recorder could impossibly provide even if the recording had been successful.

We don't see Reiichi ever listen to the tape again, except for a dream sequence at the very end. Instead, we see Reiichi in various stages of his young life researching sound. All kinds of sounds; and the more extreme, the better. He seems to have no interest in music, just in sound. Step by step, he increases the intensity of his experiments. At about the age of 18, he reaches the point of strapping dynamite around his body to experience the full impact of the detonation sound. Friends rescue him in the last moment.

Interspersed are scenes with Rei-ichi visiting a *kami shibai* (paper play) performance in a park. The *kami shibai* tells the story of a boy who can't forget his experience of the Nagasaki bombing. It becomes more and more clear that the *kami shibai* always fore-tell Reichii's next moves. Are they real or just his fantasies?

Reiichi enters university and excels with his sound studies. He has a baby with his girlfriend but the baby is unable to hear. Deaf. Reiichi is not able to develop an interest in the child. He is only focused on his sounds ... and what could be the use of a deaf child in his pursuit of sound?

When his girlfriend leaves him, he takes his frustration out on the cat. It's a very cruel scene ... but then,

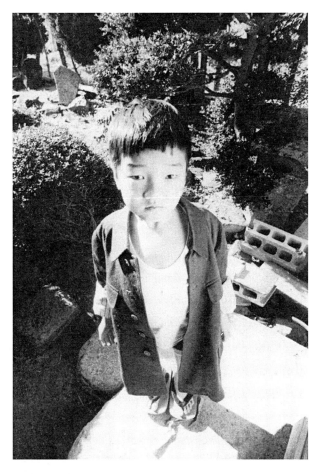

Right: Reiichi as a 5-year-old (played by Yusuke Nishida). At that age, he experi-enced the bomb (courtesy Gō Shibata). *Below:* Eighteen-year-old Reiichi (Ryuya Hasegawa) is prevented by his friends to continue in a potentially lethal sound experiment (courtesy Gō Shibata).

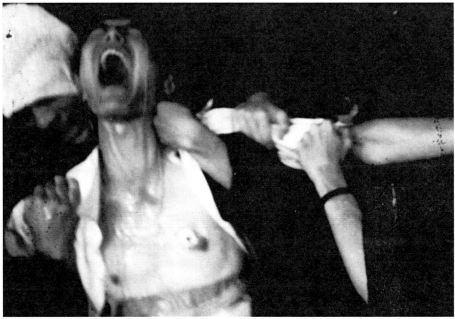

Gō Shibata in 1999, the year *NN-891102* was premiered (photograph by Johannes Schönherr).

wasn't it a cat that got him to turn the open-reel tape recorder on in the first place back on the day in the air raid shelter? The voice of the cat and the sound of the bomb may be closely linked in Reiichi's memory.

Eventually, on August 9, 2000, at 11:02 a.m. the 60-year-old Reiichi is finally able to hear the sound of that fateful day in Nagasaki again. Or is he? The soundtrack is rather lyrical, touching noise rock instrumental and the scenes go back and forth between images of five-year-old Reiichi and a 60-year-old Reiichi sitting dreamingly on his porch.

Reiichi seems to have found his peace. In the future. August 9, 2000, was still a year ahead when the film premiered in 1999. Shibata had put the end of his story into the next millennium.

Meeting Gō Shibata

In early autumn 1999, I went to Osaka to show a program of silent black and white stag movies from the 1920s. Vintage-era explicit porn. At that time, only real underground places would show films like that in Japan. The owner of the theater, the tiny Planet Studyo + 1 cinema, was Kunihiko Tomioka. He invited me to stay at his house for a few days. To my big surprise, his apartment turned out to be the campground for a large number of renegade students from the Osaka University of Arts. Parties were going on day and night in the cramped space and yet, the main focus point was not the fridge with the beer but the Steenbeck 16mm editing table in the living room. Everyone vied for their space at that editing machine.

The previous year, Kazuyoshi Kumakiri, a student of the Osaka University of Arts, had run into problems with his school. They refused to screen his graduation film *Kichiku* (*Kichiku dai enkai*, 1997), an ultra-violent account of Japanese leftists killing each other at a mountain resort in the early 1970s. Kumakiri approached Tomioka and Tomioka premiered the film in his theater.

At that time, Kumakiri learned about the editing table at Tomioka's house and about Tomioka's generally free-wheeling and open ways. He told his student friends and suddenly, Tomioka's apartment filled up with students who felt that they found a freedom there that the school could never provide. Many of them stayed on for long periods ... rolling out their sleeping bags wherever they found a space.

When I arrived, one of those students, Nobuhiro Yamashita, had just left for the Vancouver Film Festival with his slacker drama *Hazy Life* (*Donten seikatsu*, 1999). Gō Shibata however was in town. In fact, he lived in Tomioka's apartment and was busy putting the final touches on the editing of *NN-891102*.

I didn't speak any Japanese, he didn't speak English. But we immediately connected. Gō called the way we communicated "telepathy," but actually it was quite basic. We would sit down with some beers and *takoyaki* (fried octopus) in the coolest tiny bar nearby, the Hatsubei, and would just throw band names at each other. *Einstürzende Neubauten*? Agreed. *Merzbow*? Agreed. *Masonna*? Agreed. We went through the whole inventory of extreme Japanese, American and European music just by name and titles—and could talk all night that way. Shibata clearly knew well about even the furthest fringes of noise and punk. In fact, his personal background was music rather than film.

Gō Shibata's Background

I stayed in contact with Shibata over the years and in November 2004, I interviewed him for the first time. We met in an Ainu restaurant in Tokyo's Nakano ward and over a Hokkaido microbrew, fried deer and salmon, Shibata spoke about his early days.

Johannes Schönherr: Can you talk a bit about your background? You were born in Yokohama in 1975, you studied in Osaka, you worked on Kichiku...

Gō Shibata: I'm from Wakabadai, a very new town near Yokohama. Although it is very close to Tokyo, the town is very much like countryside, very isolated. In that town a lot of *bozosoku* (bikers) were around and my parents worried about me. So, they asked me to go to a small junior high school in Tokyo. They wanted to keep me away from the *bozosoku*. All my friends from elementary school eventually became *bozosoku*. My life was very much divided between school in Tokyo where the students were very smart but once I went back to my home town there were all these bad boys. I became a kind of therapist for them. Because in the world of those bad boys, they had many problems. I was listening to my friends in the hometown. I was not part of their group. That's why they could tell me their stories. Sometimes there was a problem inside the group and I was asked to go and say "sorry" to somebody in the group.

At that time, I started to make movies. It was cheaper back then to use 8mm than video. Video cameras were still very expensive. In middle school I had a friend whose father was rich and he had a video camera. I liked to make miniature model tanks and to put them into stop-motion animated films.

I was also very impressed by a Spielberg-produced film named *The Goonies* (by Richard

Donner, USA, 1985). It's an adventure story about a group of boys who go out in search of pirate treasure. I tried to make a remake of this movie with my friends. We never finished it but we were working on it for quite some while. After I entered junior high school, I decided to make a new film. I shot my friends who went to play Pachinko. That was also on 8mm. I had a script but my friends didn't follow the lines. I said, okay, let's forget the script. I wanted to film a story… but at last, it didn't work. I didn't have enough money to finish the film, so it didn't get finished. That was in Yokohama.

Which year was that?

About 1991, 1992. When I was in 3rd grade in junior high school and first grade in high school, I was shooting so many things, shooting the nature, the scenery, at that time, I was very confused. Every weekend I went to go camping at that time, together with both my friends from Tokyo and the Yokohama *bozosoku*. With those people I shot the Pachinko film that didn't get finished. I connected the footage I had with the music. Then, I started my own band.

For that film, for the soundtrack, I started the band. We played all the music that I liked, *Einstürzende Neubauten*, *Boredoms*, *Beasty Boys*, and we made a cassette tape with our recordings. Masaya Nakahara of noise band *Violent Onsen Geisha* listened to our tape and he found it very interesting. He had a record shop in Shibuya selling all kinds of independent music. Neither I nor Nakahara thought that the tapes would sell but they did. We made more than 80.000 Yen with those tapes. 1.500 Yen per piece. We made three tapes. I made the tapes at my house. This was when I was in second grade in high school.

What was the name of the band?

UNU. Just like the letters from the alphabet (*He chants*: Yu-En-Yu-En-Yu … *sounds like a Buddhist monk chanting.*) We named the band after a love hotel in Yokohama.

Most of the tapes sold in Osaka. That's when I realized that Osaka might be a really interesting place. Like, they had the *Ultra Fuckers* in Osaka and all that scum culture. I very much like the *Boredoms* who are also from Osaka. I wanted to change my environment and in Osaka were all the bands I liked. So, I decided to go there. There, I wanted to make my own film.

My family didn't have much money but I persuaded them anyway that they must send me to Osaka. To the Osaka University of Arts. In Osaka, I then played for two years in a band named *Tochika Warmers Diary*. I didn't and still don't really understand the meaning of the name of the band because it was named by other band members. It was a good name, though. We played regularly all the clubs.

The first three years I stayed in Osaka, I made music. During that time, Nobuhiro Yamashita and Kotsuke Mukai were making 8mm films at the school and Kumakiri made *Kichiku*. I was living in a very big house. I could rent the whole house for only 10.000 Yen a month, we could make any noise we wanted to make at that house. That's why Kumakiri and other friends from school came to the house to record sounds for their films. I started to get involved with those filmmakers and started to realize that I was just making music but that my reason for coming to Osaka was to make movies. So, I said, okay, now I want to make my own film. My first film was kind of work for the school, for the class. The school assignment was to make a film somehow related to a slope. I made the short film *All You Can Eat* (1996).

I was poor at that time and with my friends, we went to McDonald's, Mister Donuts, Kentucky Fried Chicken… all that junk food outlets. We went to their garbage cans outside the shops and we ate out of that. That was the inspiration for the film. All the people you see in the movie are real friends I did go to the garbage cans with, like Robin, the singer of punk performance band *Akainu*. [The seven-minute punk rock short *All You Can Eat* shows two young guys and one girl eating, eating and eating. They start with a table full of disgusting junk food, then hit the town and wolf down plants, insects and worms they find on the street. Finally resorting to cannibalism, they end up in jail where there is more junk to digest.]

Gō Shibata Talks About NN-891102

In the spring of 2013, Matthew Edwards, the editor of this book, asked me if I would be interested in contributing a text on *NN-891102*. I contacted Gō Shibata for another interview. On a hot August day, he came over to my house in Tokorozawa near Tokyo and we talked about the making and the meaning of his film.

You were a film student in Osaka. When exactly?
I studied in Osaka from 1995 to 1999. *NN-891102* was my graduation film.

Your contemporaries at the Osaka University of Arts dealt with rather recent or contemporary subject matter. Your film was very different, I think.

Gō Shibata in Tokyo, 2013 (photograph by Johannes Schönherr).

At first, I wanted to make a short film. Why? For a long film, you need drama, a story. A short film however is very similar to music. I played in a band. That was the way I wanted to express myself. In a very immediate way, like in music. Short films and music have the same atmosphere. My first idea was that a five-year-old boy experiences the atomic explosion and that he accepts that sound as music. For 55 years, he pursues that sound. In the short film, I wanted to show, however, only how he is reproducing that atomic bomb noise as a 60-year-old. But once I started to make the movie, I began to follow up on the whole story. Thus, it became a 75-minute movie. That's why my movie is different. Other people wanted to make long films from the beginning, while I started by making a short film. In the end, my film had the same length as the ones by the other folks but it was of a very different nature.

Why did you choose the Nagasaki bombing?

For two years, I visited the Nagasaki Atomic Bomb Museum on August 9, the day the bomb fell. From there, I got the idea. Actually, at first, I got the Nagasaki bomb idea and then I went there and got more ideas.

I remember you were talking somewhere about the guestbook at the museum and an entry a small boy made in there…

I went with my friends to Nagasaki to do research for the film. At the museum, they had a lot of filled-in questionnaires on display. The questionnaires asked what the visitors thought of seeing the exhibition. There were quite a lot of answers on display by small children. They all said things like "I was so moved" or "I feel so terrible." Exactly the things they were supposed to say. But one primary school student wrote: "If I had been there, I would have withstood the bomb." He had drawn a picture of Pikachu, the *Pokemon* character, next to it. I thought, "That's really a child talking like a real child. Telling his true feelings, very honest." I decided to make my movie when I read that note. Before that, I didn't have confidence in my movie idea because the content was so severe.

At that time [in the 1990s], it was taboo to mix politics and arts. If you made music or painted pictures, you were not supposed to inject comments on social problems into your artwork. That was the situation then and it may be the same now. The words of the boy and his drawing of Pikachu were so different from the pressures of mainstream thinking … it really encouraged me. I didn't know what kind of film I could make and what kind of reactions it would get. But I thought that with my movie I could get beyond the expected reactions on that historical topic.

You started out with the music before making the film?

Normally, you start out with a scenario and a storyboard when making a movie. But I wanted to start with the music. At first, we made about 30 to 40 pieces of music. But we couldn't use any of them. Some of it was really played by a band, others were just abstract compositions. It was the beginning of Japanese hiphop, it was kind of abstract breakbeats, abstract hiphop, loop rhythms. Finally we got real. There was three of us. Noel Nakanishi, Mariko Hashizume and me. We composed all the music. Noel was our main representative.

Who played the music?

We asked various Osaka bands. Like *Akainu*, for example. Mariko Hashizume played the music on the piano, Noel sampled it, made loops, then Akainu wrote the score down on paper. That way, various musicians could play the music. Noel, Mariko and I could understand the mood of the film. We could share the image of the movie via the music. If you don't have an image in your mind, you can't start making a movie.

All the actors came from the Osaka University of Arts?

Most were students at the school. The old people were not and neither the children. The actor for 60-year old Reiichi I found in a flea market. He was selling strange things. Kenji Mori was his name. He called himself an inventor. He was very famous in the flea market. He also used to be an actor. He had a powerful personality.

How many people played Reiichi?

Four people. From high school student to adult it was one actor. He was a friend from university, Ryuya Hasegawa.

The films starts with five-year-old Reiichi in an air raid shelter, playing with the open-reel tape machine. Then, the bomb struck. Now, could he record the sound of the bomb or not? It's not quite clear, I think.

The boy was just playing, trying to record the voice of the cat. At that time, the bomb explodes. The boy thought that he could record both the voice of the cat and the sound of the bomb. But maybe he couldn't record that sound.

Did he record it or not? The rest of the film is spent on him recreating the sound of the bomb.

The experience of the bomb left the boy with a trauma. The boy was just playing with the open-reel tape machine. At the same time, the world event of August 9, 11:02 took place. That those things take place at the same time and place caused his trauma. From then on, Reiichi wants to become sound himself.

The boy undertakes many experiments to research sound.

Step by step, he progresses. Japanese society and Reiichi progress at the same time. There is no border between Reiichi and society. He is a very rare person in that regard. A normal person is separated from society and politics. Film is not real. That's why I wanted to create a person who always grows in step with society. They reflect on each other.

He almost kills himself in an experiment. It looks like attempted suicide.

He didn't attempt suicide. He just wants to become sound himself.

Eventually the film jumps to the year 2000. Then, he can hear the sound of the bomb again. So, in the end, he dies becoming sound himself.

I hope so. I don't know. I wanted the audience to think that he could hear the sound again. What I wanted to express is that a person who experiences such a big event as an atomic explosion can never forget about it, can never escape it. They must always think about it for the rest of their entire life. That's a very negative energy but at the same time a very powerful energy. The kind of life Reiichi leads must be very hard. I couldn't live like that. But I wanted to find out how somebody can live like that.

In a way, Japan itself cannot separate from the explosions?

When making the movie, I didn't think about Japan and Japanese society. But yes. This way, you can say it is a symbol of Japan. Now I think of it like that.

That was done unconsciously?

Yes, exactly. Japanese always think about never engaging in another war. They can never separate from that idea. Article 9 of the Constitution expresses that. [Article 9 of the Japanese Constitution spells out that Japan will never again engage in war.]

Why did you focus on Nagasaki and not Hiroshima?

We researched. Hiroshima was an Uranium bomb, Nagasaki was Plutonium. The Americans explained that the explosion in Hiroshima on August 6 was done to end the war. They justified the Hiroshima bomb that way. I was also educated like that. But from my childhood I could not understand why it needed two bombs. I always felt strange about that. If a teacher scolded a bad student, once was enough. If he did it strongly, he didn't need to do it two times.

But the bombs in Hiroshima and Nagasaki were of different types. So, they were tests. I was surprised in the beginning. Killing people, can you call that tests?

But thinking about it, bombs are assets. So, if you want to use them as an asset, you must check its functions. Like, how many people a bomb can kill. In that way, the Nagasaki bomb was a very negative symbol. One could say that Reiichi represents Article 9. But if I had started the film with an explanation of Article 9, the film would have become very different. I started from an image, not an explanation.

You said that Reiichi wanted to become sound himself. Osaka noise musician Masonna *[Takushi Yamazaki] tried to produce the most extreme sounds possible. He said that he always wanted to find the perfect sound nobody else would be able to produce. He was big in Osaka in the 1990s.*

I often went to *Masonna*'s concerts and got very influenced by them. That was before I made the movie. Now, I realize that Reiichi and *Masonna* are very similar.

Reiichi and Masonna *tried to achieve the same.*

Masonna sounded sometimes like a rock band but more often he pursued a very extreme noise. He didn't care about time or anything, he just went to the most far-out extremes.

But actually, your movie is rather quiet, considering its subject matter.

If it had been a short film, we would have made it very noisy, like *Masonna* or *Merzbow*. But since we made this long story, the main character already exists as an extremely noisy character. That's why we didn't need extreme noise music in the film.

The shooting was all done in the vicinity of the Osaka University of Arts. But the editing was done at Kunihiko Tomioka's house. I think, you told me once that you organized a concert at the school and that started a fire and that you were kicked out of the school...

Natsukashi! [Very common but hard to translate Japanese expression, meaning "How nostalgic!" or "You remind me of the old times!"] I was already marked as a dangerous person at the school. They watched me closely. Still, I ran an illegal club, organized illegal concerts at the school.

At the end of my sophomore year, I had to choose the major that I would take. The university initially didn't want to allow me to study directing, they didn't want me to use their facilities. I had a lot of problems there. Finally, I had a big event at the school, my band played a concert, without permission. Some electrical fault in our equipment started a big fire. It was an accident but the school thought that I'm just causing problems. They prohibited me from using their equipment for editing *NN-891102*.

That sounds like something Reiichi would do. It seems like you yourself were sort of like Reiichi.

The Japanese DVD cover of Gō Shibata's *NN-891102* (courtesy Gō Shibata).

[*Laughing out loudly.*] Thinking about it now, yes, that's exactly what it was. For one year, I then did the editing at Tomioka's house. I couldn't use the school's equipment.

NN-891102 had its premiere at Kunihiko Tomioka's Planet Studyo +1 theater in 1999. The film later traveled the international film festival circuit. It is now available on DVD.

In 2005, Gō Shibata gained international fame for his second feature *Late Bloomer* (*Osoi hito*), a film about a handicapped serial killer.

Many thanks to Kayoko Nakanishi for translating the 2004 interview and to Tomoko Katayama for translating the 2013 interview.

Hiroshima Films: Cultural Contexts Before, During and After the Cold War

GREG NIELSEN *and*
MARGARET M. FERRARA

Remarkably, Hollywood has produced only three Hiroshima films—*The Beginning or the End* (1947), *Above and Beyond* (1952), and *Fat Man & Little Boy* (1989). Considering the number of Hollywood films about World War II, it is clearly significant that so few have been produced about an historical event that significantly changed history. Surprisingly, U.S. television has outdone Hollywood producing four Hiroshima films and numerous documentaries. This paper explores the multiple cultural/societal pressures, perspectives, interests, and concerns that influenced the production of Hiroshima films. In addition to the U.S. produced Hiroshima films, two non–U.S. films are examined: *Hiroshima mon amour* (France and Japan, 1959) and *Black Rain* (Japan, 1989). By investigating other cultural/political viewpoints, the American perspective comes more into focus. What emerges is a highly charged atmosphere of thoughts, emotions and reactions that reveals a subject fraught with perplexing moral ambiguities. A spectrum of cultural forces pushes and pulls against each other ranging from ethical concerns, political/military justifications, communism fears, and anti-war, anti-nuclear stances. Several primary sources are referenced in order to highlight the historical distortions and/or accuracies. They include the Hiroshima Peace Culture Foundation's Hiroshima Witness oral history program, *Hiroshima Diary* by Dr. Michihiko Haciya, and videoed statements by the pilot and co-pilot of the *Enola Gay*, the Hiroshima B-29 bomber. To date, American cinema pays lips service to the moral questions surrounding the decision to drop the bomb but is not the core concern as it is in many foreign films. American Hiroshima films emphasize military organization, technological superiority, and scientific ingenuity deemphasizing the impact of the bomb on human relationships, families, and communities.

The docudrama *The Atomic Bomb: The End or the Beginning?* starts with the following statement:

> Our nation's use of the atomic bomb remains one of the most controversial and emotional issues of World War II. Americans born before 1940, in general, cannot comprehend how anyone could be critical of President Truman's decision to end the war. Those born after 1945, growing up in the Cold War, wonder if there was not a better alternative.[1]

A film's creation and content often reflects society's current viewpoints, interests, and concerns.[2] Hollywood films are produced to make a profit. As a result, economic pressures influence the selection of images, themes, and dialogue. Many of the Hiroshima films take a U.S. military-political point of view. Often script changes were made in order to receive military equipment and Pentagon expertise. Another overt pressure, especially in the 1950s, was the House on Un-American Activities Committee (HUAC).

By examining eight Hiroshima films spanning the years 1947 through 1990, multiple cultural/societal pressures, perspectives, interests, and concerns will be brought to light. Before the Cold War, before 1949 when the Soviet Union successfully exploded their first atomic bomb, there was one U.S.–produced Hiroshima film, *The Beginning or the End?* (1947). During the Cold War, 1947–1988, three non–Japanese Hiroshima films were made: *Above and Beyond* (1952), *Hiroshima mon amour* (1959), and *Enola Gay: The Men, the Mission, the Atomic Bomb* (1980 TV movie).

From 1989 to 1990, leading up to the 45th anniversary of the dropping of the first atomic bomb on Hiroshima, four films were produced. Three were American productions, *Fat Man and Little Boy* (1989), *Day One* (1989 TV miniseries), and *Hiroshima, Out of the Ashes* (1990 TV movie). *Black Rain* (1989) was a Franco-Japanese production.

Enola Gay, Day One and *Hiroshima: Out of the Ashes* were made for television movies. *Fat Man and Little Boy* was the last Hollywood film on Hiroshima. The number one grossing film of 1989, the same year that *Fat Man and Little Boy* was released, was *Indiana Jones and the Last Crusade* bringing in $200 million. In stark contrast, *Fat Man and Little Boy* grossed only $3.5 million. It lost money. The set construction alone ran over $2 million. The television productions fared better. *Day One* won a primetime Emmy and *Hiroshima, Out of the Ashes* was nominated for two primetime Emmys.

Before the Cold War

By 1946, only a few months after the dropping of the first atomic bomb on Hiroshima, stories of the public's concerns about the dangers of atomic power pervaded the newspapers, magazines, and radio broadcasts. *Life* magazine called the splitting of the atom the "biggest event since the birth of Christ."[3] Metro-Goldwyn-Mayer (MGM) began production on *The Beginning or the End?* in 1946. This first Hiroshima film combined docudrama with romance making a fictitious Manhattan Project scientist the hero.

Almost from the beginning, MGM ran into conflicts and controversies that had nothing to do with any moral or ethical concerns by the producers.[4] By choosing the docudrama genre, director Norman Taurog was forced by legal requirements that no longer exist "to depict living, well-known public figures" only after securing their written permission.[5] The film's creative control was not completely in the hands of the director and producer. They were forced to haggle final script approval with the Pentagon and Manhattan Project scientists without forfeiting "dramatic license in the depiction of events for maximum box-office draw."[6]

Specifically, MGM chose to exercise dramatic license by showing the United States in a desperate race to build the first atomic bomb against both Japan and Germany. The Atomic Scientist Movement opposed the further development of atomic weapons. When they found out about the blatant inaccuracy, they withdrew their support for the film. Fortunately for

MGM, senior Manhattan Project scientists Robert Oppenheimer and Leo Szilard had already received fees for the film's endorsement reportedly for as high as $10,000.[7]

Still, many senior Manhattan Project officials protested the film's propaganda approach. Eventually, MGM compromised, allowing for the ethical questioning of the creation and use of the bomb by Matt, the main character. MGM received little if any disapproval from the White House and the War Department. The Pentagon determined that the film adequately portrayed military personnel, procedures, interest, and events.[8] Since much of the Manhattan Project details remained top secret, MGM cooperated with the military to insure that nothing compromised U.S. security.

William S. Parsons, assistant chief of naval operations at the Pentagon, reviewed the final script. Parsons was the naval officer who activated the atomic bomb aboard the *Enola Gay*. He disagreed with the ethical concerns expressed by Matt. The tug of war between the military justification for the bomb and the ethical concerns of scientists and others was not resolved by the time MGM wanted to start filming. MGM refused to make any further changes and the Pentagon did not attempt to force any more script changes.

Another dramatic license in the film was used to "help alleviate American guilt for destroying a target composed mainly of civilians, so that this 'entertainment film' would not oppressively burden and alienate the audience it hoped to attract."[9] Historically inaccurate, the film shows a U.S. plane dropping leaflets warning the Hiroshima civilians of the coming disaster.

For the most part, *The Beginning or the End?* justifies the use of the atomic bomb in the context of World War II propaganda. One line of dialogue expresses the consensus of opinion about the bomb in 1945 as a "necessary evil, less destructive than the prolongation of the war." Another line confirms the pro-military/government stand when after the first successful test of the bomb a character says, "Now it seems certain we can hurry the end of the war … a year less of war will save thousands of lives."

However, what remains clearly unique about this pre–Cold War Hiroshima film is the constant raising of ethical questions about the creation of the bomb and its use. A short exchange between President Franklin Roosevelt and Vannevar Bush who represented the Manhattan Project scientists, illustrates this perspective.

> Roosevelt: Atomic energy on the loose could open the way for destruction of all civilization.
> Bush: The development of atomic weaponry is inevitable, if not by this country, they by some other.
> Roosevelt: Do you have any idea how far Hitler's scientists have progressed?
> Bush: They're probably ahead of us.

Despite the ongoing tug of war between ethics and government propaganda, MGM's priority was the film's commercial success. In order to attract a female audience, they introduced a romantic subplot. During the war, Hollywood released "a glut of male-dominated combat films."[10] Consequently, the female audience stayed away. MGM would try to avoid that mistake by emphasizing the romance between Matt and his bride.

Making a scientist the main character and the hero of the war was unique to all other Hiroshima films to follow. As a pre–Cold War Hiroshima film, *The Beginning or the End?* did what could not be done in the Cold War Hiroshima films, give the spotlight to the atomic scientists. They are portrayed as the characters most in control while the military characters play a secondary role and often appear buffoon-like in comparison to the responsible and more reasonable scientists.[11] General Leslie Groves, the head of the Manhattan

Project, has a fictional subordinate who is portrayed as an opportunist and a womanizer. The actual General Groves "would not have tolerated it in the corps of engineers."[12]

In order to counterbalance the audience's expected negative reaction to the difficult moral issues surrounding the atomic bomb, MGM released the film as a B picture giving it second billing to the Red Skelton comedy *Merton of the Movies*.[13] Despite the second billing, the film failed at the box-office. According to *Variety* a Hollywood business periodical, at least seventy-five films grossed more in 1947. In recent years, however, *The Beginning or the End?* has reached a large audience since it is shown regularly on TCM (Turner Classic Movies). It is also available for viewing at the UCLA Film & Television Archive.

During the Cold War

Three Hiroshima films were produced during the Cold War. Two took a decidedly pro–American, pro–Nuclear bomb, pro-military perspective. The other weighed in on the side of peace, anti-nuclear bomb, and an end to the arms race between the two superpowers, the United States and the Soviet Union. The polarizing forces between the soul searching scientists weighing in against the further use of the atomic bomb and the political/military viewpoint advocating the strategic use of the bomb found a reincarnation in separate films rather in a single film.

Just five years after releasing *The Beginning or the End?* MGM produced another Hiroshima film, *Above and Beyond* (1952). The film business and the world had changed drastically in those few years. Besides wanting to make money at the box-office, MGM wanted to reduce the government's scrutiny of Hollywood. The House on Un-American Activities Committee (HUAC) suspected Hollywood of Communist sympathizing. MGM attempted to waylay those suspicions by producing a movie that showed the bomb as an "indispensable weapon for national defense."[14]

The political, social, and cultural atmosphere in the United States was decidedly different in the early 1950s than in the mid to late 1940s. Besides the Cold War nuclear arms race between the U.S. and the Soviets, the Korean War was in full swing. As a consequence, *Above and Beyond* does not reflect the historic context that *The Beginning or the End?* did. Rather, it has other motivations stemming from the cultural influences of the early 1950s.

In *Above and Beyond* there is a complete shift away from the ethical scientist as hero to the military hero whose devotion to country goes "above and beyond the call of duty." The action centers on Colonel Paul Tibbets, the pilot of the *Enola Gay* and the leader of the B29 squadron responsible for dropping the atomic bombs on Japan. With Hollywood and the Pentagon joining forces to show the military industrial complex as the best deterrent to the Communist menace, the military became directly involved in script development.[15]

MGM hired Colonel Tibbets as a script consultant. His stance on dropping the first atomic bomb was made clear in the 2005 BBC documentary *Hiroshima*. "I was not thinking about the people who got killed or hurt. I was thinking about the people who did not get killed or hurt." Tibbets's personal point of view is reflected in the film and aligns with the Cold War agenda. During the Cold War the moral justification for the bomb had to do with the survival of the American way of life.

This Cold War justification is reflected in *Above and Beyond* when Lucy, Colonel Tibbets's wife, says: "Somewhere at this very moment bombs are being dropped and children are being killed." Tibbets's response is swift and intense:

Lucy, don't ever say that again. Look, let's clear one little piece of morality right now. It's not bombs alone that are horrible, but war. War is what is wrong, not weapons. Sure innocent people are being killed, but to lose this war to the gang we're fighting would be one of the most immoral things we could do to those kids in there [their two boys are asleep in their bedroom].

This time MGM incorporates the love story subplot from the beginning. In fact, *Above and Beyond* is told from Lucy's viewpoint. She is portrayed as the loyal, devoted, endlessly suffering wife who stands behind her man despite the forced separation from her husband. She cannot compete with his duty to country. She comments in voice over, "In five years of marriage we were only together seven weeks."

Tibbets is portrayed as a man who places military commitments before his own life, wife, and children. He is unwavering and stoic from start to finish as evidenced by the following exchange:

GENERAL: No one's ever dropped an atomic bomb before. I can't give you any guarantee you'll come back.

TIBBETS: A guarantee didn't come with the uniform.

In polar contrast to the strong, unwavering military hero, the film's atomic scientists are portrayed as weak and unable to make important and critical decisions. Matt, the wise, responsible, and ethical scientist hero from *The Beginning or the End?* has been reduced to indecisiveness and incompetence. An example of this is shown when a group of Manhattan Project scientists are asked when the bomb will be ready:

SCIENTIST: Hard to say, maybe months ...

TIBBETS: A lot of men can die in a month.

SCIENTIST: Then the responsibility for its use must be completely and solely yours.

"From 1945 through 1947, the prevailing attitude toward members of the scientists' movement (against the bomb proliferation) had been approval and admiration, but by the end of 1947 such admiration had faded."[16] By 1949, opinion polls found growing public sentiment against atomic scientists. This decline in public favor is attributed to the conflict between what the scientists had to say about the hazards of A-bomb development and the Atomic Energy Commission's positive portrayal of atomic energy.[17]

The next Cold War Hiroshima film was released in 1959, *Hiroshima mon amour*. Directed by Alain Resnais, it was originally commissioned by the French government to be a documentary about the horrors of Hiroshima. But after traveling to Hiroshima to do some research and scout out some locations, Resnais decided to do a narrative film. Apparently, he changed his mind about doing a documentary after seeing several Japanese documentaries that he felt were "interesting and substantial."[18]

Ironically, while the film was being written and produced, France was preparing to detonate their first nuclear bomb in the Sahara desert. On June 17, 1958, French President Charles de Gaulle authorized the nuclear test (France's Nuclear Weapons, 2001). The bomb was detonated on February 13, 1960. An even deeper irony was that during this time B-52 bombers loaded with atomic bombs were in the air 24/7.

Hiroshima mon amour takes a dramatically different perspective from both *The Beginning or the End?* and *Above and Beyond*. There are no scientists or military heroes. Instead, there is a Japanese man and a French woman who are lovers for 24 hours in Hiroshima. Both remain nameless throughout the film.

The woman is an actress who is in Hiroshima portraying a nurse in an anti-nuclear bomb film. The Japanese man appears Westernized. After the war (he was a soldier during the war), he went to the university and became an architect. He asks, "Why are you in Hiroshima?" She replies, "To make a film." During this conversation she tells him it is a film about peace and that it is an international production and not solely a French film. She concludes their exchange by making a sarcastic remark: "If they make films to sell soap, why not films to sell peace." The man responds, "In Hiroshima we don't joke about peace."

The anti-nuclear bomb, pro-peace perspective resonates with the Atomic Scientist Movement. It was formed by a group of antimilitary Manhattan Project alumni who hoped to educate the public about the dangers of atomic weapons. Matt, the scientist main character in *The Beginning or the End?*, expresses similar moral reservations as the scientists against nuclear proliferation.[19]

It is important to point out that Resnais was a director involved in the French New Wave movement of the 1950s and 60s. It was made up of "a loosely knit group of French filmmakers who brought new and often subversive styles, visions ... and politics to commercial cinema."[20] *Hiroshima mon amour* does not focus on the development, creation, and dropping of the bomb. For the first time a Hiroshima film places the focus on the bomb's aftermath and the bomb survivors or what the Japanese call *Hibakusha*.

The French woman tells about her visit to the hospital where bomb victims are suffering from radiation sickness more than a decade after the initial blast. She goes into some detail describing her visit to Hiroshima Museum. The visuals reflect the horrific experiences of the Japanese civilians. There are images of twisted and burned iron, petrified bottle caps, photos of bomb victim's burns and scars, and "human skin hanging free and still writhing."

When the peace film is being shot, the film within the film, there are images of Japanese children walking in a parade each carrying a photograph of a civilian who died in the atomic blast. Others in the parade carry placards with large photos of *Hibakusha* who expose their gruesome burns.

Hiroshima mon amour was nominated for an Academy Award in 1961 for Best Writing, Story, and Screenplay written directly for the screen. Although it did not win, it was the only Hiroshima film to be nominated for an Academy Award. The Cannes Film Festival and the Directors Guild of America nominated Alain Resnais for Best Director in 1959 and 1961, respectively. The French Syndicate of Cinema Critics awarded *Hiroshima mon amour* Best Film in 1960.[21] The recognition and awards points to the fact that the American military's Cold War support of Hiroshima films featuring strong military heroes was not the only voice being heard.

Another thing that *Hiroshima mon amour* does that previous Hiroshima films did not do is open up emotional channels to the horrors and consequences of dropping the first atomic bomb. The previous black and white docudramas with their matter of fact approach did not deal with the deeper emotional and psychological impacts. Andrew Sarris concluded in his review for *The Village Voice* with:

> Even if it is too early to tell where *Hiroshima mon amour* will stand in the artistic evolution of the cinema, and let us hope this is the beginning rather than the culmination, no other film of our time so graphically reflects the alienation of individual sensibility from the brutal processes of history.[22]

More than twenty years elapsed between Cold War Hiroshima films. *Enola Gay* (1980) was a made-for-television movie based on the book by Gordon Thomas and Max Morgan

Witts. It tells the story of Colonel Paul Tibbets (played by Patrick Duffy of *Dallas* television show fame) and the training of the 509th bomber squadron. *Enola Gay* takes a patriotic and militaristic tone from start to finish that is similar to the other Tibbets semi-biographical film *Above and Beyond*. One big difference between them is the *Enola Gay* does not give as much attention to the relationship between Tibbets and his wife Lucy as does *Above and Beyond*.

The film's opening dedication superimposed over the U.S. Air Force Seal is a throwback to World War II combat films. In 1980, Ronald Reagan runs for President and wins. The Cold War is in full swing. In 1982, Reagan gives his "Evil Empire" speech about the Soviet Union and the Communists. The military man is the hero of World War II and by association the Cold War.

Accompanied by the hackneyed military snare drum and trumpet, the film's opening dedication rolls:

> On December 7, 1941
> The United States was attacked,
> And so entered a war against
> The Empire of Japan and
> The Third Reich of Nazi Germany.
> It was a war of liberation
> Fought under the Banner of Freedom.
> Young men, mostly civilians
> Willingly left their families
> And the way of peace,
> Put on uniforms
> And went to far off battlefields
> To fight and sometimes die
> For their good cause.
> This is the true story
> Of a group of those young men
> Who went to war,
> Bravely did their duty
> And, in their innocence,
> Changed all of human history.

Here the film's perspective and theme are summarized in the opening dedication. Terms like "Banner of Freedom," "good cause," "duty," and "innocence" tends to eliminate any doubt about the morality of dropping the bomb. From beginning to end, any questioning of the use of the bomb is quickly opposed. For example, in the film's first scene General Groves says, "You boys have pulled off a miracle." When J. Robert Oppenheimer, lead scientist on the Manhattan Project, expresses doubt about where the miracle will lead, Groves responds with a tone of obviousness, "Why, to the end of the war."

The film crosscuts between two primary locations, the Wendover Air Force base in Utah where the 509th trained for the Hiroshima mission and a Hiroshima, Japan military base. The film gives a cursory Japanese perspective that other U.S. Hiroshima films had not explored. By 1980, Japan was central to the United States Cold War effort hosting Air Force bases for nuclear bombers. In addition, Japan was an economic power rivaling the United States for capitalistic prowess. Nevertheless, it should be pointed out that by emphasizing that Hiroshima was mainly a military center the fact that Hiroshima was a major city with several hundred thousand civilians is deemphasized.

A third perspective gives the film an air of authenticity that could be seen as highly manipulative and propagandistic. Several Paramount World War II newsreels are strategically placed throughout the film. The first comes at the 14:30 mark. The newsreels provide a simplistic good versus evil viewpoint emphasizing the heavy American casualties and making it easy to justify the dropping of the atomic bomb.

Enola Gay claims to be a true story. Obviously, Hollywood and made-for-television production companies take dramatic license. However, there is a scene with FDR where the moral question of using the bomb or not takes place at the White House. FDR asks Colonel Tibbets, "What are your moral convictions?" Tibbets responds, "I believe we are morally bound to end this war as soon as possible with every weapon at our disposal." Roosevelt reacts by saying, "I'm inclined to agree with this position."

The film insinuates that FDR, not Truman, made the decision to drop the bomb. Again, any moral debate or doubt about using the bomb is squelched. The Roosevelt popularity and prestige trumps Truman's. Some historians question whether Roosevelt would have succumbed to the pressure to use the bomb.[23]

Even after the film is over a credit sequence tells the audience what happened to each of the main characters in the ensuing years. Again, this hammers the film's pro–American, pro-bomb, and pro-military theme that a "brave and patriotic crew carried out a necessary mission to end the war."[24] The end credits give further credence that *Enola Gay* is a "true story."

After the Cold War

On October 11 and 12, 1986, President Ronald Reagan and Secretary-General of the Communist Party of the Soviet Union Mikhail Gorbachev met in Reykjavik, Iceland. Although the talks collapsed, the progress made eventually led to the 1987 Intermediate-Range Nuclear Forces Treaty between the United States and the Soviet Union. The Berlin Wall, the symbol of the Cold War, fell on November 9, 1989. By December of 1991, the Soviet Union collapsed, breaking up into fifteen separate states. The Cold War came to an abrupt end after more than forty years.

In the two years 1989 and 1990 four Hiroshima films were produced, as many as all the previous Hiroshima films produced before and during the Cold War. With the threat of nuclear war between the two super powers waning, film producers seemed to see a renewed interest in what terrified the world for decades.

Fat Man and Little Boy (1989), produced by Paramount, is a "conventional Hollywood movie in that relationships between the characters are more important than the historical events"[25] This Hiroshima film is less pseudo-documentary than *The Beginning or the End?*, *Above and Beyond*, and *Enola Gay*, and more narrative driven.

Jerome F. Shapiro in his book *Atomic Bomb Cinema* writes that *Fat Man and Little Boy* is a remake of *The Beginning or the End?*[26] A critical viewing of both films reveals similarities, but not because *Fat Man and Little Boy* is a remake. Rather, it is because both cover the same historical material.

The military hero once again takes the central role as in both *Above and Beyond* and *Enola Gay*. However, instead of focusing on Colonel Paul Tibbets, it centers on General Leslie Groves, the head of the Manhattan Project. The theme of the all-sacrificing military man who gives up everything for his country persists. Groves has no personal life. His wife and family are never introduced. He refers to his wife as a "good wife." This implies that she is obedient, does not ask any questions, and keeps her mouth shut.

Academy Award–winning actor Paul Newman portrays General Groves. It is interesting to note that Newman was a "long-time arms-control activist."[27] He plays Groves as an infantile, single-minded, egomaniac who dominates, cajoles, and manipulates Dr. Oppenheimer throughout the film.

Oppenheimer appears to be the mad scientist driven to create the first atomic bomb without struggling with the moral issues implicit in its creation. The image of the mad scientist is visually stamped on the audience's psyche when the first test bomb is successfully detonated in the New Mexico desert. As Oppenheimer witnesses the apocalyptic explosion, his goggles reflect the light of the sun and his face ripples from the 1,000 miles per hour winds generated by the blast.

On the moral issue, whenever Oppenheimer has doubts about finishing the Manhattan Project, Groves steps in barking and biting like a stereotypical dictatorial general. For example, after Germany surrenders, Oppenheimer questions, "If we don't need it, why make it?" Originally, the Manhattan Project was started to develop a bomb before the Germans did. Groves responds by pushing Oppenheimer, "Just the threat and they're ours."

When the Chicago scientists write a petition arguing against the dropping of the bomb, Oppenheimer tells Groves, "It's a crisis of conscience." Groves responds, "You have one job doctor. Give me the bomb." Oppenheimer does superficially question the morality of the bomb. But Groves angrily responds, "Moral? Was Pearl Harbor moral? Poland, Munich, the Death March to Bataan? Was that moral? Oppenheimer finally washes his hands of the whole thing when he says, "We're not responsible for its use."

The voice of reason and conscience in this film comes out in Dr. Richard Schoenfield, a fictional Los Alamos medical doctor. He has just lost his best friend, nuclear scientist Michael Merriman, to radiation poisoning. Schoenfield confronts Oppenheimer about the secrecy and security surrounding Los Alamos and the Manhattan Project. "I think it's to keep it [the bomb] from American Jacks and Jills. This triggers a rapid exchange between them.

> OPPENHEIMER: The American people don't want to know what's going on. They want to know that their sons are alive. I'm doing everything in my power to see that they do.
> SCHOENFIELD: They are injecting the mentally ill with huge doses of plutonium at Oakridge. I've seen it.
> OPPENHEIMER: I don't know about that. But will it be big enough to stop all wars forever? If you want to ask a question, ask that.
> SCHOENFIELD: Oakridge isn't building two or three bombs it is set up to build thousands. Hey, Oppenheimer, Oppenheimer you ought to stop playing God.

Fat Man and Little Boy does not end with the bombing of Hiroshima. Instead, the individual losses of the central characters are emphasized especially the scientist who developed the bomb. The devastating effects of the bomb on the civilians of Hiroshima are not shown or even mentioned.

Day One based on the book of the same title by Peter Wyden was also released in 1989. Aaron Spelling (famed *Charlie's Angels* producer) produced it as a made-for-television movie. It takes a wider, more comprehensive look at the Manhattan Project with a significantly more ethical element than *Fat Man and Little Boy*. General Leslie Groves once again is the central military character. Brian Dennehy plays Groves as dominating, single-minded, and cowboyish, much like Newman's Groves.

Groves takes the status quo position that "if we succeed, we'll win the war and save countless American lives." Throughout the film, Groves justifies the development and dropping of the bomb. For example, at a meeting in Washington, D.C., where government and military leaders gather to discuss the issues around using the bomb, Groves argues that the Japanese will never surrender. He reminds them how 22,000 Japanese civilians in Saipan committed suicide rather than be captured.

After the bomb was successfully tested in New Mexico he says, "We developed a weapon that can end this war and save thousands and thousands of American lives. Isn't that something? His aide responds, "It's amazing General." Groves replies like a cowboy gunslinger. "It sure as shooting is."

The Chicago scientists led by Leo Szilard, the film's man of conscience, submit a petition against the use of the bomb. Groves suppresses it and comments as if he thinks he is the Commander in Chief not President Truman. "I've got all the authority I need to drop the bomb."

The film begins with Szilard leaving Berlin in order to escape the Nazis. "I take Hitler seriously." He continues his chain reaction research in America. He wants to make sure the Nazis do not develop and use an atomic bomb first. Several times throughout the film Szilard expresses his concerns about the bomb's creation. After an initial experiment he reflects, "The world is headed for trouble; the world is headed for grief." Later, he comments after the successful test of the first nuclear reactor, "This day will go down in history as a black mark against mankind." When Germany surrenders he reacts, "This changes everything. As men of conscience we must now prevent America from dropping the bomb on someone else."

"*Day One* expresses concerns for the possibility of an arms race that the historical figures mostly lacked."[28] In the context of 1989, the threat of nuclear war had been a menacing reality for decades and the film takes dramatic license by playing on that fear. Szilard goes to Albert Einstein expressing his concern that "if we drop the bomb we'll start an arms race." After Roosevelt dies, Szilard requests a meeting with Truman. "We know Russia will become an atomic power soon. Russia will build bombs in an arms race that will end in both Russia and America being destroyed."

One major difference in *Day One* from other Hiroshima films with powerful military protagonists is that some military leaders disagree with using the bomb. This more than likely would have been impossible in an American made Hiroshima film before the end of the Cold War. General Marshall warns, "The implications of the bomb go far beyond the implications of the present war." General Eisenhower expresses his concern. "Japan is already defeated. Dropping the atomic bomb is completely unnecessary. We don't need to do it to save American lives." Admiral Leahy insists that "the Japanese were already defeated and ready to surrender" and that by using the bomb America has "adopted ethical standards common to the barbarians of the dark ages."

Unlike *Fat Man and Little Boy*, *Day One* does end by recognizing the horrendous consequences and devastation caused by the atomic blast. The Los Alamos scientists watch slides showing the physical devastation and human casualties caused by the bomb. Many of the photos had not been readily available to the general public before. As the scientists watch, the camera captures their anguished looks and remorse. One scientist is sickened by the sight and leaves the room to throw up. Robert Oppenheimer, the leader of the Los Alamos scientists, observes, "the reaction has begun."

The Japanese film *Black Rain* (1989) takes an even more sobering perspective on the horrific effects on the Japanese A-bomb victims and survivors. The film was shot in black and white during a time when most were shot in color. The central characters are Shige, his wife Shigeko, and their niece Yasuko. They experience the flash, the blast, and the radio-active black rain.

For the first time on film, the agonies of the bomb victims are reenacted in visceral detail. Two sequences, one from 4 minutes to 12 minutes and another from 33 minutes to 46 minutes, graphically portray what happened to Japanese civilians after the flash. There are images of people in the throes of death, hands and arms held away from the body with dripping flesh, carbonized bodies, children crying for their mothers, and dead bodies floating in the Ōta River.

These images accurately reflect the oral history created and preserved by the Hiroshima Peace Culture Foundation. Starting in 1986, they have recorded the testimonies of the bomb victims, the *Hibakusha*. Every year the testimony of 50 *Hibakusha* have been recorded and edited into 20-minute segments per person. This collection is titled *"Hiroshima Witness— Hibakusha Testimony"* and can be found on the following website: http://www.pcf.city. hiroshima.jp/virtual/VirtualMuseum_e/visit_e/est_e/panel/A6/6204.htm

The transcripts can be read online at http://www.inicom.com/hibakusha/.

American films, except for *Hiroshima, Out of the Ashes*, emphasize military organization, technological superiority, and scientific ingenuity in order to end the war as quickly as possible. The moral issues and ethical questions are not the core concern of American Hiroshima films.

Black Rain and other Japanese atomic bomb films like *Rhapsody in August* "focus on the impact of the bomb on human relationships, families, and communities."[29] The drastically different dramatic and artistic representation of Hiroshima by the American and Japanese filmmakers provides some "evidence for the potent and fluid relationship between films and their social context."[30]

Most of the film takes place in 1950 in a small agricultural town, Fukuyama. Yasuko's aunt and uncle want to find a marriage partner for their niece. Unhappily, no one wants to marry her because she is an "untouchable," a bomb victim. The Korean War and the threat of more nuclear devastation terrify the family.

They listen to a radio broadcast:

American President Truman has declared that he would consider using the atomic bomb against the Communist Chinese army in Korea. He stated that he hoped that the atomic bomb would never be used, but the final decision about using the atomic weapons would be made by the commanding officer in the field. This statement was in a 14 article declaration…

Uncle Shige turns off the radio, reacting to the announcement: "Humans are obstinate creatures. We are strangling are throats. An unjust peace is better than a just war. Why can't they understand that?"

Throughout the film bomb victims die of radiation sickness. A neighbor, Shokichi, says, "The flash has overcome me at last." He is nearly blind. An exchange between Shokichi and Shige speaks to the exasperation and mindlessness of nuclear warfare.

SHOKICHI: Why did the Americans drop the bomb? Even if they hadn't done it Japan's defeat was already certain.

SHIGE: They said it was to end the war quicker.

SHOKICHI: Then why didn't they do it to Tokyo?

SHIGE: I don't really understand it.

SHOKICHI: I won't be at peace if I die without understanding why. I can't take it that I'm going
     to die like this.

Shokichi dies a few days later followed in the next months by Shigeko and Shige.

Hiroshima, Out of the Ashes (1990) is the only American Hiroshima film that shows
the dropping of the first atomic bomb from the Japanese perspective, from ground zero
and the surrounding area. Still, a military centered justification for the bomb is established
early in the film. An A-bomb flight crew watches a training film that establishes Hiroshima
as a center for munitions factories and military installations. In addition, it is identified as
the "home of Japanese Steel" and the headquarters of a Japanese division.

After this is established, the film introduces multiple protagonists on August 5, 1945.
There is Yoshi the Japanese schoolboy, a Japanese doctor, the German priest, the pregnant
Japanese-American woman, and even American B-29 airmen who are held prisoners in
Hiroshima Castle. About thirty minutes into the film the bomb drops, followed by the flash
of light and the blast of wind. For the rest of the film, the audience witnesses the devastation
of the bomb on the personal lives of each protagonist.

The horrendous immediate aftermath of the bomb shows burned and charred bodies,
children being burned alive in the rumble, a burned baby on a mother's back, flesh dripping
from hands, and the black radioactive rain. The films end credits read that the "research
for the film was provided in part" by *Hiroshima Diary: The Journal of a Japanese Physician,
August 6–September 30, 1945*, by Dr. Michihiko Hachiya. The University of North Carolina
Press first published the diary in the United States on the tenth anniversary of the Hiroshima
bomb.

Reading Dr. Hachiya's eyewitness account is spellbinding. It is clear his descriptions
influenced the film's horrific images. For example he writes:

> I paused to rest. Gradually things around me came into focus. There were shadowy forms of
> people, some of whom looked like walking ghosts. Others moved as though in pain, like scare-
> crows, their arms held out from their bodies with forearms and hands dangling. These people
> puzzled me until I realized that they had been burned and were holding their arms out to pre-
> vent the painful friction of raw surfaces rubbing together [3].[31]

Overall, *Hiroshima, Out of the Ashes* does not argue for the morality of one side over
the other. Instead, it is decidedly antiwar. The characters evolve toward the pacifistic *war
is wrong* perspective. One character, for example, Mr. Togawa says, "Nobody's fault—must
blame everything on stupid war."

Having American military men bomb victims in the film adds a powerful perspective
and perhaps provides more empathy for the devastating story of Hiroshima. According to
Hiroshima in America: Fifty Years of Denial, there were twelve American prisoners of war
who perished in the blast.[32] After the blast, three American soldiers escape and hide in a
cesspool in order to survive the heat and flames. One dies the first night while the other
two, after leaving the cesspool, are stoned by an angry Japanese civilian mob. A Japanese
officer rescues them.

The antiwar theme continues when the older American, Pete, says to the younger one,
Tom, "It sure looks different from the air." Tom responds, "Yeah, well, they started it." Pete
reacts, "So what, it makes no sense." Again, at the end of the film after Japan surrenders,
the antiwar theme is expressed when Tom thinks a Japanese guard is going to kill him. The
guard says, "I want you to live. I want you to see what one bomb did to my city so you can
go back and tell your people this must not happen again. You are not my enemy. War is

our enemy." The camera pans from Tom's point of view to a lifeless wasteland that was once the thriving city of Hiroshima with a population of 350,000 civilians.

While all the other Hiroshima films are politically charged and controversial, *Hiroshima, Out of the Ashes*, a made-for-television movie originally broadcast to coincide with the 45th anniversary of the bombing of Hiroshima, avoids the controversy by blaming war itself for the bomb. There is almost a "philosophical resignation" that is not present in the other American produced Hiroshima films and is articulated by a character that recites a Japanese Haiku, "Now that my house has burned down, I have a better view of the moon."[33]

After the Cold War: Since 1990

English journalist Ronald Bergan wrote an article titled *Why Hollywood Ignores Hiroshima* for the Sunday Guardian on August 15, 2010. He ponders the question: why are American films so reluctant to depict the Hiroshima bombing? When you consider the number of Hollywood films about World War II, the fact that Hollywood has made only three films about an event that ended the war in the Pacific is more than remarkable and clearly not without significance. Bergan points out that "nowhere in American cinema do we see one victim of the bomb, one burning corpse, one person dying of radiation, one deformed child."[34] Only the made-for-television movie *Hiroshima, Out of the Ashes* (1990) shows the bomb's victims.

Now, more than 65 years after the horrific event, "the omission seems even more astounding."[35] Bergan speculates that the United States suffers a collective guilt around the fact that it is the only country to have used a nuclear weapon on a civilian population. He argues that it cannot be because the "subject is too appalling."[36] Endless Hollywood films have graphically portrayed horrendous events. Toni Perrine suggests in her book *Film and the Nuclear Age: Representing Cultural Anxiety* that "it is not surprising that few commercial narratives have engaged a subject fraught with perplexing moral ambiguities."[37]

In the twenty plus years since the last Hiroshima film, a dozen or more documentaries about Hiroshima have been produced. The most ambitious of these was three-hour television miniseries *Hiroshima* shown on the fiftieth anniversary of the first atomic bomb. Still, it was not produced by Americans, but co-produced by Canadian and Japanese companies.

Strictly speaking it is not a narrative film. It is a kind of hybrid documentary and docudrama that stages elaborate reenactments interspersed with actual film footage from the World War II film archives of several countries. A unique aspect of this ambitious production is the first hand accounts by eyewitnesses to history. They include observations and statements by government and military officials from the United States and Japan, Hiroshima bomb victims, and crewmembers of the *Enola Gay*.

Another reason that American Hiroshima films have not been produced in the last twenty years can be attributed to the controversy that exploded over the Smithsonian exhibit of the *Enola Gay*. It was scheduled to open on the fiftieth anniversary of the Hiroshima A-bomb. Veteran groups, one led by Paul Tibbets, and conservative media fought the proposed exhibit that included the various historical controversies and the bomb's devastation to bomb victims both physically and psychologically.[38]

Outraged critics of the proposed exhibit were successful in having it changed to preserve the traditional American view concerning World War II and how it ended. The current

Smithsonian exhibit consists only of a section of the *Enola Gay* with a recording by Paul Tibbets describing the plane's restoration. "Only the Hiroshima bomber is displayed now, without context or explanation, as just another great American plane, like the *Spirit of St. Louis* or the *Kitty Hawk Flyer*."[39]

In recent years, two documentaries *White Light, Black Rain* (2007) and *24 Hours After Hiroshima* (2010) separate themselves from the orthodox propagandistic docudramas and documentary films of the past by showing living witnesses to the horrors of the bombing, the stories of the *Hibakusha* survivors. *White Light, Black Rain*, produced by Japanese-American Steven Okazaki, was shown on HBO and is currently available through Netflix. *24 Hours After Hiroshima* is a National Geographic production in their popular series *National Geographic Explorers* and is rebroadcast from time to time on the National Geographic cable channel.

Chapter 9 of *White Light, Black Rain* is particularly remarkable. A segment of the 1950s popular television show *This Is Your Life* documents the life of a *Hibakusha*, the Rev. Kiyoshi Tanimoto, a leader of the Hiroshima Maiden Project that arranged for free plastic surgery in America for many deformed by the bomb.

Captain Bob Lewis, co-pilot of the *Enola Gay* spoke, "and looking down from thousands of feet over Hiroshima all that I could think of was: my God, what have we done?" Captain Lewis, who was visibly anxious and genuinely sorry about the bomb, shakes the Reverend Tanimoto's hand and gives him a check contributing to the Hiroshima Maiden Project while saying, "On behalf of the entire crew that participated in that mission ... I'd like to make the first contribution."

With the World War II generation passing away and documentaries showing the world multiple perspectives, will Hollywood tackle the subject more directly? It remains to be seen. James Cameron, director of the two highest grossing Hollywood films, *Avatar* (2009) and *Titanic* (1997), plans on producing a film about the bombings of Hiroshima and Nagasaki. He optioned the book *The Last Train from Hiroshima* by Charles Pellegrino, "a non-fiction account of the World War II mission to drop an atomic bomb on Hiroshima and of the bombing's victims."[40]

Controversy and polarization has already plague the pre-production and scriptwriting phase of the proposed Cameron Hiroshima film. Publisher, Henry Holt & Company has stopped printing and shipping the book amidst allegations of glaring inaccuracies by some scientists, historians, and veterans. Cameron defended the author when he wrote, "So there must be a reason for the misunderstanding." He added that the film does not "have a shooting script and no decision has been made to proceed in the short term."[41]

Conclusion

This essay began with the quote:

> Our nation's use of the atomic bomb remains one of the most controversial and emotional issues of World War II. Americans born before 1940, in general, cannot comprehend how anyone could be critical of President Truman's decision to end the war. Those born after 1945, growing up in the Cold War, wonder if there was not a better alternative.[42]

This polarity of viewpoint continues to be an incendiary one. The World War II generation has continued to vehemently attack those "revisionists" who question the use of the bomb.

Now that those born before 1940 are passing away, Paul Tibbets, pilot of the *Enola Gay*, died at 92 on November 1, 2007, maybe Hollywood and American cinema will do what they have not done so far, create Hiroshima films that tell stories that grapple with the morality, guilt, and the short and long term influences on human lives.

To date, American cinema pays lips service to the moral questions surrounding the decision to drop the bomb but is not the core issue as it is in many foreign films like *Hiroshima mon amour*, *Black Rain* and the Canadian/Japanese docudrama *Hiroshima* (1995). Furthermore, the impact of the bomb on human relationships, families, and communities has received minor attention as compared to Japanese films like *Black Rain*, *Rhapsody in August* (1991) and *Hiroshima no pika* (2005).

With the recent nuclear plant disaster in Japan resulting from the April 7, 2011, Great East Japan 9.0 earthquake, the Japanese collective memory of Hiroshima and Nagasaki has resurfaced. On the one hand, the U.S. responded with humanitarian aid and Red Cross donations. On the other hand, there was an irrational fear of nuclear fallout and the panic buying of potassium iodine. It may just be that as long as there is the possibility of nuclear accidents and the threat of deliberate nuclear bomb detonations polarizing reactions will surface and find expression in a range of human emotions.

Notes

1. *The World War Two Atomic Bomb: The Beginning or the End?* (U.S., 2003), written by Linda Kaye.

2. J.A. Evans, *Celluloid Mushroom Clouds: Hollywood and the Atomic Bomb* (Boulder, CO: Westview Press, 1998).

3. *Life Magazine*, "No," 1947.

4. J.A. Evans, *Celluloid Mushroom Clouds: Hollywood and the Atomic Bomb* (Boulder, CO: Westview Press, 1988).

5. *Ibid.*, p. 28.

6. *Ibid.*

7. *Ibid.*, p. 29.

8. L. Suid, *Guts and Glory: Great American War Movies* (Reading, MA: Addison-Welsley, 1978).

9. J.A. Evans, *Celluloid Mushroom Clouds: Hollywood and the Atomic Bomb* (Boulder, CO: Westview Press, 1988), pp. 31–32.

10. T. Doherty, *Projections of War: Hollywood, American Culture, and World War II* (New York: Columbia University Press, 1993), p. 153.

11. J.A. Evans, *Celluloid Mushroom Clouds: Hollywood and the Atomic Bomb* (Boulder, CO: Westview Press, 1988).

12. N. Reingold, "MGM Meets the Atomic Bomb," *Wilson Quarterly* 157 (Autumn 1994), p. 161.

13. J.A. Evans, *Celluloid Mushroom Clouds: Hollywood and the Atomic Bomb* (Boulder, CO: Westview Press, 1988).

14. *Ibid.*, p. 47.

15. *Ibid.*

16. P. Boyer: *By Bomb's Early Light* (New York: Pantheon, 1995), p. 30.

17. *Ibid.*

18. S. Kolbowski, "After Hiroshima Mon Amour," *Art Journal* (Fall 2007), p. 81.

19. J.A. Evans, Celluloid Mushroom Clouds: Hollywood and the Atomic Bomb (Boulder, CO: Westview Press, 1988).

20. R. Brown, "Hiroshima Mon Amour," *Cineaste*, 1959.

21. "IMDB (Internet Movie Data Base) Pro."

22. A. Sarris, "Hiroshima Mon Amour," *Village Voice*, November 24, 1960.

23. T.A. Perrine, *Film in the Nuclear Age: Representing Cultural Anxiety* (New York: Henry Holt, 1998).

24. *Ibid.*, p. 55.

25. *Ibid.*, p. 30.

26. J.F. Shapiro, *Atomic Bomb Cinema: The Apocalypse Imagination on Film* (New York: Routledge, 2002).

27. T.A. Perrine, *Film in the Nuclear Age: Representing Cultural Anxiety* (New York: Henry Holt, 1998) p. 65.

28. *Ibid.*, p. 58.

29. *Ibid.*, p. 74.

30. *Ibid.*

31. M. Hachiya, *Hiroshima Diary: The Journal of a Japanese Physician, August 6–September 30, 1945* (Chapel Hill: University of North Carolina Press, 1955), p. 3.

32. R.J. Lifton and G. Mitchell, *Hiroshima in America: Fifty Years of Denial* (New York: G.P. Putnam's Sons, 1995).

33. T.A. Perrine, *Film in the Nuclear Age: Representing Cultural Anxiety* (New York: Henry Holt, 1998), p. 60.

34. R. Bergan, "Why Hollywood Ignores Hiroshima," *Guardian News and Media,* August 15, 2010, p. 1.

35. *Ibid.*

36. *Ibid.*

37. T.A. Perrine, *Film in the Nuclear Age: Representing Cultural Anxiety* (New York: Henry Holt, 1998), p. 65.

38. I. Buruma, "The Over the Bomb," *New York Review of Books* 42, No. 14 (1995): 26–34.

39. *Ibid.*, p. 29.

40. D. Itzkoff, "James Cameron Defends Hiroshima Book Author," *New York Times*, March 5, 2010, p. 1.

41. *Ibid.*

42. *The World War Two Atomic Bomb: The Beginning or the End?* (U.S., 2003), written by Linda Kaye.

Bibliography

BOOKS

Bergan, R. 2010a. "Why Hollywood Ignores Hiroshima." 2010.

_____. "Why Hollywood Ignores Hiroshima." *Guardian News and Media*, August 15, 2010. http://www.guardian. co.uk/film/2010.aug/15/hollywood_hiroshima-ronald-bergan-films.

Boyer, P. *By the Bomb's Early Light*. New York: Pantheon, 1985.

Brown, R. "Hiroshima Mon Amour." *Cineaste* 1959.

Buruma, I. "The Over the Bomb." *New York Review of Books* 42, 14 (1995): 26–34.

Doherty, T. *Projections of War: Hollywood, American Culture, and World War II*. New York: Columbia University Press, 1993.

Evans, J.A, *Celluloid Mushroom Clouds: Hollywood and the Atomic Bomb*. Boulder, CO: Westview Press, 1998.

Hachiya, M. *Hiroshima Diary: The Journal of a Japanese Physician, August 6–September 30, 1945*. Chapel Hill: University of North Carolina Press, 1955.

Itzkoff, D. "James Cameron Defends Hiroshima Book Author." *New York Times*, March 5, 2010.

Kolbowski, S. "After Hiroshima Mon Amour." *Art Journal* (Fall 2007): 81–84.

Lifton, R. J., and G. Mitchell. *Hiroshima in America: Fifty Years of Denial*. New York: G.P. Putnam's Sons, 1995.

Pellegrino, C. *The Last Train from Hiroshima: The Survivors Look Back*. New York: Henry Holt, 2010.

Perrine, T.A. *Film in the Nuclear Age: Representing Cultural Anxiety*. New York: Henry Holt, 1998.

Reingold, N. "MGM Meets the Atomic Bomb." *Wilson Quarterly* (Autumn 1984): 157.

Sarris, A. "Hiroshima Mon Amour." *Village Voice*, November 24, 1960.

Shapiro, J.F. *Atomic Bomb Cinema: The Apocalypse Imagination on Film*. New York: Routledge, 2002.

Suid, L. *Guts and Glory: Great American War Movies*. Reading, MA: Addison-Wesley, 1978.

FILMOGRAPHY

Feature Films

Above and Beyond (U.S., 1952). Screenplay by Melvin Frank.

The Beginning or the End? (U.S., 1947). Screenplay by Frank Wead.

Black Rain (JP, 1989). Screenplay by Shohei Imamura. Based on the novel by Masuji Ibuse.

Day One (U.S., 1989). Teleplay by David W. Rintels. Based on the book by Peter Wyden.

Enola Gay: The Men, The Mission, the Atomic Bomb (U.S., 1980). Teleplay by Millard Kaufman and James Poe. Based on the book by Gordon Thomas and Max Morgan Witts.

Fat Man & Little Boy (U.S., 1989). Screenplay by Bruce Robinson.

Hiroshima Maiden (U.S., 1988). Teleplay by Jean O'Neill, Tom Shima, Steven Hensley and J. Miyoko Hensley.
Hiroshima mon amour (FR, 1959). Screenplay by Marguerite Duras.
Hiroshima no pika (JP, 2005). Written by Toshio Maruki. Based on the children's book *Hiroshima No Pika*.
Hiroshima: Out of the Ashes (U.S., 1990). Teleplay by John McGreevey.
Rhapsody in August (JP, 1991). Screenplay by Akira Kurosawa. Based on the novel by Kiyoko Murata.

Documentaries

24 Hours After Hiroshima (U.S., 2010). National Geographic Channel.
Hiroshima (CAN, JP, 1995). Teleplay by John Hopkins and Toshirō Ishidō.
Hiroshima: BBC History of World War II (GB, 2005).
White Light, Black Rain: The Destruction of Hiroshima and Nagasaki (U.S., 2007). Written by Steven Okazaki.
The World War Two Atomic Bomb: The End or the Beginning? (U.S., 2003). Written by Linda Kaye.

Hiroshima: An Interview
with Director Roger Spottiswoode

MATTHEW EDWARDS

Few films have attempted to accurately portray the events leading up the Allies' decision to drop the atomic bombs on Hiroshima and Nagasaki and explore the myriad of
complexities that brought about their usage. An exception to this rule is the Canadian and
Japanese co-production of *Hiroshima*, a made for television docudrama that weaves fact
and staged re-enactments to create an engrossing, historically accurate and moving portrait
that is both objective and unbiased, leaving the viewer to ultimately decide whether the
bombings of Hiroshima and Nagasaki were necessary. What the film does set out to achieve,
and successfully, is to chronologically re-tell the events from the perspective of both the
U.S. war cabinet and the Japanese war cabinet, through staged recreations based on historical research and through real documentary footage and firsthand accounts of survivors
and combatants. Adopting such a cinematic tapestry is one of the film's major strengths,
as well as dividing the directorial duties between critically acclaimed British director Roger
Spottiswoode and respected Japanese filmmaker Koreyoshi Kurahara (director of domestic
Japanese hits like *Nankyoku monogatari* [1983] *and Gate of Youth* [*Seishun no mon*, 1981],
which he co-directed with Kinji Fukasaku of *Battle Royale* [*Batoru rowaiaru*, 2000] fame.
Kurahara is also fondly remembered for his Nikkatsu films such as the superb *Black Sun*
[*Kuroi taiyō*, 1964] and *The Warped Ones* [*Kyōnetsu no kisetsu*] in 1960. Both directors utilized their own crews, employing their own cinematic styles to create a film that lives long
in the memory and one that refreshingly tells the story of the bombing from both the U.S.
and Japanese government's perspectives as a means of getting closer to the truth and as a
means of presenting what happened objectively and fairly.

In *Hiroshima*, Kurahara directed re-enacted Japanese segments of the film and his
stylized and methodical direction adds a new layer to the film, by way that cinematically
and technically it is distinctly Japanese in mood and feel. Though this is at odds in style
and execution to the rest of the film, it ultimately works as Kurahara gives the viewer a
better understanding of the intricacies of the Japanese war machine and how the peace
fraction in the Japanese cabinet were eventually drowned out, despite sympathies from the
emperor. The film clearly shows that despite their protestations, they are rendered ultimately
impotent as the Japanese military went hell-bent on adopting its "Basic Policy for the Future
Conduct and War," whose manifesto was for all Japanese nationals between the ages of 15
and 50 to commit national *seppuku* in its defense of its homeland. Surrender was not an
option in a country where death was seen as honorable and the emperor was revered as a

deity. As Kurahara brilliantly shows, a peaceful solution would only be accepted by the Japanese on their terms, which they naively tried to mediate through the Soviets, terms which we see in the U.S. segments as unacceptable and not in line with the surrender conditions drawn up at Potsdam. When the bombing of Hiroshima does arrive, Kurahara shows a confused government still entrenched in their desire for a bloody land battle with General Anami espousing that millions of American servicemen will die at sea, on the beaches and on land. It is only when the Soviets declare war

Hiroshima director Roger Spottiswoode (courtesy Roger Spottiswoode).

on Japan that the government realize the game is up. In capturing the last flickering embers of the war cabinet before their surrender, Kurahara is supported by a series of fine performances from his fellow countrymen. The acting by Naohiko Umewaka as the emperor, Tatsuo Matsumura (of cult favorites *Harakiri* 1962 and *Samurai Rebellion,* 1967) as Prime Minister Suzuki and Ken Maeda as General Anami, are uniformly excellent which help elevate the film to that of a masterwork.

Naohiko Umewaka gives a sublime performance as Emperor Hirohito, in Roger Spottiswoode's and Koreyoshi Kurahara's brilliant docudrama *Hiroshima* (courtesy Roger Spottiswoode).

Hiroshima, while being a co-production with Canada, and featuring a heavily Western presence in production, is still an important film in the arsenal of Japanese atomic cinema. With funding coming partly from Japan, Kurahara directing the Japanese scenes with his own crew and a host of stalwarts from the Japanese film industry and acclaimed *Black Rain* (*Kuroi ame*, 1989) writer Toshirō Ishidō gaining co-writing credits with John Hopkins, the film is as much a Japanese film as it is a Western film, despite the fact that the film has had very little exposure in Japan. Whether this has been attributed to the sensitive matter of Japan's failure to own up to its colonial past and wrongdoings during the war, one can only speculate. For Kurahara, this must have been a shame for domestically the film has never had any significant distribution. The opposite is true for Kurahara's other foray into the *Genbakudan* genre, focusing his cinematic lens previously on the repercussions and legacy the bombings had on ordinary Japanese people. In the tragic *A Record of Love and Death* (*Ai to shi no kiroku*, 1966), Kurahara tells a story of the doomed romance of a *Hibakusha* survivor and his lover, who is played by actress Sayuri Yoshinaga. Not widely seen outside of Japan, this Nakkatsu film charts the relationship of Kazue and Yukio who are brought together after Yukio accidentally knocks her over outside the music shop where she works. Drawn together, the two become close but Yukio harbors a secret: he is a *Hibakusha* who developed radiation poisoning when he was four; it soon transpires that he also an orphan to the bomb (both his parents were killed in the bombing). When the radiation effects take hold of him once more, Kazue wills Yukio to recover, but to no avail. With Yukio's passing, Kazue makes the ultimate self-sacrifice by following her lover into death. Such downbeat *Hibakusha* romances were played out in other Japanese films such as *A Story of Pure Love* (*Jun'ai monogatari*, 1957) by Imai Tadashi.

While the Japanese segments add a degree of classiness to the film, the plaudits for the final work should go to Roger Spottiswoode for steering the whole enterprise into a cohesive and flawless work. Clearly Spottiswoode realized when tackling a subject such as the atomic bombings with a limited budget a different tact was required. Seeking to make a film that was not only historically factual but equally not diluted due to the constraints opposed on him through lack of finance, his solution was to infuse the film with found documentary news footage and staged scenes. This masterstroke sees Spottiswoode blur the lines from what is real and what is not. So engrossed the viewer becomes into the film, he or she sometimes forget that he or she is watching Kenneth Welsh playing Truman and not Harry Truman himself. So realistic is the film at times that one almost feel as if Spottiswoode and Kurhahra, to some degree, were actually there and filming the discussions of both parties. Spottiswoode also deserves credit for eliciting such a wonderful performance from Welsh as Truman and for creating an element of sympathy for his character. He highlights the magnitude of pressure Truman was under to make a decision and rightly points out that Truman was moved to act by the need to bring about the end of the war and he had no real understanding of the true horrors of what lay in store for nuclear bombing.

In May 2014, I had the pleasure of interviewing Roger Spottiswoode for this collection and to talk about his experiences making *Hiroshima* and what compelled him to make the film. I thank him for his generosity in giving up so much of his time for this book. It is a film that he is rightly proud of and one that will be considered a vital addition to Western and Japanese cinema's depiction of atomic bombings on film.

Matthew Edwards: *Let's start by talking a little about your background as a filmmaker? Readers will recognize you as the director of many cinematic favorites such as Tom Hanks'*

Turner and Hooch, Terror Train, Tomorrow Never Dies, Air America *and the editor on* Sam Peckinpah's Straw Dogs *and* Pat Garrett and Billy the Kid. *How did you get involved in filmmaking?*

Roger Spottiswoode: I started out making commercials and I grew up in a film household. My father made documentaries and moved to Canada in 1940 to make propaganda movies to encourage America into the war. He did make some films but the Japanese took care of that, before very much was done, with Pearl Harbor. So I grew up watching lots of documentaries and because I didn't get along with my father, I went into a different career mission making commercial features. And then I found myself making films like *And the Band Played On* and *Hiroshima*, which had documentary elements to them.

How did you get involved in Hiroshima?

I was approached by Showtime Network to make a film about Hiroshima, starting from the time Truman and Suzuki took office, which was around the same time [Editor's note: Harry S Truman was elected to office April 12, 1945, and Kantarō Suzuki on April 7, 1945]. So it was very easy to tell a story about the main characters and their motives for dropping the bomb. I found this very interesting, especially through our research of their letters and diaries. Was it about the Russians? Was it to stop an invasion? How did it come about? I also had to ask myself, "Who else is going to get a chance to do this?" So I decided to add the Japanese perspective to the story which I felt was essential. So we approached the Japanese director Koreyoshi Kurahara to direct the Japanese segments of the film. He was a very, very nice man. Sadly he is dead now.

Was Hiroshima *a personal and emotional film to make for Kurahara? He lived through the war and was indoctrinated to fight to death, like many people were by the Japanese government. Elements in the war cabinet were prepared for a national seppuku or self-sacrifice, weren't they?*

Hiroshima was a very personal film for Kurahara and he felt it was his last opportunity to make something about the war. He was indoctrinated to fight to the death, you're right. He told me so many stories connected to the war and the atomic bombings, which we brought into the movie. The Japanese thought white protected you from the atomic blasts, which is not explained in the film. There is a scene in the film where the Japanese are wearing white sheets. It is so mystic and strange. When he was fifteen years old, he was in a regiment training to be a *kamikaze*. Imagine training to be a *kamikaze*! He told me he was being prepared, like modern day jihadists, to be a suicide bomber. He was going to be buried on the beaches, breathing only through a bamboo pipe. When the tanks arrived on the beach he would have been expected to jump out of the sand and jump on the tank and detonate their grenades. He would have died on the beaches. Only the Japanese defeat and age saved him, he said that to me. It was a great dishonor at the same time, but he survived because of it. He is a great director and took on the Japanese side and did it very well, indeed. I find his side is far more interesting than our side.

How was the film received in Japan? It was a Japanese-Canadian co-production as well?

The film was only played once in Japan, after midnight. It was a Canadian and Japanese co-production and part of the co-production treaty was the screenings. At the Japanese screening I don't think anybody watched it which is unacceptable.

I find it strange that Hiroshima *was a Japanese co-production yet they tried to "hide" the film. From my personal experience of living in Japan, they have a tendency to forget or not teach about their past wrongdoings.*

They have never acknowledged what they did in China. They killed over ten million people, by hand. It was not done in concentration camps where you could pretend not to know about it. It was done publicly, with everyone participating in beheadings and machine gunning. It was horrific.

The younger generations have no idea about what happened during World War II as the Japanese government censors this part of history.

You're right and the same applies to China. They know all about Japan but they don't know that Mao killed more people than Hitler and Stalin.

So the film hasn't had any repeated viewings in Japan?

No. I screened the film at the University of Toronto. I went to a meeting about Hiroshima there. The cultural attaché was there and asked to see the film, so I sent it to him. He sent me a very nice note afterwards. It is a hard film. It really is. Japan has become a slightly different country but not completely.

And the Japanese have only shown it once, in a midnight showing?

Yes, as far as I know. I had a couple of wonderful Canadian producers in Robin Spry and Cellin Gluck who helped get behind the picture here in the West.

Hiroshima *is what you have called a docudrama. What do you mean by that?*

I feel *Hiroshima* is essentially a documentary and we filled in the missing parts of the documentary with renditions of what happened. We made it historically accurate. There is no added drama. I tried to recreate a timeline of events and meetings from both sides and interweave into that the use of real-life interviews and documentary footage in order to tell a wider story. We also wanted to tell the Japanese side, so we got in touch with Koreyoshi Kurahara to direct those scenes. They did it their way, though completely fact-based and non-biased. I must say, Kurahara's footage was very Japanese and shot more rigidly than I had asked [laughs].

Did you encounter any difficulties marrying your directing styles and visions when making the film? The final results would indicate not as you both seem to blend your respective angles well.

The biggest difficulty was process of *mokusatsu* because you can have a meeting, as would happen frequently, and a translator would be sitting beside me in this meeting interpreting and we would agreeing to something after discussing it at length. And then we say "well we thought we had agreed to it," and we would work out from the Japanese side that it was an absolute no. They will never say no. They never do. And that happened all the time. The language difficulties, no, it's not language its cultural difficulties. I hoped we tried to illuminate a little bit of the complexity of this cultural difficulty in the film with the *mokusatsu* story. It is true that when Prime Minister Suzuki says *mokusatsu* to the troops he didn't understand how the radio worked. That was one of the things that became clear in the letters we read as part of the research for the film. It was fascinating. It was weird because Suzuki never really understood the radio. So here was this guy in Japan who had no idea if he was on the radio to the Japanese troops he could be listened to by the Americans and then they would misinterpret *mokusatsu*. Anyway, it was fascinating trying to portray the complexity of how they felt differently. Some of them would have surrendered. The foreign secretary would have done, the prime minister would have done as would the head of the navy. But, Anami was never going to and he was in charge.

There is a scene that I didn't shoot that came out of two sets of diaries, which I deeply regret. I can't even remember why ... actually, I didn't shoot it as I felt they were too jokey; too offensive. But I was wrong. It really happened. After the emperor said they were going to surrender, after that meeting, they filed out and three people went into the men's room. These three: the minister of the navy [Mitsumasa Yonai], the foreign secretary [Shigenori Tōgō] and next to the foreign secretary was Anami. And Anami said to the one either side of him, "The American navy is in the harbor, right now! They are coming. I've held back the planes. I haven't used the planes." Which he didn't, he never protected the cities. He was saving them for the invasion. So he had the gasoline and the planes and he said, "I'm going to take out the navy this afternoon." And the foreign secretary said, "Are you out of your mind? Did you not just hear the emperor say that we have surrendered?" And Anami said, "Yes. And when we have taken out the navy he'll have to reconsider because we'll be back at war with them and now they won't have a navy and we'll be ahead. That's the way we got to go." And the head of the navy said to Anami, "If I was the Americans and I had a third bomb I would drop it on us, right now." I guess they ended up telling him that. Anami didn't end up committing suicide until the next day.

Which is depicted in the film, isn't it?
   That's right.

The style of the film is very effective in that you create a rich tapestry of staged re-enactments combined with documentary footage and first hand testimonies of witnesses recounting their personal stories of the war. Why did you adopt this docudrama approach for the film? Was it budgetary reasons?
   We knew, or we hoped, there was a lot of footage. We started a little research and realized there was more footage than most people had seen. So we proportioned a lot of money to that. I also thought that there were things that we would never be able to reproduce well. We looked at old war films, and they do it fairly well, but they really can't do what we do. So we incorporated a lot of footage that had not been seen before. I did think that we could create a world by using old footage that would be more convincing than a one we would put into a film if we could somehow blend the two together, like Woody Allen had done in *Zelig*. Although I didn't think we could do it quite as sophisticated as we didn't have the budget. But we wanted to do something like it and I think we found a way to do it. We found this documentary footage before we shot—a lot of it, not all of it—we knew what we had. We could bring people into the meetings and then have our actors do the meetings and then have them come out and they are all relating to the same thing, because we could identify what happened in the meetings. So it emerged as a possible way of doing it on a wider canvas and we could find a form that did not have to be so big to produce, which immediately limits you and makes it a more difficult production and less believable.

I thought the differing styles worked effectively. For example, your real footage of Truman walking into a meeting room and then cut to the staged footage inside was really effective.
   In the introduction, just to play with the form, we showed you both people all the time [Truman and Kenneth Welsh as Truman]. All the way through the film you see real footage of Truman which we couldn't have shown had we not included the documentary footage.

In Hiroshima *you use firsthand testimonies that are interwoven into the film's narrative? Who filmed these? Both you and Kurahara?*

No, I was present at a couple but Matthew Asner did most of these testimonies. He is a very nice documentary filmmaker who came aboard the film and part of our team and did a remarkable job. We came across these people who we knew were survivors who had these remarkable stories to tell. And I like *Reds* enormously. The people who give the history in that film are very effective. I thought we can take off our hats to Warren Beatty and do the same. We shot a lot of film. We have wonderful footage that has never been used and I've always wanted to use it. We have the best two hour film on the survivors of the atomic bombings. Well, I could have if I can find someone willing to edit it.

Do you think you will ever get the opportunity to complete it?

I've been trying to get a university to do it. I need a film school to do it because it will take a while and we can't get anyone to put up a lot of money for the project. The people who will want it will be the Smithsonians and libraries. This is something people should be able to see in fifty years' time to know what the bomb is really like. It is part of our collective history. But you have to understand that it is hard to make a program on this now. It is hard to finance it commercially. So it has to be funded some other way.

I thought the bombing sequence of Hiroshima was expertly put together. The scene builds up a sense of dread and tension and ultimately sadness as we witness the tragic force of the bombs. Were you pleased with the way you handled this scene?

You always think you should have done things better, but it was a very strange experience having the *Enola Gay* there on set. It was flown up to Montreal and we had it for a week. It is an ugly and unpleasant plane and the people who brought it to us didn't like it either, because of its history and because it is a dreadful plane. It doesn't work well and it is lethal. You can't parachute out of it. You have to take your parachute off to get out of the window. You have to take your parachute off to get out of the escape hatch. So there is no chance of standing on a wing of a plane and putting your parachute on. The pilots hated it and everyone loathed it. So it was an odd thing, but having the real plane there, and knowing what happened, made it interesting and I somehow had to dramatize that more and make a big scene out of it and also make clear that the people who dropped the bomb didn't really understand what they were doing. I wanted to show how this monstrous thing had come about and how it had to been done. Truman, I do believe, felt he had to drop the bomb. He got sick of losing more and more people. I just wanted to try and make everything human.

Some of the crew did express remorse after the bombings.

We tried to get that across in the film. We also have interviews with people below like the young boy who became a doctor because of his experiences in Hiroshima. That is an amazing story. It was an effort to try and make sure we had a clear view of what happened on both sides.

The documentary footage you used in the film of the destruction of the bomb on Hiroshima and Nagasaki, and the injuries inflicted on its peoples, is particularly moving and graphic. Did you feel that it was essential to not flinch when exposing the brutality of war and the effects of the atomic bombings or did you assert some restraint?

Absolutely. There is lots of disturbing imagery, but it is the most disturbing event of the twentieth century. One should know what it was. My goodness, we only showed three or four minutes in the whole three hour film. One does feel you need to show this. I don't think we over did it? Remember, the film was made at the end of the Cold War and there were still people sitting around suggesting that we should nuke them all, the *Strangelove* thing. This was made not long after the Berlin Wall had come down. The Right was still of the opinion that we should blow up people if necessary.

Kenneth Welsh is brilliant as Harry Truman.

Yes, isn't he!

What was it like working with him on the film and how did he get involved in the project?

He's a delightful actor and looks very much like him [Truman]. It was the first time he played Truman and repeated the role in the television series *Haven*. He really wanted to do a good job and he really worked at it and he was terrific. He had great compassion for Truman and we gave him a lot of research to read, the ad libs in the script, he read the books and looked at the tapes. He's wonderful. As soon as I heard his voice I knew he was right for this part.

I thought he was great. Both Welsh and Timothy West, as Churchill, played their roles well.

They did, as did Wesley Addy who plays Stimson. He was marvelous. With his silences, and when he doesn't comment very much he was eloquent in the extreme. He disapproved of everything. He was generous to Truman but so deeply disliked what was being said and done. I tried to get the scene with Byrnes going without much dialogue and I think they both did it. They were both very good. I was incredibly lucky. The Canadians allowed me to bring in many Americans, a lot more than we would normally have on a Canadian production. They made exceptions for that role.

The film throws up many important questions such how we place enormous powers in hands of individual people, of which both U.S. and Japan were guilty of. It is interesting the scene when the voice of reason, Leo Szilard is brushed off quickly.

It is one of the remarkable moments about that piece of history. Szilard really invented the bomb. He sent his notes off to Einstein and he talked to him and said, "Yes, it works." Szilard is one of the fathers of the bomb and he absolutely understood, and imagined, the Cold War and what would happen if it was even tested. Let me go sideways for a moment. One of the things that I found fascinating making this film was that I had imagined that we would come up with an answer as to why the bomb was used. Was it the Russians? Was it this, was it fear of them? Was it fear of this or that? What was the answer? Was it cynical? I honestly thought there would be an answer. What began to emerge from the research was almost everything was true but they were concurrent truths. There were people who were afraid of this, there were people who didn't give a shit about Japan but who wanted to drop the bomb just to scare the Russians. There was Truman wanting this and Szilard who didn't believe in dropping the bomb and had to be diverted away. It is possible, or maybe it is just me, that much of history is like this. We look for single answers to things. Why did this happen? What was the actual reason? And the real reason doesn't exist as there are multiple things going on at the same time. It is a very fluid situation and it is very hard to pin down what was exactly the main reason or voice that was the loudest. Obviously, Byrnes in a way. Yet what can you say about Byrnes? He was probably a horrible man. Yet America survived and Hitler didn't because when Byrnes took office, a long time before Truman, he became responsible for arming the army. Roosevelt gave him the job of making sure they had enough tanks. He somehow got hold of the German weapons, or information on German weaponry, and understood what no one in the American army would say that the German weapons were better. He was an enormously cold-hearted and tough character and he said that the German's had a much better army, better soldiers and better weapons and we will never catch up. But he saw that America could out produce the Germans on people and weapons by 20:1, not 10:1 nor 5:1. So this cold, ruthless character who later insisted on using the bomb and slowly cut off all the escape hatches in the debates did not in the end make the final choice because Truman did prevent him from doing that. What I'm trying to say that it is complicated. One can demonize people but at the same time they weren't have got that far without them.

I think you achieve that. In the film you don't set out to demonize anyone. You play the film simply as this is what happens in chronological order without passing too much judgment. It would have been easy to demonize the Japanese and take the stance that the bomb had to be dropped to prevent a land invasion.

Who knows if the Japanese were right? The Japanese believed, and I think they were right, that if they had managed to kill over a million Americans on the beaches, America would have sued for peace. At some point, during the first landings, all these people would have died and they would have said that you can have Asia and we'll have the West. It's hard to second guess all of that. Would we be happy if Hitler was still over in Germany? Would we have settled? America argues now whether they should have killed 200,000 Japanese when maybe only 100,000 Americans would have died. That's what American generals thought their losses would be if they invaded Japan. The Japanese sensed the losses they could incur on America would have been much heavier and far more accurate. That was the surprising part of our research. That was what the Japanese military was figuring out and the amount of training that they were doing for girls and young men like Kurahara to become *kamikaze*, meant that it was no longer just planes or torpedoes it was a whole Jihadist culture going on in Japan which the Americans were unaware of at the time and which they would have discovered at a huge cost when Americans, Australians and Canadians tried to land in Japan. That's a hard thing that even historians today aren't debating, but we were, partly through our footage and partly through very, very good research through private diaries and letters and digging up more than what was in the books.

Because I made *And the Band Played On*, it taught me that dates are incredibly important. If you can figure out the exact order of what people knew when and dramatize it, or put documentary footage together, it is very interesting because one doesn't always have that clearly. It is through history books that we learn this but once we see it on film it is incredibly compelling. I did it for *And the Band Played On*. Look at what Reagan said. We put Reagan footage into that film and it is devastating. We know that he knew. Now we understand the history of AIDS and we know that he was told and his comments are appalling. At the time it was hard to say that because they seemed insensitive and no one seemed to really know what was going on. They really show what was going on at the CDC (*The Centers for Disease Control*). I know they spoke to the government and this wasn't always published. The head of the government knew what was going on. Then war becomes very interesting and that was true of Hiroshima.

One of the most memorable sequences in the film is when Truman is having breakfast on the war ship Augusta *and announces to the crew the attack on Hiroshima, where he describes it as "the greatest thing in history." Shortly after we see the tragic consequences of his actions making his words sound exceedingly hollow. I felt that was a powerful moment in the film. Was that your intention?*

Yes, he says those things in the film because he said them. That is word for word what he said. Actually, his actual lines were not shown but we got all that extremely accurate and a lot of the stuff on the Augusta is real footage, not all of it, but everything is true. Later in the film we see them seeing the first photographs, do you remember?

Yes, I do.

He can't face showing them to anyone. And Stimson says, "I wish the world never had to know about this." And Byrnes is saying "we should show people where we spend our money." I think it is a wonderful scene but it is about all of those issues and I think in the heat of the moment they knew they had ended the war. On Augusta, Truman's grandiose has not really understood the implications and I think that is fair comment. Yet he is deeply affected later when he knows what it was but I think also deeply unrepentant. I'm sure he had terrible sorrow for having to do that but he did believe he was saving lives, which he was.

That leads on to question that people are quick to criticize Truman and America for dropping the bomb. Is it wrong for historians to question the motives of men who lived through a war we never had to endure?

I must say that I ended up having quite a bit of sympathy for him because how does one stop the war? Right now we've got Hawks trying to say Obama should go back to war again with Iraq. This is insane! How does one end a war, particularly World War II, as there were so many people dead? And it was still going on and all Truman's generals were planning an invasion of Japan and that was the only way to stop them. Basically, the fanatics were in charge [of Japan]; people who believed in national suicide of a country with a hundred million people.

They look upon the emperor in Japan as a deity in Japan and if he had said "fight to the death," the Japanese would have done so.

You're right, and they were fighting to the death. Everyone now says that the Americans should have offered a way out sooner and that the Japanese would have surrendered sooner, but I don't know. If they had started negotiating with the Japanese I don't think they would have gotten anywhere. At the same time, they were wise enough to retain the emperor. One can argue about that as he was a war criminal. He had gone to China and killed about ten million people. That is a colossal number.

I tried to interview the emperor's brother for the film. I did interview him during a long meeting with him where I tried to persuade him to be one of the voices [one of the talking heads in the film]. I offered him the end of the film. I knew the brother had gone to China, that had been made clear through several letters, and that he disapproved of what was going on there. People were being murdered on an incredible scale. The military was furious with him and had him sent back in disgrace to Japan. We had an introduction and we talked for an hour or two and I said to him about this clear evidence of his not approving of what had happened [in China] and would he like to add to that, or comment on it now for history? He didn't dispute what I was saying. He just said, "Well, I don't know about whether one can add to history. Anyway, if you film me you can edit it." And I said, "Well, that is true. But I will give you an absolute contract between the company and you and your lawyers and we will not cut anything. We will give you whatever you need; one or two or three rolls of film. And we will not put a pair of scissors to it, or we will allow you to make the cuts. We would be very happy to do that." We felt he would add to the film, but sadly in the end he wouldn't do it. I thought it was a long shot, but sadly there are still so many people in Japan who believe they have nothing to apologize for and that they were doing the right thing and that they didn't complete the job.

Look what happens when Japanese prime ministers, like Shinzo Abe's in 2013, visit to pay their respects at the controversial Yasukuni Shrine, which honors World War II criminals and soldiers. This invariably stokes up anger from China and South Korea and widespread condemnation from the global community. Yet sadly, Japanese people don't necessarily understand what went on during the war as they aren't taught about their past in schools. It is hidden and that's a frightening part of it, I think.

Well it is. You're absolutely right. Actually, what is interesting is that I did a film in China…

The Children of Huang Shi *with Chow Yun Fat?*

Yes. In rural China in all the schools we visited they know about Stalin, Lenin and of course Hitler. All the people we now know to be war criminals. We now know that Mao killed more people than Stalin and more than Hitler. In the famine he killed seventy million Chinese; consciously and knowingly. Yet nowhere in the Chinese school books is this acknowledged. There was a great famine in China in the sixties but this was attributed to natural causes. You cannot meet a Chinese person outside government, or in government, for that matter, who knows the real truth. Chinese people's knowledge of their own history is incredible. They know a lot about what Japan did during the war but they don't know what Mao did. So both Asian countries live a complete lie.

Hiroshima *is a film you are very proud of, isn't it? Are you pleased with the final results and is there anything you would change?*

I would like people to keep on viewing the film. If I could, I would go back and shoot one or two missing scenes, one of which I mentioned earlier. There are a couple of others. I would probably have a slightly longer version. I know it is hard to watch as it is [laughs], but I am pleased with it. Many people made it and it is an enormous collective work, so I'm proud of it but in a very collective way. Kurahara's direction and the Japanese footage I feel is extraordinary and terrific. He absolutely made that. The script is a wonderful thing. I just wish we could have shot a little bit more.

Can you find any justification for the dropping of the bombs, especially Nagasaki?

I think I believe what the film shows that General Anami would have gone on had the emperor not have stopped. No question they would have gone on after Hiroshima, which they did. Nothing changed. The military would have gone on after Nagasaki. The Japanese were right. At that point America only had two bombs—well they had three but one was used in the desert [Trinity site at the Alamogordo Bombing and Gunnery Range]. Eventually I think the Japanese would have lost, but more people would have died. I don't know whether they would have gotten around to an invasion. I don't know. I don't know how to fault people who are there to try and prevent more losses on your side. Where is their responsibility to the people who started this? The Japanese during the war were mass murderers; a country that massacred China and behaved appallingly in Burma. People were dying…. I don't know how you can rationally say that they didn't have the right to stop the war immediately. I think it is second guessing to say that this should have never happened. I think it is a tragedy that the bombings had to happen.

I see this also from a slightly different perspective. It is not in the film but during the process of finding documentary footage for *Hiroshima* I came across a treasure trove of footage from an airbase in America. When the Russians took Berlin they went into the *Reichstag*, and all the ministries, and took everything out. Everything. They took every picture, every sculpture, every paperclip, every document and every piece of film. They found all sorts of home movies that the generals took of slaughtering Jews and people who they shot from this, or that, massacre. There were Hollywood movies that Hitler watched in the evenings. The Russians took everything out. They put it—all the documents/films—somewhere in Moscow and did very little with it. Though, they did look through it. The Americans did the same with the Japanese. The War Ministry took everything from Japan and filed it and put it away in creates. In 1994, the people in charge of the security of these documents—a very enterprising person, a military officer in charge of its safe keeping—started looking at the documents for the first time in 48 years. He knew it was in danger of being destroyed when it was 50 years old. What he discovered from the War Ministry wasn't just documents but home movies by the Japanese. Japanese soldiers took 8mm cameras with them and they filmed stuff and sent it home where it was confiscated by the Japanese military police. They would look at it and then it would be deposited by the government into their vaults and not sent onto the families. We saw some of this footage and it is awful. It is an army of occupation having fun killing people. It is very hard to watch that kind of stuff and keep a balanced view. You know that footage can never be shown because there is no reason to make the Chinese even more upset, by reminding them. It won't help anyone. During war, terrible things happen—no doubt on both sides. However, trying to end a war is extremely difficult. They ended it in the only way they knew how. Mixed motives, I'm sure. But at the same time, after the war America gave out an enormous amount of money and treasure to help rebuild Japan. They did, unlike our politician's now. They put Japan back in a way that it has now become a democratic nation which has been peaceful, like Germany.

It is very hard to judge people. We know the positives are very good and whether the negative part was unnecessary or an adversary? I didn't know going into the film. I saw the film represents—and it's not my point of view—it has become my point of view, I didn't chose that footage for a reason; that is what we found. It makes it clear that Truman does drop the bomb and celebrates it, which is awful to watch. But it shows how Stimson absolutely hated the idea and that it was wrong in every way and that Byrnes was a sort of a monster. It is very complicated and it is the best I could do and I still stand by it. That's kind of what happened and I'm not in a position to judge it. Whilst I can see all sides to the argument, with regard to whether using the bomb was right or wrong, I'm just grateful that I didn't have to be there to make that decision.

White Light/Black Rain: The "Atomic Films" of Steven Okazaki

Matthew Edwards

Few American filmmakers have been willing to tackle the subject of the atomic bombings and depict the horror and tragedy of one of darkest moments in human history. Yet Steven Okazaki, a Japanese-American by birth, has dared to delve his documentary lens into the realms where few choose to look. His Hiroshima and Nagasaki trilogy makes Steven Okazaki as one of the crucial documentarians in the West on the subject in the last thirty years. Unbiased, non-politicized, balanced: his moving films brim with a quite sadness and fury at the suffering endured by the Japanese *Hibakusha* and the dangers of nuclear warfare. His films do not look to attribute blame just an overriding sense that such an atrocity, whether morally right or wrong, cannot be repeated. *Survivors* (1982) and the Academy Award nominee *The Mushroom Club* (1985) deal with the lives of those Japanese, and Japanese Americans, damaged by the bombs and who continue to suffer social discrimination and psychological issues as they come to terms with their physical and emotional scars as they wrestle with the trauma inflicted on their psyche and person. *White Light/Black Rain* (2007), Okazaki's Emmy and Sundance nominated documentary, is a brilliant and harrowing film that once again reminds us that the events on August 6 and 9, 1945, should not be forgotten. The film has won numerous plaudits and has proven Steven Okazaki as one of America's most vital and important filmmakers working in the medium today.

I contacted Steven in May 2014, and he so generously gave up a huge amount of his time to be interviewed for this book. I am very grateful for his kindness and all his effort in making this interview come to fruition.

Matthew Edwards: *What is your background in film? How did you get involved in documentary film/television?*

Steven Okazaki: Since childhood, I wanted to be an artist, a painter, but I changed my mind when I was about to start college and decided to study film. I felt it would force me out of my cocoon and push me out into the world more. After college, I just wanted to make films, any kind of films, any genre. I didn't have any connections in Hollywood and I wasn't keen on spending years working my way from third assistant to second assistant, so I stayed in San Francisco and starting making documentaries.

Your film Survivors *(1982) tackles the problems encountered by* Hibakusha *victims and the trauma and psychological effects inflicted on them on both a personal and social level. What prompted you to make a documentary about these survivors?*

My sister was taking a class at San Francisco State University and was writing on a paper on Hiroshima and Nagasaki survivors living in the United States. Many Japanese Americans have roots in Hiroshima, and many American servicemen married women from Nagasaki, so there were a fair number of atomic bomb survivors living in the U.S. My sister dropped the class, but I got interested. I was very taken by these nice 50-year-old Japanese women who had survived one of the most horrible events in human history.

Also, at that time, many films had been made about the making of and the decision to use the atomic bomb, but the films all featured scientists, historians and military experts, but no people who experienced the bomb first-hand. This seemed arrogant and racist to me.

Was it harrowing for the participants to recall their memories of the Hiroshima and Nagasaki bombings? As a Japanese-American filmmaker, was this an emotional experience for you too?

I met two *Hibakusha* (atomic bomb survivors), both men, one in Los Angeles, the other in the Bay Area, who were unhinged by their experience. They were crazy. They went through so much horror as children, they couldn't process what they experienced. They were both erratic, nervous, couldn't hold jobs, couldn't lead normal lives. Both of them poured out their stories the moment I met them, but then when I tried to arrange to film them, they became paranoid and refused to talk. So it's important to remember with my documentary (and others) that it's about the people who survived, not just physically, but emotionally.

But everyone else was eager to talk. Most of them never had an opportunity to share what they'd been through. When they were younger, they didn't want to burden others with all that terror and pain. And when they were older, the people around them, their spouses and children, avoided the subject. Of course, it's always on their minds, it's not something easily forgotten. So when we arrived wanting to know everything, the stories just come out.

I felt honored to hear their stories. I've interviewed hundreds of *Hibakusha* and I am always fascinated and moved.

The Mushroom Club was more of personal journey into the atomic bombings. What was the genesis for tackling the subject again?

I wasn't happy with *Survivors*. I didn't have the filmmaking skill or emotional maturity to make it when I did, and I promised myself that I would return to the subject someday. In the meantime, I visited Hiroshima whenever I could and collected stories, talked to people, spent hours doing research in the Peace Museum and sitting in the Peace Park just thinking about it.

I was planning to make an ambitious, as comprehensive as possible, feature-length documentary for the 50th anniversary of the bombing in 1995, but then the Japanese and American funding for the project was cancelled at the last minute, so I wasn't able to do the film.

I was very disappointed. And when the 60th anniversary of the bombing approached I decided I couldn't rely on any big foundations or TV networks for funding and I just took my Sony digital camcorder to Hiroshima and starting filming with the help of my wife, Peggy Orenstein, and my friend, Tomoko Watanabe. The film was short and done for very little money, but it was something.

How did you find Yuriko Hatanaka and the other members of the Kinoko Kai? Her story is heart-breaking and reveals the true wretchedness of atomic warfare and the impact the bombing has had on future generations of Japanese citizens?

In the 1960s, RCC-TV, a local TV station in Hiroshima, made a short documentary called *The Small-Headed Children*, about babies exposed to radiation in-utero. I saw the film, learned that the parents of the children had formed a club called *Kinoko Kai* (*The Mushroom Club*) to lobby for help from the Japanese government, and I went to meet Mr. Hatanaka who was the leader of the group. He was incredibly kind and patient, taking care of his daughter who was 55 years old, but with the mental and physical capacities of an infant.

I understand that White Light/Black Rain *was originally envisaged ten years previously but both your American and Japanese backers reneged on the project. Why was this? Were they concerned that the documentary would potentially be viewed negatively towards them? How frustrating was this for you?*

I was devastated to realize that 50 years after the bombings the story was still being censored. Neither funder told me directly why they were backing out, they just did it, but it was obvious. The American funder backed out when veterans groups started applying political pressure, wanting to eliminate the point of view of the *Hibakusha*. And the Japanese funder thought I was too critical of the way the Japanese government treated the *Hibakusha*, after the war and now.

You finally found support through HBO, who have supported what could be described as a challenging film as the topic is still emotive for American audiences. Can you tell us about the film's production? I understand you met with over 500 atomic survivors and interviewed over 100. How did you eventually choose the 14 that were featured in the film?

I had completely given up on making my dream documentary about Hiroshima and

Promotional release of Steve Okazaki's Emmy nominated documentary *White Light/Black Rain: The Destruction of Hiroshima and Nagasaki* (courtesy Steve Okazaki).

Nagasaki. But I wanted to do something to mark the 60th anniversary of the bombing so I made *The Mushroom Club*, a small personal film, a token of my appreciation to the people in Hiroshima who had been so kind to me over the years. And while I was putting the last finishing touches to *The Mushroom Club*, I got the call from HBO. The president of documentary programming, Sheila Nevins, said she wanted me to make an ambitious, comprehensive film on Hiroshima and Nagasaki, and I was like "What? Well, I'm making this little film called *The Mushroom Club*." And she said, "Great, we'll help you finish that, and then you can make the big film." So it was HBO that instigated the project, not me. At that time, HBO was producing a big dramatic series about World War II in the Pacific, from the American side, and I think she wanted to show another side of the war. It was Sheila that made it happen. I had given up.

But, as I noted, I had been thinking about it for twenty years, so when HBO said, "Go, do it," I thought about it for one more day, then hit the start button. Sometimes, when you're making a documentary there's this wonderful momentum that pushes you through the production and that's how it was with *White Light/Black Rain*. People in Hiroshima and Nagasaki were so excited about the film, there was so much energy coming at me, I just caught the wave and filmed and edited and filmed and edited, and nine months later the film was done.

The interviewees? Well, from 1980 to 2005 I had talked, formally and informally, to about five hundred *Hibakusha*, extraordinary people with incredible stories. But by the time we made the film the majority of them had died. So I pre-interviewed a hundred new *Hibakusha* for *White Light/Black Rain*. The only survivors I knew from before were Keiji Nakazawa and Shigeko Sasamori, who as one of the Hiroshima Maidens and now lives in Los Angeles.

For the fourteen *Hibakusha* in film, I looked for different personalities and different experiences. I wanted some specific things. Since Catholicism is an important part of the Nagasaki story, I found two women who were in a Catholic orphanage at the time of the bombing. It was luck that a friend introduced me to Dr. Hida, who was a young Army doctor at the time and took care of people immediately after the bombing. I did a lot of casual pre-interviews with groups and individuals, and when you meet the right person you just know it. You say, "Wait, don't tell me anymore until we can film it."

The film is a little unbalanced, favoring Nagasaki survivors. Nagasaki people are very open and direct. I love Hiroshima people, but they are very cautious and polite. They're very conscious of what other people think. Outspoken people in Hiroshima are often criticized for showing off. So most of Hiroshima survivors I interviewed didn't live in Hiroshima and were freer to say what they feel.

When making a film like White Light/Black Rain, *was it difficult not to censor yourself and to not make the film too horrific and intense?*

I've learned a lot about making documentaries from Sheila Nevins. She's inquisitive and fearless. The first very rough cut of *White Light/Black Rain* was kind of poetic. I was very concerned about not upsetting the viewers too much, taking them by the hand through this very difficult story. Sheila challenged me, asked me why I had taken such a gentle approach to such a horrible event. I told her I was worried about people turning the channel as soon as the first black and white footage of the human suffering came on. She told me adamantly not to hold back for the sake of the viewer, that this was my opportunity to tell the truth of what happened without censorship. She told me to "show and tell us everything" and that's what I tried to do. It's painful for people to watch the film, but remarkable how many stay with it. I feel very gratified by how open and responsive people are to the film.

There is a startling moment at the start of White Light/Black Rain, *when you interview a cross section of Japanese youngsters and they are unable to recognize the date of the atomic bombing of Hiroshima? Did this ignorance surprise you? Having lived in Japan and knowing the significance the bombings have in their teaching in Junior High and Senior High education, I was most shocked. For me, it made your documentary even more vital that we must not let future generations forget this tragic moment in history in fear we may repeat it.*

Yes, I was shocked. The Japanese crew was shocked. Nearly everyone who sees the film is shocked. But none of them knew; we didn't cut anyone out. We walked down Takeshita Dori in Harajuku which is where the Junior High school kids flock to on the weekend and not a single person we filmed knew the significance of August 6, 1945. I said, "Okay, that's how we'll open the film."

There's a remarkable scene in the film when you show a clip from This Is Your Life *episode of* Hibakusha *survivor the Rev. Kiyoshi Tanimoto, leader of the Hiroshima Maidens Project, when he meets for the first time Captain Bob Lewis, co-pilot of the* Enola Gay. *It is both a crass yet captivating and moving moment with Captain Lewis seemed genuinely upset and remorseful for his actions.*

Yes, the *Hiroshima Maidens* story is fascinating. Twenty-five young women who went to America for plastic surgery operations in the 1950s. For me, the shocking thing is that they put the two survivors behind a screen so we only see their silhouettes.

At one point, I thought of doing a separate film on the Maidens, but only two were willing to participate. The others felt abused by the Japanese media and public, and didn't want any more attention.

Through researching the film, and when interviewing American servicemen responsible for the atomic bombings, did you encounter genuine remorse for their actions?

No, none of the Americans expressed remorse. I think, if they did, if they took any responsibility for the bombings, it would be more than anyone of them could bear. And I think that's fair. They didn't know about radiation. They were soldiers, following orders to fly the plane and push the button. Their superiors and their government made the decision, not them.

We were lucky to get interviews with four key American participants in the bombings. They're all dead now. They were willing and open to share their stories. Of course, I asked all of them what they felt about all the horror and suffering the bombs caused. Morris Jeppson was the most sympathetic. He clearly had thought about the people who suffered and died, as opposed to blocking it out as the others had. Theodore Van Kirk held to the party line: "It was war, it saved American lives, no regrets, didn't lose a night of sleep over it." He attended one of the screenings of the film and was uncomfortable being on the stage with one of the survivors. Harold Agnew was a scientist and thought like one. It was an exciting experiment for him. Lawrence Johnston, also a scientist, spoke honestly, but guardedly. After the interview, he accused me of setting him up. He said he didn't expect me to be Japanese. I thought some of them might react that way, but felt it would be wrong to tell them in advance that I was Japanese American and that my father fought in Italy, Germany and France with the U.S. Army, to prejudice them one way or the other. My position was that we ask the questions and they answer them however they choose to.

What is interesting about your documentaries is that there is very little anti–American sentiment from Hibakusha *survivors, just the view that atomic warfare should never be repeated. Did this surprise you? Any bitterness seems more directed at the discrimination* Hibakusha *survivors have, and continue to, suffer in Japan.*

I don't think it's possible to live a fulfilling life and feel that much anger and bitterness. It will destroy you, hurt the people around you, taint every good thing in your life, make you crazy. Initially, many survivors hated America, but then Americans arrived in Hiroshima and Nagasaki and they weren't demons. They were people like them, and many of them wanted to help.

Also, the Japanese are very pragmatic. The war was over, they had to find food, rebuild their homes and get on with life. The new mantra was "Peace." Japanese have a lot reverence for that word. And a lot of them are very disturbed that Japan seems to be moving away from it.

In both The Mushroom Club *and* White Light/Black Rain *you interview the late inspirational Manga artist and writer Kenji Nakazawa (Barefoot Gen). His story has had a profound impact on many artists and filmmakers. What memories do you have of working with him on your films?*

I think *Barefoot Gen* is the most important, most powerful, most honest depiction of the Hiroshima bombing. I put it above any other book or film. I have a huge amount of admiration for Nakazawa and I couldn't imagine making the film without him. His testimony was indispensible.

Working with him? Well, he was kind of cranky with me. Totally cooperative, but cranky. I realized later that he would have been much warmer if I had a woman do the interview. My friend Tomoko Watanabe and her daughter Kuniko Watanabe worked with him and told me how kind, funny and warm he was.

How have Japanese audiences responded to your films?

The Japanese response to *White Light/Black Rain* was incredible. It played in hundreds of movie theaters and in Tokyo at Iwanami Hall for four months, sold-out for most of the run. Peace groups, famous artists and movie stars supported it. Then it showed on NHK and got great ratings and repeat broadcasts. There was no censorship.

I was overjoyed by how both the American and Japanese audiences responded to the film. I think both appreciated that the film wasn't manipulative propaganda, that I just let the people who were there tell their stories.

A[nime]-Bomb: An
Interview with *Hibakusha*
Director Steve Nguyen

Matthew Edwards

Anime and the atomic bomb as a spectacle has been a frequent motive used in the post-apocalyptic visions and imaginations of Japanese animators and their creations, as films like *Akira* (1998) and *Barefoot Gen* testify. Yet, one of the most interesting atomic bomb films to emerge in recent years is *Hibakusha* (2012), a short American animated film that chronicles the life of atomic bomb survivor Kaz Suyeishi, and directed by Steve Nguyen and Choz Belan. With a nod to Japanese anime, and the work of Masaaki Yuasa, the film charts the story of Kaz Suyeishi who at the age of 17 experienced the bombing of Hiroshima. Having spent a lifetime talking to audiences about the bombing and the impact, Nguyen and Belan felt compelled to document her life; her story. Their film is a moving and sad portrait of the effects of the bomb and a film that resonates with the need to find peace. The film, like Suyeishi's message, does not pass judgment nor point the finger; it doesn't ask why the bombings happened. What is refreshing about Nguyen's and Belan's vision is that they tackle the aftermath of the bombing and the obliteration of not only the city of Hiroshima, but also its inhabitants and their injuries and scars. These scars, and the legacy of the bomb on *Hibakusha* survivors, on both a physical and psychological basis, are explored during the film which culminates in a brilliant scene when Suyeishi encounters Captain Tibbets in a live TV debate where he is unrepentant of his actions and argues that the dropping of the bomb was necessary to end the war. Overwhelmed by this, Suyeishi collapses. This scene expertly capsulates the impasse this part of history has created over this issue; primarily between Japanese and Americans. In another great sequence, Suyeishi mistakes the *Enola Gay* for a beautiful angle spreading her wings in the sky. Moments later we bare witness to the Angel of Death wreaking misery and destruction on Hiroshima, reducing the city to a red flaming inferno of twisted metal, burning homes and rubble, all beautifully recreated by animators at StudioAPA.

In May 2014, I was fortunate to interview co-director Steve Nguyen about the film and why adapting Suyeishi's story was so important to him. I thank him for the generous amount of time he put into the interview.

Matthew Edwards: *How did you get involved in film animation?*

Steve Nguyen: I've always been a huge graphic novel fan since I was an early teen, so my formative years were spent developing ideas stemming from old Marvel and DC comics.

The first instance that I've used animation was in a documentary series I produced called *L I F E* when I was attending university. Each episode consisted of three to five minutes of animated documentary going into abstract topics. The idea was mostly inspired from Richard Linklater's, *Waking Life*.

Your animated film Hibakusha *charts the early life of atomic bomb survivor Kaz Suyeishi. How did you meet her and what inspired you to commit her story to film?*

I was introduced to Kaz through a family friend about seven years ago while attending a lecture at our temple. Her story about living in Hiroshima during the 1945 atomic bombing was

Co-director Steve Nyugen (courtesy Steve Nyugen).

something I considered making into a graphic novel. It was halfway through the writing process that I realized that this would make for a great film. Animation hadn't even come into the picture until I watched the animated documentaries, *Persepolis* (2007) and *Waltz with Bashir* (2008). The way those memoirs were captured were so visually moving to me that I scrapped my graphic novel idea and decided to commit to an animated film concept with Kaz's memories as the subject of focus.

Was securing finance for the film difficult? The subject matter is still an emotive subject in the U.S.

Mushroom cloud over Hiroshima. APA Studio beautifully captures the ferocity and monstrous scale of the nuclear attack in Steve Nyugen's and Choz Belen's *Hibakusha* **(courtesy Steve Nyugen).**

It was extremely difficult because nobody wants to invest in an animation catered to adults. The most challenging phases during this time were doing the market research, convincing people to fund the film, and filling out the extensive applications. The financing for a majority of the film came from independent donors, crowd sourcing, and the Documentary Channel before they were replaced by Pivot. Once we had established an income stream, the funding came throughout different stages of the production.

American film has generally shied away from the subject of the atomic bombings, especially Hollywood cinema. Why is that? Did you consciously want to readdress this issue?

Our focal point wasn't necessarily the atomic bombings, but more about Kaz's growth as a woman learning to overcome a powerful adversity in her life. We wanted to emphasize the issue of peace as an important theme throughout the film, and less about the war. I felt it was more important to see the struggle in her story rather than the numerous casualties and glorified American pride that most Hollywood war films want to focus on.

In the film, Kaz recalls that the Enola Gay *resembled an angel spreading her wings. It is a very powerful image in the film as this was based on Suyeishi's own recollections of the bombing. Did you feel a sense of importance to get that scene right?*

Whenever you make a very personal film, you want to make sure you get every detail right. Taking one statement from a very personal story and transforming it into a work of art is going to be a challenge. We just wanted to create the angel metaphor in our own light. From there, it's up to the audience and the critics to define it.

The narrative of the film takes place during different time frames? Was this a difficult aspect to incorporate into what is essentially a 40-minute film?

It was definitely complex, but manageable! Once we did the research on the Hiroshima

Angel of Death. Suyeishi mistakes the *Enola Gay* for an angel spreading its wings in the sky. Moments later Hiroshima is reduced to a red flaming inferno of destruction and horror (courtesy Steve Nyugen).

subject matter, we thought it would be creative to take pieces of Kaz's memories from 1945 and weave them throughout her present day recollections like a quilt. It's a common film mechanism that is used quite often.

Talk us through the animation process. How did you achieve the look and feel of the film? Did you visit Hiroshima and the peace dome as research for the film?

Our process was extremely disorganized that it almost drove our art directors and sound engineers nuts. The original rough-cut of our film was about a 20 minutes of live documentary of Kaz speaking vividly about the bombing and what she endured directly afterwards. My co-director, Choz Belen, and I used it as a reference for the animatic phase. We went through an insane journey of taking a year and a half to finish the animation because we decided to alter our script halfway through production. Instead of working on a 20-minute piece with 5 minutes of animation, it eventually evolved into a 45-minute fully animated piece.

Most of our ideas stemmed from graphic novels, and we wanted that to be the essence of *Hibakusha*. We wanted to use real life models to capture the realism of our animation through a modern lens.

As far as research goes, we based the film on multiple consultation from actors, museum patrons, documented photographs, constant communication with other community members, and publications about Japanese-American relations revolving around that time were what we based the film on. I just learned so much from the stories that I heard, and it was incredible to recreate and discover all of these places have still remained intact. A year after we completed the film, I was able to collaborate with the United Nations non-profit organization, Global Zero, for a follow-up documentary titled *Hiroshima Revisited*. It's on YouTube somewhere, but everything that we've covered in the animation was revisited again in this documentary.

Kaz and Asako encounter a solider on Ground Zero (courtesy Steve Nyugen).

Top: Kaz's younger brother Shōzō writhes in pain from his horrific injuries inflicted from the bombing. Nyugen and Belen remind the audience of the physical scars borne by many people as a result of the nuclear blast (courtesy Steve Nyugen). *Bottom:* Colonel Paul Tibbets being interviewed by Peter Mack. Unrepentant of his actions he argues that the dropping of the bomb was necessary to end the war (courtesy of Steve Nyugen).

Your approach to the film's animation reminded me of Masaaki Yuasa's brilliant Mind Game *(2004) and Studio 4°C. Did the work of Japanese animators and their films inspire the artistic vision of the film in any way?*

    That's funny that you mention because I'm a huge fan of *Adventure Time* and Masaaki Yuasa's body of work. But yes, anime was a huge inspiration for *Hibakusha.*

Kaz describes the pain and suffering she has endured throughout the years as a result of radiation sickness. Many people who survived the initial bombing of Hiroshima would later develop radiation sickness as a result of their exposure to radiation. For hundreds and thousands of people, the horrors of Hiroshima didn't end through the initial bombing (courtesy of Steve Nyugen).

From an artistic point of view, how did you achieve the post-atomic landscape we see during the film? Did you refer to archival documents?

Kaz managed to keep a few scrapbooks and photo albums with vintage photographs of what Hiroshima looked like before and after the bombing. She also mentioned very specific colors that she remembered in her memories—so blue, red, and black were very recurrent throughout the film's flashbacks. Whatever we couldn't find or replicate, we used our creativity to fill in the gaps.

*How did you come to work with voice actor William Frederick Knight (*Ghost in the Shell *and* Paranoia Agent*)? Was* Hibakusha *a story he felt that needed to be told?*

Back in 2010, I worked with William on an action project called *Dilated*. I knew he had a prominent voice-over history when we casted for him, so I decided to reach out to him to see if he would be interested in doing a table read for the *Hibakusha* rough script. After the first read, I think we sold him on our portrayal of the Colonel. William was incredibly supportive of our production, so much so that he lent both his voice and image to our cause, and I can't thank him enough for that.

What reception has the film received in America?

It's been great. The veterans, anime enthusiasts, college students, film patrons, and Nisei community have given us tremendous support throughout the entire process. There are always a few skeptics that have minor critiques about the legitimacy of the film. I can understand why they have these views, but I don't necessarily agree most of the time.

What reactions has the film had in Japan? Has the Japanese anime community got behind the film?

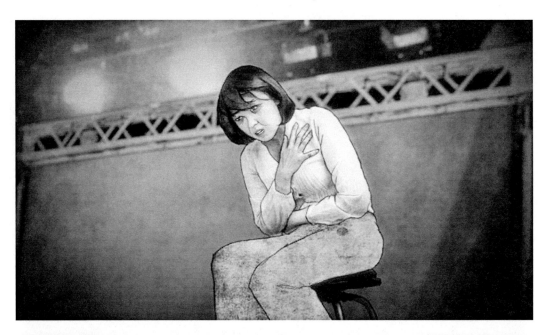

Top: Overcome with stress at Colonel Paul Tibbets comments, Kaz collapses. One of the key scenes in the excellent *Hibakusha* (courtesy of Steve Nyugen). *Bottom:* Kaz's flashback takes her back to her classroom where she recalls students being given instructions to take cover in case of a bomb or air-raid (courtesy Steve Nyugen).

I haven't been to any of the official screenings in Japan, but from what I hear, it has been well received. I know people have watched it. Not only in Japan, but all over Asia. There were quite a few articles that I have come across, and they seem to speak highly about *Hibakusha*. When it screened at the Hiroshima Peace Museum, there was some criticism that the film didn't address the plight of the *Hibakusha* enough.

I understand that the film was dedicated to American Society of Hiroshima-Nagasaki A-bomb survivors. Hopefully it will keep awareness of the bombings alive in the U.S. Was that part of your thinking?

I believe that the film will always serve that purpose.

You co-directed the film with Choz Belen. How would you describe your working relationship?

He's a genius. I learned a lot from him, and I still do to this day. I love to learn in any collaboration that I'm a part of, and we were heavily tested both emotionally and physically throughout the *Hibakusha* production. We still continue to collaborate to this day, but we live in different states, so we don't get together like we often did in the past while we were touring for the film. Regardless, he's still my partner and will always be.

Your film shows the personal tragedy and human cost associated with the bombings and the lives that were destroyed. How did you both approach the task of depicting the horror and suffering and the ordeal the Hibakusha *had to endure? Did you impose any form of self-censorship so that not to make the film too difficult for audiences?*

The important issue was to highlight Kaz's experience of the bombings and let the audience understand what it meant to be a survivor in her eyes. The message was not to blame others for what happened, but to help other people understand what had happened to the *Hibakusha*. I wanted the audience to go through this experience in a world that they weren't familiar with, and I think the design of the animation is intended to produce that effect.

Choz and I came to a mutual agreement that all the casualties of war depicted in this film had to be done tastefully because we did not want to take away the focus of the original message.

Hibakusha *is a film not about the past but one about the future. The overriding message is seemingly one of peace and that such an act [the atomic bombings] should not be repeated. Would you agree?*

Absolutely.

The plot sees Suyeishi come face to face with Pilot Paul Tibbets during an NBC interview. It is an emotional scene as you show Tibbets unrepentant for the bombings which causes Suyeishi great anguish. Was this based on fact or was it fictional?

This is 100 percent fact. We took an excerpt verbatim from Colonel Tibbets, and it was basically what he had said in the film. We just decided to frame it this way in order to give the Kaz character a sense of closure and open up a pathway for her to unleash all of her inner feelings.

Interestingly, Tibbets' reaction during the film is one that is shared by many who live through the war and felt the actions of Truman and its allies were justified and ended total war. Can you find any justification in the dropping of the bombs?

I've always said that films have the ability to build bridges between human beings and open up dialogue between opposing sides. In reality, I know that it does not bring immediate change in the world in the form of politics or people's decisions. Every decision has its benefits and its consequences, but I want people to understand that this atomic bombing actually happened. Thousands of people died instantly that day. Most of them were children, women, and the elderly. Once you see the film, it puts everything about the Hiroshima incident into perspective.

Hibakusha: Our Life to Live:
An Interview with Director
David Rothauser

Matthew Edwards

Flying under the radar of other contemporary films on the Hiroshima and Nagasaki bombing is *Hibakusha: Our Life to Live*, a compelling and neglected piece of work in the atomic bomb cycle of films. Since 2010, this moving and emotionally difficult film has been steadily gaining positive reviews and supporters in America and Japan and from the United Nations as it has begun to reach out to a wider audience. This steady rise can be attributed in part to the film's inclusion in the Uranium Film Festival and their unique spectrum of films relating to the nuclear threat. Directed by David Rothauser, an actor, playwright and filmmaker whose acting credits include *The Longest Night* and the television series *Kennedy*, the film is shot as a docu-drama; it blends elements of documentary footage within the framework of a fictional story in order to project to its audience the dangers of nuclear warfare. Combining news reel footage, first hand testimonies of atomic bomb survivors from Japan, Korea and America and footage of the participants of the 60th Anniversary Peace Ceremonies in Japan, the film is bound together through the fictional story of a young girl named Yoko who befriends a *Hibakusha* survivor named Nakanishi. It is their relationship that sets them off on a journey into the legacy of the bombings and the *Hibakusha* experience, which culminates, after Nakanishi's sudden death, in Yoko visiting Japan to attend the peace ceremony.

While the personal stories of the *Hibakusha* are the most haunting aspect of the film, lingering in the mind long after the film has finished, Rothauser's stylized renditions also lend a powerful punch. During one of the fictional re-enactments in the film, Rothauser presents the bombing of Nagasaki during an intimate and traditional Shintō wedding. At first we see the wedding party reveling in the day, before Rothauser inserts footage of the U.S. planes on route to Nagasaki. We see the bomb fall from the underbelly of the plane onto the city below and a blinding light fills the screen, vaporizing the wedding party. At once Rothauser plainly shows the true horror and personal tragedy that befell so many people on that fateful day and why such a weapon should never be used again.

In August 2014 I contacted Mr. Rothauser who kindly agreed to be interviewed for this collection and to talk about his experiences making the film. I thank him for his warm generosity and for sharing his experiences on making what is a very emotional and thought-provoking film that keeps the message of the atomic bombings alive for future generations.

Peace activist on stilts in Nagasaki in *Hibakusha: Our Life to Live* (courtesy David Rothauser).

Matthew Edwards: *What motivated you to make a film about the bombings of Hiroshima and Nagasaki?*

    David Rothauser: Years ago, when I was living in New York, I read a book by John Hersey entitled *Hiroshima*. You're probably aware of it. I had grown up with the war and I

Hidekazu Harada and "Yoko" (Tsumugi Yoshida) visit Hiroshima (courtesy David Rothauser).

had known all about the bombing. In fact, as a child we were all excited about the atomic bomb. We all had nuclear rings that we would send away for from a cereal box. We had these nuclear rings that we would wear and you had to go into a dark closet to see the nuclear movement in the ring. That was the only way could see it. In a dark closet! But as I grew order I read this book and I realized the long-term effects of radiation and I said to

Wedding Party: Eiji Nakanishi and family (courtesy David Rothauser).

myself: "this is horrible. This means not only the Japanese, who were bombed, but it means anyone else who is in contact with that form of radiation. That means us. It means our family and their kids, one generation after another." And I realized the horror but I wasn't a filmmaker then and so I didn't have the means to really express it until later on when I studied filmmaking and began making films and then got to a point where I could actually do something. Someone introduced me to two *Hibakusha* survivors; one from Hiroshima and one from Nagasaki. And I interviewed them and I didn't even know why I interviewed them, I just wanted to. One thing led to another and I was introduced to more survivors and then in 2005 I decided I was going to make a film and began filming. I went to Japan and we filmed other Japanese survivors. That's how the whole thing got started.

I also realized at that time that I wanted to draw a connection between the older generation with the younger generation because many people in Japan—especially the younger generation—know next to nothing about the atomic bombings. So I was able to craft part of the film that was fictional and the other part with interviews from survivors. The fictional part we worked with a little girl who was not an actress and with a musician who was one of the survivors. In the film he teaches her music and takes her on a fictional journey to Hiroshima to experience the peace ceremony that happens every August 6. So that's how we got started with the film.

It is interesting that you tried to draw a connection between the younger and older generations in the film and that the younger generation knew little about their past. Did you find this shocking?

Yes, but we also met people from the younger generation who were passionate about telling the story of Hiroshima and Nagasaki. But that was generally in the Hiroshima and Nagasaki area. Outside of that, people seemed uninterested or it didn't make an impression on them. They were disconnected, is the best way to put it. And there was censorship in Japan right after the bombing. The Japanese don't like to dwell on negative things. They are very upbeat people. Even the survivors, were upbeat. So it was hard to find people who wanted to dwell on the bombings.

How did you set about writing, producing and financing the film?

We met a number of survivors in New Jersey and Boston and there was a film festival going on at two universities in the Boston area about Hiroshima and Nagasaki. And so I went to the festival and I met four survivors from Hiroshima and Nagasaki. That was also the day we actually began filming the interviews with them, after they had agreed to that.

The reality of nuclear warfare. A mother nursing her baby after the Nagasaki bombing (courtesy David Rothauser).

Then through independent resources we raised enough funding to go to Japan, to film the survivors. For example, one person paid our airfare to Japan and back, another person invited us to live in their home while we were filming and someone donated us a van and did research and took us to all the locations that we needed to go. So we got a lot of in kind services. All the funding was independent. There was no corporate funding, no large funding.

It sounds like many people got behind the film and your vision.

Yes, they became passionate about it. I felt really moved by the way they responded to it, both the Americans and the Japanese.

Did you encounter any opposition in America or Japan in terms of the project?

One of my oldest, and best, friends from New York—and I would call him a Conservative Intellectual [laughs]—and we meet all the time and we discussed this. His point of view is War will always happen and it continues to happen and that we should have bombed the Japanese a year before we did and he comes up with all these arguments. The only thing that stops me from killing him is his sense of humor [laughs]. He is as negative as you can be about that whole subject matter and the atomic bombings. He has no compassion for what happened. I don't come across this a lot, but occasionally I meet people who are very rigid in that way.

Some people do still strongly believe that it was the right thing to do, that America was justified in dropping the bomb and that is saved countless American lives and a land invasion.

Those are the arguments but none of them hold water. It is just speculation. No one really knows what would have happened if we had landed troops on Japanese soil. We don't know. They may have said, "We give up, this doesn't make any sense." We just don't know. To say that it saved a million lives is an excuse as far as I'm concerned.

How did you meet, and get hold of, Hibakusha *survivor Eiji Nakanishi? His story is so remarkable and yet so moving, especially with the physical scars he has had have to live with.*

He was the first survivor I met in America, in New Jersey, and he played folk music. He sang in a band that played Japanese and English folk tunes. He gave a talk in Princeton, near the university. I was so moved by his talk and his music that two years later I invited him to be part of the film, and he agreed.

One of the fascinating aspects of your documentary is that it centers not only on the plight of Japanese Hibakusha, *but also American and Korean* Hibakusha. *There is still an overriding ignorance toward this issue in the West in that there were thousands of Koreans and some Americans who were injured and killed by the bomb. Was this something you wanted to make clear, how the bombings had a wider impact on us globally and not just the Japanese?*

I purposely wanted to do that and cover even more survivors if I could. We approached Chinese survivors living in Japan but they refused to be interviewed for the film. I can only surmise that it was because the wound was too deep for them. They just couldn't talk about it; be a part of the film. So we respected that and didn't push them.

How did you get on interviewing the Korean Hibakusha?

My wife is Korean so she introduced me to Korean survivors in Korean and we met others in Japan. The Koreans that I interviewed in Korea, some of them said that they were happy that America dropped the bomb on Japan because it ridded them of Japanese captivity. The problem was that many of the survivors, both the Japanese and Koreans, were prejudiced against by their own people. So when they returned to Korea people didn't want to have anything to do with them; and the same with the Japanese survivors in Japan who were discriminated against. So there was that problem. The Koreans that I interviewed were really angry about the whole thing and that they didn't get the medical attention that the Japanese were getting.

That came across in the film. They were certainly more bitter and angry than the Japanese, who were more resigned in a way. It's the Japanese way, I suppose. They are very a pragmatic people.

Yes, I think so. I teach Japanese students here in Boston area. They are college students and they come over for a semester or a year and a half, and they are all that way. They process things very differently from other people.

In terms of style, you spoke earlier that the film is very much a docu-drama in that you include a fictional narrative to bind the film together, why did you adopt this approach?

My background is in theater and I started out as an actor. When I started my filmmaking career I wanted to combine what I had learned as an actor with what I could do as a filmmaker. I didn't want to do pure documentaries. I wanted to do something that involved a conflict that actors have to deal with. I had done other films and those films were essentially docu-dramas. I did one about Bertolt Brecht and Un-American House Activities Committee and we used a transcript of a congressional hearing that Brecht was called to on suspicion of being a Communist and we dramatized it. The film became very successful because it was pretty well worked out. Then I did another film on the Sacco and Vanzetti case (*Diary of Sacco and Vanzetti*, 2004), which was a famous court case in America. So I have been using that form. With *Hibakusha: Our Life to Live*, I wanted to open things up. I didn't want to make a film about the mushroom cloud that everyone is bored with, by now. It's the same thing over and over. So I wanted to get a ground level approach to what happened and I tried to do that by having the bomb drop on the peace festival in 2005. And then we went to Nagasaki, I wanted to show the bomb being dropped on a very intimate wedding ceremony to show an intimate thing that happened to a small number of people, so we took that approach.

I felt that technique was very effective. I personally think the film turned out exceptionally well.

I was in on every editing session and worked very closely with the editor. I had storyboarded the whole film, prior to filming. So I knew exactly what I wanted. We got pretty much everything we were looking for. I had a feeling that it would be pretty good but then you never really know till you have seen the completed film. Right now I think the film is too long, but people sit through it and don't turn away from the screen. I have seen it a thousand times, so I have lost perspective. But people seem to really appreciate it.

Nagasaki survivor Hidetaka Komine (courtesy David Rothauser).

What would you change about the film, if you could go back now? What would you do differently?

I would have a different opening. It has not been accepted by most film festivals.

Why is that?

I don't know. They don't tell you. They just reject it. My feeling is that the opening isn't as dramatic enough to grab or hold their attention, and it becomes a little bit too talkie at the beginning. I'm not sure. I would probably change the beginning a little more and make it more dynamic, rather than just spoken. But I don't really know.

But it is part of the Uranium Film Festival.

Yes, it played in Rio de Janeiro. The director of the festival told me afterwards that when he first saw the film he didn't like it. He said it was the only one about Hiroshima and Nagasaki, so he included it. But when he saw it a second time he said that this was a really good film. Maybe people don't look at it carefully when they first see it at the festival, or judging it for a festival.

It is a very challenging film. It is holding up a part of our history here in the West that we don't like to see, or a shameful part of our history.

It is and people don't want to deal with it.

This may have played a part, especially when you consider that Hollywood has rarely tackled the subject.

You're right, but have you seen *Dr. Strangelove*? That's my favorite. I love the way they use humor because if you sometimes talk too much on a serious level you lose your audience. You have to infuse it with some other kind of human experience to keep them with you. I think that movie does it really well. I have actually written a new play about the bomb called *Genie in the Bottle*. It a play about a nuclear scientist in the military who is the human personification of the bomb and he doesn't know it, nor does any of the other characters in the play. I would love to make a film but I'm exploring making a play first.

I thought the semi-autobiographical character of Davey was very effective in the film. It shows how war films and American propaganda had come to view the Japanese as vermin and an enemy that needed to be eradicated by any means hence we see jubilation after the bomb is dropped. What was growing up in a post–Hiroshima or Nagasaki U.S. like?

Growing up in that period, World War II, it was a couple of things that I really felt deeply: one was the excitement of war, from a child's point of view. We had a lot of propaganda movies in America about the war. We all thought this was great stuff. We even went so far as to put a bomb, a real bomb, not an atomic bomb but a regular bomb, in the lobby of a movie theater and if you paid twenty-five bucks you could sign your name on the bomb in chalk and they would drop the bomb. Of course, I did that. It was all very exciting, but there was also the element of fear that I didn't expect. One night I was dreaming that the German's came over and bombed our town I was living in. It did something to my stomach; it created an emptiness inside my stomach. I was terrified. In the morning I woke up and I crept over to window to see if it really happened. I didn't know. So there were these two things, the propaganda movies and all these heroes who get killed in the movies and are back in the next one, so for a kid that is great stuff. No one dies in a war. That was my experience growing up. We were all very happy about winning the war and we were great; we were the good guys and God was on our side. The Japanese were bad and evil. I believed all that junk. It was only much later that I began to realize what at happened.

So you felt it was important to put that former self into the film and how you bought all that propaganda?

I'm not sure if I was successful, but I tried to make a link between the child who is also interested in science and the adults who make science. I tried to draw a link between the child feverishly trying to make a bomb in his lab and the adults doing the same thing. I am not sure it was successful.

Why do you think that?

Because no one has ever mentioned it to me after seeing the film; no one has ever mentioned anything about it. For me it was successful in the film to make it, but I don't think the audience got it.

I thought it was effective but then again Hibakusha: Our Life to Live *is a film that allows viewers to react differently, on their own personal level. That is one of the films strengths, I believe.*

I interviewed a number of academics who I was making another film about. One of them was a professor at Massachusetts Institute of Technology and I said to him: "Can you draw a link between a child's passion and excitement for nuclear weapons and a young scientist?" And the professor said that most of the scientists at Los Alamos working on the atomic bomb were very young, the average age was about twenty-five. And that they came with a vision that young people have today with technology. They were excited by just the technology but completely forgot what they were making; or didn't know.

During your film, Yoko becomes fascinated with the drawings and pictures of Hibakusha survivors. Was this a way of bringing their experiences to life in the film? The drawings are so poignant and moving, especially the simplistic drawing of the burnt out trolley and the charred remains of the victims strewn in the carriage and lining the floor.

Yes, it was and I tried to foreshadow that with the elderly *Hibakusha* and the young girl. We filmed that on a burned out trolley that had been rebuilt. What I was trying to show that she was alone on the trolley saying goodbye to him and then she disappears out of the window, you never saw her, and he is still waving. I was hoping that would give an intense loss—the elderly man waving to the child who isn't there. The next image is then the burnt out trolley. I was trying to convey some emotional impact there.

Another moving element in the film is when you see Hibakusha *victims and 9/11 relatives coming together to sue for a common peace. I found that very powerful.*

I think at the time I was developing the film I met people who had lost relatives and family in the 9/11 attacks and I knew that the stone from the Peace Abbey in Massachusetts was being taken to Japan and they were going to march with it from Nagasaki to Hiroshima. So I knew about that. And I wanted to include that in the film. Actually, I couldn't be there for the beginning of the march but through email I was introduced to a Japanese filmmaker and we worked out a plan whereby she would film the opening of that march. She was confused because of the language barrier and I tried to explain what I wanted by email and somehow she managed to understand everything that I was trying to get. She got it all! I couldn't believe it. She captured it so well.

Has the film received much exposure in America and abroad?

The film has been received very well. The first place we showed it was at the United Nations, during the Non-Proliferation Treaty conference in 2010. What was interesting was that there were people from lots of different countries; some from Germany, some from

西電話局

八月七日……
焼けて赤くなった、
電車が天満町に止まり
何かと思えば……
人間の黒焦げが電車
の中から点点と外に倒れ
もう炭と云って良い
人間の炭……
信じられない事だった。
無隊さんがムシロを
掛けていた。
まさか全市が一瞬に
して灰になり、死の町と
化すとは……あまりの
ショックに頭が変になり
そうだった。
本当に広島は壊滅
そういうか？
遠くから西電話局
が良く見える

1120

Burnt Out Trolley. A heart-breaking drawing from a *Hibakusha* survivor (courtesy David Rothauser).

Japan, Korea and American talk-show host Phil Donahue came to the viewing of the film at the UN and his comment right after the film was shown was "this film should be shown forever." That was quite a strong comment, from him. There was a lady from Germany who told me I should take the film to Germany and show it there. People were very moved by it almost everywhere I have taken it.

There were some people who took issue with my portrayal of Franklin D. Roosevelt. They felt I fooled around with a timed sequence with him promising the American people he would never send their sons to a foreign war. That was done a year before the Japanese bombed Pearl Harbor. They felt I took license with that. Others did not and defended me. So I had reactions coming from both sides. But mainly the reaction has been positive.

Has the film had much coverage in Japan?

We showed it in Hiroshima, Kyoto and Osaka. It got a really positive response. When we showed the film in Hiroshima, we got invited by the *Japan Times* to do an interview. They wrote a whole article on the film. We have had a really good response from the Japanese people. Overall it was very positive.

However, in Nagasaki they refused to show it. I sent it to people in Nagasaki and they saw the film but they misinterpreted it. They felt that the film was promoting a positive aspect of nuclear war and in particular they didn't like the way I treated the Nagasaki survivors. They felt I didn't explore certain individuals enough and give them enough coverage. They weren't happy about that and refused to show the film. Later on, one of the people who rejected the film, who I have met, contacted me a year later to say that they were really happy with the work I was doing and that they wanted to try and get the film shown in Nagasaki. So far that hasn't happened. I haven't pushed it but I will try again to get the film shown there.

Going back to Phil Donahue, how did he become attached to the film as narrator? Was that after the UN showing? I understand that you originally did a voice-over for the film.

We needed a narrator for the film and I had narrated one version of the film. It was ok, but I'm not well known and I wanted to get a named person on there. I thought of him because he has a great voice and I liked his television program he had in the U.S. It was very controversial and direct. So I got the name of his agent in New York and called her up and asked her what the chances of him narrating my film? She said send me a rough cut of the film and I'll show it to him and see what he says. And I did. I sent her a rough cut of about fifteen minutes and he got right back to me to do the narration. He came to Boston and we took him to a studio and we did the narration one afternoon. He was terrific. I sent it to him before. He did the whole thing in an hour and twenty minutes. He was easy to direct. He struggled to get some of pronunciation clear but in no time he was able to do it.

Hibakusha: Our Life to Live *is definitely a film that needs to be seen. We need to keep the topic of the atomic bombings alive for future generations because people are still suffering to this very day as a result of Hiroshima and Nagasaki. We should never use a weapon like that again...*

Talk show host Phil Donahue (left) with director David Rothauser (courtesy David Rothauser).

Yes, you are right. But the situation has become somewhat critical in Japan because of the new prime minister Shinzō Abe. If he is successful in dropping Article 9 and building up the Japanese military to world class standards that means he has to complete with the nine other nations that have nuclear weapons. That would mean in order to compete Japan has to have a nuclear weapon. Which I think would be horrible.

But look what happened in Fukushima!

You're right. You'd think that would be enough to convince them. Actually, the Japanese people really don't want a military. I think 59 percent of the Japanese population said that they wanted to keep the Peace Constitution.

In the film, you show disgraced former defense minister Fumio Kyūma state that the bombings of Hiroshima and Nagasaki were necessary to end the war. What did you make of his comment? Such a comment in Japan is akin to political suicide.

I think it was government propaganda, because America has been such a critical part of the new Japanese constitution. But America likes to pull strings. As you may know, four years after the constitution was written, America tried to get Japan to drop Article 9 and go to war against North Korea. Fortunately, Japan wouldn't do it. But America has been chipping away at that. What Kyūma said was, I think, part of the relationship and secret pact that Japan has with U.S. that motivated that comment. And once someone comes out in public and makes an outrageous statement like that, even if they are fired, or they apologize, it is too late. The statement has been made. And that is part of the whole process that they go through, behind the scenes.

Is there still a prevalent belief in America that the bombs needed to be dropped or is that attitude changing, especially with filmmakers like you questioning the use of such a weapon?

It is hard to say. I know now, at this time, there are more small towns and communities that come out in America with commemorations of Hiroshima and Nagasaki. So I think it is increasing, in that way. People tend to be middle-aged and some young people get involved. I think there is a more positive realization of what nuclear weapons means. But overall, it is impossible to say. For example, members of my own family would never discuss the bombings and if they do it is from a negative point of view, in that we should have bombed them more without reasoning through it or looking at it in an open mind. People are distracted by daily life here to an extent where everything is relatively easy if you are middle class in America. To talk about the war, or any war, even in the Middle East, there is little discussion going on, aside from academics. Among the population at large I never hear it. So I don't know.

Did this lack of discussion on the bombings influence your decision to make this film?

I was hoping to generate a positive response from people and to tell the story of the survivors. I felt their stories were important to tell and should not be forgotten. Some stories should always be remembered. I was hoping that by giving the *Hibakusha* survivors the chance to tell their stories in the film that it would generate a positive response from audiences. I think the film does generate a sympathetic response. I don't think the film generates a response where people will go out and do something to try and prevent this for happening again. I'm not sure if I hit that note.

I have been working since with *Women's International League for Peace and Freedom* to bring a version of the Japanese Article 9 as an amendment to the U.S. constitution and I'm finding that most people who I talk to about that are totally confused or seems to them like a fantasy idea. But I point out that Japan has lived in peace for almost 70 years. It is a perfect example that it can be done, but they don't understand it. So I don't think I have been at all successful [laughs]!

Looking back at the film, what are you most proud about?

To have told the story with the focus on Eiji Nakanishi. I felt it was important to have told his story, especially after he passed away half-way through the filming. I felt then it was most important to focus on him.

I don't know if I am proud. I am happy that I completed the film and I am happy that audiences seem to derive something good out of the film. I guess that is what I am mainly proud about. That people can come away from the film with something that means something to them.

I showed the film recently in a small church near Boston and we had a problem with the projector and they could not control the sound. They played the film from a laptop and the sound was laptop quality being projected. So we were all sitting there straining to hear what was being said and I was watching the audience and thinking, well they are not falling asleep. I was horrified because the sound was terrible. But a woman came up to me afterwards and thanked me and she said she was so happy that I had shown the film. The other audience members seemed appreciative of the film, despite the poor sound, and gained something from the film.

All That Remains: An Interview with Ian and Dominic Higgins

Matthew Edwards

Dr. Takashi Nagai's story is not new to the cinematic world. A survivor of the nuclear attack on Nagasaki, a physician, radiologist convert to Catholicism and subsequent peace activist, his bestselling book *The Bells of Nagasaki* charted his experiences caring for the sick and dying in the aftermath of the bombing. His story has been dramatized in Japan firstly in 1950 by Shochiku in *The Bells of Nagasaki* (*Nagasaki no kane*), directed by Hideo Ōba and scripted by Kaneto Shindō and secondly by Keisuke Kinoshita in the 1983 drama *Children of Nagasaki* (*Kono ko wo nokoshite*).

Fortunately, Dr. Nagai's story has been retold for a third time. Interestingly, his remarkable story has inspired British filmmaker brothers Dominic and Ian Higgins (*Finding Fatima*) of Major Oak Entertainment to dramatize his life into a new stunning feature. Shot primarily in the U.K., and utilizing state of the art computer effects, the film chronicles Dr. Nagai's life and the bombings of Nagasaki in a moving and brilliant portrait of one of history's forgotten "Saints." Gathering interest in both Japan and in the West, the film reminds us of the horrors of atomic warfare and keeps the memory of the bombings fresh in the minds of future generations. I caught up with both Dominic and Ian in May 2014 to discuss the film, Dr. Nagai and the bombings of Hiroshima and Nagasaki. I thank them both for the effort, energy and time that they put into the interview. I am deeply grateful to include their film in the anthology and for helping to bring Dr. Nagai's story to a wider audience.

Matthew Edwards: *What made you decide to chronicle the experiences of Dr. Takashi Nagai and the atomic bombing of Nagasaki? Did Dr. Nagai's* The Bells of Nagasaki *have a profound impact on this decision?*

Ian: We came across the story of Dr. Nagai while researching a previous film which touched upon the atomic bombings of Hiroshima. We bought a copy of *The Bells of Nagasaki* after reading a quote which stated Dr. Nagai deserved to stand alongside the great men of the 20th century such as Ghandi and Martin Luther King. As filmmakers we tend to be drawn to "forgotten stories and heroes" and the fact we had never heard of this man really intrigued us.

Dominic: Nagasaki is also often referred to, with some justification, as the forgotten A-bombed city. After reading *The Bells of Nagasaki*, which is a recording of his own personal experiences surviving the atomic bombing, we knew we had to at least try to make this film. It's a book that should be read by most people.

267

Dr. Nagai's heroism—his treatment of atomic bomb victims and work as a peace activist—is a story very few people have heard about in the West. Why is that?

Ian: We've asked ourselves this question many times. During his life time he was a celebrated figure and his books became bestsellers, read throughout the world. I think most of the world now wants to forget what happened in Hiroshima and Nagasaki because even now, 70 years later, the bombings are still claiming innocent victims—in the form of diseases brought on by exposure to radiation; this makes it harder to justify their use.

Dominic: I think Nagasaki is a city that is very much in the shadow of Hiroshima. Someone once said, "Hiroshima is bitter, noisy, highly political. Its symbol would be a fist clenched in anger. Nagasaki is sad, quiet, reflective. Its symbol: hands joined in peace." Dr. Nagai did not believe in aggressive, noisy protesting, he only believed in peaceful means, his works encourage quite mediation. Such people find it harder to have their voices heard.

Dr. Nagai's story had been previously dramatized in the Japanese film Bells of Nagaskai *(Nagasaki no kane), directed by Hideo Ōba and scripted by Kaneto Shindō. Did you refer to Ōba's work during the making of* All That Remains, *and did it have any influence on your own film?*

Dominic: Actually we were unable to track down a copy of *Nagasaki no kane* as it's no longer available—which is a great shame. We really wanted to view a copy as we consider

Dr. Nagai fights the bomb. A dream sequence from the brilliant *All That Remains* (courtesy Dominic and Ian Higgins). *Bottom:* Red inferno. Devastation and horror in Nagasaki (courtesy Dominic and Ian Higgins).

this film to be quite important because the director, Hideo Ōba visited Dr. Nagai and the film was screened for him at Nyokodo. It was also one for the first films to deal with the atomic bombings and was filmed on location in Nagasaki.

Ian: I think our film is quite different from Hideo Ōba's film in that as far as we know, *Nagasaki no kane,* mainly deals with Takashi Nagai's life leading up to the bombing and for oblivious American censorship reasons, deals quite briefly with actual bombing of Nagasaki.

Dominic: There was a later film made about Dr. Nagai, *The Children of Nagasaki* (*Kono ko wo nokoshite,* 1983) directed by Keisuke Kinoshita and once again it's a film that is impossible to find in English. We did manage to find a version with French subtitles though! It is a film with some merit, but it feels quite superficial in regards to being a biopic on Takashi Nagai.

Very few western films have been made about the atomic bombings, especially in the U.S. Why is this and was this something that you consciously wanted to re-address?

Dominic: When we first started out researching the film we came across a quote from an American film critic that said, "American films always view the atomic bombings of Japan from a distance." And that is very true, when we think of films like Spielberg's *Empire of the Sun.* We wanted audiences to understand what Dr. Nagai experienced and that meant we needed to convey something of that horror.

Ian: I think anything to do with the atomic bombings of Japan is quite contentious here in the West, most of the victims were innocent civilians—women and children. Perhaps it's just easier for us to concentrate on the terrible crimes committed by the Japanese military during World War II. Dr. Nagai's story is one of ordinary humans, victims of a war they really knew little about. It's certainly not easy listening to a survivor talk of their experiences and sadly, with each passing year, the anniversary of the bombings seems to be mentioned less and less in the Western media. With film, we can reignite interest in this subject and help to keep the memory alive for generations to come.

How did you raise financing for the film?

Dominic: We originally funded the film ourselves and then turned to crowd funding, through a site called *Indiegogo*—basically it works by offering people the opportunity to donate money to the film in return for a "perk" such as a copy of the finished film, artwork or even a credit in the film.

You have stated that the film is a docu-feature? What do you mean by that term and what can audiences expect from the movie?

Ian: When we started out we envisaged something that had the gritty authenticity of a documentary but the emotional power and poetic visuals of a dramatized film. As we started to work with the actors and develop the scenes the drama aspect just expanded and evolved.

Dominic: The film started as a docu-drama that grew in scope and vision into a full feature film. But it retains some of its documentary aspects especially in its use of archive footage, most of it USAF (United States Air Force) stuff. It really adds a level of authenticity to the whole experience, just knowing that real people, real locations and real events are helping us to tell a more complete story.

Has the film generated much interest in Japan?

Ian: We've started to pick up real interest in Japan with the *Asahi Shimbun* running a big story on it and other interest being expressed from organizations and individuals on the back of that. I think the interest mainly comes from the fact that we're a Western film company making a film about a very Japanese story.

How did you come to cast Leo Ashizawa in the role of Dr. Takashi Negai and Yuna Shin as Midori?

Ian: We spent a long time casting these roles as we were looking for actors that had both the talent and screen presence that would lift them off the screen. The moment we saw Leo and Yuna reading lines, we knew we had found the right actors—there was a real sense of truth to the way they delivered their lines, we sensed them connecting to their characters.

Dominic: When we called them back for a second casting session, we got them to read lines from a scene together and the chemistry between them was just so right—casting these roles was one of those magic moments.

Stylistically, how did you approach the filming of the All That Remains? *The film was shot mostly on HD digital film and with a green screen, I believe.*

Ian: The stylistic approach to *All That Remains* was very much to create something that looked like a cross between live-action and animation. This was both an artistic choice and a practical one. Without a huge Hollywood budget this style gave us the confidence to tackle big scale scenes such as the atomic bombing as it allowed us to blend CGI, live action and archive footage more seamlessly on the limited budget we did have.

Dominic: With CGI, we can create any environment or set-piece we want and from a stylistic point, it allows us a lot of creative freedom.

Ian: It does mean though many more hours in post-production compositing elements and adding backgrounds.

Dominic (center) and Ian Higgins directing Leo Ashizawa in *All That Remains* (courtesy Dominic and Ian Higgins).

I understand that the film was primarily filmed in Birmingham, England, with some principle photography taking place in Japan. How did this impact on you re-creating an authentic Japanese feel to the film and what problems did you encounter?

Ian: This was the main reason for us to rely so heavily on green screen, it allowed us to not only create the right setting but the right period too. We really wanted this film to have the feel of classic Japanese cinema and as part of our research, we immersed ourselves in Japanese films of the 1940s and 1950s, I think in the end, it was the films of Yasujirō Ozu who influenced us the most—the contemplative stillness found in his films was something we really wanted to capture in *All That Remains.*

Dominic: The major problem we faced was finding Japanese or East Asian cast. We were lucky to find a small but tight knit acting community based mainly in London.

To help us re-create a feeling of being in Nagasaki it was absolutely crucial for us to fly out and spend some time in Nagasaki. We literally walked everywhere through Nagasaki taking pictures for research purposes. Some of these pictures would serve as material for some of the film's many Matte Paintings.

Because there are not really any locations in England that could double up for Japan, that meant that almost every shot in the film needed to either be created with CGI or digitally altered to look more authentic.

During the making of the film you worked alongside both students and teachers at Nagasaki University and the photo division of the Nagasaki Atomic Bomb Museum. How important was this for you when recreating on screen the horrific aftermath of the bombing?

Behind the scenes shot from Dominic and Ian Higgins' *All That Remains* (courtesy Dominic and Ian Higgins).

Dominic: We contacted Nagasaki University because their students had been involved in a project to re-create a CGI model of pre-bombed Nagasaki. During the project they had been working with Mr. Yoshitoshi Fukahori, head of the Committee for Research of Photographs and Materials of the Atomic Bombing, who himself was a survivor of the bombing. This was going to be invaluable for our research, both for gaining some insight into what Nagasaki looked like before the bomb was dropped, and for what it was like living through that eventful day.

Mr. Fukahori actually remembers seeing Dr. Nagai walking past his house on his way to work—these living links to that time and place were invaluable to us.

Ian: This was very important part of our research, as they had so much visual reference material. They also set up interviews for us with *Hibakusha*.

The movie's visual effects and CGI were created by Pixel Revolution Films. How did they set about recreating the Japanese and post atomic landscape that you envisaged for the film?

Ian: Pixel Revolution Films is our own production company and all the effects were created by Dominic and myself, so we didn't have to relay our vision to someone else, but the downside was that we had to do all the work ourselves! Each of the effect shots started from a description we read or were told, or an archive photo, we then used a mixture of CG renders and photographic material to build up the digital set-pieces. We spent months working on nothing but the FX shots, it was pretty grueling.

Dominic: We worked from countless photos and film footage from the USAF to recreate the landscape. We also relied on the testimonials we had from the *Hibakusha* we had interviewed as well as the descriptions from book sources such as *The Bells of Nagasaki*. In that book Dr. Nagai described the landscape as looking like "The universe stripped bare." Sentences like that really paint an invocative image in the mind.

Aside from using CGI, I understand that you opted for more traditional methods of special effects?

Ian: We are big believers in mixing techniques, both old and new. Alongside the CG shots we used model miniatures because sometimes these just proved to be the best tool for the job. There's a scene where one of the bells from the cathedral (which was right under the atomic explosion) is unearthed from a pile of rubble and raised on a makeshift stand and these shots were created by mixing CG backdrops, live-action actors and a miniature model for the bell itself.

Dominic: The special make-up effects too were a mix of traditional and digital prosthetics. We really utilized the best of both worlds.

How did you approach filming the victims of the atomic bombs and their injuries? Was recreating such horror traumatic for the cast and crew?

Ian: Before we even picked up our cameras we spent several weeks planning the atomic bombing scene, storyboarding and designing shots. We discussed our requirements with our co-producer Nigel Martin Davey who then sourced some wonderful locations.

We filmed the scene over a period of several days stretched out over months; we spent four days on a demolition site and various locations that had plenty of rubble strewn about. We also spent several days shooting in the green screen studio. We had so many extras that we had about eight make-up artists working altogether on the aftermath sequence. We had a great crew also who were willing to really get their hands dirty and do whatever it took to get the shot we needed. You can't underestimate the value of a good crew when working on such a technically and emotionally demanding scene.

Dominic: It was very difficult, we were adamant about creating something that felt authentic but how far could we take it without making it unwatchable?

We experimented with taking various stylistic approaches with the bombing scene. One of the most powerful scenes of an atomic bombing can be seen in *Barefoot Gen,* the 1983 animated version. It was nightmarish and surreal—and yet far more vivid and real than any other depiction we had seen. This film became a big influence on us.

Before we started filming any of the aftermath scenes, Leo Ashizawa and the other cast members who were involved in these scenes, watched several reels of USAF footage—some shot only months after the bombing. It was surprisingly good quality and in color. It was all there, the immense structural damage and the horrific physical injuries inflicted upon the cities inhabitants.

We agreed with Leo that we wouldn't show him any of this footage until we were ready to film these scenes. This way the footage felt raw and fresh.

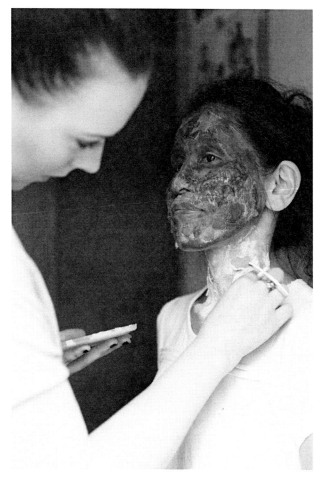

Behind the scenes make up of *Hibakusha* survivor (courtesy Dominic and Ian Higgins).

We also gathered many written testimonials from survivors and passed them on to Leo to study.

These documents not only describe the bombing in great deal, they also relate the terrible physical and mental trauma all of them suffered and continue to suffer to this day.

Ian: Leo is an actor who takes his research very seriously and during his preparation for the role he read as much as he could on Dr. Nagai and the A-bombing, including books written in Japanese that were out of bounds for us.

This dedication and commitment to research was one reason he was able to bring so much to the part of Dr. Nagai and to the film.

Dominic: When we came to filming the scenes of the victims our make-up team worked from photos, it was a very long and intense part of the filming production. But everybody on the team was dedicated to trying to create something that felt real.

We discussed ways of faithfully depicting the keloid scaring with our lead make-up artist Vera Fenlon—who did an amazing job with creating so many prosthetics. However, we found traditional make-up techniques could be quite restrictive in some cases. So we opted to create "digital prosthetics" on some of the victims.

Top: Nagasaki feels the full force of "Fat Man," a light akin to a thousand suns (courtesy Dominic and Ian Higgins). *Middle:* The Black Rain falls. Leo Ashizawa as Dr. Takashi Nagai in *All That Remains* (courtesy of Dominic and Ian Higgins). *Bottom:* Scorched corpses. Dr. Nagai is led through a hospital corridor by a nurse (courtesy Dominic and Ian Higgins).

Ian: The sound design was also something we spent a lot of time developing and working on. Even though we are very visual film-makers, sound design is so important to us. One example is how we use singing in the film to represent the transcendental quality of the human spirit. During the bombing we have a sequence where school girls are singing a hymn as everything burns around them, but as they sing the wind and flames are roaring

Dr. Takashi Nagai returns home to his beloved Nagasaki to find the destructive ruins of the scorched city (courtesy Dominic and Ian Higgins).

angrily as though attempting to drown out their voices and so we have this real battle going on in the sound-scape.

Dominic: Another big influence on the sound design of the bombing sequence came from the many eye witnesses descriptions from both Japanese and Americans, who described the mushroom cloud as looking like it were alive. We wanted this thing to feel like a living monster on the rampage, a terrifying giant that just wants to consume or smash everything in its path.

Ian: For me, I think one of the most difficult parts of filming this sequence was when we were working with the child actors, one of them burst into tears during his performance—I felt terribly guilty because he had been so looking forward to his scene. Probably the most moving scenes for us all though was one involving Dr. Nagai and a young woman played by actress Yuriri Naka who is physically and mentally scarred by the bombing, revealing the secret guilt each feels for surviving the bombing while their loved ones perished.

Dominic: I think one of the most emotional moments on set happened with an elderly lady who was playing one of the victims. In the scene she reaches out and takes the hand of a dying girl. But during the shoot, the elderly lady started to cry. Afterwards she explained that she had grown up in Hiroshima just after the war and remembered vividly seeing the *Hibakusha* and the destruction left behind in the city. When she held the hand of the girl, she was literally connecting to her past.

It reminded me that these events are not so long ago.

It is well known that Dr. Nagai was a convert to Christianity, however it less known that Christianity in Japan is different from Western Christianity, in that Japanese "Kristians" incorporate elements of Buddhism and Shintoism into their teachings. Did you look to educate audiences on this aspect of Japanese Christianity in the film, and how the Japanese have a gift of taking an existing concept and subverting it to make it their own?

Dominic: Wherever Christianity has spread it as incorporated certain cultural influences and in Japan we find a form of Christianity that has absorbed elements of eastern philosophy and culture.

A beautiful example of this is Nyokodo. Dr. Nagai chose to end his days living in a little hermitage he named Nyokodo (As yourself hermitage)—he was very much following an ancient Japanese tradition by living a hermit lifestyle yet his little hut bares a Christian inspired name.

Ian: This was something we found fascinating. Christianity has been in Japan longer than it has in America, the first missionaries landed in Japan in 1549, yet its years of oppression are still within living memory and even today it is very much a minority religion, so perhaps here we find something akin to the earliest form of Christianity. This was the overriding feeling we had after spending the night in Nara as guest of Father Paul Glynn, the Australian author of an autobiography on Dr. Nagai entitled *A Song for Nagasaki*, and his parishioners. Fr. Glynn has immersed himself in this Japanese form of Christianity and is a quietly spoken, meditative man, much like Dr. Nagai. For us it was more important to convey this feeling of purity and serenity.

Your previous films, 13th Day *and* Finding Fatima, *also deal with the issue of faith and Christianity. Is it fair to conclude that this a theme that permeates throughout your work?*

Ian: I would say we are often drawn to spiritual themes, themes that explore the purpose of our lives and the transcendental power of faith, even in the most harrowing of circumstances. These are universal themes not limited to any one religion and it's something we find really interesting in the human psyche.

Dominic: There is a transcendental and dreamlike nature to film and we are very much drawn to stories that contain themes of salvation and redemption. I guess ultimately, these are themes that really explore what it is to be human.

Many people in Nagasaki wrongly assumed they had been spared from Le May's U.S. bombing offensive due to the city's Christian links. Are you surprised the U.S. deployed an atomic bomb on the city?

Ian: This was a very interesting premise for us as filmmakers, Dr. Nagai was a convert to Christianity (very much against his father's wishes) and in a time when Western religion was generally frowned upon in Japan, in fact Dr. Nagai was once arrested and interrogated because of his Christian beliefs, so on a personal level, the atomic bombing really becomes the ultimate test of this new found faith. Indeed, Dr. Nagai eventually came to view the bombing as "divine providence" a conclusion that initially, and understandably, shocked and divided the other *Hibakusha.*

Dominic: Nagasaki was actually a secondary target. I believe the original target was Kokura, but dense cloud cover on the day forced the bombing crew to turn back. The crew did not have enough fuel to fly back to base on Tinian Island. This left the crew with two options, either head back to Okinawa and drop the bomb over the ocean or head to the secondary target. The order came in to drop the bomb on Nagasaki.

Although Nagasaki had suffered several smaller bombings during the previous months it had been spared from the firebombing that had devastated other cities. Was the reason it had been left relatively unscathed to allow for a detailed study of the effects of an A-bomb?

Dr. Nagai did initially struggle to make sense of the bombing, and when Japan capitulated on August 15 he was very much a man defeated. His overriding emotion at that time was anger. He even refused medical aid to a patient.

The only way he could make sense of it all was by turning to his faith. Nagasaki has a rich history of Christian martyrdom. So I think it's true to say that this terrible disaster strengthened Dr. Nagai's faith, by enabling him to feel a connection to that past. Christianity teaches that there is redemption through suffering and sacrifice. This ideal gave him comfort and strength.

Original British poster of Dominic and Ian Higgins' *All That Remains* **(courtesy Dominic and Ian Higgins).**

During the Funeral Address he gave for the 8000 Catholic Victims of the Atomic bomb on November 23, 1945, Dr. Nagai uses the word "*hansai*" which means sacrifice. For Dr. Nagai, Nagasaki was a sacrificial lamb that had to be sacrificed for peace.

For me, Dr. Nagai's story is essentially a journey about faith and forgiveness. Was it this idea that you wanted to explore in the film?

Ian: Very much so. The most remarkable thing about the story of Dr. Nagai is that he was a man with every reason to hate, but through his work he preached only forgiveness. But, there was another aspect to his journey that we found fascinating and explore in the film, as Dr. Nagai's faith deepens wars are fought with ever increasing technological advancement, so we have this duality of a man's spiritual evolution against the evolution of warfare, culminating in a weapon that could destroy all of civilization. Ultimately faith is the triumphant force.

Dr. Nagai's book The Bells of Nagasaki *was originally suppressed by the American occupying forces, its publication only approved when an appendix was added detailing Japanese atrocities in the Pacific War. What are your thoughts on the suppression of his work and the suppression of all films/literature about the bombing in the immediate aftermath of the war?*

Dominic: I remember when we were in Nagasaki someone handed us a first edition copy of *The Bells of Nagasaki* with the appendix ripped out. I think censoring history can be a dangerous thing. It is important for us to learn from the past.

In regards to the American censorship, I can understand that back in 1945, the American government did not want too much information leaking out about the atomic bombings. The war was finally over and the war in the Pacific had seen some of the most brutal fighting with devastating loss of life, especially among American servicemen. There was a sense of justification for the two atomic bombings; everybody had believed that it had brought an end to the conflict.

Ian: But, I think the censorship of anything related to the atomic bombing served to increase the suffering of a demoralized and defeated nation (even more so for those who had actually survived the atomic bombings). It was effectively taking away their voice and hiding them away from the world. When Dr. Nagai's book, *The Bells of Nagasaki*, was finally published in 1949 the cathartic effect it had on the Japanese people was overwhelming and resulted in it becoming a bestseller. The Occupying forces saw only the negative connotations of allowing the media to reveal the truth (or at least some of it) to the public and not the good it would do. The books of Dr. Nagai and, a little later, films such as *Children of Hiroshima* (1952) helped heal wounds that had been left to fester.

Also it had a very negative effect on a more global scale, as it gave a very misleading and quite positive image of the atomic bomb in the West.

Dominic: What remains a tragedy is that Takashi Nagai wrote prolifically about his experiences of surviving and living in the aftermath of the bomb, yet most of these books and essays were never available in English and are no longer available even in Japanese.

Ian: There are reels and reels of color film shot by the USAF when they entered Nagasaki shortly after the bombing. All this footage is in the public domain, but it remained hidden for decades—nobody knew it existed; we've included some of these reels in our film.

Do you believe there was any justification for the dropping of the atomic bombs?

Ian: There is a strong argument that suggests that Japan was on the verge of capitulation when the first bomb was dropped. This is supported by President Eisenhower—then Supreme Commander of all Allied Forces—who is quoted as saying, "I was against it on two counts. First, the Japanese were ready to surrender, and it wasn't necessary to hit them with that awful thing. Second, I hated to see our country be the first to use such a weapon." Also having spent many months reading and listening to accounts of those who survived the atomic bombings, watching archive footage of the aftermath and visiting the Atomic

Bomb Disease Institute of Nagasaki where survivors and their children and grandchildren are still being checked for signs of "atom bomb disease," I would find it impossible to answer yes to this question.

Dominic: Admiral William Leahy, the highest ranking member [*sic*] of the U.S. military at that time, is also quoted as saying, "The Japanese were already defeated and ready to surrender because of the effective sea blockade and the successful bombing with conventional weapons. My own feeling was that in being the first to use it, we had adopted an ethical standard common to the barbarians of the Dark Ages. I was not taught to make wars in that fashion, and that wars cannot be won by destroying women and children."

Although I think it is important to add that it is easy for us to sit here and look back in judgment. Most of us alive today did not experience that war. But, what I struggle with is the notion that it is ever right to use a weapon of such destruction. The fallout from these bombs is still being felt generations after they were dropped.

Appendix: Japanese Titles of Films Referenced in Text

The Affair at Akitsu (*Akitsu onsen*, 秋津温泉, Yoshishige Yoshida, 1962)

Affairs Within Walls (a.k.a. *Secrets Behind the Wall*, *Kabe no naka no himegoto*, 壁の中の秘事, Kōji Wakamatsu, 1965)

Akira (Katushiro Ōtomo, 1988)

All Monsters Attack (*Gojira-Minira-Gabara: Oru kaijū daishingeki*, ゴジラ・ミニラ・ガバラ オール怪獣大進撃, Ishirō Honda, 1969)

Antarctica (*Nankyoku monogatari*, 南極物語, Koreyoshi Kurahara, 1983)

Assassination of Ryōma (*Ryōma no ansatsu*, 竜馬暗殺, Kazuo Kuroki, 1974)

Atomic Bomb Home (a.k.a. *Summer of Prayer*, *Natsu no inori*, 映画「夏の祈り」, Katsumi Sakaguchi, 2012)

Barefoot Gen (*Hadashi no Gen*, はだしのゲン, Tengo Yamada, 1976)

Barefoot Gen (*Hadashi no* Gen, はだしのゲン, Mori Masaki, 1983)

Barefoot Gen: Explosion of Tears (*Hadashi no Gen: Namida no bakuhatsu*, はだしのゲン 涙の爆発, Tengo Yamada, 1977)

Barefoot Gen 2 (*Hadashi no Gen 2*, はだしのゲン2, Toshio, Hirata, 1986)

Barefoot Gen 3: Battle of Hiroshima (*Hadashi no Gen Part 3: Hiroshima no tatakai*, はだしのゲン Part 3 ヒロシマのたたかい, Tengo Yamada, 1980)

Battle Royale (*Batoru rowaiaru*, バトル・ロワイアル, Kinji Fukasaku, 2000)

Battle Without Honor and Humanity (*Jingi naki tatakai*, 仁義なき戦い, Kinji Fukasaku, 1973)

The Bells of Nagasaki (*Nagasaki no kane*, 長崎の鐘, Hideo Ōba, 1950)

Black Rain (*Kuroi ame*, 黒い雨, Shōhei Imamura, 1989)

Black Sun (*Kuroi taiyō*, 黒い太陽, Koreyoshi Kurahara, 1964)

Blood Is Dry (*Chi wa kawaiteru*, 血は渇いてる, Yoshishige Yoshida, 1961)

Children of Hiroshima (*Genbaku no ko*, 原爆の子, Kaneto Shindō, 1952)

Children of Nagasaki (*Kono ko wo nokoshite*, この子を残して, Keisuke Kinoshita, 1983)

Children of the Beehive (*Hachi no su no kodomotachi*, 蜂の巣の子供たち, Hiroshi Shimizu, 1948)

Coup d'etat (*Kaigenrei*, 戒厳令, Yoshishige Yoshida, 1973)

The Effects of the Atomic Bomb on Hiroshima and Nagasaki (*Hiroshima, Nagasaki ni okeru genshibakudan no kōka*, 広島長崎における爆弾の効果, Nippon Eigasha, 1945/1967)

Eros Plus Massacre (*Erosu + gyakusatsu*, エロス＋虐殺, Yoshishige Yoshida, 1970)

Evil Spirits of Japan (*Nihon no akuryō*, 日本の悪霊, Kazuo Kuroki, 1970)

The Face of Another (*Tanin no kao*, 他人の顔, Hiroshi Teshigahara, 1966)

The Face of Jizō (*Chichi to kuraseba*, 父と暮せば, Kazuo Kuroki, 2004)

Fires on the Plain (*Nobi*, 野火, Kon Ichikawa, 1959)

Gamera (*Daikaijū Gamera*, 大怪獣ガメラ, Yuasa, Noriaki, 1965)

Gate of Youth (*Seishun no mon*, 青春の門, Kinji Kukasaku and Koreyoshi Kurahara, 1981)

Ghidrah, the Three Headed Monster (*San Daikaijū: Chikyū saidai no kessen*, 三大怪獣 地球最大の決戦, Ishirō Honda, 1964)

Ghost in the Shell (*Kōkaku kidōtai*, 攻殻機動隊, Mamoru Oshii, 1995)

Godzilla (*Gojira*, a.k.a. *Godzilla*, ゴジラ, Ishirō Honda, *1954)*

Godzilla Against Mechagodzilla (*Gojira tai Mekagojira*, ゴジラ×メカゴジラ, Masaaki Tezuka, 2002)

Godzilla Final Wars (*Gojira fainaru wōzu*, ゴジラ ファイナルウォーズ, Ryuhei Kitamura, 2004)

Godzilla, Mothra and King Ghidorah: Giant Monsters All-Out Attack (*Gojira, Mosura, Kingu Gidora: Daikaijū Sōkōgeki*, ゴジラ・モスラ・キングギドラ 大怪獣総攻撃, Shūsuke Kaneko, 2001)

Godzilla Raids Again (*Gojira no gyakushū*, ゴジラの逆襲, Motoyoshi Oda, 1955)

Godzilla Tokyo S.O.S (*Gojira Mosura Mekagojira Tōkyō Esu Ō Esu*, ゴジラ×モスラ×メカゴジラ 東京 SOS, Masaaki Tezuka, 2003)

Godzilla 2000 (*Gojira nisen: Mireniamu*, ゴジラ2000 ミレニアム, Takao Okawara, 1999)

Godzilla vs. Biollante (*Gojira tai Biorante*, ゴジラvsビオランテ, Kazuki Ōmori, 1989)

Godzilla vs. Destoroyah (*Gojira tai Desutoroia*, ゴジラvsデストロイア, Takao Okawara, 1995)

Godzilla vs. Hedorah (*Gojira tai Hedora*, ゴジラ対ヘドラ, Yoshimitsu Banno, 1971)

Godzilla vs. Mechagodzilla (*Gojira tai Mekagojira*, ゴジラ対メカゴジラ, Jun Fukuda, 1974)

Godzilla vs. Mechagodzilla II (Gojira tai Mekagojira II, ゴジラvsメカゴジラ, Takao Okawara, 1993)

Godzilla vs. Megalon (*Gojira tai Megaro*, ゴジラ対メガロ, Jun Fukuda, 1973)

Godzilla vs. Space Godzilla (*Gojira tai SupēsuGojira*, ゴジラvsスペースゴジラ, Koichi Kawakita, 1994)

H-Man (*Bijo to ekitainingen*, 美女と液体人間, Ishirō Honda, 1958)

Hiroshima (ひろしま, Hideo Sekigawa, 1953)

The Human Vapor (*Gasu ningen daiichigō*, ガス人間第一号, Ishirō Honda, 1960)

I Live in Fear (*Ikimono no kiroku*, 生きものの記録, Akira Kurosawa, 1955)

Invasion of Astro Monster (*Kaijū daisensō*, 怪獣大戦争, Ishirō Honda, 1965)

Ju-On: The Grudge (*Juon*, 呪怨じゅおん, Takashi Shimizu, 2003)

Kichiku: Banquet of the Beasts (*Kichiku dai enkai*, 鬼畜大宴会Kazuyoshi Kumakiri, 1997)

King Kong vs Godzilla (*Kingu Kongu tai Gojira*, キングコング対ゴジラ, Ishirō Honda, 1962)

Kwaidan (*Kaidan*, 怪談, Masaki Kobayashi, 1964)

The Lunchbox (a.k.a. *The Charred Lunchbox*, まっ黒なおべんとう, Tatsuharu Kodama, 1990)

Matango (*Matango*, マタンゴ, Ishirō Honda, 1963)

Mind Game (*Maindo geimu*, マインド・ゲーム, Masaaki Yuasa, 2004)

Mother (*Haha*, 母, Kaneto Shindō)

Mothra (*Mosura*, モスラ, Ishirō Honda, 1961)

Mothra vs. Godzilla (*Mosura tai Gojira*, モスラ対ゴジラ, Ishirō Honda, 1964)

The Mysterians (*Chikyū bōeigun*, 地球防衛軍, Ishirō Honda, 1957)

Nagasaki Angelus Bell 1945 (*Nagasaki 1945: Angelus no kane*, NAGASAKI 1945 アンゼラスの鐘, Seiji Arihara, 2005)

Neon Genesis Evangelion (*Shin Seiki Evangerion*, 新世紀エヴァンゲリオン, Hideaki Anno, 1995–1996)

Night and Fog in Japan (*Nihon no yoru to kiri*, 日本の夜と霧, Nagisa Ōshima, 1960)

NN-891102 (Gō Shibata, 1999)

An Obsession (*Tsumetai chi*, 冷たい血, Shinji Aoyama, 1997)

On a Paper Crane: Tomoko's Adventure (*Tsuru no note: Tomoko no bouken*, つるにのって とも子の冒険, Seiji Arihara, 1983)

Onibaba (鬼婆, Kaneto Shindō, 1964)

Paranoia Agent (*Mōsō dairinin*, 妄想代理人, Satoshi Kon, 2004)

Pitfall (*Otoshiana*, おとし穴, Hiroshi Teshigahara, 1962)

Rashomon (*Rashōmon*, 羅生門, Akira Kurosawa, 1950)

Rhapsody in August (*Hachigatsu no kyōshikyoku*, 八月の狂詩曲, Akira Kurosawa, 1991)

Ring (*Ringu*, リング, Hideo Nakata, 1998)

Rodan (*Sora no daikaijū Radon*, ラドン, Ishirō Honda, 1956)

Sakuratai 8.6 (*Sakura-tai chiru*, さくら隊散る, Kaneto Shindō, 1988)

School of the Holy Beast (*Seijū gakuen*, 聖獣学園, Norifumi Suzuki, 1974)

Shin's Tricycle (*Shin-chan no sanrinsha*, しんちゃんのさんりんしゃ, Tatsuharu Kodama)

Silence Has No Wings (*Tobenai chinmoku*, とべない沈黙, Kazuo Kuroki, 1966)

Stray Dog (*Nora inu*, 野良犬, Akira Kurosawa, 1949)

Terror of Mechagodzilla (*Mekagojira no gyakushū*, メカゴジラの逆襲, Ishirō Honda, 1975)

Tomorrow/Ashita (*Tomorrow: Ashita*, TOMORRO/明日, Kazuo Kuroki, 1988)

Town of Evening Calm, Country of Cherry Blossoms (*Yuunagi no machi, sakura no kuni*, 夕凪の街 桜の国, Kiyoshi Sasabe, 2007)

Varan the Unbelievable (*Daikaijū Baran*, 大怪獣バラン, Ishirō Honda, 1958)

The Warped Ones (*Kyōnetsu no kisetsu*, 狂熱の季節, Koreyoshi Kurahara, 1960)

Woman in the Dunes (*Suna no onna*, 砂の女, Jūzō Itami, 1964)

Women in the Mirror (*Kagami no onntachi*, 鏡の女たち, Yoshishige Yoshida, 2003)

Wuthering Heights (*Arashi go oka*, 嵐が丘, Yoshishige Yoshida, 1988)

About the Contributors

Julia **Alekseyeva** is a fourth year Ph.D. candidate in comparative literature at Harvard University with a secondary field in film and visual studies. Research interests include the films of Japan, France, and the USSR, particularly political avant-garde and documentary practices. She has taught courses on art and filmic representations of modernity and the modern city.

Mick **Broderick** teaches media and cultural theory and practice at Murdoch University, Western Australia, where he is associate dean (research) in the School of Arts. He has published extensively on the nuclear era, trauma and the apocalyptic with translations into French, Italian and Japanese.

Matthew **Edwards** is the editor of *Film Out of Bounds* (McFarland, 2007) and editor of a forthcoming collection on Klaus Kinski. He is an elementary school teacher.

Margaret M. **Ferrara** is an associate professor in secondary education social studies at the University of Nevada, Reno. Her research interests include civic education and single gender classrooms.

Yoshiko **Fukushima** received a Ph.D. from New York University and is an associate professor at the University of Hawaii at Hilo. She is the author of *Manga Discourse in Japanese Theater: The Location of Noda Hideki's Yume no Yūminsha* (Kegan Paul 2003; Routledge, 2005) and she studies the use of comedy and the role of comedians in wartime Japan.

Junko **Hatori** is a board member of the biennial Hiroshima Peace Film Festival. She is a freelance interpreter and translator working with numerous NGOs across Japan.

Tienfong **Ho** is an art and film historian who specializes in the history of monuments and contemporary art. She teaches art history as an adjunct professor at Temple University's Tyler School of Art and is a film instructor for the interdisciplinary course cluster "Disaster, War and Rebuilding in the Japanese City" at Bryn Mawr College.

Jason C. **Jones** is an assistant professor of Japanese at the University of Wisconsin, Milwaukee, where he teaches courses on Japanese film, Japanese pop culture, subtitling, translation, and academic writing in Japanese. His research interests include Japanese film, Hollywood and Japan film remakes, and Japanese consumer and popular culture.

Kenji **Kaneko** is a freelance English-Japanese translator and independent researcher. He is interested in Asia Pacific studies, international relations, Asian studies and Japanese studies. He is involved in a research project that explores Spanish language learning as a heritage language in Peruvian communities in Japan.

Robert **McParland** is the author of *Charles Dickens's American Audience* (Lexington, 2010) and *Writing on Joseph Conrad* (Infobase/Chelsea House, 2011), and the editor of *Film and Literary Modernism* (Cambridge Scholars, 2013) and *Music and Literary Modernism* (Cambridge Scholars, 2006). He is an associate professor of English and chair of the Department of English at Felician College.

Keiko Takioto **Miller** was a high school French teacher prior to becoming an assistant professor of French and Japanese and director of the Asian Studies Program at Mercyhurst University. She is writing a manual for teaching Far Eastern ideographs to learners of non-ideographic traditions that integrates the art of *shodo*, or Japanese calligraphy.

Yuki **Miyamoto** is an associate professor in the Department of Religious Studies at DePaul University. She is the author of *Beyond the Mushroom Cloud: Commemoration, Religion, and Responsibility After Hiroshima* (Fordham University Press, 2011) and researches discrimination and radiation, recently focusing on Minamata disease in the wake of the Fukushima accident.

Senjo **Nakai** teaches communication theories as a member of the faculty of Communication Arts, Chulalongkorn University, Thailand. Research interests include cross-cultural communication, folk media, popular culture, and informal forms of communication media, such as rumor, gossip and graffiti.

Greg **Nielsen** is a doctoral student at the University of Nevada, Reno, focusing on the use of film as a teaching tool in the classroom. He is the author of several books, articles, and screenplays. His master's degree project, the historical film *Hiroshima,* was a quarterfinalist in 2008 for the Francis Ford Coppola screenwriting contest Zoetrope.

Tony **Pritchard**'s research interests include aesthetics, critical theory, film, and media archaeology. He teaches at Western Washington University in Bellingham, Washington.

Freelance writer Johannes **Schönherr** joined the anarchist Kino im KOMM cinema collective in Nuremberg after his arrival in the West and became involved in setting up American underground shows. He is the author of *North Korean Cinema: A History* (McFarland, 2012).

Shannon **Stevens** is an assistant professor of communication studies in the Department of Communication Studies at California State University, Stanislaus. A former journalist, she also advises *The Stanislaus Signal* student newspaper and enjoys researching and applying the tenants of critical pedagogy in the newsroom and the classroom.

John **Vohlidka** is an assistant professor of history at Gannon University. He specializes in early modern European history, with special emphasis on Tudor-Stuart history and the Reformation. He also teaches a variety of courses, such as comics and culture, the history of the future, and post-atomic Japan.

Index

Abe, Shinzo 238, 265
Above and Beyond 52, 211–212, 215, 217–218, 226
Academy Awards 216
Addy, Wesley 235
Adventure Time 250
The Affair at Akitsu 153
Affairs Within Walls 2, 8, 9, 99–110
Aioi River 12, 151
Air America 231
Akira 6
All Monsters Attack 60–61
All That Remains 2, 267–279
All You Can Eat 204–205
Allen, Woody 233
And the Band Played On 231, 236
Aoyama, Shinji 8
Arihara, Seiji 7
Armageddon 50
Article 9 (Japanese Constitution) 172–173, 182, 208, 265
Asahi Shimbun 79–80, 85–87, 187, 269
Ashizawa, Leo 270, 273–274
Asner, Matthew 234
Assassination of Ryōma 172
Atomic Bomb Casualty Commission 167, 173, 191
Atomic Bomb Dome 177–178, 180
Atomic Bomb Home 9
August 6, 1945 5, 11, 71, 112, 114–116, 120, 132, 140, 142, 150, 163, 174, 179, 191, 240, 244, 257
August 9, 1945 5, 12, 71, 140, 200, 206–207, 240
Augusta 237

Bacon, Francis 96, 98
Barefoot Gen (anime, 1983) 2, 6, 106–109, 111–123, 166, 169, 187, 199, 245, 273
Barefoot Gen (film, 1976) 7
Barefoot Gen (manga) 111–123
Barefoot Gen: Battle of Hiroshima 7

Barefoot Gen: Explosion of Tears 7, 166
Battle Royale 228
Battle Without Honor and Humanity 8
The Beast from 20,000 Fathoms 58
Beatty, Warren 234
Beautiful Kirishima 174
The Beginning or the End? 52, 211–215, 226
Belan, Choz 246–248, 253
The Bells of Nagasaki (book) 267–268
The Bells of Nagasaki (film) 73–76, 195, 267–268
Bergman, Ingrid 101
Berlin Film Festival 8, 9, 81, 99
Black Rain 2, 8, 115, 124–139, 151, 161, 163–164, 168, 180–181, 186, 211–212, 220–221, 225–226, 230
Black Sun 228
Blood Is Dry 153
Blowing Up Paradise 49–50
Bockscar 12
A Boy's Marbles 7
bozosoku 203–204
Breathless 174
Bresson, Robert 101

Cannes Film Festival 75, 79, 216
Chichi to kuraseba see *The Face of Jizō*
Children of Hiroshima 2, 73–80, 143, 150–152, 155, 278
The Children of Huang Shi 238
Children of Nagasaki 74, 267, 269
Children of the Beehive 72–73
Children of the Beehive: What Happened Next 73
Cibot-Shimma, Miho 7
Civil Censorship Detachment 70
Civil Information and Education Section (CIE) 72–74

Continental Distributing, Inc. 82
Coup d'état 153

Daiei Studios 59
Dallas 217
Darabont, Frank 3
Day One 212, 219–220
DC Comics 246
Death March to Bataan 219
Diary of Sacco and Vanzetti 260
Dilated 251
Dr. Strangelove 261
Documentary Channel 248
Donahue, Phil 264
Donner, Richard 203–204
Duffy, Patrick 217

Edwards, Gareth 3
The Effects of the Atomic Bomb on Hiroshima and Nagasaki 72
Einstein, Albert 220, 235
Einstürzende Neubauten 203–204
Eisenhower, General Dwight 77, 84, 86, 278
Emmerich, Roland 3
Emmy 212, 240, 242
Empire of the Sun 269
Enola Gay 11, 16, 114–115, 191, 194, 211, 213–214, 216–217, 223–226, 234, 244, 246, 248
Enola Gay: The Men, the Mission, the Atomic Bomb 212, 216–218
Eros Plus Massacre 153
Etō, Jun 70, 76, 143
Evil Spirits of Japan 172

The Face of Another 2, 88–98
The Face of Jizō 2, 8, 150–151, 154–155, 171–183, 188
Fat Man 12, 195
Fat Man and Little Boy 211–212, 218–220, 226
Finding Fatima 267, 276
Flusser, Vilém 89, 92, 97–98
Frederick, William *see* Knight, William Frederick

Friday the 13th 141
Fukasaku, Kenji 8

Gate of Youth 228
Genbakudan 1, 5, 6, 8, 10, 75, 230
Gere, Richard 6
Ghidrah, the Three Headed Monster 60
Ghost 176
Ghost Dad 176
Ghost in the Shell 251
GHQ SCAP 72
Gigan 60
Godard, Jean-Luc 174
Godzilla (creature) 3, 17–67, 86
Godzilla (1984) 35–55, 62
Godzilla (1985) 44–55, 62–63
Godzilla (1998) 35, 49–50, 53, 64
Godzilla (2014) 3
Godzilla Against Mechagodzilla 65
Godzilla Final Wars 35, 56, 65
Godzilla King of the Monsters 37–43, 47–49
Godzilla, Mothra and King Ghidorah: Giant Monsters All-Out Attack 60
Godzilla Raids Again 59
Godzilla Tokyo S.O.S 65
Godzilla 2000 64
Godzilla vs. Biolante 63
Godzilla vs. Destoroyah 63–64
Godzilla vs. Hedorah 60
Godzilla vs. Mechagodzilla 62
Godzilla vs. Mechagodzilla II 64
Godzilla vs. Megalon 61
Godzilla vs. Space Godzilla 64
Gojira (film, 1954) 1–3, 6, 17–67, 140–141
Good for Nothing 153
The Goonies 203
Gorbachev, Mikhail 218
Great Artiste 16
Ground Zero: Documents of Hiroshima 9, 10
Groves, Leslie 213–214, 217–220

H-Man 6, 59
Hachiya, Michihiko 222
Halloween 141
Hanks, Tom 230
Harada, Yoshio 154, 177
Harakiri 229
Hashimoto, Kōji 36, 62–63
Hatanaka, Yuriko 162, 241–242
Hazy Life 203
HBO 224, 242–243
hibakusha 1–3, 5–6, 8–10, 26, 56, 63, 65, 71, 75, 77–81, 85, 102, 104, 108, 112–113, 119, 122, 128, 131, 147, 151–152, 161–162, 166, 186, 191, 196, 216, 221,

224, 230, 240–243, 245, 254, 257, 262–266, 272
Hibakusha (film, 2012) 2, 246–253
Hibakusha: Our Life to Live 2, 254–266
Hidashi no Gen: Jiden 111–123
Hidashi no Gen: Watashi no Isho 111–123
Higgins, Dominic 2, 267–279
Higgins, Ian 2, 267–279
Hira, Mikijirō 90
Hirata, Akihiko 35
Hirata, Toshio 7
Hirohito, Emperor 14, 15, 181, 229
Hiroshima (BBC documentary) 214
Hiroshima (book) 255
Hiroshima (film, 1953) 2, 75, 77–87, 150, 227
Hiroshima (film, 1995) 155, 223, 228–239
Hiroshima Chamber of Commerce 72
Hiroshima Diary: Journal of a Japanese Physician 211, 222
Hiroshima in America: Fifty Years of Denial 222
Hiroshima Maidens 79, 86, 224, 244
Hiroshima no pika 225
Hiroshima mon amour 100, 102–106, 109, 153, 211, 215, 227
Hiroshima Municipal Government 72
Hiroshima, Out of the Ashes 212, 221–223, 227
Hiroshima Peace Memorial 119–120, 142, 158, 192, 241
Hiroshima Revisited 249
Hitler, Adolf 220, 238
Honda, Ishirō 3, 6, 19, 31, 54–56, 58, 61, 76, 140, 144
House on Un-American Activities Committee (HUAC) 212, 214, 260
The Human Condition 174
The Human Promise 153
The Human Vapor 6

I Live in Fear 5
Ibuse, Masuji 124, 127–130, 135, 137, 151, 163, 180
Ichihara, Etsuko 151
Ichikawa, Kon 174
Ifukube, Akira 32
I'll Not Forget the the Song of Nagasaki 85
Imamura, Shōhei 124–139, 170, 180
Independence Day 48, 50
Indiana Jones and the Last Crusade 212
Inoue, Hisashi 154, 156, 171–183

Inoue, Mitsuharu 174
Invasion of Astro Monster 60
Ishidō, Toshirō 230
Itō, Sueo 72
Iwanami Film Production Company 173, 177, 182
Iwasaki, Akira 72

The Japan Confederation of A- and H-Bomb Sufferers Organizations 1, 84, 194, 198
The Japan Council Against Atomic and Hydrogen Bombs 184
Japanese Teachers Union (JTU) 75, 77, 79–81
Jet Programme 1
La Jette 92
Ju-on: The Grudge 141
Jurassic Park 50

kaiju eiga 56, 83, 141–142, 144
Kamiya Etsuko's Young Days 174–175
Kamiyachō Sakura Hotel 175
Kayama, Shigeru 58
Kayoko, on the Day of Cherry Flowers Blooming 172, 174
Kichiku 203–204
Kimura, Takeo 177
Kinema Junpō 74, 80–81, 86–87
King, Martin Luther 267
King Kong vs. Godzilla 59
Kinoko Kai 241–242
Kinoshita, Keisuke 74, 267
Kinugasa, Teinosuke 143
Kitamura, Kazuo 151
Knight, William Frederick 251
Kobayashi, Ippei 85
Kobayashi, Masaki 174
Kodama, Tatsuharu 7, 8
Koizumi, Junichirō 174
Kon, Satoshi 6
Kondō, Nobuyoshi 162
Kōno, Fumiyo 185–199
Korean *hibakusha* 196, 259
Kumakiri, Kazuyoshi 203–204
Kurahara, Koreyoshi 155, 164, 170, 228–239
Kuroki, Kazuo 8, 154, 170–183
Kurosawa, Akira 3, 5, 6, 8, 56, 64, 66, 151
Kwaidan 75
Kyūma, Fumio 265

Late Bloomer 209
Lehay, William 279
Lewis, Bob 224, 244
L I F E 247
Linklater, Richard 247
Listen to the Voices from the Sea 171
"Little Boy" 11, 46, 111, 191
Little Boy, Big Typhoon 175
The Lost World: Jurassic Park 48

Lovers in Cuba 172
Lucky Dragon No.5 6, 38, 58, 75, 78
The Lunch Box 7
Lupin III 187

MacArthur, Lt. Douglas 71
Madhouse 6
Major Oak Entertainment 267–279
Manhattan Project 27, 29, 36, 212–213, 215–217, 219
Manichi 79–80
Marker, Chris 92
Marvel 246
Masaki, Mori 6, 7
Masao, Adachi 107
Masonna 203, 208
Matango 6
Matsumura, Tatsuo 229
Matsushige, Yoshito 71, 151
Mechagodzilla 60, 64–65
Meguminooka Nagasaki Genbaku Home 9
Merton of the Movies 214
Merzbow 203, 208
Metro-Goldwyn-Mayer (MGM) 212–215
Mind Game 250
Miyazawa, Rie 154, 177
Mizoguchi, Kenji 142, 180
Mori, Kenji 207
Morikawa, Tokihisa 141
Mother 75
Mothra 6, 59–60, 66, 141
Mothra vs. Godzilla 36, 59–60, 63
Murakami, Fuyuki 38
Murata, Takeo 58
The Mushroom Club 161–162, 240–241, 243, 245
The Mysterians 6

Nagahara, Shūichi 43
Nagai, Takashi 2, 73–74, 267–279
Nagasaki Angelus Bell 1945 7
Nakadai, Tatsuya 90
Nakata, Hideo 3, 140–149
Nakazawa, Keiji 6, 7, 111–123, 166, 169, 187, 199, 245
Nanjing 70
Nankyoku monogatari 228
National Geographic 224
Neon Genesis Evangelion 6
Nevins, Sheila 243
Newman, Paul 219
Nguyen, Steven 2, 246–253
NHK 134, 161, 187, 199, 245
Night and Fog in Japan 100
Night of the Living Dead 176
Nightmare on Elm Street 141
Nippon Eigasha 72
NN-891102 2, 8, 200–209
No More Hiroshimas 72

Noh 3, 176
North Korea 5
Nostalgia 180
Nyokodo 275

Ōba, Hideo 73–74, 170, 175, 267–268
An Obsession 8
Odagiri, Ichiun 128–129
Ōe, Kenzebaurō 154, 173, 182–183, 186, 195
Okazaki, Steven 2, 161, 167, 170, 224, 240–246
Okuda, Mariko 153
On a Paper Crane: Tomoko's Adventure 7
Onibaba 75, 142
Ōoka, Shōhei 71
Oppenheimer, J. Robert 27, 29, 97, 213, 217–220
Osaka University of Arts 202–208
Ōshima, Nagisa 100
Ōta, Yōka 195
Otowa, Nobuko 150
Ozu, Yasujirō 270

Pacific Rim 140–141
A Page of Madness 143
Paranoia Agent 6
Pat Garrett and Billy the Kid 231
Pearl Harbor 2, 13, 19, 63, 65, 118, 120, 152, 172, 219, 231, 262
Peckinpah, Sam 231
Perry, Matthew 126
Persepolis 247
The Pickpocket 175
Pink Film (*pinku eiga*) 9, 99–110
Pitfall 89
Pixel Revolution Films 272
Planet Studyo + 1 cinema 202, 209
Poitier, Sidney 176
Pokemon 206
post traumatic stress disorder 18, 19, 24, 26, 29–33
Potsdam Proclamation 12, 14, 229

Rambo III 44
Rashomon 83
Reagan, Ronald 44, 45, 217–218, 236
Record of Life and Death 164, 230
Red Dawn 44
Red Heat 44
Reds 234
Resnais, Alain 100, 102–106, 155, 170, 215–216
Rhapsody in August 6, 56, 64, 151, 221, 225, 227
Ring (1998) 2, 8, 140–149

Ring (2002) 141
Rocky IV 44
Rodan 6, 59–60, 141
Romero, George A. 176
Roosevelt, Franklin 213, 218, 235, 262
Rothauser, David 2, 254–266
Rugrats 35, 36

Sakaguchi, Katsumi 9
Sakai, Sachio 39
Sakuratai 8.6 75
Samurai Rebellion 229
Sasabe, Kiyoshi 170, 190–191, 197
Sasaki, Sadako 7, 142
School of the Holy Beast 9
Sekigawa, Hideo 2, 75, 77–87
Seven Years Diary (Nananen no ki) 186
Shibata, Gō 200–209
Shikibu, Murasaki 95
Shimizu, Hiroshi 72–73
Shimura, Takashi 36, 141
Shin, Yuna 270
Shindō, Kaneto 73–75, 77, 79–81, 85, 142–143, 150, 152, 155–156, 170, 267–268
Shin's Tricycle 7, 8
Shochiku 72, 74, 79, 153, 174–175, 267
Shōnen Jump 111, 119
Showtime Network 231
Silence Has No Wings 172
The Simpsons 34, 35
The Small-Headed Children 242
A Song for Nagasaki 276
South Park 35
Spelling, Aaron 219
Spielberg, Steven 203, 269
Spottiswoode, Roger 2, 155, 228–239
Stalin, Joseph 102, 103–105, 107–108, 238
Stone, Oliver 155–156
A Story of Pure Love 230
A Story Written on Water 153
Straw Dogs 231
Stray Dog 8
Struck by Black Rain 121
Studio APA 246–247
Summer Girl 141
Survivors 240–241
Suyeishi, Kaz 246–253
Suzuki, Kantarō 231–232
Suzuki, Norifumi 9
Suzuki, Tatsuo 177
Szilard, Leo 213, 220, 235

Tadashi, Imai 230
Takabayashi, Shinichi 175
Takarada, Akira 40
Tale of Genji 95
The Tales of Heike 129

Tales of Moonlight and Rain 142, 180
Tanabe, Masaaki 9
Tanaka, Tomoyuki 19, 58
Tardieu, Jean 171
Tarkovsky, Andrei 180
Taylor, Telford 15
Terror of Mechagodzilla 62
Terror Train 231
Teshigahara, Hiroshi 88–98
Tetsutani, Shinichi 7
This Is Your Life 224, 244
Tibbets, Paul 214–215, 217–218, 223–225, 246, 250, 252–253
Tinian Island 276
Tobenai chinmoku 173–174
Toei 3
Toho 3, 8, 32, 45, 48, 50, 56–59, 64, 182
Tōhoku earthquake and tsunami 85, 98, 117, 120, 140, 157
Tokyo firebombing 14, 15, 51
Tomioka, Kunihiko 202, 209
Tomorrow/Ashita 8, 172, 174, 176, 181
Tomorrow Never Dies 231
Town of Evening Calm, Country of Cherry Blossoms (film) 185, 190–191

Town of Evening Calm, Country of Cherry Blossoms (manga) 184–199
The Town of Evening Calm: The Real Condition of 1953 (novel) 195
Trinity test 88, 97
Truman, Harry S 11, 13, 14, 77, 155, 192–193, 198, 211, 221, 224, 230–231, 233, 235–237, 239
Turner and Hooch 230
Turner Classic Movies 214
24 Hours After Hiroshima 224

UCLA Film and Television Archive 214
Ultra Fuckers 204
Ultraman 61
Unit 731 70
Urakami Cathedral 176
Uranium Film Festival 254, 261
Urayama, Kirio 170

Varan the Unbelievable 59
Verbinski, Gore 141
Vietnam War 104, 174
Violent Onsen Geisha 204

Wakamatsu, Kōji 8–9, 99–110
Waking Life 247
Waltz with Bashir 247
The Warped Ones 228
Weekly Shōnen Jump 7
Welsh, Kenneth 230, 233, 235
West, Timothy 235
White Light/Black Rain: The Destruction of Hiroshima and Nagasaki 167, 224, 227, 240, 242–245
Woman in the Dunes 89
Women in the Mirror 2, 8, 151–153, 155
World War Z 140
Wuthering Heights 153

Yagi, Yasutarō 79
Yamada, Tengo 7
Yoshida, Yoshishige 152–155
Young Days 174
Yuasa, Masaaki 246, 250
Yukichi, Fukuzawa 132
Yumechiyo nikki 161–164, 170
Yun Fat, Chow 238

Zeami, Motokiyo 129
Zelig 233